2010
COACH OF THE
YEAR CLINIC
NOTES

LECTURES BY
PREMIER HIGH SCHOOL COACHES

Edited by Earl Browning

COACHES CHOICE™

www.coacheschoice.com

ISBN: 978-1-60679-109-7

ISSN: 1945-1202

Telecoach, Inc. Transcription: Emmerson Browning, Kent Browning, Tom Cheaney, and Dan Haley

Diagrams: Steve Haag

Book layout and cover design: Bean Creek Studio

Cover photos (Dale Mueller, front and back): Rob Moyer, Ft. Thomas, Kentucky (www.robmoyer.com)

Special thanks to the Nike clinic managers for having the lectures taped.

Coaches Choice
P.O. Box 1828
Monterey, CA 93942
www.coacheschoice.com

Contents

Contents

THE 3-4 DEFENSE ALIGNMENTS AND ADJUSTMENTS

Paoli High School, Indiana

First, I want you to know, we did not turn the program around alone at Paoli High School. When we took over at Paoli, it was not a pretty situation. There had not been a lot of success in the program over the years. It takes a lot of people to build success. It takes the kids, obviously. They have bought into what we are trying to do. It also takes a great coaching staff. Just like most everyone else in high school coaching, we do not get to pick and choose our kids. We take what we get, and we do the best we can with it.

We are a 2A school with an enrollment of 466 students. We break up our coaching staff by having three offensive coaches and three defensive coaches. I serve as defensive coordinator and linebacker coach. I coach four positions in our defense. If I have anything to say offensively, sometimes they will listen, and sometimes they just tell me to shut up. I could not do it without those offensive coaches.

We took over the program in 2006. From 2000 to 2005, they won 11 games. They gave up a lot of points. Going into the 2006 season, we felt good about ourselves. However, we ended up giving up more points, and we didn't win a single game. Sometimes, it gets worse before it gets better. Sometimes, you just have to believe in what you are doing. We run a flex bone offense, and we run a 3-4 defense. That is what we believe in, and we stick to it. We stuck to that offense and defense, and we gave up nearly 40 points a game that first year. As we pressed on, we continued to get better. Sometimes, when a team is not successful, you get a lot of offensive-minded people wanting to change things because that is the fastest way to get recognized.

DEFENSIVE PROGRESSIONS

	2000/05	2006	2007	2008	2009
PPG	36.1	39.6	20.4	16.1	7.6
YPC		8.0	4.8	5.0	2.9
Third Down		60%	67%	67%	75%
T.O.	Margin	-20	+10	+22	+21
W-L	11-49	0-10	6-5	10-2	13-1

KEYS TO OUR SUCCESS

- Defensive attitude
- Player development
- Player's trust
- Player commitment
- Consistency (staff, schemes, etc.)
- Weaknesses of the defense (Players need to know this.)
- Player knowledge

We had to develop a defensive attitude. That was not just with our football program; it was throughout our school and community, and it was the same with our basketball program. We continued to stress defense, and our kids have taken to that.

For player development, we have what we have. We do not get to go out and choose our kids. There is not a whole lot going on in Paoli, Indiana. I don't know if any of you have been skiing there, but we do have a nice ski resort. However, that is about it.

We have to develop our kids. Our coaching staff does a great job. Through the months of January and February, we are coaching our coaches. Every Wednesday night, we have a clinic night, from our youth coaches to our high school coaches. Everything is being implemented from the third grade on up. We do some things on Sundays with our younger kids before they get to high school to develop them. We do spring football with our junior high. In Indiana high schools, we do not have spring football. We will work with the junior high kids for a month, much like a college would, and we will have some scrimmages with them. We have summer camps, where we encourage attendance.

We feel it is important to get the players' trust. We must get their trust somehow, some way. They have to believe in what we are teaching them. I was talking with one of our seniors recently. He was an eighth-grader when we came in. I was trying to sell him that we are going to have success. All he had seen in his time at school was defeats. I think he made the weight room three times coming into his freshman year. He did not have much hope in the program.

Some way, you have to get trust and commitment from your kids. We tell them you have to do what you need to do today so you can do what you want to do on Friday nights. We tell them you have to have some pain and suffering somewhere. He can be humiliated in the game, or he can suffer along with his teammates in the weight room and on the practice field. In the last few years, our kids have gotten much better with their commitment.

With consistency in our staff, our schemes, and everything that we do with the kids, they know what to expect. My job each day is to train kids in the weight room and outside the weight room. When they go in the weight room on Monday, they know what to expect. They are not dealing with unknowns.

We talk with the players about their weaknesses. We feel it is important for our players to know their weaknesses. There are weaknesses in everything we do. Your kids have to be aware of that. You have to give them knowledge to help them improve. Coaches can watch all the tape we want, but if our coaches do not know what they are doing and do not teach what the kids are going to see on Friday night, they are at a disadvantaged. We spend a lot of time educating our kids on what they are going to see. There may be things they see on film

that we have not talked about or we have not shown them before.

We know we are going to have to be able to adjust and adapt very quickly on game night. We play so many kids both ways that it is hard to coach kids in a game on Friday night. We do have the halftime when we make our changes, but there is not a lot you can do in the amount of time you have. There is very little coaching time during the game. However, halftime is critical for us because we have so many kids playing both ways. Our kids did a nice job of listening and making adjustments at halftime this year. We did not give up a single point during the third quarter of last year.

We are going to run a base defense out of a 3-4 look. We are going to see a lot of run-oriented offenses.

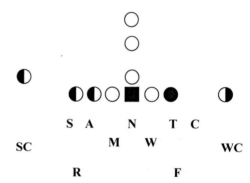

Diagram #1. Base Defense vs. Pro

Our interior three guys, our anchor, nose, and tackle go with the defensive line coach, and he coaches those three positions. They averaged about 180 pounds this past season across the board, including our outside backers. We want speed on our defense. We do not play big, slow guys on our defense. We want speed on the field. Our nose is going to be a two-gap player. He is going to have to be able to play two gaps. However, on the snap of the ball, he is playing only one gap. He has to recognize what that center is going to do. We want kids who are quick and technically sound in that nose position. He has the playside A gap.

With our anchor tackle, we are going to try to funnel everything inside. Big plays happen on the perimeter, and that is why we want to funnel everything inside. If there is a tight end, the anchor tackle is going to be in a 5 technique. He has to play that edge and read that block. Our tackle will play a 4 technique to the backside if there is no tight end. He will be head-up on him, and the guy will have to release inside our pass rush.

We have our Cat backer outside our tackle. Most of the time, we are going to rush our Cat backer. We will set our Sam backer to the tight end every time. We take one of our best players, one whom we feel can match up with that tight end the best. Our Cat backer is going to go to the backside. When we play an undersized linebacker, that is where he plays. He is going to be a fast kid, and we are going to be playing games with him.

We play our inside linebackers off the ball, no closer than five yards, and we want them moving. The only two guys who are not covered are those two offensive guards, and we want our inside backers to beat those guards. We have worked a lot on that. The Mike and Will are in a near-back read. In the I formation, we read the fullback.

Position: A
Alignment: 3 technique
Key: Guard
Vs. Run: B gap
Vs. Pass (2): Rush draw/screen

Position: N
Alignment: Zero technique
Key: Center
Vs. Run: Playside A gap
Vs. Pass (2): Rush draw/screen

Position: T
Alignment: 3 technique
Key: Guard
Vs. Run: B gap
Vs. Pass (2): Rush draw/screen

Position: C
Alignment: 5 technique/tight end 9 technique
Key: Tackle/tight end, near back
Vs. Run: Primary force
Vs. Pass (2): Contain rush/draw/screen

Position: S
Alignment: 9 technique
Key: Tight end
Vs. Run: Primary force
Vs. Pass (2): Contain rush/screen

Position: M
Alignment: 3 technique/4.5 to 5 yards
Key: Near back
Vs. Run: Playside C gap, backside A gap
Vs. Pass (2): Strong hook/curl

Position: W
Alignment: 3 technique/4.5 to 5 yards
Key: Near back
Vs. Run: Playside C gap, backside A gap
Vs. Pass (2): Weak hook/curl

Position: SC
Alignment: 5x1
Key: End man on line of scrimmage
Vs. Run: Secondary force
Vs. Pass (2): Flats

Position: R
Alignment: 8 to 10 yards over tight end
Key: End man on line of scrimmage
Vs. Run: Alley player
Vs. Pass (2): Deep half

Position: F
Alignment: 8 to 10 yards and one yard outside
Key: End man on line of scrimmage
Vs. Run: Alley player
Vs. Pass (2): Deep half

Position: WC
Alignment: 5x1
Key: End man on line of scrimmage
Vs. Run: Secondary force
Vs. Pass (2): Flats

As far as the weaknesses in the defense, we are weak against the play-action pass, and we are weak against misdirection. Our kids know that. We coach them up on this. We will do a drill where they read through the near back, and pick up the guard as the secondary read. If the fullback leads us left, and all of a sudden the guard pulls and we get a down block, we have to adjust for that on the fly. We will spend a lot of time working on that move.

We are deep, and we are going to out athlete those guys. We are going to play two guys who want to get to the football. Our senior Mike linebacker is 190 pounds and not all that fast. Nevertheless, he had 416 career tackles in three years of playing varsity football. He could get to the football. Our junior Will linebacker has tools to be even better. They have to get to the football.

Our corners are in a cover-2 shell. We will press our corners 95 percent of the time. We get up there and take away an outside release. We are going to follow those guys into our safety. They are going to be our secondary run support. Our Sam linebacker is our primary force. Our strong corner and our weak corner are our secondary force. So our Sam and Cat are primary; they don't let things get outside of them. If they get a tight end who releases inside of them, they will squeeze and get to the quarterback. If they get any type of hook blocking scheme, they are going outside, and we let our backers run. Again, we are banking that their guards are not going to get to our linebackers.

Our safeties are 7 to 10 yards back, and they have over the top. We will show a cover-2 shell, but we bring those guys in the box a lot. We will put nine in the box a lot because we play a lot of run teams. If we run a cover 3, where we are in a stack, we will have a rover. Our free safety was 6-foot, 195-pound kid he could come up and make plays. He was also a kid who we wanted back in cover 3 because he has good ball skills.

Sometimes, we bring our backers off in a spread situation. We stick where we have our Sam linebacker on man coverage if they have a real good tight end. We take our Cat and play bump and run if they try to isolate a good receiver out there.

We do a lot of things based on what the opponent is trying to do to us. Our weak corner is going to be our better corner. We are not going to play a cover 2 against a trips set. If we see a trips set, we are going to go to a cover 3. We are going to bring our rover up. Our weak corner is going to be isolated because we call quarter-quarter-half, so that our weak corner will have a lot to deal with. We have a fast defensive back, cover guy at the weak-corner spot.

The slower kid is going to be the strong corner. We are going to read the receivers. Our corner is playing the #1 receiver, but he is reading the #2 receiver. He must have good vision. We talk as if we are playing as a blind person would play. How would a blind man play? He would have to feel the receiver. The same thing up front is true. I tell our Sam that he has to feel for the receiver, and then he can look. However, you play that block by feel.

It is the same thing with our corners. If we line up and have him inside, we know he is going to release; our eyes go inside as soon as the #2 receiver comes of the ball. I have to zone off and get him as a corner. That takes a lot of work. They have to trust in what we are teaching them to get the job done.

Our philosophy is this. We are going to stop the run. A lot of times, we keep five men down. We can rush five, and we might bring a Mike linebacker and play games inside. One thing you have to watch for is when teams start running the option on you. They run our backs downfield, and they try to get the ball outside our end.

A big thing there is our kids have to understand this concept. We use the term "plumbers" on defense. You have to check for leaks. Where is the pressure coming from? If we have a Mike backer and a nose stunt coming, we are going to overload the box and go to a tight-end set. We play games on the interior. The outer defenders are plumbers. We know we are going to get the leaks.

If the quarterback breaks outside, you are going to take care of the problem. If you get a screen pass or a draw, you are going to have to take care of it. The kids are educated to know about our weakness, and they must adjust.

Our inside backers are reading the #2 receiver to the #1 receiver. Still, you have to match up to the receivers. The Will backer might have to help the weak corner if the #2 receiver is in the backfield. He can help him on the slant route. They have to communicate that information on the coverage.

This is our base defense versus different offensive sets. This is how we cover the four formations and how we adjust on each formation.

First is the double tight-end set (Diagram #2). Our weakside corner is up tight on the outside of the Cat.

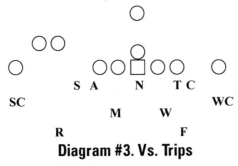

Diagram #2. Vs. Double Tight Ends

Next, we have a trips set (Diagram #3). Our weakside corner is lined up outside, but he is not as deep as the free safety.

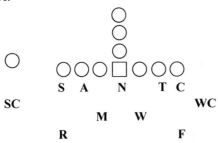

Diagram #3. Vs. Trips

If we get twin sets to both sides of the formation, we play the corners outside and the safeties inside on the slots (Diagram #4).

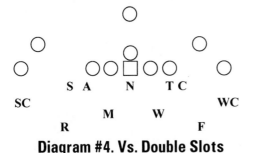

Diagram #4. Vs. Double Slots

If we see the no-backs set, we play the frontside the same as we played trips, and we play the backside with the corner outside and the free safety inside (Diagram #5).

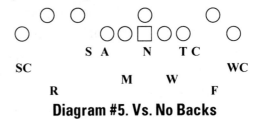

Diagram #5. Vs. No Backs

We do not like a lot of double tights because if that Cat is a little undersized, we might have a rough time. He has to realize that the weakside corner is in cover 2, and he is right there to help him out. We tell those guys that nobody get outside wide. It is zero width. You tighten up. You are going to have a corner helping you immediately on run support. We have to make sure we are knocking the snot out of that tight end so he doesn't get a free release.

Against the doubles, we play games. We will take our Sam and Cat and widen them out. Their job is to force the ball back inside. Can we play inside #2 and still force that ball back inside from that position? Yes, we can do that.

Against trips, we rotate the free safety. Mike has to read #3 to #2 to #1. That is what we teach. Read progression is where we have to get the job done. Versus no backs, it is going to depend on what we are facing, but we will probably widen Sam and our Cat. Obviously, we will have to make some adjustments on those.

We are starting to get the types of players we want, so this season we moved around a lot more on defense. We angled a ton of times, and we practiced it a bunch. We started moving the defensive players on the angles. In essence, we are going to post snap to a heavy look (Diagram #6).

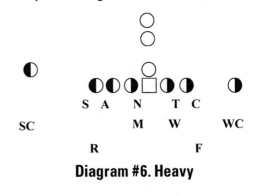

Diagram #6. Heavy

We are shifting to the heavy side, or the strongside. We take the nose man and play him in a 1 technique. We play a 3 technique with the tackle. The Cat can squeeze down a little, where he can force the ball inside. We adjust our backers. The Mike linebacker plays the A or B gap. We can play heavy, but this season we angled to it, rather than lined up in it. We were able to do this because we had speed. I like this defense because we can play games, and we do stunt often. Here are the heavy responsibilities.

Position: A
Alignment: 5 technique
Key: Tackle
Vs. Run: C gap
Vs. Pass (2): Rush draw/screen

Position: N
Alignment: Zero technique
Key: Center
Vs. Run: Playside A gap
Vs. Pass (2): Rush draw/screen

Position: T
Alignment: 4 technique
Key: Tackle
Vs. Run: C/B gap
Vs. Pass (2): Rush draw/screen

Position: C
Alignment: Ghost 6 technique / tight end 9 technique
Key: Tackle/tight end, tackle/tight end, near back
Vs. Run: Primary force
Vs. Pass (2): Contain rush/draw/screen

Position: S
Alignment: 9 technique
Key: Tight end
Vs. Run: Primary force
Vs. Pass (2): Contain rush/screen

Position: M
Alignment: 2 technique/4.5 to 5 yards
Key: Near back
Vs. Run: Playside B gap, backside A gap
Vs. Pass (2): Strong hook/curl

Position: W
Alignment: 2 technique/4.5 to 5 yards
Key: Near back
Vs. Run: Playside B gap, backside A gap
Vs. Pass (2): Weak hook/curl

Position: SC
Alignment: 5x1
Key: End man on line of scrimmage
Vs. Run: Secondary force
Vs. Pass (2): Flats

Position: R
Alignment: 8 to 10 yards over tight end
Key: End Man on line of scrimmage
Vs. Run: Alley player
Vs. Pass (2): Deep half

Position: F
Alignment: 8 to 10 yards and one yard outside
Key: End man on line of scrimmage
Vs. Run: Alley player
Vs. Pass (2): Deep half

Position: WC
Alignment: 5x1
Key: End man on line of scrimmage
Vs. Run: Secondary force
Vs. Pass (2): Flats

I covered how we play heavy against the pro set. Against the two tight ends, we play heavy to the wideside of the field (Diagram #7). On the backside, we have the tackle come down to the 3 technique, and the Cat plays a 9 technique.

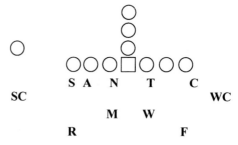

Diagram #7. Heavy vs. Double Tight

If we face trips, we still play the heavy look to the trips side (Diagram #8). The strong corner and

```
Free    F
Rover   R
Zeke    Z
Stud    $
Sam     S
Will    W
```

1. OLB must flip
2. ON/OFF: blitzing or not. If on: Zeke=Zebra   Stud=Snake
3. END and OLB call own movements
   a. Fire
   b. Solid
   c. Eagle
   d. Hatchet
   e. X
   f. Others…..

4. Set of blitzes for certain formations. Found on wrist bands of players
5. 2 backs or trips = MUST BE IN COVER 3
6. 1 back or Balanced = MUST BE IN COVER 2
7. If Zeke is ON: Wk corner automatic MAN, Safety looks to #2. Automatic "SWITCH" Call. Switch will be on either side depending who is ON.
8. "Tight" Zeke and Stud are both ON
9. Cover 2 Zebra: Zeke is ON (Switch on wk side)
10. Cover 2 Snake: Stud is ON (Switch on st side)
11. Corners in Cover 2 = 3-4 yards   Read #2, Play #1
    Safeties in Cover 2 = 10=12 yards
12. Any Blitzes (Sending 6) Cover 0
13. Any Blitzers "NEVER PASS A BACK" If he goes out, you break off and go with him.
14. Don't blitz a wing/veer team
15. In cover 0 "22" call. "Us 2 got them 2". (inside outside man)
16. Cover 4. Wk Corner= ½, Rover=1/2, St Corner= ½ Free is left to roam & help on run.
17. State blitzes = SAM
18. Metal blitzes = WILL
19. ILB Blitzes…..OLB Pitch and Peel
20. ILB if man blocks, rush through (Blitz and engage) take him to the QB
21. OLB Fire only on 1st down, I backs, and Cheat I
22. 3 deep on option
23. NO PRIMARY RUN SUPPORT FROM CORNERS! (only secondary)
24. FS Pop pass on strong side
25. WC Pop pass on week side
26. Blitz out of STRONG and STACK
27. Run WEAK for 1 back, and some 2 backs
28. STRONG DUECE, "G" schemes (guard moving teams) WING T
29. Wk option teams cover 4.

strong safety are deep on the wide receivers. On the backside, we have the weakside corner on the split end, and the free safety is keying the tight end.

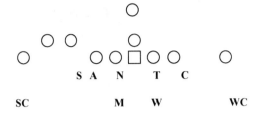

Diagram #8. Heavy vs. Trips

Against the double slot, we align heavy to the wideside of the field (Diagram #9). The corners and safeties on each side have the two wide receivers. The Mike and Will linebackers key the fullback.

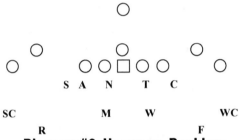

Diagram #9. Heavy vs. Doubles

We play to the wideside of the field if we see a no-back set (Diagram #10). We still have the Cat on the line of scrimmage. The Mike and Will linebackers key the inside receivers and drop to their zones.

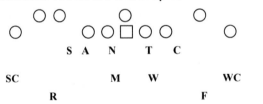

Diagram #10. Heavy vs. No Backs

In tight formation, we have our anchor and tackle in 3 techniques (Diagram #11). The question that comes up is this: How do we adjust our linebackers?

Our backers are playing to the B-gap side. We have to widen them a little. Then, we have a C-gap player. Our kids have to understand that we have to take away the audible to a sneak, and then bump

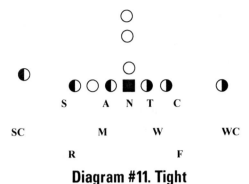

Diagram #11. Tight

outside. The fact the quarterback can run the sneak forces our backers to hesitate on the bump outside. That is one of the weaknesses here.

Here are the tight responsibilities against the pro set.

Position: A
Alignment: 3 technique
Key: Guard
Vs. Run: B gap
Vs. Pass (2): Rush draw/screen

Position: N
Alignment: Zero technique
Key: Center
Vs. Run: Playside A gap
Vs. Pass (2): Rush draw/screen

Position: T
Alignment: 3 technique
Key: Guard
Vs. Run: B gap
Vs. Pass (2): Rush draw/screen

Position: C
Alignment: 5 technique/tight end 9 technique
Key: Tackle/tight end, tackle/tight end, near back
Vs. Run: Primary force
Vs. Pass (2): Contain rush/draw/screen

Position: S
Alignment: 9 technique
Key: Tight end
Vs. Run: Primary force
Vs. Pass (2): Contain rush/screen

Position: M

Alignment: 3 technique/4.5 to 5 yards

Key: Near back

Vs. Run: Playside C gap, backside A gap

Vs. Pass (2): Strong hook/curl

Position: W

Alignment: 3 technique/4.5 to 5 yards

Key: Near back

Vs. Run: Playside C gap, backside A gap

Vs. Pass (2): Weak hook/curl

Position: SC

Alignment: 5x1

Key: End man on line of scrimmage

Vs. Run: Secondary force

Vs. Pass (2): Flats

Position: R

Alignment: 8 to 10 yards over the tight end

Key: End man on line of scrimmage

Vs. Run: Alley Player

Vs. Pass (2): Deep half

Position: F

Alignment: 8 to 10 Yards and one yard outside

Key: End man on line of scrimmage

Vs. Run: Alley player

Vs. Pass (2): Deep half

Position: WC

Alignment: 5x1

Key: End man on line of scrimmage

Vs. Run: Secondary force

Vs. Pass (2): Flats

We get a little wider, and we free up the Will backer so he can run. Mike is now a C-gap player. The coverage all stays the same. We worked a lot on covering those guys up, reading the blocks, and reacting to them. If you are a down lineman, you have to knock the snot out of your man, and you cannot let him run free. Our kids need to know we want that front line to eat up the blocks, and we do not want to get upfield. We want Mike and Will to be free to run to the ball and make plays.

Here is the tight look against the two tight-end set (Diagram #12). Our noseman is head up with the center. Our Tackle and Anchor are in 3 techniques. The Sam and Cat are in 9 techniques.

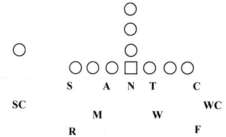

Diagram #12. Tight vs. Double Tights

We generate a lot of pressure out of our tight set. Sometimes, we use a four-man front that we call our G look. We do not do it often because I do not feel comfortable with it at this time. I would much rather take our outside linebackers off, and play a three-man front and bring some pressure with the stunts. I like that better than playing a four-man front. I think it is easier to adjust to and our kids have picked it up.

Our alignment against the trips look is similar to the double tight set (Diagram #13). We can play games with the inside people, but we have to be able to cover the wideside of the formation with our strong corner and strong safety. We can play Sam or Mike on the inside receiver, or have them cover the flat and hook zones.

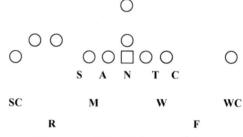

Diagram #13. Tight vs. Trips

Against twins to both sides, we line up the same as we do on all tights (Diagram #14). We can rush the Sam or Cat from the outside, or they can play pass defense.

When we see a no-back set, we want to apply pressure up front (Diagram #15). Again, we can rush five, or we can rush seven to apply pressure on the quarterback.

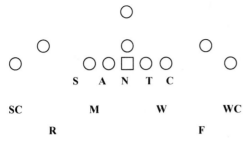

Diagram #14. Tight vs. Doubles

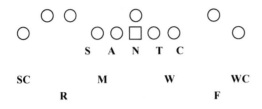

Diagram #15. Tight vs. No Backs

Against the spread looks or the doubles, we play a lot of cover 3 or cover 1. Our Will linebacker has to be the adjuster. If we are in cover 1, the rover has the #2 receiver, and the corner has the #1 receiver. The weak corner has #1 to his side. Will has the #2 receiver. Mike is going to move. We are going to play games and try to get immediate pressure, so our coverage guys do not have to run for very long. If we cannot get pressure with our stunts, we are not stunting. We are going to find that out very quickly, because we are asking too much from our coverage guys.

If we give the offense 4 to 6 seconds to throw the ball, it is too much time. In our man coverage, we are going to take away all inside routes. We are going to force them to throw the fade, and we are going to be physical with the receivers.

In cover 3, we are going to show it and disguise it. Against doubles, we have a strong corner lined up on the #1 receiver. If it is cover 3 or cover 1, he is going to shift late, and the rover has the inside receiver or #2 receiver. Will is on the #2 receiver inside on the weakside. If we play cover 3, we are going to read the #2 receiver to the #1 receiver . Versus trips, Will is our adjuster. If we are in a cover

3, the Will and Rover set up so they do not give it away. We are going to run man coverage, or we are going to play cover 3, but we do not want to give it away.

We keep things simple by necessity. You do not always have the brightest kids. Sometimes we have intelligent kids, but not always. Depending on the game plan, we might call all the defensive plays on the field. Every week we will have special checks based on the scouting report. The kids know we have calls based on what the opponent does.

If we see a two-back team, that is what we are setting up our defense to stop. If they come out in a one-back set or a spread look, we have a check call. We have a one-back check and a spread check. Each week, no matter what they come out in, we have a check for it. We have a defensive check for it. Our kids are not going to look as if they are confused. They may recognize the set late sometimes, but we are going to have them understand what we are going to do against each look.

What we run in the defense, we set up for each formation. We have checks for each formation. It starts on Monday, and we teach it all during the week. We go over the checks every day in practice.

Our kids get a game tape every week. It will have their previous game on it, and they get a grade sheet. We are giving them every tool possible to be successful. They have got to want to be successful. They have cutups on all the plays. We have a sports edit system. They turn in their tape on Friday and pick it up again on Monday. It has their scout packet included. Our kids are good kids. They watch tapes with each other and spend a lot of time with each other. They were a special group this past year. I hope teams that follow them will do the same thing.

I hope you have gotten something from this lecture. It has been an honor for me to speak to you. Thank you.

DEFENSIVE COVERAGES AND BLITZ SCHEMES

North Allegheny Senior High School, Pennsylvania

North Allegheny Senior High School is 11 miles north of Pittsburgh. We are the second biggest school in western Pennsylvania, and we play in the highest classification there. It is an honor to come down and speak here today. A good thing about coming way down here is that we do not play any of you, so I can give you all of our secrets.

Last year, we gave up 7.1 points per game, which was the least amount of points in western Pennsylvania in our classification. We had a good season. We lost in the playoffs 14-10 to a team we had beaten three weeks earlier 28-3; so apparently we did not have it totally figured out.

My plan is to go through all this and show you as much as I can, with a lot of X's and O's and no stories that take up our time. The packets I gave you have spaces so you can draw in some things. Now, what you have in your packet is how it looks before you see the movement on the screen, so you guys can just draw in what you see and not worry about having to draw all 22 players. You can see how just a little bit of movement affects the whole scheme.

KEY POINTS OF PRESENTATION

- Base 4-4 with coverage system—Outnumber your opponents (with leverage and balance)
- Blitz to confuse opponents
- Zone blitz schemes
- Force, point, and cutback

Base 4-4

Our scheme is a 4-4 scheme (Diagram #1). We set it up with R, T, H, S, and TC always aligned to the tight end side. Our splitside guys are the E, N, M, W, and OC, and our FS always aligns to the strength of the formation. In this way, we are always going to match strength to strength.

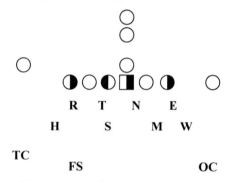

Diagram #1. Setting the Defense

We are the North Allegheny Tigers, so to get into our base 4-4, we call *Tiger*. I use the word Tiger so our players will think *Tiger equals tight*. That means we are setting the front to the tight end. Our rush end is in a 7 technique, our tackle is in a 3 technique, our noseguard is in a shade or 1 technique, and our end is in a 5 technique. We call Tiger to set the front. If we call *Tiger G*, we are just telling the noseguard to line up in a 2 technique instead of a 1 technique.

The second front that we use is called *over* (Diagram #2). We call it over because the noseguard and the tackle have moved over a gap. The rush has moved from a 7 technique over to a 5 technique, and the Hero has reduced to the 9-technique area. It is now more of a 50 type of look. The secondary and the Will linebacker stay the same, but our Stud and Mike linebackers move back one gap toward the tight end. That is what we call our *over front*. If we call *over shade*, the nose moves from a 2 technique to a shade, or 1 technique on the center.

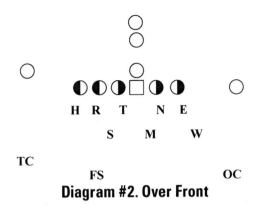
Diagram #2. Over Front

DEFENSIVE COVER SYSTEM

Our cover system has three ways of calling the defense, based upon the formations we might see. If the formation has two backs, then we are looking at two receivers on one side and one receiver on the other. If the formation has one back, then we are either looking at a 2x2 receiver set, which we call *ace deuces*, or we are looking at trips. They can be in empty, but empty is a form of trips. We can talk about unbalanced and other variations, but we will see two backs, one back (ace deuces), or one back with trips.

With that concept, the first part of our defensive call will be the front and any stunt we want to run. For example, *Tiger G Mike cross*, tells our front to align in Tiger G, and it tells our Mike linebacker to run a blitz and cross with the defensive lineman in front of him. That is the beginning part of the call.

The second part of the call is our coverage call. For example, if we call *Tiger G Mike cross 7-3 Baltimore*, 7-3 Baltimore is the coverage call. Since most high schools use the same personnel in all their formations, we have to fit our pass coverage to the formation that we see out of the offensive huddle. To do that, the first number, 7, is the coverage we will check to if they come out in two backs. If they come out in ace deuces, then we will play the coverage indicated by the second number, 3, which is a form of cover 3.

Finally, we use cities to indicate the coverage we will play to trips; in this case, it is Baltimore. Baltimore and cover 3 go together because Baltimore is a form of cover 3 that we play against trips.

Cover 7 Rules

If we call *Tiger 7-3 Baltimore* and they come out in two backs, we are playing cover 7. Our corners are deep-half players. The Hero and free safety read the tight end. If the tight end blocks, the free safety becomes the extra run defender. He is the ninth man in the box, while the corners are worried about any play-action pass with receivers over the top. That is how we play that.

If the tight end releases to the outside, the Hero will jump him (Diagram #3). With that, the corner plays for the deep threat. If he gets a vertical push, he is on top and the free safety is the robber underneath. We have taken away the curl/flat combination. When the free safety sees the outside release, he can bounce over and rob the curl without worrying about being a deep defender. On the backside, the corner is over top of everything, with the Stud, Mike, and Will linebackers playing underneath coverage.

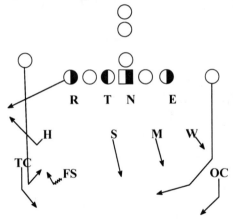

Diagram #3. Y Releases Outside vs. Cover 7

If the tight end crosses inside, the free safety will run with him (Diagram #4). When Hero reads the tight end inside, he gets underneath the #1 receiver. With the tight end crossing, #1 is probably running some kind of deep inside route, so we have Hero underneath him and the corner over the top. On the backside, we will probably see some sort of vertical route with the corner over the top. Stud, Mike, and Will are underneath players for any kind of play-action or waggle. We should be in good shape.

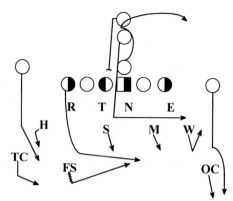

Diagram #4. Y Crosses Inside vs. Cover 7

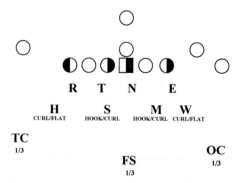

Diagram #6. Cover 3 vs. Ace Deuces

The corner is the half-field player over the top. So if we get a vertical release by the tight end, the toughest play for the free safety to cover is the vertical release and then the tight end breaks outside (Diagram #5). It is just like the inside man-to-man. The corner knows that Hero will work underneath #1 when he reads a vertical release by the tight end. He knows the free safety is jumping the tight end. Because he is getting help underneath, the corner knows he can help on the outside route by the tight end.

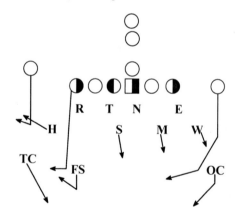

Diagram #5. Y Releases Vertical vs. Cover 7

Cover 3 Rules

If we call Tiger cover 7-3 Baltimore and they come out in ace deuces, we are playing cover 3 (Diagram #6). Our corners have the deep outside thirds, and our free safety has the deep middle third. Hero and Will are curl/flat players, and Stud and Mike are hook/curl players. Against any form of ace deuces, we will check to cover 3.

Baltimore Rules

If we call *Tiger cover 7-3 Baltimore* and they come out in trips, we are playing Baltimore (Diagram #7). Baltimore is a form of cover 3, and the B in Baltimore means we are bumping linebackers. They are sliding to the trips. Of course, if we are playing a team with a great running back, we have the option of not bumping all the way out. Mike is the guy whose alignment changes the most, so he is the one who adjusts to the specific threats and the game situation. If Mike walks all the way out, then our Stud becomes a two-gap player, so we have to understand that when we make our adjustment call.

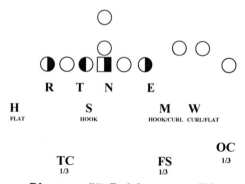

Diagram #7. Baltimore vs. Trips

If we see trips to the tight end side and an extension on the backside, the same principles apply (Diagram #8). We have called *Tiger cover 7-3 Baltimore* and we see trips to the tight end, so we check the coverage to Baltimore. We are bumping our linebackers to the trips. We have matched the strength of the formation, we are in a sound alignment, and we should be in good shape.

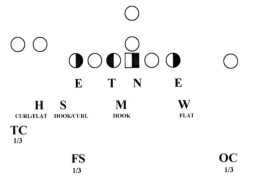

Diagram #8. Baltimore vs. Trips to Tight End

It is easy to get into our coverage system no matter what defense you play. If you are a 50 guy, a stack 3-5 guy, or if you are a 4-4 guy, you can fit this system in. If our opponent comes out in two backs, we check 7 and that is easy. Then, if the back motions to the split end side, we just check 3. The Willie moves with him, the free safety moves with it, and we adjust on the fly. We communicate coverage checks with a color system so we are not yelling out the coverage.

It would be the same way if the back motioned to the tight end side. That becomes a trips formation, so we would check to Baltimore, the linebackers would bump to the trips side, and the safety would adjust. We are in good shape.

Omaha

Omaha is our *roll defense* against a trips look. We are rolling our secondary instead of bumping our linebackers (Diagram #9). If we want to keep our two linebackers inside to defend a strong running attack or blitz the passer, we will roll the free safety down to the #2 receiver and roll the Will linebacker back to the middle. We have a little weakness on the backside here, so we will just cover the split end man for man, but we gain a bit of an advantage on the trips side.

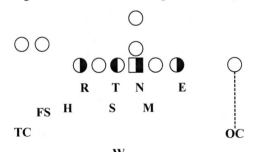

Diagram #9. Omaha vs. Trips to Tight End

If it is trips away from the tight end, we will roll the free safety down to the #3 receiver (Diagram #10). That way, if #3 motions back across to a 2x2 set, the free safety can roll back to the middle of the field. Our Omaha rule moves our tight corner to the middle of the field and assigns Hero to the tight end man for man. The inside backer covers back out away from trips, and all of our roll alignments work with the man for man stuff that I will show you.

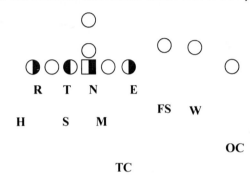

Diagram #10. Omaha vs. Trips

BLITZ TO CONFUSE OPPONENTS

If we call *Tiger Stud 7-3 Baltimore*, we are simply blitzing our Stud linebacker in the A gap with the tackle stunting into the B gap. Nothing else changes and we are playing our regular coverage system behind it. We are in great shape.

If we call *Tiger Stud cross 7-3 Baltimore*, the tackle stunts down hard in the A gap and the Stud crosses and blitzes in the B gap. As in the previous call, nothing else changes. You can see how you can be a simple 4-4 team. We can call a blitz with the coverage system behind it being able to adjust.

Blitz Man Protection Side

The coverage system and the blitz concepts are really the key things that we try to do. We can adjust the coverage systems by putting forms of cover 2 in there, forms of man, and forms of man free. I will show you a couple of different calls and different rules within the package so you can see how they fit.

With blitzes, we have to know what team we are playing and what their protection scheme is. Typically, dropback pass protection has a gapside and a manside. We have to know what side we are blitzing according to what blitz we are going to call.

If we want to blitz a 2x2 set and we know that the gap protection side is to our left, then we may want to blitz and confuse the other side, which would be the man protection side (Diagram #11). On that side, the guard and tackle would have our noseguard and end, and the back would have Mike or Will, whichever comes. If both come, there would be a guy uncovered and that would be a hot read for the quarterback.

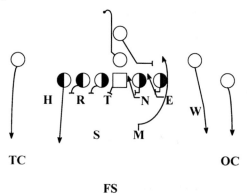

Diagram #11. Blitz and Confuse Manside

The back is the weakest pass blocker, so we are going to blitz him, make him move, make him hit, and match him to our best blitzer. The worst scenario would be our best blitzer on their worst blocker, and that would be if they protect it right and match up the way they are supposed to. We are only bringing three to that side and they are protecting with three, but what we are trying to do is confuse them. We will bring our noseguard and end inside to get their linemen moving with them and maybe occupy their back. Then, we will bring the Mike backer around so the back will have to adjust and move to try to get him. That is a favorable set of match-ups for us.

Blitz Gap Protection Side

The next part of it is the way we would blitz the gap protection side. They have three blockers for three gaps, so if we blitz that side, we will bring four and outnumber the protection (Diagram #12). On the manside, our noseguard and end will work hard to make sure the quarterback stays in the pocket. On the gapside, we will bring the Stud inside to make

sure all three gap blockers are occupied, and we will bring the Hero off the edge. It may be a little tough to cover behind it, so we may have to adjust the free safety and the Will alignments.

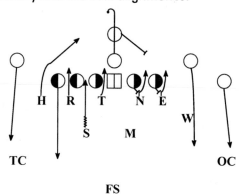

Diagram #12. Outnumber Protection on Gapside

Cover Zero Rules

We will also blitz with six people by bringing two linebackers along with the front four. When we do that, we are playing a form of man-to-man coverage. We have rules for all our man coverages. We will call *Tiger 0-10 Atlanta* (Diagram #13). This means we will play cover zero against two-back sets, cover 10 against ace deuces, and Atlanta against trips. Atlanta alerts the roll guy that he has the back out, but these are all forms of cover zero.

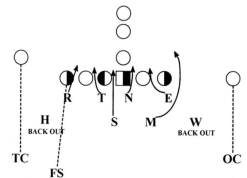

Diagram #13. Tiger Stud Mike Cannon 0-10 Atlanta

Stud means we are bringing our Stud linebacker, and *Mike cannon* means we are bringing our Mike linebacker through the C gap. Against the two-back set, our corners cover the #1 receivers, our outside linebackers cover the #2 receivers if twins, but they cover the back out if not. Our free safety covers the #2 receiver to the tight end side, but if there is no #2 receiver on that side, he plays alley away and has back out.

Against any ace deuces set, we will check to cover 10 (Diagram #14). The corners have #1, the outside backers have #2, the free safety has back out, and the inside backers are involved in the blitz. It is simple for our kids.

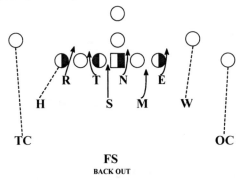

Diagram #14. Tiger 0-10 Atlanta

Against any trips formation, we will check to Atlanta (Diagram #15). The corner to trips has #1 and the corner away has #1 only if he is extended. If he is not extended, we will roll to the middle of the field and cover back out. The free safety inverts to trips, covers #2 if there is a tight end and #3 if there is not a tight end.

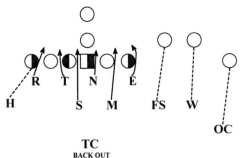

Diagram #15. Atlanta

The Atlanta rules seem like a lot when you write them down, but they are really easy for our kids. If our Hero is on the trips side, he covers #2 if there is no tight end and #3 if there is a tight end. Away from trips, he covers #1 if #1 is not extended, but he inverts to the middle of the field and covers back out if #1 is extended. If our Will is on the trips side, he covers #2, and away from trips, he rolls to the middle and covers back out. Notice we are lining up with the roll players just like Omaha.

If we get tight end trips, we will leave Hero on the tight end because he is most likely our worst man-to-man defender (Diagram #16). We could be in trouble against a really good tight end, but we are bringing six people on the blitz. Our secondary will be just fine if our Stud linebacker can get to the quarterback, so our variety of blitzes will protect our man coverage.

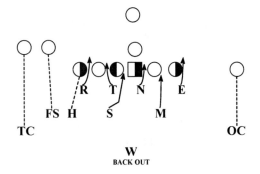

Diagram #16. Atlanta vs. Trips to Tight End

Motions

The cover zero rules allow us to adjust the coverage to two-back sets, one-back sets, and trips. The design of the coverage gives us the match-ups we want and the easy adjustments to the various sets without affecting the blitzes we have called up front. That holds up when we see motion. Whether the motion changes the formation from pro to twins, from two back to one back, or from ace deuces to trips, the coverage rules I have given you allow our kids to make easy adjustments in the secondary while our kids involved in the blitzes are unaffected. You cannot use motion to dictate to us when or how we will blitz because we are in control.

Cover Zero Blitz Schemes

You have seen our Tiger Stud Mike cannon blitz, against manside protection and against zone side protection when we are in cover zero. Now, I want to show you three more blitzes (Diagram #17). We also run *Tiger G axe*, where we line up in Tiger G and cross blitz our Stud and Mike linebackers in the A gaps.

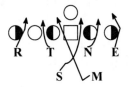

Diagram #17. Tiger G Axe

We run *Tiger nasty Will*, where we bring our Will linebacker off the edge, our end inside, and our noseguard across the center to the strong A gap (Diagram #18).

Diagram #18. Tiger Nasty Will

Finally, against a double-slot formation we run *over G Stud Mike*, which gives us a great match-up for our linebackers (Diagram #19).

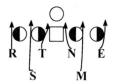

Diagram #19. Over G Stud Mike

Zone Blitz Schemes

When we go to our zone blitz scheme, we are trying to trick the offense. We want the blocker to think he is blocking somebody who is a dropper. If the call is *dart whip drop three*, the dart part of it says D gap to our players, and we line up similar to our Baltimore alignment (Diagram #20). The D-gap guy is our blitzer. The *T* in dart says that our tackle is the dropper. We are going to bring the rush down inside and make the offensive tackle try to block him. That will free up our Stud linebacker off the edge. The tackle will occupy the offensive guard so he will not help on our rush end, and then he becomes our dropper. Our zone blitz schemes are all based on three-deep, three-under coverage, and bringing five on the blitz.

The *whip* part of the call is the backside part of it. The *W* means that we have our Will linebacker coming off the edge with the noseguard and end blitzing inside. On the frontside, we work the #2 and #3 receivers, same as Baltimore, and the backside is over the top, same as Omaha.

Against ace deuces, we are still running dart whip, but now the Hero is the D-gap guy, so we bring

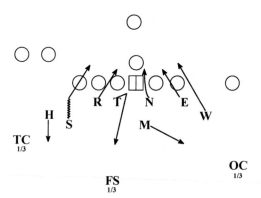

Diagram #20. Dart Whip Drop Three

him off the frontside edge and replace his drop with the Sam linebacker. Since Will is removed, we run the whip with our Mike linebacker and replace Mike's drop with Will. Everything else remains the same.

If we call *string whip drop three*, the whip part remains the same as I just described, but the *S* and *N* in string refer to the Stud and the noseguard (Diagram #21). We will bring our tackle outside to make the offensive tackle take him, and then create a 2-on-1 inside with our Stud and nose on the offensive guard. Now, our rush end is the dropper and we are three-deep, three-under, bring five.

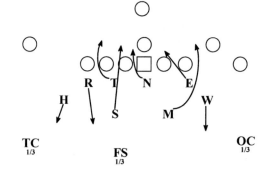

Diagram #21. Sting Whip Drop Three

The simplest zone blitz to install is the *Stud cross Mike drop three* (Diagram #22). We bring the ends up the field, the tackle inside, and Stud in the B gap. Mike blitzes his B gap and the noseguard is the dropper. The coverage is the same.

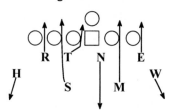

Diagram #22. Stud Cross Mike Drop Three

Leverage With Force

When we install a defense, we all want our guys to pursue the football, but in our system, there are three kinds of players in pursuit—there are force guys, point guys, and cutback players (Diagram #23). The force guy has got to know who he is. Against the sweep, the Hero has to know he is force and he has to turn everything back to everybody else. He becomes the fencepost, so he gets up there and squeezes the play as hard as he can. Now, we are in a position where everybody else can fly to the football.

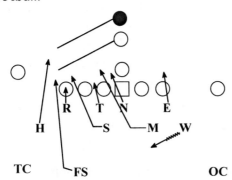

Diagram #23. Leverage With Force—Sweep Play

The free safety can be right at it, the Stud can be right at it, and the Mike can be right at it. Those guys are fliers. The linebackers are scraping. The linemen are beating blocks, and everybody is flying to the ball, but there needs to be somebody who is watching our rear ends.

That player is our Will linebacker. He is our cutback player. We use the term *BCRS* with our kids, which means in order, bootleg, counter, reverse, or screen. When the play goes away from our Will linebacker, in his brain he repeats B-C-R-S and lets nine guys make the play over there. He becomes the guy who has to make the play if the ball comes back. The corner is also back there to help, but it is Will's responsibility. When he says B-C-R-S to himself, which is enough time to slow him down and keep him in position to make the play.

If we see a lead play up inside, we apply the concept in the same way (Diagram #24). The Mike is the force guy. He will hit it, drill it, and drive it back. The Sam and free safety are point players, Hero is the cutback player, Willie is the bounce player, and the corners are over the top.

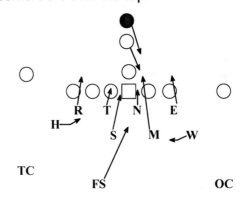

Diagram #24. Leverage With Force—Lead Play

I did not go over our Cover 1 rules today. I will be around later to discuss anything you are interested in reviewing. Thank you.

GOAL LINE AND 4-2-5 DEFENSIVE PACKAGE

Brooke High School, West Virginia

Thank you. I appreciate the opportunity to be with you to share what we do with our defense. We run an aggressive attacking defense. Our base alignment is the 4-2-5 look. Between 70 and 80 percent of the time, we are blitzing or attacking in some form or fashion. Because we do blitz so much of the time we must stress two areas in our defense. We must stress tackling and pursuit. Because of the lack of depth, we do tackling practice without pads. Our basic philosophy is to attack the offense with movement and blitzes. We hang our hat on a man-blitzing defense. We feel the most important part of tackling is getting to the ball. You will hear me talk about the three Rs of defense: read, react, and run.

I do want to talk briefly about the type of personnel we need to run this defense. For the front four, we want players who have played linebacker but were not starters. We take the big linemen and move them to the offensive side of the ball. We are willing to sacrifice size for speed. Our defensive ends are just slightly smaller than our linebackers and linemen.

We like the traditional-size linebackers. We want them strong enough to stop the run, and fast enough to defend against the pass. We play with two strong safeties, one free safety, and two corners.

I want to talk about a couple of quotes about teaching and coaching.

Coaching consists of team preparation, devising game plans and schemes to defeat opponents. When you are coaching, you are dealing with strategies, different offenses and defenses, and putting in plays to take advantage of skills, strengths, and weaknesses of your players. The measure of a coach is the quality development of his system, and has been distilled into winning.

Teaching consists of instruction and training of individuals in the fundamental skills of the game, and in teaching players how to play, instead of how to run plays. The measure of a teacher is not in winning, but in the fundamental soundness and skill level of the players taught. A player with excellent fundamentals and skills can play successfully in any system.

—Jay Bilas, "America Needs More 'Teaching' From Its Coaches" (ESPN.com)

Basketball is overcoached and undertaught. The United States produces the best "athletes" in the game, but not necessarily the best basketball players.

—Pete Newell, legendary coach and teacher

He is absolutely right, and it is finally catching up with us, as is the rest of the basketball world. What is the reason for this happening?

Problems

- Instant gratification.
- It takes time to teach and instill discipline.
- Too focused on winning instead of developing players.
- High school coaches get less practice time than ever and less access to the kids. Practice time cannot be wasted.

What does it take to have a successful defense? I do not care what scheme you teach and believe in. There are special points to consider if you want to be successful on defense:

- Scheme: Teach it, and believe it (indoctrination).
- Progression teaching: Paint by the numbers.
- Position-specific movement: Do not drill just to drill.
- Pursuit: Put bodies in the picture.
- Tackling: Technique is the key.
- Takeaways: We must practice creating turnovers.

Look at your scheme. Does your philosophy fit within your scheme? Your base defense and how you play the secondary are all-important when it comes to your scheme.

Scheme

- Split-4 philosophy
  - ✓ Defend gap-control defense
  - ✓ Blitz gap-cancellation defense
  - ✓ Coverage: Man or zone

Practice Planning

- Teach by progression.
- We call it paint by the numbers.

Position-Specific Movement

- Choose or develop drills that fit your scheme.
- The drills must have a reason (do not drill just to drill).
- Simulate game reactions.
- Specific drills
  - ✓ Leverage drill
  - ✓ Triangle drill

Pursuit

- Specific drills
  - ✓ Sideline drill
  - ✓ Digit drill
  - ✓ Pass pursuit drill

Tackling Progression

- Technique of the tackle
- Footwork for the tackle
- Approach to the tackle
- Finish the tackle
- Video

Causing the Turnover

- Practice creating the turnover.
- Circuit train turnover drills.

DEFENSIVE PHILOSOPHY

There are two schools of thought when discussing defensive philosophy of football. One school believes that it is the job of the defense to stop the opposing offense from scoring. The defense will be sound and react to the offense. The second school of thought places the defense's responsibility on a slightly different level. We believe it is the responsibility of the defense to return the ball to the offense and to keep the opposing offense from dictating the pace of the game. Whether it is done by creating turnovers or by holding the opposition to a three-play series, it is critical that the ball stay in the opponent's hand for as little time as possible. This will also accomplish the first task. If they don't have the ball, they can't score. The following is a list of priorities in our defensive philosophy:

- We must challenge the offense, not just defend it. We will actively attack the offense.
- The number-one purpose of the defense is to regain possession of the ball for the offense. We must emphasize the creation of turnovers and forcing the offense into long-yardage situations.
- We must force the offense into low-percentage forms of attack (such as long passes or trick plays) to assure that they will have a higher probability of making mistakes and stopping themselves.
- As with any defense, we must be able to bend but not break. Most high school offenses cannot drive the ball the length of the field or for more than eight plays without making at least one mistake. When it occurs, the defense must be able to capitalize. We must regain possession of the ball.
- As with all football teams, it is important to adapt the defense to fit our personnel.
- We also believe it is important to line up in multiple fronts. Different alignments confuse blocking assignments and create more practice time for opposing offenses. The use of multiple stunts can also serve the same purpose.

- Without aggressive players, no defense will succeed. We want at least eight guys in the picture within a three count of the initial contact. We practice it this way.

Our defensive rules:
- Move on move.
- Play the defense called.
- Communicate.
- Attack.
- Pursue.
- Hit, hit, hit.
- Get the ball.

Defense mode:
- Identify
- Communicate
- Execute

SECONDARY PLAY

We only play three coverages. We play man-free, a three-deep zone, and a two-deep zone rotation. Now, within those three coverages, we have a variety of different techniques we use.

Listed are the different techniques we use within our coverage package:
- *Bump:* The defensive back aligns to the inside shoulder of the receiver and delivers a blow with the off hand based on the wide receiver's release. The aiming point of the jam is in the breastplate of the shoulder pads. On an outside release, we will force the wide receiver wide and progress to running on the inside hip.
- *Press:* The defensive back aligns as if he is in bump technique. Just before the snap or at the snap, depending on speed, the defensive back will drop into coverage. We can roll off into man coverage or zone coverage, depending on our game plan. We hope to slow the quarterback's read long enough for our pass rush to have an effect.
- *Loose:* This is our off-man technique. We will align according to the split of the wide receiver. We will read the initial drop of the quarterback and progress into our man coverage from there. We

base it on a three-step or five-step drop of the quarterback.
- *Base:* This is our off-zone technique. We want it to look the same as our loose technique. We will read the EMOL (end man on line) to the quarterback and progress into our zone coverage from there. We will play a three-deep and two-deep scheme from this technique.

CREATING TURNOVERS

We pride ourselves on the ability to create turnovers, and a big part of that is practicing how to create the turnover. During a 10-minute period of our defensive practice, we run a circuit drill where everyone on the team will practice stripping the ball in three different ways. The strip drills are as follows:
- *Punch Drill:* If we cannot see the ball as we approach from behind, or we can see the ball as we approach from the front, then the ballcarrier is carrying the ball high. Therefore, we want to punch up at the ball as we tackle. Swing the hands up between the ballcarrier's arms and body as contact is made.
- *Swat Drill:* If the opposite is true, and the ball is visible from behind or is not visible from the front, then we will swat down on the ball as we make contact with the ballcarrier.
- *Rip Drill:* If we have the ballcarrier standing up and our people are on him, then we use the rip technique. The defender lifts up on the elbow and pushes down on the wrist to create a twisting motion with the arm. This will most always result in a fumble.

In the next segment, I want to get to the X's and O's and talk about our defensive front package. We have an end, tackle, nose, and rush end on the front. Our strongside linebacker is the Strike. The backside outside linebacker is the Bandit. Will is the weakside linebacker, and Mike is the strongside linebacker.

I want to show you the front four, the linebacker's alignment, and the technique for each front. First is our base 33 front (Diagram #1).

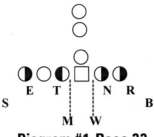

Diagram #1. Base 33

End: 6i technique
Tackle: 3 technique
Nose: 3 technique
Rush: 5 technique.
Strike: 4x3, force/insurance
Mike: A gap to flow
Will: A gap to flow
Bandit: 3x3 force/insurance

If we bring the Bandit down on the line of scrimmage and move the nose tackle down into the A gap, we have our split 32 look (Diagram #2).

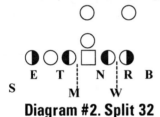

Diagram #2. Split 32

End: 6i technique
Tackle: 3 technique
Nose: 2i technique
Rush: 5 technique
Strike: 4x3, force/insurance
Mike: A gap to flow
Will: B gap to flow
Bandit: 7 technique, force/fold

To run the same defense on the tight-end side, we move the Strike up on the outside of the tight end (Diagram #3). That is our tite 23 call.

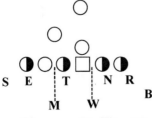

Diagram #3. Tite 23

End: 6i technique
Tackle: 2i technique
Nose: 3 technique
Rush: 5 technique
Strike: 9 technique, force/fold
Mike: B gap to flow
Will: A gap to flow
Bandit: 3x3, force/fold

If we want to bring both the Strike and Bandit up on the line of scrimmage, we call switch 22 (Diagram #4). It is an eight-man front with the two linebackers in the C gaps. If the offensive back offsets to the force man, he should slide to the end of the line of scrimmage.

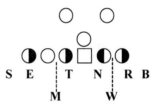

Diagram #4. Switch 22

End: 6i technique
Tackle: 2i technique
Nose: 2i technique
Rush: 5 technique
Strike: 9 technique, force/fold
Mike: A gap to flow
Will: B gap to flow
Bandit: 9 technique, force/fold

If we want to slide the linebackers to the weakside, we call over 31 (Diagram #5). The Mike is in the strongside A gap, and the Will is in the weakside C gap.

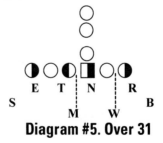

Diagram #5. Over 31

End: 6i technique
Tackle: 3 technique

Nose: 1 technique

Rush: 5 technique

Strike: 4x3, force/insurance

Mike: A gap to flow

Will: B gap to flow

Bandit: 3x3, force/insurance

We can bring the strongside end and tackle down to the inside gaps and play our slide 41 look (Diagram #6). The weakside plays the same as they did on the over 31 call.

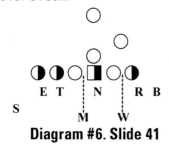

Diagram #6. Slide 41

End: 6i technique

Tackle: 4i technique

Nose: 1 technique

Rush: 5 technique

Strike: 4x3, force/insurance

Mike: A gap to flow

Will: B gap to flow

Bandit: 7 technique, force/fold

If we want to play on the outside shoulder of the strongside line, we call our tuff split 32 alignment (Diagram #7). The Strike plays a 9 technique, the end is in a 5 technique, and the tackle moves to a 3 technique. The nose plays a 2i, and the rush end plays a 5 technique.

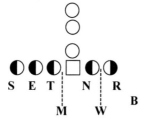

Diagram #7. Tuff Split 32

Strike: 9 technique, force/fold

End: 5 technique

Tackle: 3 technique

Nose: 2i technique

Rush: 5 technique

Mike: A gap to flow

Will: B gap to flow

Bandit: 3x3, force/insurance

If we want to switch the tackle and the Mike, we call tuff switch 22 (Diagram #8). It is the same call for the backside. The Strike and end play the same techniques. It is a change-up for the tackle and Mike.

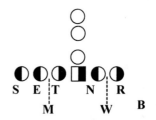

Diagram #8. Tuff Switch 22

If we want to move the nose man outside and bring the Will in the A gap, we call "tuff tite 23" (Diagram #9).

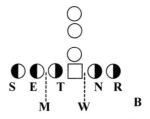

Diagram #9. Tuff Tite 23

Strike: 9 technique, force/fold

End: 5 technique

Tackle: 2i technique

Nose: 3 technique

Rush: 5 technique

Mike: B gap to flow

Will: A gap to flow

Bandit: 3x3, force/insurance

Our tuff base 33 is a split 4-4 look with the Mike and Will inside over the A gaps (Diagram #10). The Strike is on the outside of the tight end, and the Bandit is off the line on the weakside.

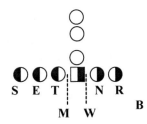

Diagram #10. Tuff Base 33

If we want to move the Will backer over to the B gap, we will call tuff over 31 (Diagram #11). The nose plays on the outside of the weakside guard. We have the same alignment for the other front people.

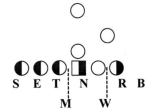

Diagram #11. Tuff Over 31

GOALS FOR OUR G-CAT DEFENSE

I want to spend a few minutes on the goal-line defense. We use the G-Cat from the six-yard line in. We have set goals for our G-Cat goal-line defense:

- We will stop the offense from scoring a touchdown.
- We must hold offense to a field-goal attempt.
- We must take away the offense's best green-zone plays.
- We must stop the play-action pass and option with G-Cat.
- We will not give up a score on a trick play.

We establish special takeaways for our G-Cat defense:

- After a tendency breakdown, we will determine the plays to stop.
- Our goal-line period will be designed to stop these plays.
- Any adjustments to G-Cat will be made to stop these plays.
- We will always make sure to stop the play-action pass and option.

G-Cat: Base Alignment, Assignment, Responsibility, and Rules

The Base Alignment Rules: Both defensive tackles will align in a 2i technique. As the ball gets closer to the goal line, the alignment of the defensive tackles will reduce as well. By the time the ball is inside the one-yard line, the defensive tackles are eye-to-eye with the offensive center.

Responsibility: A gap and quarterback wedge play—The defensive ends both align in a 4 technique.

Responsibility: C gap to the B gap squeeze—The outside linebackers both will align in a head-up technique. Against a tight end, the outside linebacker will play a man-press technique on the Y-end. Against no tight end, the outside linebacker will play an edge technique. Versus a slot, the outside linebacker will play a man-press technique on the #2 receiver. Against trips, the outside linebacker will make a help call and man-press the #3 receiver.

Responsibility: Man-press or edge technique—The corners or defensive backs play an edge technique to a closed side. Versus an extension, the corner will play man-press technique on the #1 receiver.

Responsibility: B gap to fill or B gap to scrape—The Mike linebacker will play over the ball and read backfield flow. On an "I am down" call, the Mike will slide, aligning to the B gap. Mike has no pass-coverage responsibility in G-Cat.

Responsibility: B gap to fill, C gap to scrape, or edge technique—The Buck linebacker aligns stacked on the defensive end and reads backfield flow. Versus an extension, Buck makes an "I am down" call and plays the edge. He has no pass-coverage responsibility when aligned in the high B gap.

G-Cat: Explanation of Defensive Techniques Used in Successful G-Cat

Edge Technique: Technique used by the player on the edge of the defense.

- Versus run: Player is responsible for force versus run his way.

- Versus pass: Player is responsible for BOB (back out of backfield).
- Versus option: Edge player is responsible for the pitchman.
- Possible edge players: Corner, outside linebacker, Buck.

Man-Press Technique: Used to cover the quick receivers of the formation.

- Corner: Plays man-press on #1, who is extended from the formation.
- Outside linebacker: Plays man-press on the tight end or #2 extended from the formation.
- "Help" call: Outside linebacker may also play man-press on #3 versus a 3x1 set.

Stack Technique: Buck linebacker when he is aligned "high" versus formation

- Buck aligns stacked on the defensive end, who is playing a 4 technique.
- Action to: Buck will fill downhill into the C gap.
- Action away: Buck will find the run-through lane to the ball.
- Versus option: Buck will take the quarterback; on the edge, he takes pitch.
- Versus pass: Buck will run through C gap for contain or pull-up.

Squeeze Technique: Used by defensive end when aligned in a 4 technique on the offensive tackle.

- Premise: Defensive end cannot allow the offensive tackle to release inside to 2nd level.
- Gap control: Defensive end plays C gap but is a squeeze player in B gap. Note: In other words, there is no B gap (denied by defensive end).
- Versus pass: Defensive end is the contain rush adjusting off Buck's rush.
- Versus option: The defensive end is the quarterback player (he may have help on the quarterback).

First, I want to show you the G-Cat against a power set (Diagram #12). We are on the goal line from the six-yard line in. Our inside linebackers can go to either side. We are basically in a 6-5 goal-line set.

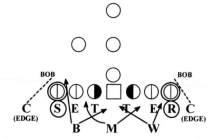

Diagram #12. G-Cat vs. Power Set

If the offense splits the back and X-end, we take our corners and cover them one-on-one. We tie the Strike on the tight end man-to-man. The Bandit and rush end both play the edge (Diagram #13). They can give a call to let the other defensive secondary players know what they are doing. The corner can give a call to let the inside backers know he is out of the base defense and is playing man-to-man on the splitback.

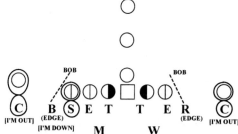

Diagram #13. G-Cat vs. Pro Set

The tackles take care of the inside gaps to prevent the sneak. The down linemen keep the blockers off the linebackers.

I see my time is up. I hope this has given you some ideas on setting up the even front defense and the adjustment you can make from a multiple 4-2-5 defense. Thank you.

THE NO-HUDDLE 4-4 BASE DEFENSE AND DRILLS

Greensburg Central Catholic High School, Pennsylvania

I am going to tell you a little about our program. The one thing I want to tell you is that I know nothing about the defense. I hired a defensive coordinator and told him to run the defense. I told him he would never hear from me except on the sideline when things are going bad. I will simply ask him, "Are you going to stop that, or what are you going to do?" We allow all the coaches on the defensive side of the ball to do their own thing.

I think the thing that has made me successful is that when I worked for other people, they allowed me to coach. The head coach has to let his assistant coaches do what they do best. He has to allow them the freedom to coach. The reason we made it to the state finals this year had a lot to do with us hiring a young coach who had previously played for us. He played at the University of Toledo, and adding him to the staff took us over the hump. I am old-fashioned, so I let him do his job and stayed out of the way.

We play a base 4-4 defense. We do not blitz very often. We teach our players how to play the base defense. We start our program in the winter by getting our players in the weight room. We have a good weight program. We have a Max Sled in our weight room, and every day that we lift, we work on the sled. The sled has an indicator that can register the power you are hitting it with and at what speed. The stronger our players are, the better our defense is.

This year, we forced 57 turnovers with 27 of those being interceptions. We are good in the defensive secondary, but where we dominate is in the defensive line. Our players are very strong. Our two tackles bench over 400 pounds, and they are both back next year.

We started at Central Catholic in 1995. The first year we were there, we scored 100 points and gave up 219 points. You can figure we were not very good. After that first season, we started getting better on the defensive side of the ball. This year, we played 16 games and gave up an average of nine points a game. We gave up 158 points, but 36 of them came in the Mount Pleasant game. We lost the game 36-35 and neither team played any defense.

If you can play good defense and beat people up front, you have a chance of winning. We have a large squad, and I try to play as many kids as possible. We play two-platoon football. I know there are teams that play their players on both offense and defense for four quarters. I do not think they can give you much when they are tired. We ask our players to play six quarters. They play all four quarters on the side of the ball that they excel in and two on the other side of the ball. That gives us many options during the game.

This year, we used six different defensive tackles and four different defensive ends. We work our players hard during practice and reward them with playing time. I am an old-fashioned coach. We line up and run the ball at people. Until I hired some younger coaches, we did nothing but run the power.

We try to play offense and defense the same. That means we play both *physically*. The secret for our success is that we work hard in the weight room and use as many players as possible in the games.

Dan Mahoney, my defensive coordinator, was instrumental in installing this defense and deserves the credit for its success. He is at Syracuse

University today with a recruit. Now, I want to turn the lecture over to my linebackers coach, and he will take you the rest of the way.

DAVE KEEFER

I am happy to be speaking here today. I agree with Coach Colosimo when he says the reason we are successful is the cohesiveness we have on our staff. We are close and discuss all the things that go into the game plan. I give all the credit to Coach Colosimo for giving us the latitude to do the things we do.

We play a 4-4 defense, but that does not mean we do not get into other looks defensively. Our philosophy is very basic. We win many games in the off-season because we have a great off-season training program. We do power lifting and plyometrics. This morning, before we came over here, we had a Saturday morning workout. On Saturday mornings, we will have 25 players come in to work out.

PHILOSOPHY

The defensive philosophy of Greensburg Central Catholic football is to outwork, outpractice, and outplay the opponent throughout the year, both out of season and in-season. This can be established through the total commitment of the best 11 players who are committed to playing to the best of their ability on and off the field. This does not necessarily mean the best athletes.

In our philosophy, we want to outwork our opponents in the off-season and in-season. We want to get the players committed to playing to the best of their abilities. The players must have confidence and get the mind-set that they are better prepared than their opponents are. That mind-set will create competition within the program.

The other mind-set you must create is making the players think they are the toughest guys that ever existed. They need to think that teams fear them. This is my eighth season at Central, and you have to hammer that into your players. That is what we try to do. The players know coming into the program, they are going to have coaches that are going to be tough on them. The coaches respect them, but they are going to be tough on them and drive them.

Our practice organization is very systematic. We take one thing after the other, and every session is 15 minutes in length. Once you start belaboring a point, you start losing your players. You have to be highly organized in what you do or the players start to get bored. It is not as it used to be when the coach told the team he was going to get two hours of good practice if it took him three hours to do it. It is very difficult to do that anymore with the types of players we deal with.

These players today think they are entitled to start, and if they are not going to start, they may not want to play at all. We have to switch gears and capture these kids. You cannot beat kids into the ground anymore and expect them to play for you. You can do that, but they have to want to play like that. You can achieve it, but it takes a high degree of organization and caring.

They do not understand that the first 30 minutes of our practice is spent conditioning. They think we are just working drills. We do it that way so we do not have to spend 15 to 20 minutes at the end of practice doing conditioning sprints.

Our off-season conditioning program and our weight program is excellent. We change things up in the program and keep them interested. You cannot give a player a program and tell him to work on it. Every two to three weeks we change what we are doing. The players do not get bored, and all the muscles groups get the work they need. We change the program so the muscles have to adapt to the new program.

Fundamentals, practice, and hard work are the only way we can achieve success. Commitment to the position coach's directives to gap control, pursuit, technique, and desire, as well as off-season weight room and conditioning, will lead to this goal. Nothing short of this will lead to our desired results.

We swarm on defense. That goes back to the way we practice. We emphasize getting to the ball. One of the things I brought from another school was the no-huddle defense. If you watch any film on us, we do not huddle. Our players are where they are supposed to be in all points and times.

We put the time in on film study. It may look like we are stunting, but we do not stunt that much. It may look like that, but tendencies of the offense dictate that. If we have a linebacker flying to the B gap, the offensive formation dictated his play. If we find a team that is running the B gap from a particular formation 80 percent of the time, we want the linebacker firing that gap regardless of his key. He is attacking the B gap right now, and we will take the 20-percent chance they are running somewhere else.

This year, we had 57 turnovers in 15 games. That was the most turnovers we have ever had at Central Catholic. Our offense turned the ball over seven times during the season. That is a plus-50 turnover ratio. We have a knack for getting the ball. We emphasize taking the ball away from the offense. Plus 50 turnovers is pretty darn good, and that is one of the reasons we were successful this year.

I would recommend the no-huddle defense. As soon as the offense comes out in a formation, we have automatic calls we use. Some teams start out in a power I formation, and the next thing you know they are in a spread formation. Our players are ready for those types of situations. The coaches on the sideline signal coverages and alignments to the players on the field. They look to the sideline for signals, but they really do not need to. We have automatic coverage formations. They look to the sideline to make sure they are calling the right coverages. We are a multiple coverage team. We can play basic zone coverages and man coverages.

Our players are not scrambling to get where they are supposed to be. They know where to line up because it is automatic to them.

The calls we make reflect a certain way to set the defense. If the offense comes out in a certain formation, we have a certain set we play to that formation. If the offense comes out in something that is very different than what we have prepared for, the players know the hand signals and they know which coach to look for. In that case, the coach calls the defense.

Down-and-distance is very important for the defense. They must know what situational downs are and what the offensive tendencies are in those areas. We need to address the turnover issues and what defenses we execute best in a game situation. Sometimes we think we have a great game plan. However, for some reason, things do not work. We have to be prepared to change things in the game plan.

We make a plan to stop a power and the offense starts running a trap and they are successful at it. I have always had the philosophy, as a defensive coordinator, that a defense cannot stop everything. We will make adjustments to stop the trap, but we are going with the percentages and tendencies of the offense to develop a game plan. We are going to game plan to stop what the offense runs the most. They may have some success with another play, but through game adjustments, we will stop that play.

Be positioned correctly to play your gap responsibility. This boils down to fundamentals. Traditionally, everyone aligns with a technique numbering system. We do not do that. We align our defenders by numbering each offensive lineman with #1, #2, and #3. #1 is the inside shoulder position. #2 is the head-up position, and #3 is the outside shoulder of the offensive player. We do that for the down linemen and linebackers. Our terminology is different, but I believe it is simpler for the defenders to understand.

A 5 technique, for us, is a #3 position on the offensive tackle. We changed this in the last two years and it has helped our players. We did the same thing with our coverages. We do not number the coverages. We use colors to designate the coverage. We call *white*, *silver*, or *maroon*. We game plan for the coverage and coach up the ones we are going to use. We can always run the other coverages, but we do not think we will use them in a particular game. We practice the one we feel fits the game plan and change or adjust during the game.

On defensive front, stunts, and coverages we want to be in the best situation to run them. That comes down to game planning and film study.

DEFENSIVE GOALS

- Under 100 yards rushing
- No big plays over 20 yards
- Win turnover battle
- Score as a defensive unit
- Pursuit
- Tackling

The design of the 4-4 defense is to stop the run. The main staple in most high school programs is the running game. If you stop the running game, you stop most high school teams. That does not mean we are going to play the 4-4 exclusively, but it will be our primary base defense. We are going to design alignments and adjustments to fit what the game plan calls for. We set these goals to get into the minds of our players. In high school football, if you stop the run most of the time you are going to win.

We want to stop big plays. We consider anything over 20 yards as a big play. We want to limit any plays over 20 yards. I mentioned earlier the trap play. It does not matter if the offense is successful with the trap. If teams want to use the trap as a way to beat us, God bless 'em. We will let them trap, but eventually, we will stop it. Plays that run for 5 to 10 yards, we do not worry about. We are going to be solid fundamentally across the board, and we feel the trap is not a play that will beat us. If they trap one player, we get him to improve his technique and he stops the trap.

The linebacker has to be ready in his stance before the ball is snapped. We start in the stance and play fundamentally from there. As soon as the linebacker stands up and gets out of his fundamental football position, that means they are *looking* instead of *playing* his technique. That is one of my pet peeves.

We feel you must win the turnover battle. I mentioned earlier that we had a plus-50 turnover ratio this year. In high school, college, or the pros, the team that wins the turnover battle usually wins the game.

We want to score as a defensive unit. We had two returns for touchdowns this year. We had an interception and a fumble return for a touchdown this year. We have transition drills we use in practice for that very scenario. If a player intercepts the ball, we have a procedure that the defense goes through to try to return that ball for a score. If a player intercepts a ball, our defense does not stand in one place. We transition from defense to offense and try to score.

I feel like pursuit is an important point for any defensive football team. We have daily pursuit drills we do in our defensive periods. In those drills, we assign landmarks for the players to the ball. This is not a tackling drill. We have the cones set up on the sideline and the defenders are playing their techniques and running to their assigned landmark.

Every day we start our practice off with a tackling drill. We do tackling drills in every scenario. We do open field tackling, sideline tackling, or goal-line tackling. We have a tackling circuit and a turnover circuit. We rotate through the circuit, which takes 15 to 20 minutes. We have five stations in the tackling circuit.

In our tackling circuit, we teach the goal-line tackle, three-dummy scoop, low-ball block, open field tackle, and lateral slide and attack. In the turnover circuit, we do recovery and secure, fumble recovery, club and rip, club and punch, and interception. We do this at every defensive practice and try to instill that into our players. We do the circuits at the beginning of every practice. We take pride in and try to hang our hat on *turnovers*.

I want to talk about some of the drills we do. The first one is a pursuit drill (Diagram #1). We do this daily. We have a rabbit, who is a fast offensive player. The drill starts with the defense on the sideline. The coach blows the whistle and the defense sprints onto the field and gets into their defensive alignment. A coach standing in the shotgun position tosses the ball to the rabbit. He must go outside the cones and up the sideline. This is not a tackling drill, and they do not stop the rabbit. He runs the entire sideline as the defense pursues.

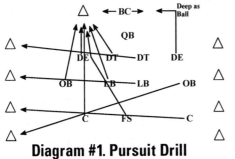

Diagram #1. Pursuit Drill

The outside linebacker gets up the field as the force player. The playside defenders go straight to the ball. The corner and safety react to their fits on the outside linebacker. The corner forces from the outside to the inside. The rush end goes to the ball. The Sam linebacker scrapes to the ball, and the rest of the defense pursuits to the cones on the sideline. The defensive end opposite the path of the ball is the trail pursuer and watches for any reverse, bootleg, or misdirection plays. The Will linebacker slow plays the backside and takes the last cone in the opposite sideline. He is the last defender in the pursuit angle.

We are not just coaching pursuit. We are developing a mentality of the defense, and it is a great conditioner within practice. During our season, we do not do much conditioning after practice. We work them at high speed in 15-minute segments in practice to get their conditioning done. If they are running around and busting their butts in 15-minute segments, they are getting the conditioning they need.

One of the principle changes we had this year was in-season weight lifting. Monday is our film day. We watch our game film and the scouting film. We go over the scouting report and do the clerical stuff on that day. We started doing some heavy weight lifting on that day. I think that helped us during the season. We were in much better condition and so much stronger heading into the playoffs. I felt we were stronger than any team we played in the playoffs. Usually teams start to weaken as the season drags on. Our players got stronger during the season because of the way we set up our conditioning.

We have another pursuit drill we use in our pass-rush scheme (Diagram #2). The defensive linemen get into their stance and rush the passer. They use their primary pass rush moves. They use the swim, rip, or whatever technique they choose. The secondary and linebacker drop into their coverage zones. The quarterback throws the ball into an area of the field, and the defense pursues to the ball. Everyone has to drive to the ball no matter where he throws the ball. The emphasis in the drill is *proper angle*. If you practice these things, you stand a better chance of your players doing what you want. You have to emphasize to the corner away from the throw that he has to get into the proper angle and go to the ball.

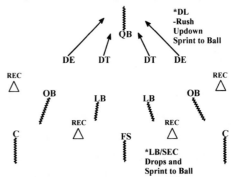

Diagram #2. Pass-Pursuit Drill

We use a drill where the freshmen get the crap kicked out of them. It is an *interception drill*. We use it in our 7-on-7 drill (Diagram #3). This is an interception transition drill. We place bag holders in the field at assigned spots. We drop into coverage and the quarterback throws the ball into a zone. We intercept the ball. At that point, everyone turns and picks out a bag to block. The bag holders have to be tough to hold the dummies when defenders are attacking them with a full head of steam. This is a very aggressive drill and the emphasis is on that.

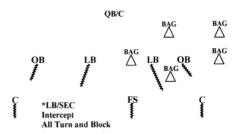

Diagram #3. Interception Drill

We use a *box-and-hip drill* (Diagram #4). It is a simple drill with a ballcarrier, defensive lineman, linebacker, and defensive back. The ballcarrier runs the ball outside a cone and up the sideline. We align the defenders in levels to the inside of the cone. They must pursue from the inside to the ballcarrier focusing on the inside hip. They frame the hip and run to the ballcarrier. The box part of the drill is to get outside the ballcarrier and force him inside. They work to the outside hip of the ballcarrier and force him inside.

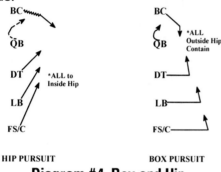

HIP PURSUIT   BOX PURSUIT

Diagram #4. Box and Hip

We teach the angles and the adjustment to those angles in this drill. We use all our drills and work hard in them because everything the player does has to be second nature. You must play with speed on defense. If everything is second nature, you are not thinking about what you must do—you are playing.

When we get into the season, we back off on the physical drills we use in the pre-season. This drill is a *three-level Oklahoma drill* (Diagram #5). The drill is set in a 10-yard area. On the line of scrimmage are an offensive lineman and a defensive lineman.

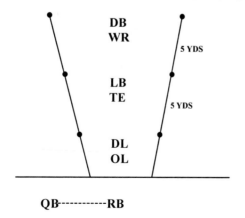

Diagram #5. Three-Level Oklahoma Drill

Five yards behind the line of scrimmage is a tight end and linebacker. Five yards behind the linebacker is a wide receiver and a defensive back. We have a quarterback and a running back behind the line of scrimmage. The drill is set in a triangle with the apex of the triangle being the running back. As the back reaches each successive level, the drill area becomes wider. The end of the drill is 10 yards wide.

The defenders have gap responsibilities they must play. They cannot choose a side to run around. We snap the ball and we have three blockers and three block defenders doing combat. The back runs the ball and must stay inside the cones marking the triangle areas of the drill. He cannot go outside the drill. The object is to defeat the block and pursue to the ball. If we make the tackle at the first level, the defenders at the second and third level continue to shed the blocker and get to the ball. If the ballcarrier is still up, we finish the tackle. If he is on the ground, we break down around him.

We use a tackling circuit in practice. Every defensive player goes through the tackling circuit. We have five stations within the circuit. We do goal-line tackling, three-dummy scoop, low-ball block, open field, and lateral slide and attack. The goal-line tackling is a close quarters drill that simulates the goal-line situation. It is not a finesse drill. It is a back trying to score and a tackler trying to stop him.

We have three dummies on the ground. The defenders walk over the three dummies. We roll a ball out at the end of the dummies, and the defender bends his knees, scoops, and scores. The low-ball drill is the third station. We roll the ball at the tackler with a back coming behind it. The defender plays the ball off his feet and makes the tackle. The ball that we use in this drill does not come in after practice and it is heavier from the weather. It is big and extremely heavy. The defender has to exert pressure to get the ball away from him.

The open field tackling is all about the feet coming to balance, and moving laterally. You must keep the head up and the eyes on the target. The lateral slide and attack drill is done off cones. We have cones representing alleys. The back runs along the cones and turns up in an alley. The tackler mirrors the back and attacks as he turns up in the alleys.

We do this tackling circuit every day. The thing that we try to emphasize in tackling is to tackle with the palms coming up. If the player brings his palms up, the hips dip. The motion of bringing the palms up brings the hips into the tackle. If you bend at the waist and bring up your palms, you align the angles for power and explosion. We emphasize *palms up* and *rip with the hip*. That is a strong tackling position.

Another thing we emphasize once we make the contact is to step on the toes of the ballcarrier. If we do that, the defender gains leverage and takes the ballcarrier off the ground. We emphasize those two minor details of tackling daily.

We do a turnover circuit daily. We do this daily because we want this to be second nature. We have five stations. We have recovery and score, fumble recovery, club and rip, club and punch, and interception. When you work the club, rip, and punch, make sure to work both sides of the ballcarrier. We work the drills coming from behind the ballcarrier. We punch the ball out, club over the top of the arm, and grab and rip the ball. It is common to see our players going after the ball. That is what we teach.

I want to talk a little about our alignment (Diagram #6). We align our defense to the strength of the offense. In our base alignment we play with a rush end aligned in a head-up-to-outside alignment on the tight end. He plays with his outside arm free. The strongside tackle plays in a 3 alignment on the outside shoulder of the guard. That alignment will vary from a tight to loose 3 technique.

The outside linebacker to the strongside is three yards outside the tight end and two yards off the ball. The noseguard is on the inside shoulder of the backside offensive guard. The backside end aligns in a 5 technique on the offensive tackle. The backside linebacker's alignment will vary with the receivers to his side.

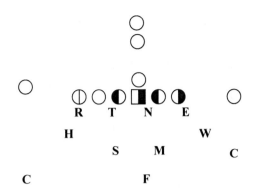

Diagram #6. Base Alignment

The inside linebacker to the strongside aligns in the A gap. The weakside linebacker aligns in the B gap. Last year, we had small linebackers. If you play with small linebackers, get them deeper and wider in their alignment. We may play him as deep as six yards off the ball. The reason we do that is because the offensive tackle outweighs him by 50 pounds on average. If he stayed tight to the line, the tackle came up the field, turned inside, and sealed him off. The depth gave the linebacker a chance in space to work on the offensive tackle.

We have stunts that we run but they are situational in nature. We slant our defensive line, but we base everything on scouting reports. We slant the defensive line in both directions. When you slant the line, you readjust the linebacker's gaps. We play a lot of base defense.

PAT DAWSON—DEFENSIVE LINE COACH

I played offensive line in college. When I came to Central to coach, I tried to think of the things that offensive linemen did not like from the defensive linemen. The answer was *hands*. The biggest thing a defensive lineman can do is get his hands into the offensive lineman. We want to use the hands to *stop the pressure* from the offensive linemen.

We play a 3 technique and a 1 technique, and we are never heading up on the offensive linemen. I always preach to work *half the man*. We do not want to work down the middle of a blocker. High school players have a tendency to lower their heads and try to explode and run over the blocker. We try to eliminate that and have them work half the man.

We want the defenders to work with their inside hand on the sternum and the outside hand to the elbow to shoulder pad. When we work on the seven-man sled, we work movement off the football. We use a ball to initiate movement, but we also use cadence to make them concentrate on the movement of the ball. We use the hard counts to try to cause them to jump. When we come off the ball, we want to see the hand placement of the defenders. We want them to be snapping the hands into half the blocker and controlling him.

We work on stance every day in practice. We want 60 percent of their body weight on the hands and 40 percent in their hips. I want the off hand up. If the off hand is not up, you cannot get the jab in the punch. On movement, I want the hands to fire. You cannot do that if your jab hand is down.

We work multiple defenders at a time working on an escape move. We align in the shoulder technique and come off the ball. We jab, work half the man, lock out, and make a move. The big thing we teach them is to perfect one move. If they are good with the rip, perfect it. If they use the shrug or swim, perfect that move. If each player will perfect one move, the defender will be a better player.

We want our players to play situational downs. Through tendencies and coaching, we get the defensive line to change their stance when they suspect a pass. In the no-huddle defense, the defensive linemen look at me on the sideline. We give them a signal to get into a pass-rush posture and rush the passer. We want them to narrow their stance, put more pressure on the hands, and perfect their pass move. Last season, we made only three mistakes that put us in the wrong mode. That was good for 16 games.

We take the responsibility to make the calls. We watch more film than the players watch and can better make those judgments. Three blows in 16 games is not a bad percentage. We make run/pass calls for our defensive line all the time.

We are a gap defense. The 3 technique wants to shoot his hands, replace the heels of the offensive lineman, disengage, and make the play. We rode them all year long about pursuing down the line. We wanted them running to the sideline on their pursuit angles every play. We want them to play their gap, pursue, and play over someone else. We want them to be playmakers.

The biggest drill we work is the hand-placement drill. We work this for 15 minutes daily. We put an offensive lineman and a defensive lineman in a perfect hook-up position. This is a fit-up drill. We stand behind the defensive lineman and signal the offensive lineman what to do. On the signal, the offensive lineman tries to go one way or the other to block the defender. The defender has to lock out, get separation, work a move, and escape. That is the best drill we do. This drill carried over to the games.

COACH COLOSIMO

I am sorry to cut you off coach, but we are out of time. I have enjoyed my time here, and I hope we gave you something you can use. If we can be of assistance, we will be around all weekend. We can talk all the football you like. Thank you for your kind attention.

WING-T ADJUSTMENTS WITH THE MIDLINE

West Memphis High School, Arkansas

I appreciate the opportunity to speak with you today. How many of you run the wing-T? How many of you run the option? Good! I am not going to go into a long introduction. I am sure you have seen all the introductions you care to see. We are going to go into football. We are a wing-T team. We have been a wing-T team for 30 years. We are a fullback trap, Buck sweep, waggle plays, and all the rest of the wing-T plays. That is what we are all about. We live in the wing-T, and we love it.

As we started playing better teams, and teams that were well-coached athletes, they put us in a bind. So, we wanted to go to something on offense that would give us an advantage. If they go to a 3 technique and really squeeze down, it makes it hard to run a trap, and we love to run the trap. We needed something to go to where we could run the ball up the middle. We did not want to give up that inside play. Because of this, we went to the midline.

When I started going to the clinics in the 1980s, coaches lied to me. They said, "If you are going to run the option, you have to be committed to running the option." They said, "You have to spend 30 minutes every day on it, and you have to rep it up, and get everything down pat." That is a lie. However, if it is your base offense, that is probably what you need to do. However, for us it is a complementary play. It is a play that we run and teach in boot camp in the spring. We run that play when the trap play is not working. As long as the trap is working, you will never see the midline play from us. We do not spend that much time on the midline.

Our junior high schools do not run our offense. We have three junior high schools, and none of them run the option. When we get those young players, they do not even know how to spell option. We spend the time in the spring teaching them the option offense. In addition, during two-a-days, we run the option a lot. Once the season gets going, we run one 10-minute session once a week on the option. When we go to our team session, we run it three or four times in that scrimmage. That is it. We still feel we can run it on Friday night.

During the season, we are going to spend our time on the fullback trap play. We spend our time with the trap, the Buck sweep, and the waggle pass. We are not going to spend a lot of time running the option, but it can still be successful. If the trap works, you will never see the midline option. It has been a real good complementary play for us.

Any time you put in a new play or a new concept, or complementary play, you need to make it easy on the offensive line. You need to do something that is very, very simple for the lineman. Let me go over the blocking rules for our midline 40 and 48 option at this time:

- Quarterback Read: First man head-up or outside offensive guard (audible to slide if there is a noseman)
- Center: Noseman or backside
- Playside Guard: Protect A gap
- Playside Tackle: Protect C gap
- Playside End: Protect D gap (or loop inside if two defenders are threatening the C gap)
- Playside Back: Loop inside offensive tackle to the inside linebacker
- Backside Back: Pitch route
- Backside Tackle: Head-up or protect C gap
- Backside Guard: Head-up or protect B gap

The playside tackle has the C gap. How do you take the C gap? It is up to that kid. What we want is for somebody to line up in a stance and pancake that guy in front of him. That is the way we once ran it.

When we get a defender that runs a 4.4 40 and weighs 185 pounds playing a 7 technique, it is tough to block him. We got to the point where we would actually show pass on the play, and we were running the midline play. We had a tackle showing a pass block, and we were able to block the 7 technique. I do not care how he does it, but the main point is to get the guy blocked

We like to go get the defenders, but we will have the tackle show pass to help with the blocking. Sometimes, we have to step outside and rooster-fight with that 7 technique. I do not like to do that, but it is better than letting that 7 technique come all the way due to the quarterback.

The playside tight end is to block the D gap. It is very simple. The end and tackle block outside. The only exception to that is, if you have two C-gap players, as in a 4-3 look. If you have a 6 technique or a 7 technique lined up outside, and you have the Sam linebacker behind him, it is the 4-3 look. You do not know who the C-gap player is going to be from the stack. We can have the tackle block outside, and we loop the tight end inside the tackle to pick up the linebacker. We may decide not to run the play at all if we get two C-gap players.

The only guy who has to be a good blocker on this thing is the playside guard. He protects the A gap. We want to run the play where there is a 3 technique. He is going to do it just as he does a fullback trap. He is going to dip, he is going to rip inside, and he is going to get up on that linebacker in the A gap. That is how we teach it.

If the defensive lineman lines up in the A gap, our quarterback should check us out of that play. If they have two people in the A gap, we should check off to a base play. We tell the quarterback that any time the playside guard blocks a lineman, it is an automatic keep for him. He bellies the fullback he normally would, but the quarterback is going to keep the ball.

The rest of it is very simple. The center blocks the backside A gap. The backside guard has the B gap, and the backside tackle blocks the C gap. All they are doing is keeping people out of the way on the backside.

The playside halfback, wingback, tailback, or whoever is on that side has to loop underneath the tackle to block the inside linebacker for the quarterback. We want to high-low that inside backer. The guard is coming at him low, blocking for the fullback. The wingback is coming in high, blocking for the quarterback. They are both blocking the same guy, but they are blocking for two different people, depending on who is going to get the ball.

The fullback trap is our baby. That is what we want to do. If they stop that, we run the midline. The midline is not going to work unless they are trying to stop the fullback trap. Our fullbacks have to be tough. They hate the midline because they are going to be hit hard and often. They have to really be tough.

We teach all the reads too, but in the end, 95 percent of the time the midline is a quarterback run play. It is a misdirection play out of the wing-T. We teach the quarterback to read, and give it to the back if we tell him to hand it off. However, he isn't going to give it because it is a quarterback run play.

After the midline, we put in the veer option. You can run the veer to the tight-end side or the split-end side, but we usually run it to the split-end side. In the wing-T, all the action happens to the tight-end side. Again, we run it to the split-end side. We block it just like the dive play. This is our veer 45 and 46 option.

Veer Option Rules

- Quarterback: Read first man head-up or outside the offensive guard (audible to slide if there is a nose).
- Center: Nose or backside
- Playside Guard: Protect the A gap.
- Playside Tackle Protect the C gap.
- Playside End: Protect the D gap (or loop inside if two defenders are threatening C gap).

- Playside Back: Loop inside the offensive tackle to the inside linebacker.
- Backside Back: Pitch route
- Backside Tackle: Head-up or protect the C gap.
- Backside Guard: Head up or protect the B gap.

The blocking is very simple. The playside back is very important; he has linebacker to the safety. If the linebacker does not take the fake, he better block him. If he takes the fake, then he goes on to the safety.

I have four pass plays I want to show you. The first one is not a Delaware wing-T pass play. We call it our wingback delay pass (Diagram #1). We fake the Buck sweep. The tight end runs an eight-yard flag. The wingback is going to delay just a little bit, and he is going to run a seam route. If he ends up running a post, then he will run into the other safety. Our split end will run an out-and-up, but we probably will never throw it to him, unless our coach in the press box tells us they are not covering him.

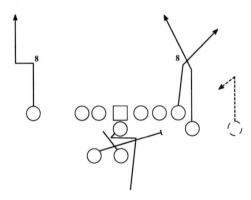

Diagram #1. Wingback Delay Pass

We can run this play with the tailback at the wingback position. We can use the play on our dropback-action passes as well. It is effective against the man defense. If the corners are up tight, it is a good play on the wingback side. I will show each of the passes at the end of the lecture so you can see how we run each pass.

We block our pass plays three different ways. The first way we call "load." If they run a shade nose, or if they blitz a lot, we want the fullback in there filling after the fake.

Our next pass is our wingback delay Z-Up pass (Diagram #2). It is the same action as the wingback delay, and we still fake the Buck sweep. Now, the wingback is going to run a speed-out route, where he runs a five-yard out route, and then just turns it on down the field on the wheel route. We have not run this much because it is a longer throw for the quarterback. Our quarterback has to have a much better arm to throw the pass.

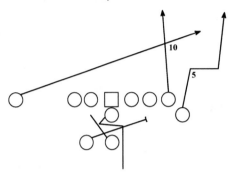

Diagram #2. Wingback Delay Z-Up

We tell the tight end to run straight at the safety. He wants to keep the safety away from the wingback. It is a hard throw because it is a deep route. Nevertheless, if they are in man-to-man, the wingback can beat the defensive man on the out-and-up. Most of the time, the corner is playing real tight because he's protecting against the Buck sweep.

We fake the Buck sweep on the delay pass. It is effective against a tight corner reacting quickly to our buck sweep. We think our wingback is a better athlete than your corner.

We also run the buster pass (Diagram #3). We call it buster because it is a cover-3 buster. It is the same principle as four vertical. We are looking directly at the safety. We roll out to the right, and our eyes are on the safety. We think the safety is going to turn and take off toward the tight end and release the wingback. If he does, we plant our foot, and we are going to throw to the tailback in a seam route.

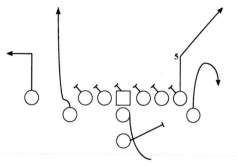

Diagram #3. Buster Pass

We read the safety on the buster pass. If the free safety rolls to the tight end, we throw to the running back or H-back. If the free safety stays in the middle, we work a high-low route with the wingback and tight end. It is effective against a one-safety look. When the outside linebacker is covering our running back, we feel we have a big advantage on the defense. If they are in man-to-man, that means the outside linebacker is covering the tailback, and we like our options with the outside linebacker covering the tailback. If they are in cover 3, and the safety moves, we are going to hit him for a big play. If they are in cover 3 and the safety does not move, it is not going to work, so the quarterback goes to a high-low read, similar to a smash route read. No matter what formation we're in, and we run it out of different formations, the inside receiver is going to run a flag, and the outside receiver is going to run a curl underneath the flag.

The next pass play we have is what we call Minnesota (Diagram #4). We run this against a press man coverage, or on any 1-on-1 situations. Our receivers take an outside release and run full-speed, running the fade route. If they can catch that cornerback in 10 yards, the quarterback should throw the fade. If the receiver cannot catch the corner within 10 yards, he puts the brakes on, squares off, and the quarterback throws the out route.

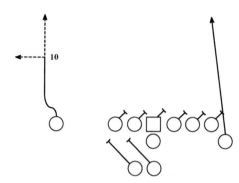

Diagram #4. Minnesota Pass

The play has been a great first-down play for us. We let the kids decide if we are going to run a fade route or an out route, based on how the corner plays. They like to throw the fade because they think it is more fun. It is like calling two plays at once. We run this pass against a team that likes to play man-coverage. In addition, we run it against a team that plays three-deep coverage. We do this because we have the 1-on-1 option.

That is all I have on the tape. I will be around if you have questions. Thank you very much.

ODD STACK 3-5-3 DEFENSIVE PACKAGE

North Gwinnett High School, Georgia

I have been lucky to be on the speaking circuit lately. It is an honor to be here. I am a blunt, straight-up person. What I want to do is to help you find something that you can take back and use with your team. I like these clinics because you get to meet so many people and talk a lot of football. We had a big game this year. We opened up with Prattville, Alabama. They ranked in the top five or six in the nation. Prattville played in the Classic in Cincinnati a couple of years ago. I have been in the Cincinnati area and I have talked to the coaches at Colerain High School and St. Xavier High School. What we talked about with them came in handy when we played Prattville.

People come to clinics for different reasons. I sat up in the room last night with a bunch of local coaches and we talked a lot of football. That is what the clinics are all about. I want to stay on task and shoot through some things I think will help you. When I sit down to talk football with coaches, I am not necessarily interested in the defense you run. I want to know what you run, where it came from, and why you run it.

When I started out in coaching, we ran a 50 defense. At the next job I had, we ran a 4-2 type of defense. When I went to Knott County Central in Kentucky, we ran a 50 slant defense. We played with 145-pound tackles and a noseguard, and we slanted them strong and weak. That scheme came back into play when we put the defense in that we run now. I went to Lexington Catholic to coach, and we installed the 4-3 defense and ran it for 14 years. We played cover 3 and cover 2 and stunted occasionally. When I went to Hazard High School, we had some good-looking athletes. We had good safeties when I was there. At Hazard, we played a lot of 4-3 with quarters coverage. I like the quarters coverage, but we were not a big pressure type of team. I had good athletes, and I did not want to get in their way. However, I did not trust them enough to play straight man-to-man.

Next, I went to North Broward Prep in Florida. We ran a 4-3 defense with the under front. We took our Sam linebacker, angled him, and played quarter coverage over the top of that alignment. When we started doing that, we brought more pressure into our scheme.

When I went to North Gwinnett High School, Bob Sphire was the head coach. He was a spread offensive coach that wanted the tempo of the game run as fast as possible. He liked the 3-5 because of the fit, the tempo, and the way it helped us in practice. This defense fits his offensive ideas. He told us the opponent will bust a long touchdown on you sometimes, but the turnovers we will produce will outweigh the risks.

The thing I liked about the 4-3 defense was the shade techniques we played and our ability to force the double-teams. However, I wanted to slant and go at the offense in two or three different ways. This is what we came up with and we play it well.

NORTH GWINNETT HIGH SCHOOL

I want to show you some things about our school:
• Located in Suwannee, GA
• 3,400 students
• Gwinnett county public schools
   ✓ 126 schools in county
   ✓ 18 5A schools in our county
   ✓ 4 5A schools in our town

- GHSAA, Region 7, Class 5A
- We were the fourth staff in four seasons when hired
- Prior to our arrival, playoffs three times in 52-year history
- Outstanding administration

Before we got there, North Gwinnett had been knocked around a lot. We put together a great staff. I was a head coach for 12 years, and I know you must have a good staff to win. You have to find people that fit what you are planning. If you are a young coach and working with a head coach or an older coach, you will learn something every day. No matter what you do, it always comes down to being in a great situation, being around good people, and having an opportunity to be successful. I do not care where you go or how many different jobs you have, that is what you are looking for. If you find that, get the best out of it and whatever happens will happen.

We have had a lot of success, but we have not won the state championship yet. We have to compete with 18 other 5A programs in our county, and we had to do something different to build our image and increase our attractiveness to potential athletes. We started to play nationally ranked teams like Prattville. That stirred the interest in our school.

Quickly, I want to show you our defensive philosophy.

PROGRAM PHILOSOPHY

- Lexington Catholic offensive and defensive philosophies matched, ending in 2005 state championship
- Help establish tempo; can control it on both sides of the ball
- Exciting style of play
- Play in the extremes
- Bob Sphire philosophy: Throw it all at them at once, and then go back and reteach; no spoon feeding

Fifteen minutes into our spring training, you will see the offense and defense going at each other 90 miles an hour. It is blood and guts in a blitz period. We have a five-minute blitz period where someone is going to win and someone is going to lose. You have six coaches and 50 players on each side of the ball going at it. We must have that part of our package in the first day of spring practice.

Package Philosophy

We have a package philosophy. This is not clinic talk. This is what we do.

- Be multiple but simple
- More than one way to defend a scheme; never be locked into a front/coverage; never be dictated to...
- Sound against the option
- The ability to attack and overload any blocking scheme
- Ability to play a shade technique, a slant technique, and a read technique
- Zone and man coverage with ironclad adjustments
- Our scheme forces our opponent to adjust, not vice versa

Never be dictated to is a mind-set. If you do not watch yourself, particularly on defense, you will worry about what the offense is doing. You need to run the defense and let the offense worry about how to handle your defense. You have to work harder than the offensive coaches to cover all the things they run. If you are not careful, you will end up with too much defense. You can play this defense against teams that are bigger, faster, and better and hold your own. Our scheme is going to force the opponent to adjust. The offensive tackle will not see one technique from the defender all night long.

We are going to disguise what we do. There is movement before the snap and movement after the snap. We are going to disguise the coverage and stem the line. We will walk the linebacker and safety men up, back, and do many different things.

We want to present as many looks as possible to force our opponent to spend practice time preparing for us. We want to create a major burden for them. We want them to spend more time on us than on anyone else that they play. Strategically and tactically, we want to be more creative and more intelligent than anyone we face. We want to play in the extremes.

We want to force our opponent to make decisions before and after the snap. Never allow them to just line up and tee off on you. Line up one way, and attack out of another look. After watching us on film, we want two individuals to be concerned. We want the quarterback to be concerned and the head coach to be concerned about the quarterback. We want him to worry about protecting the quarterback. The opponent has to find ways to protect their quarterback. When they see the quarterback getting killed on film, they will adjust their practice schedule.

You do not have to hit the quarterback every time, but you have to be around him. That makes him uncomfortable in the pocket.

The 3-5-3 defense provides the best chance to adapt to all styles of play. Every year we play the defense it has changed. One year, we played with a stunting front and cover 1 and zero in the secondary. Now, we play a lot of match-up zone coverage. We are getting the same results as we did in man coverage, but it allows us to play the run better. In this coverage, we can play the four vertical patterns. We have to tweak the defense and improve the package because of the teams we are starting to schedule.

We are an attack, gap-control defense. All defensive linemen are responsible for one gap that is pre-determined by the huddle call. We will line up pre-snap and play great technique by attacking the offensive linemen or the tight end, or we will slant to our gap responsibility using our quickness to offset our opponent. All linebackers are two-gap players depending on flow. The outside Buck and Will linebackers play either B gap or C gap. On flow to them, they play C gap. On flow away, they play B gap.

Our goal is always to outplay the other team's defense. Stats give you an indication of how your defense is playing. However, there are only three stats we are concerned with. They are *points allowed, turnover ratio,* and *quarterback touches.*

It is imperative that the defense gives the ball to the offense on turnovers as much as possible. On average, each team will have 12 offensive possessions per game. If we can take the ball away on three of those possessions, we have eliminated their scoring opportunities by 25 percent. You do not always have to have highly talented athletes to play defense. The one thing that you must possess is a great desire to get to the ball. This is something that we stress and practice daily.

We are complicated, and we have a lot of personnel packages. We had a number of injuries last year. Teams try to formation us to dictate our fronts and coverages. If you do only one thing in your adjustment, the offense is dictating to you how to play. We set our defense to what the offense does best and make our adjustments to what they do. We are going to force the offense to do other things. In the league we play in, you must stop the run. I know they throw the ball more in Kentucky than we do in our league. However, if the ball is in front of your defensive backs and it is not going over your heads, you have a chance.

From 2006 to 2009, we have added to and adapted our package. The first year, we played more base than anything. In the following years, we added coverage packages and blitz packages to fit our personnel. However, we continued to play top programs from across the nation.

We divide our defense into three component parts. The front is made of the down linemen and three linebackers. They play in three tandems. The Mike linebacker and nose tackle are one of the tandem parts. The Buck and Will linebackers and the defensive ends are the other two parts.

SCHEME IS DIVIDED INTO THREE PARTS

- Front six defenders play in three tandems
  - ✓ DL must play shade technique, master slant technique
  - ✓ LB flow read and adjustments, primary run defenders

- Adjusters: Rover, dog, and free
  - ✓ Rover is LB/DB, dog FB/LB
  - ✓ Free can be dog type player (big on run support)
- Corners
  - ✓ Must be able to play 1/4, 1/3, zone coverage, and man (no primary run support)

In our base alignment, we play with two defensive ends aligned in a 4 technique head-up the offensive tackles (Diagram #1). We have a nose tackle in a 0 technique head-up the center. We play with three linebackers in a stack position behind the down linemen. They are five yards off the ball. The Buck linebacker aligns to the tight end side. The Mike linebacker aligns in the middle, and the Will linebacker aligns away from the tight end. The Rover is a strong-safety type that goes to the tight end side. The dog is the fullback/linebacker type and plays opposite the Rover. In the base alignment, the corners are one yard inside and seven yards deep on the wide receivers. That alignment will change with our coverages. The free safety is 11 yards deep in the middle of the defense.

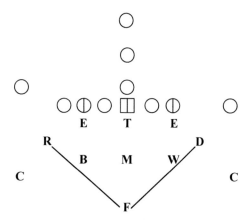

Diagram #1. Base 3-5-3, Cover 3

When we slant, we have to utilize our speed. We use what we call a *veer slant*. We do the exact same thing an offensive tackle does on a veer block. When we slant, we are going inside, keeping the shoulders parallel to the line of scrimmage. We rip with the outside arm and get skinny coming inside. If we meet a trap blocker, we use a wrong-arm technique. We played small players at this position last year. People could not block us, and we were getting in the backfield.

Our linebackers are no different from anyone else playing this defense. The Mike and Buck linebackers read the fullback, and the Will linebacker reads the tailback in a two-back set. They play flow. If there is a one-back set, they all read the single back on their first step.

The corners must be able to play quarters, thirds, and man coverage. We do not teach press man coverage. We play five yards off the receivers. If we have corners that can cover, we play straight. However, we switch most in-and-out routes and banjo the coverage. The corner plays the hips of the receiver and keys where he is going. The *banjo technique* is all about the eyes. The corner aligns on the outside hip, and if it goes to the inside, there will be some type of out pattern coming to him. This has worked very well for us. When our personnel get better and are ready, I will let them press, but that all happens in practice.

We played five different option schemes this year. The free safety is the extra man in the option scheme. He has to be big in run support. In the four years I have been at North Gwinnett, we have had two free safeties. Both of them were average football players with below-average speed, but you could not block them.

I want to get into the nuts and bolts of what we do. These are our main elements of our defense.

MAIN ELEMENTS

- 30 stack technique fronts (Strong, 55, 55 strong, stack)
- Change-up fronts (Bear, Okie, angle)
- Aggressive slant package, which enables us to use speed over size
- Relentless pressure package where we can bring four, five, six, and possibly seven defenders
- Three zone coverages and three man coverages with adjustments that are sound in all situations

In the strong front, we shade the ends and nose to the strongside of the set. The tackle shades the center to the strongside. The ends play a 5 technique to strength and a 4i technique to the weakside. The Buck linebacker is at five yards in a 4i technique. The Mike linebacker aligns at five yards in a weakside shade on the center. The Will linebacker is at five yards in a 5 technique. The dog and Rover backs are 3x3 yards outside the tight end. The corners are 7x1 yards off the wide receivers, and the free safety is 11 yards deep over the center.

In the *55 front*, the defensive ends move into a 5 technique on the outside shoulder of the offensive tackles. The Buck and Will linebackers move up to three-and-a-half yards, and the Mike linebacker moves back to six yards. The perimeter players have the same alignment as the strong front.

The *55 strong* is a combination of the two fronts (Diagram #2). The ends align in 5 techniques, and the nose aligns in a strong shade as he did in the strong front. The linebacker depth is five yards on this front, and the perimeter players are the same.

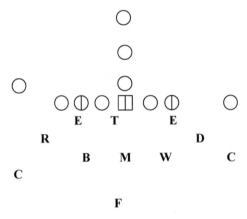

Diagram #2. 55 Strong

The *stack front* moves the defensive end into a 4 technique head-up the offensive tackles. Everyone else in this front is the same as the base front.

We can change up the fronts with Bear, Okie, and angle fronts. In the Bear front, the defensive end moves into a 3-technique alignment, and the Buck and Will linebackers move to the outside in a 6 technique on the tight end or a 5 technique on the tackle. We like to stunt from the Bear front (Diagram #3). The *Okie front* is a straight 5-2 defensive alignment. Because we play so many run teams, we had to get defenders closer to the line of scrimmage. We walk the Rover up on the tight end,

and he plays hip to hip on the line of scrimmage and does not come off for pass coverage.

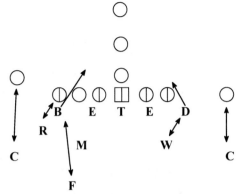

Diagram #3. Bear Front

The *angle front* is our 4-2 look (Diagram #4). We shift the down linemen to the weakside and walk the Buck linebacker down into a 6-technique position on the tight end. The strongside defensive end aligns in a 3 technique, and the end to the weakside aligns in a 5 technique. The nose tackle moves to a 1 technique to the weakside. The Mike and Will linebackers align in stack positions behind the 3- and 1-technique linemen.

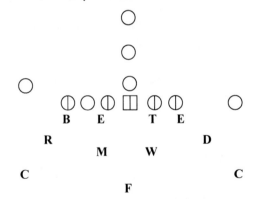

Diagram #4. Angle Front

We can move the three-man front as a unit with *slash, whiz, pinch,* and *out calls*. The slash and whiz calls are slant calls to the strongside and weakside (Diagram #5). The nose tackle slants to the strong A gap and uses an evasive technique. He rips to the offensive lineman's heels with his eyes inside. The defensive ends do the same thing, and the linebacker steps opposite the defensive line move. The whiz move is the same movement weak. The pinch movement is an inside movement by the ends. The out movement is the opposite movement by the defensive ends.

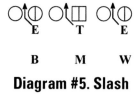

E   T   E

B   M   W

Diagram #5. Slash

We will set our defensive strength to the tight end 80 percent of the time. We can set the strength to the field or boundary (if we have scouted tendencies). We have the ability to set the strength to the strong receiver side. We also have the ability to use a "check with me" system, which determines our front, based upon our opponent's offensive formation.

If the offensive set is balanced in the middle of the field, we will always declare the strongside to our left because most teams are right-handed. Our Mike will give a *lucky* or *ringo call*, which is left and right for the front. If the tight end lines up on the left, Mike will yell, "Lucky, lucky." Our safeties will give *lightning* and *rocket calls*, which is the passing strength of the formation.

When we make our defensive calls, the first thing we call is personnel. We call the front, stunt, second stunt, and the coverage.

DEFENSIVE CALLS

- Personnel
- Front (with tag)
- Stunt (with tag)
- Second stunt (with tag)
- Coverage (with tag)

Example: Strong Green

In this defense, the front is a strong front and green coverage, which is cover 3. There is nothing tagged which means we are playing base defense and cover 3.

Example: 55 Blood Cross Green Disguise

In this defense, we align in a 55 front with a blood-cross stunt by the linebackers. Blood is a strongside, two-linebacker stunt. The coverage is cover 3, but we are going to align in another shell

and move to cover 3. We align in disguise coverage and roll to a cover 3 in the secondary. We either use wristbands with the defensive call, we signal the defense, or I yell what I want.

The linebackers have four flow reads. They read fast, hard, split, and counter flows. The fast-flow read for the linebackers is a wide play to the outside (sweep). The hard reads are both backs in the same hole with the ball inside (isolation). Split flow is one back inside and one outside (option). Counter flow starts one way and goes the other (misdirection).

The overhang linebackers are the cutback players. We use *pull calls* to get them into different alignments. We can pull them to the line of scrimmage if we like. We have gotten into zone blitzes and used the pull call to get the linebacker into a position to blitz. We can pull the linebackers into double coverage on a receiver.

In the *55 front*, the linebackers align in a 4i technique at three-and-a-half yards deep. They read the near back through the guard. If we align a defensive end in the 4i technique, his read is the same as the linebackers.

COVERAGE

We play six primary coverages:
- Green = Three-deep
- Blue = Two-deep
- Orange = Four-deep
- White = Four-match
- Purple = Five-match
- Black = Man-free

I do not have time to get into the coverages, but we can change the force players by adding words or running blitzes or stunts. We can force with the corner, Rover, dog, linebacker, defensive end, or free safety. An example of the coverage is *strong white* (Diagram #6). This coverage is set against a trips set. The Will linebacker makes a pull call and shifts the backers to the openside to cover the gaps. The Rover is a flat player to the trips side. The corners align at 7x1 and play a quarter of the field. The free safety aligns 10 yards deep, splitting the #1 and #2 receivers, and plays a quarter of the field. However, he is keying the #3 receiver strong.

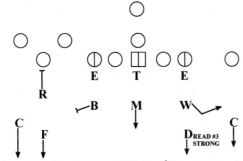

Diagram #6. Strong White (Four-Match)

This is a quarter-coverage defense. In our coverages, we number the receivers moving from the sideline to the inside (Diagram #7). The widest receiver is the #1 receiver. The next widest receiver is the #2 receiver. The third receiver in the trips set or the running back in the backfield is the #3 receiver. We number the receivers from the sideline to both sides. In a quarters coverage, the #2 receiver will tell everyone how to play the coverage.

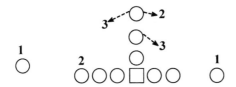

Diagram #7. Numbering of Receivers

We move our defense at all levels. In the defensive line, we run line games between the defensive ends and the nose tackle. The line game I am going to show you is a *loop weak* (Diagram #8). I will show this from the Bear front. The 0 technique twists to the weakside B gap. He comes off the butt of the defensive end. He is doing the loop technique. The weakside defensive end crashes the A gap and becomes the penetrator. The defensive end goes first and wants to occupy the guard and hold the center from getting outside. The strongside defensive end is B-gap player. The Buck linebacker is aligned in a 6 technique and slants into the C gap. The Mike linebacker is aligned at five yards and is head-up the center, and the Will linebacker plays a 5 technique.

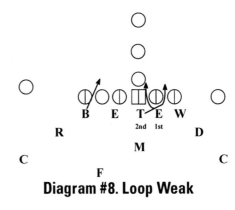

Diagram #8. Loop Weak

At the second level, we can run one-, two-, and three-man stunts involving the Buck, Mike, Will, Rover, or dog. This gives a four-, five- or six-man pressure scheme. If we want to send one blitz runner, we simply call the position we want to blitz. If we call *55 Buck*, the Buck linebacker shoots the B gap. That is his gap of responsibility and he blows it. If we call *55 Rover*, the Rover blitzes off the edge of the defense. We can also add the word *twist* to the call and the down lineman and the linebacker run an in-and-out movement from their position. A *Buck twist* call sends the defensive end into the B gap and the Buck linebacker blitzes the C gap.

If we want to bring five-man pressure, we add another linebacker into the stunt. We have a war-and-blood package. That package brings two linebackers from the same side. The *war stunt* for us is the Mike and Will linebackers running through their gaps to the weakside of the defense (Diagram #9). The Mike linebacker blitzes the A gap, and the Will linebacker blitzes the B gap. The nose tackle slants into the strongside A gap. The defensive ends on these packages are C-gap players. If we run a *blood stunt*, the Mike and Buck linebackers run through their gaps on the strongside. It is the opposite stunt to the other side.

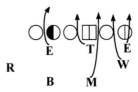

Diagram #9. War Weak

If we want to add a sixth man to the scheme, we tag another linebacker stunt. We just showed you the war stunt. This time, we will tag that stunt with a different look, plus we add a Buck twist to the strongside. We add *X* to the war stunt and switch the gaps for the Mike and Will linebackers. The stunt is *55 war X switch Buck twist* (Diagram #10). Since we are sending all the underneath coverage, we play a purple coverage in the secondary.

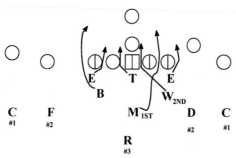

Diagram #10. War X Switch Buck Twist

Purple coverage is a man scheme. In purple coverage, the Rover and dog stay over the top of the #2 receivers to their side. They jump all out routes by the #2 receivers. The corners stay over the top of the #1 receiver to their side. The free safety has the #3 receiver. The corners, the Rover, and the dog play banjo coverage and switch crossing patterns between the #1 and #2 receivers. They must play with their eyes and communicate.

We can also run blitzes with our third-level defenders. The corners and free safety can get involved with this game.

I will be around, and I am ready to talk some football. Thank you for your attention.

THE SPREAD OFFENSE ZONE READ PLAY

Cheshire High School, Connecticut

Thank you. Before we get going, I want to tell you about our history. I hope that you can take something from this talk that will help you in your program. Just take whatever works for you. I enjoy going to clinics, and I do pick up an idea here and there. Just because this information works for us does not mean it is going to work for you. It must fit into the things you are doing. You must keep your personnel in mind. We went to the spread offense because we felt we had the people to do it.

Looking ahead, we feel we have the personnel to stay in the offense a few years. We are committed to this system. Our eighth grade, seventh grade, and sixth grade teams are using the same system. This offense can be run in the lower levels of football. It does not matter what system you use; just be sound fundamentally in what you are using.

I am an option coach. We have talked to a lot of other people. We went from the option to the spread offense. We went just the opposite of the option in our offense. We went to things I never thought we would run offensively. We are running things we said we would never run. I played at Western Connecticut State University for Paul Pasqualoni, and Steve Addazio was my offensive line coach. When Steve Addazio came to Cheshire High School, we took the things we were doing at West Conn and ran them at Cheshire High School. We were a wishbone team. In our first year, we did not get out of the wishbone. It took us until the eighth game of our second season before we were able to run the option out of the I formation.

We ran an I-formation option or double-slot option team until last year. Now, we are a spread option team. We have taken the spread offense, and we are running the option out of the spread formation. We are going to throw the ball, and we run all of the screens, but we are an option team first.

We are a Tony Franklin System team (www.tonyfranklinfootball.com). It is our spread offense. Everything we do is out of the no-huddle. This system supplied us with our pass and screen game. When we are talking about the option, we are talking about the play-action pass. We have the simple concepts of the quick passing game, and the stretch plays. That is about it.

The System has allowed us flexibility with the run game. Just because we are a System team, does not mean we have to do everything they do. They encourage you to have a change-up. Our change-up is the option.

In 2008, we were 55 percent run and 45 percent pass. In 2009, we were 75 percent run and 25 percent pass. Even though we are a spread team, we were 75 percent run. Very seldom do we have a tight end in the game. We are running the football.

We have averaged almost 370 yards game since joining the System. When I looked at the stats from 2008 to 2009, we were only five yards different from one year to the other, even though we are running a completely different offense this year.

TONY FRANKLIN SYSTEM BASE CONCEPT

We are a no-huddle team. We are calling our plays from the sideline. Everyone has a wristband with 135 plays on it. It puts the pressure on the coaches to get the kids in the right place. It is difficult for the quarterback to come to the line of scrimmage and make the right calls with all of the different ways the defense plays today. The coaches read the defense. We get information from the coaches up in the press box down to the sideline. We call the play. We want our offense to be able to run the best play possible. We are looking for match-ups. We want to get our players into space against defenders that cannot tackle.

One other thing about running the spread offense is this: I do not want to say the defense is unpredictable, but there is just so much you can do on defense. If we run a 2x2 look, the defense has to cover the four receivers. After they cover the four receivers, the defense only has so many players they can put in the box. If you have a certain number of players in the box, we are going to throw the ball.

We were talking about personnel earlier. Our X- and H-receivers usually line up on left side of the offense. We go X, Y, Z, across the formation. The H is just the middleman on the left side. The Y and Z usually line up on right side of the formation. We are usually a 2 X 2 team. Our featured back is the F-back. The F's alignment changes play to play. He knows where he has to be on each play. Our offense forces defense to be more "predictable."

Let me talk about our alignments. Our offensive line is looking at two- to two-and-a-half-foot splits, with the head on our center's hip. From the first day of fall practice to the last day of spring practice, we yell at our kids to widen their stance. It is unbelievable that we have to remind the linemen about their splits. They just do not listen to us and continue to squeeze down on their splits.

We can run our formations with a tight end on any of our offenses. All we have to do is to tag the play with our special calls. If we want to tag a play, we add the word "yo" to the formation. If the end is tight, it is a three-foot split. If he is not tight, he splits five yards, depending on the pattern and the play. The quarterback sets at five yards deep. The off receivers are one yard deep, and X and Z spread wide. We want them wide. They may be a little tighter, depending on the play. As a rule, they are going to be one yard deep, and they line up on the numbers or wider. The F's alignment varies; as a rule, he lines up on the inside leg of our offensive tackle, and one yard behind the quarterback.

Our two-back formations are colors. Our blue formation tells the H-back he lines up on the left side of the formation behind the tackle. The F-back is on the right side of the formation (Diagram #1). If we want to flip the formation, it would be a green formation.

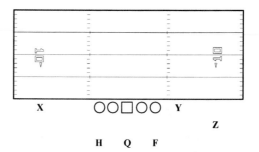

Diagram #1. Blue Formation

If we call blue left, we are going to take the Y-end and put him on the other side of the formation (Diagram #2). We run a lot of our option game out of the two-back set.

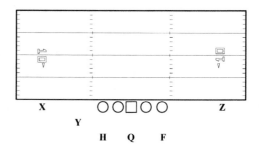

Diagram #2. Blue Left Formation

Our ace formation is a standard 2x2 set with the H-back on the left side with the X-end (Diagram #3). The Y and Z split to the right side.

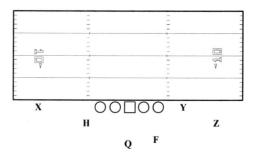

Diagram #3. Ace Formation

On ace yo, the Y-end is in the tight-end position (Diagram #4). Yo is our tag call. As you recall in the ace formation, the Y-end splits to the right side.

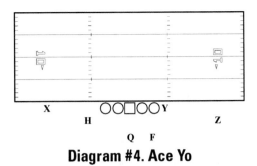

Diagram #4. Ace Yo

If we want to get into a trips set, we call ace left (Diagram #5). Left tells the Y-end that he goes to the other side. Everyone else is where he would normally be in the ace formation.

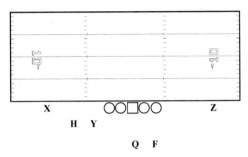

Diagram #5. Ace Left

The early formation brings the H-back over to the right side for our trips set (Diagram #6). The H-back is between the Y-end and the Z-back.

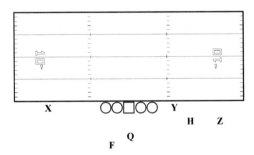

Diagram #6. Early Formation

I want to talk about the zone read play. We decided if we are going to run the ball. If we face a six-man box, we can run the zone read play. We block five defenders and read one of them. If we face a seven-man box, we can run the zone read, but we have to get another blocker, or we have to get another back in the box. It could be by bringing the tight end inside, or we can motion a back to account for one of the defenders.

One of the difficult things to do on defense is to play assignment football. Watching coaches teaching the defense to play the option, the correct way, is a pain in the butt. You have the quarterback, you have the fullback, and you have the pitch; that can be tough to teach.

What we want to do is to stretch the field with the formations. We throw the football to keep the defense spread. VWe force the defense to play assignment football and to defend the whole field. We are giving teams a lot to prepare for week after week.

We go into each game with four or five different options, in addition to all of the passes and our screen game. We need all of this offense just to keep the defense guessing on what is going on.

Zone-blocking assignments depend on the defender we are reading on the play. Usually, we are going to read the end man on the line of scrimmage. We do have a lot of variations. We change the way we run the plays so the defense does not get a handle on what we are doing. We change the "give" key up to keep the defense guessing. We do not let the defense know whom we are reading on each play. We are not going to line up and run the same play the same way repeatedly. We are going to change it up and try to keep the defense on their heels.

The offensive line needs to know who the give key is. We base the give key on how we are calling the play. With the wristbands we use, we have gotten very specific with the assignments. For the left tackle, if I call "blue 22," he is going to look down at his wristband and will read "zone right." It may read "block defensive end." We keep things very simple.

We must know whom we are reading (usually the end man on the line of scrimmage). Working from read key, we work with someone to the second level. This is the way we teach the play.

We want to be physical on the blocks. Teams see us in a spread offense, and they think we are a soft offensive team. They think we are a passing team. We are not. We want to run downhill and whack people.

Quite often, we see a 4-2 box defense. We are going to run our 32 zone play (Diagram #7). The tackle is going to block the end. The center and guard are going to work on the nose up to the Sam backer. If we face the 3 technique on the playside, the guard is going to fan block him. The backside tackle has a shade man in the gap, and the tackle is releasing upfield to the Mike backer.

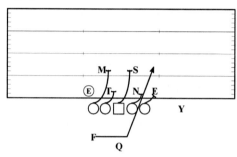

Diagram #7. 32 Zone vs. 4-2

Against the under defensive look, we are shading the other way now (Diagram #8). We may allow the right guard to step down to get a piece of the noseman before he releases upfield on the Mike backer. This is a tough block for both guards. Our line was young this year as we had to replace five starters from the year before. We are still reading the backside end. That is how we block the 32 zone against the under look.

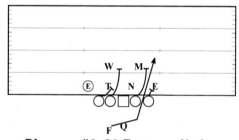

Diagram #8. 32 Zone vs. Under

We see a lot of the 3-3 stack defenses. We still run the 32 zone to the tight-end side (Diagram #9). The callside guard and tackle are going to work on the end and backer. The center and backside guard are working on the nose and Mike backer. The backside tackle releases inside and up to the Will backer.

We do see some 3-2 defensive looks with the Will and Sam backers wide outside (Diagram #10). The onside guard and tackle work together. The center and backside guard have the nose and inside

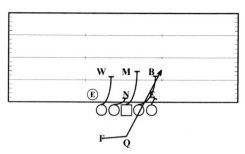

Diagram #9. 32 Zone to Tight End vs. 3-3 Stack

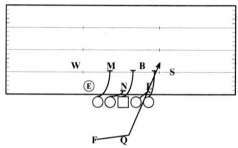

Diagram #10. 32 Zone to Tight End vs. 3-2

blitz by the backer. The backside tackle has the Mike backer. Both the center and strong playside tackle are reading the onside backer. If the backer comes inside, the center comes off the nose block and picks him up. If the backer stays outside, the tackle has him.

If we face a true 50 defense and we want to run our 32 zone, we are going to bring another blocker on the line. The defense is playing an under look with a shade nose, a 5 technique, and a 9 technique (Diagram #11).

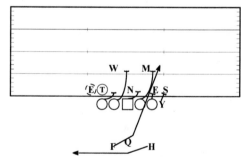

Diagram #11. 32 Zone to Tight End vs. Under (Shade, 5, 9)

We ask the Y-end to block the Sam backer on the line of scrimmage. The onside tackle and guard block the end and Mike backer. The center and backside guard have the nose and Will backer. The tackle is releasing inside. We read the defensive tackle, and pitch off the end.

I want to talk about the offensive line stance. I learned everything about the offensive line while working with Steve Addazio and working with George DeLeone when he was up at Syracuse. Everything I learned then is now out the window. Because of the nature of the offense we are running now, we are in a two-point stance. This is what we want on our stance:

- Feet under the armpits
- Toe-to-heel stagger with inside foot up
- Rest inside forearm on front thigh board
- Rest back arm on back thigh
- Comfortable position

For the left side of the line, getting that inside foot up gets a little awkward at times. The stance may be awkward but they can still get out of the stance. They can come downhill and hit defenders.

When we talk about getting in the stance, since we are in the no-huddle, the linemen come up to the line of scrimmage, and they are ready to go. We are calling the plays from the sideline, so the linemen are kind of hanging out until we call the play. It is a comfortable position for them. For the defensive linemen, they are down in their stance. The waiting for the play wears on them after awhile. This is particularly true in a clock-kill situation, and you want to take the air out of the game.

The best thing they did in football was to have the back judge put his hand up. The line is ready to go, and they are waiting for the quarterback to call the play. The quarterback waits for the back judge to put his hand up, and then we are snapping the ball. The entire time the defensive line is sitting there in their stance. That is tough on them.

I will touch on some offensive line drills we use. We do things with the line that we learned from George DeLeone. We get them on the grid squares. We set them up five yards apart and five yards deep. We get everyone back so we can get everyone at once. We had 30 offensive linemen this year. We had two coaches working with them. It is a lot to try to get reps for 30 players. We only have the kids for about 12 minutes during the individual period. It is

because of the nature of our offense, we do more team periods.

- Grid squares
- Stance, one step
- Stance, one step, punch
- Stance, one step, punch on sled (with drive)
- Duck walk on boards
- Fit drill with partner
- Fit drill with linebacker
- Live 2-on-2
- Half line with stunts
- Full line with stunts

We get them in the grid squares, and we work the stance, one step drill. We have them take one zone step with the right foot. We give the kids reps on this both ways.

Next, we go stance, one step, punch. All we are doing is punching air right now. We want them to get used to the motion. From here, we go to the sled and have them do the same drill on the sled. It is stance, one step, punch on the sled. The players offset slightly on the sled. They take one step and punch the sled. Then, we do the drill and add the drive on the sled. We go stance, one step, punch, and drive. They drive the sled until they hear the whistle.

One thing we have picked up is this: the typical play is going to last for about five seconds. Therefore, we drive the sled for about five seconds. We do not have them drive the sled for 20 yards, just five seconds.

We do other drills for footwork. I have learned over the years that a lot of the fundamental drills we can do to develop footwork we do not have to do at full speed. If we do a simple duck walk drill, we do not have to do it going 90 miles an hour. We can just work on the feet. We get the boards and put them at a 45-degree angle. They take a zone step, and work down the board.

The coaching points on the drill are this: they take a good first step, and they get their hands back. They are pounding their feet into the ground. When they have to make contact, they want to have a solid base. They do not want to get up on their toes.

We are going to look at a hard zone block. We are simulating a zone block. We get two players in a position where they have taken the first step and are in the initial contact phase. We put the forearm up in a good position. We are getting them cheek-to-cheek, and then we are going to drive the defender back. We want the defender to give some resistance so the blockers can get a realistic look at what is going on. We want them to get their eyes on the linebacker. We want four eyes on the linebacker.

We come back and do the same drill, but this time we add a linebacker. The linebacker is stacked behind the down man. He can be shaded one way or the other. We want to get push on the down defender and drive him back into the linebacker. At the last minute, the blocker where the linebacker comes off releases to pick up the linebacker. The other offensive lineman knows he must take over the block on the down lineman when the one blocker comes off the double-team block to pick up the linebacker.

The next phase I will stand behind the linebacker and tell him where to go and when to go. The linemen hit, drive, and then pick up the linebacker.

The next phase is to go live. It is just the two down linemen and the linebacker. It does not matter if we have a tight end and a center, or a guard and a tackle; it does not matter who is working in the drill because of the zone concepts all the blocks are the same. We work the zone block and then getting up to block the next level. We want push first on the block.

Then, we put the line together, and we add some stunts to the drill. I will show you some cut-ups later on picking up the linebacker.

- Push (this is the number-one priority); stay on the double-team.
- Get cheek-to-cheek with four eyes on the linebacker.
- Come off at the last minute for the linebacker.
- Get on them, and keep the feet moving.
- Take them where they want to go, and let the backs be athletes.

Ideally, this is what we want to do on the zone play. If we cut the linebacker loose, and he is out of the run-through, we are getting three yards on the play. If we leave the man on the line of scrimmage, we get nowhere. We get nothing done. We want to get cheek-to-cheek and four eyes on the linebacker, to come off the block at the last minute, get on the linebacker, and keep the feet moving.

Our feature back is the F-back. At times, we do consider the H-back as a featured back. I am not sure why he is the H-back. Where did the H come from? For a lack of a full definition, we will call him the hybrid back, or H-back. He can be a wide receiver, or he can be a running back. What we have done is this. We have some backs who are just Hs, and we have some receivers who are just Hs. We have a few players who can do both a receiver and a running back. Some of our Hs are going to be working as running backs, but most of the time it is just the featured back. Following is what we are looking for in the running back stance:

- Feet under the armpits, balanced
- Hands on hips
- Knees bent, flat back, and eyes up
- Alignment—varies by play

We do not want the hands on the knees because the hands are hot. We want them to look like an athlete when they are in the featured back stance. The alignment is going to vary from play to play, depending on what we are trying to do.

We had nine fumbles this year. We had three fumbles from the featured back. Only one of those three fumbles was by a starting F-back. That is very good for the entire season. We only put the ball on the ground one time from the F-back. We emphasize in every drill we do: ball security.

Running Back Drills

- *Purpose:* Used to teach basic fundamentals and stress the importance of ball security
- *Tempo:* Jogging
- *Organization/Set-Up:* Partner up

Strip Drill

This is a pre-practice drill. We call "Partner up," and everyone gets a football. First, they jog nice and easy for 10 yards. We want the ball high and tight.

- Go 10 yards with the ball in each hand.
- Make sure the defender is giving good effort in an attempt to get the ball loose.
- The coach should also try to get the ball.

The coach grabs at the ball and tries to strip the ball. After they get 10 yards, they switch the ball to the other hand and come back the other way.

Coaching Points:
- Keep the ball high and tight.
- Cover the nose of the ball.
- Pump the arms, and rub the nipple raw.
- Switch the arms, reaching over the top to the nose of the football, then drag across the chest to the other arm.

Another drill that we use is another pre-practice drill. It serves a couple of purposes. We work on their agility, their elusiveness, and you work on ball security. We call it the 45-degree cone drill.

- *Purpose:* Pre-practice drill designed to work on sticking the foot in the ground with proper head/body alignment and bursting out of cuts. Used to improve cutting ability, elusiveness, and change of direction.
- *Tempo:* 50 percent to 75 percent
- *Organization/Set-Up:* Align cones five to eight yards apart at a 45-degree angle. Align last cone five yards away from the end zone. Finish with a burst or a move into the end zone.

We want to simulate something as if we are scoring a touchdown. We want to finish the drill strong with some type of action. When the players hit that last cone, we want them going full speed.

Coaching Points:
- Coach head and body alignment.
- Stick the foot in ground hard. Don't round off.
- Don't overstride when sticking.

- Sink hips, and get chest over toes when sticking.
- Throw the elbow to get out of the break.
- Accelerate for a step or two out of the break.
- Use good form-running technique.
- Keep eyes up. Don't look at the ground.
- Switch the ball to the outside hand on each stick of a cone.

We stress the head and body alignment. We have to force them to stick their foot in the ground on the cuts. Get them used to doing that, and it will carry through to our receiver drills and on everything else we do. We stress "stick the foot in the ground." We do not want them to round the cuts off at the cones.

I want to talk about our quarterbacks. Our quarterback is five yards deep on the spread offense. Our quarterback does not call the cadence. The quarterback indicates he is ready for the snap of the ball. The center is the one who calls the cadence. The only people that need to hear the cadence is the offensive line. The five linemen can hear the center's call much better. The center on each play will identify the defensive front, identify the Mac, set the pass protection, and then look between his legs.

When our quarterback is ready, he gets in his stance. We want his eyes up with the hands out in front of him. Following is a list of what we stress in his stance:

- Balanced feet, under the armpits
- Athletic stance—Knees bent, flat back, eyes up, don't hunch
- Hands extended, ready to receive the snap
- Usually toes at five yards
- Be a fluid athlete, not a robot

We talk about catching the snap on the shotgun offense. We want the eyes of the quarterback to follow the ball into his hands. He must realize if he is going to run the option, before he can read his key, he must catch the snap. If it is a high snap, the quarterback must get his eyes up and concentrate on catching the ball. He should not just put his hands up high and look at the defense as he catches the ball. He needs to keep his eyes on the ball until he secures the snap. He must follow the football.

One of the things coaches are guilt of is of overcoaching kids. We want our quarterback to be an athlete and not a robot. Let them do what feels comfortable to them.

We do a drill for the quarterbacks that we call the ride-and-decide drill. This drill goes back to our triple option days. We spent a lot of time working on the mesh drill. We do this drill sometimes in the individual drills, but a lot of times it is a post-practice drill. We do not have to spend a lot of time on the drill.

We get a line spacer, and we have a second quarterback to step up and snap the ball to the first quarterback. We have a coach run the "give" reads. If we have defensive players run the drill, it wears them out. We get a coach to run the drill because he can give us the give read we want to work on.

When the quarterback gets the snap, he is reading the backside end man on the line of scrimmage. He takes a small, six-inch step. His feet are at a 45-degree angle. We are looking downhill at the defensive end. The running back takes a six-inch step. His aiming point is the playside leg of the playside guard. The quarterback gives a soft squeeze on the football.

This is what we tell our quarterbacks: "This is where you must decide who you want to carry the football. Do you want the running back with the ball, or do you want the quarterback with the ball?" How we coach that is going to determine who has the ball more often in the offense. We tell our quarterback if the end can get downhill and tackle that featured back, he should pull the football.

It is the easiest option play there is. We want to keep the ball in the belly of the running back as long as we can. We do not want the ball in the mesh to go beyond the front hip of the quarterback. If we ride the ball past the front hip, the ball is going to be on the ground. As the quarterback sells the ride, he has to soft-squeeze the ball. If he decides to put the ball into the belly of the running back on the give, he must give the ball and then come outside and carry

out the fake. The secondary should have no idea who has the football. We insist the quarterback carry out the fake. The play is no good if the quarterback gives the running back the football and then turns around and watches the play.

If the quarterback pulls the ball on the fake, he pulls the ball out and puts the ball back in his belly. If the quarterback leaves the ball hanging out after he pulls the fake, it will be knocked out of his hands, and it will be on the ground.

Quarterback Ride-and-Decide Drill

- *Purpose:* To teach the quarterback to execute the zone read properly and maintain ball security
- *Tempo:* Three-fourths to full speed
- *Organization/Set-Up:* Coach or player snaps the ball to the quarterback. He takes a six-inch step and pivots to the backside defensive end. He has two hands on the ball, and he is reaching with the ball away from the line of scrimmage into the mesh area with the back. He will read the defensive end. If the end crashes inside and shows his numbers, the quarterback will quickly pull the ball back into his belly and replace the defensive end, getting upfield as soon as possible. If the defensive end hangs, drops, or gets straight upfield, the quarterback will give the ball to the running back and protect himself.

We rep this drill repeatedly. It gives the quarterback non-violent reps. We are looking for ways to rep our plays without killing the players in practice.

Coaching Points:

- If the quarterback is in doubt or unsure of a read, he should give the ball to the running back; think give, and react to pull.
- If the exchange is bobbled, the quarterback can follow back into the hole to avoid the unblocked defensive end.
- The quarterback should pull straight back into his belly to avoid the running back from knocking the ball away as he runs through.
- The quarterback is responsible for read and pull; the running back is responsible for proper mesh.

- The running back should be patient to the hole and explosive through it.
- The running back reads the first down lineman playside for his cut.

The next part of the play is the pitch phase. We run the pitch phase several ways. We can move the H-back inside. We can motion the H-back. We can get into a trips set and bring the H-back into the pitch phase. We can run trips, bring the H-back into the dive position as the read back, and bring the F-back on the pitch phase. We have run the zone play, and our pitch phase was the bubble screen off the zone play. We were reading the zone, and throwing the bubble screen off the defender on the pitchman. There are a lot of ways to run the play. You are only limited by your imagination. This is something we work on in the ride drill.

Coaching Points:
- The running back is responsible for pitch relationship, which is one yard behind and four yards outside of the quarterback.
- The quarterback attacks the outside shoulder of the pitch key hard and works to get the ball pitched. If he comes hard upfield, the quarterback turns up under him and then gets back outside as if on a sweep.
- The quarterback wants to keep the pitch low and slightly in front of the running back. We tell the quarterback to stop, look, and pitch.

- Give or retreat after the pitch as a hit is probably coming.
- We teach a basketball pitch as opposed to thumb-under pitch.
- As the quarterback pitches the ball, he follows through on his motion.
- We do not want the quarterback on top of the man he is pitching the ball to on the play.

We have several zone-read variations. We have flexibility to run the play out of many different formations and motions. In addition, we run solid screens, which are play-action screens.

We can run the zone read as a double or triple option. What we are teaching the quarterback in the two backs when there is no pitch phase of the read play is that we want to replace the give deep. We want the quarterback to get his shoulders downhill and go toward the line of scrimmage. We work on this every day.

As I said before, we can change the player who we want to catch the pitch on the option. We can line up in two backs, and have one of those players take the pitch. We do this to change our offense to take advantage of what the defense is doing.

I have cut-ups of all of these plays, where you can see how we run the zone and option plays. If you have questions, I will be here throughout the clinic. Thank you for your attention.

A SOUND APPROACH TO THE SPREAD OFFENSE

Edgewater High School, Florida

Gentlemen, you are looking at an old high school football coach who ran the I-formation offense for 32 years. Over those years, I collected ideas from all over the United States on the I-formation offense. We won a state championship, and was runner-up in the state finals. We won a bunch of football games.

The last year we ran the I formation, and we had six offensive linemen who signed scholarships with major colleges. In addition, the tailback and a wide receiver signed a scholarship with a major college team. We got beat in the second round of the playoffs. I knew the night we lost in the playoffs that I could not run the I formation and coach any longer. It was not fair to our players. We had that many good players, and we just were not doing a good job with the material we had.

I had a coaching staff who were older in years. Some of them were former players who had come back to coach with me. Some of my coaches had been with me for 25 years or more. The offensive coordinator had been with me for 28 years. He is a great football coach. We worked well together for a long, long time.

Today, it is hard to hire a high school football coach, especially in the state of Florida. You do not have much to choose from for various reasons. Our economy is down. Schools are not hiring football coaches. They are hiring teachers in English, reading, and math. I went to the principal and told him I wanted to hire a football coach. The first question they asked was, "What can he teach?" You cannot hire PE teachers or history teachers today. They have to hire teachers who will help students pass the state-required test. It is hard to find coaches who can qualify as teachers in the fields they are hiring today.

At the end of the year, I got together with two of my coaches. One of the coaches was my line coach. He played for me. He was the first all-state player I had. I told them we were going to make a change in our offense for the next season. "We are not going to run the I-formation offense anymore. I know you have been coaching with me for a long time. We are going to change the offense."

The past year, all of the Florida state football championship games were in Orlando at the Citrus Bowl. That included the championships for Class 1A to Class 6A. After we got beat in the playoffs, I went to see every game in the state championships. I went to all of the games. Only two out of the 12 teams in the state finals that were not running a spread offense. The other 10 teams were running a spread offense. I knew then there was something special about the spread offense. I did not know what it was, because I knew nothing about the spread offense. The bottom line is: we changed our offense to the spread offense. I made my coaches change.

I had met Urban Meyer two years before because he wanted one of my big offensive linemen. He came to our practice. I bet he thought I was crazy. His team was running the spread offense and running an offense that was wide open, and here we were still running the I-formation offense.

It was not an easy thing to get the assistant coaches to agree to change. When you are coaching with guys who are older and have been with you for a long time, it is hard to get them to change. Change does not come easy. This is especially true when you have been successful. The other coaches looked at me and asked, "Why do we have to make all of these changes?" As the head coach, I was convinced we needed to change to the spread offense.

At Christmas vacation time, we implemented the spread offense. What I did not tell the assistants was the fact I had been doing research on the spread offense for about a year. I called coaches, I got cut-ups from college coaches, and I watched different games and teams that ran different spread schemes. Before I started doing the research, I did not know much about the spread offense.

After getting all the information on the spread offense, I was convinced I was not going to be a coach who threw the ball 60 to 65 times a game. I did not want to do that. We had some small players, but they could run well. I wanted to keep the same philosophy that we had in running the I formation. We wanted to run the football 60 percent of the time and throw the ball 40 percent of the time. The coaches bought into this concept. Before, when we were running the I formation, we ran a lot of play-action passes, sprint-draw plays, and screen passes. The concept of running the football 60 percent of the time helped sell the spread offense to the older staff members.

Our school changed the last two years. We went down from an enrollment of 3,300 students. The economy in Florida is starting to hurt everyone. Now, we were losing students, and we were losing football players. We do not have as many kids coming to our school now.

The first thing I did in installing the spread offense was to visit four or five schools that ran the spread offense. If we were going to commit to throwing the football 40 percent of the time, I wanted to make sure that our pass-protection scheme was as sound and simple as it could be.

I am not a know-it-all coach. I am going to tell you everything I do from the heart. This works with my players. We all know if you get negative plays in high school football, you are probably going to lose. If you get fumbles, interceptions, if you get trapped, if you get holding calls against your offense, you are probably going to lose a bunch of games. We

wanted to make sure that did not happen. Every college coach I talked with told me this: "If you are going to run the spread offense, make sure the pressure on the quarterback comes from the outside and not inside."

If you have something on offense that works for you, that is great. I took that advice from the college coaches, and I fit it into our system and with our players. If we were going to turn a defender loose, we were going to turn them loose outside the tackle box. We were determined to make sure our quarterback did not have a defender in his face. We could sit around for days and draw up defensive schemes to defeat what I am going to show you on pass protection. This protection worked for us.

This is the best thing I learned about football by going to the spread offense. In our first year, we were not very good. We had 11 players who had to have an operation for one reason or the other. We were not a good football team. We were struggling to be 5-5. The more formations we gave the defense, the less number of defenders they put in the box. When we were an I-formation team, we never saw that happen. We saw seven, eight, and even nine men in the box before, but never did we see teams reduced the numbers they put in the box.

We went through the first eight games of that first season, and no one wanted to listen to what we were doing. We prepared for each team each week. We coached them up for what to expect. No one wanted to listen to what we were saying. When we started getting better at the end of the season, we got a lot of attention, but no one wanted to listen. We went to the negative for me. I could not believe that was how it was going to turn out.

I wanted to keep the offensive concepts I had learned from college and pro coaches over the years. I wanted to make sure we could still run those types of plays. We wanted to keep our pass protection and our blocking rules for our plays. We included those plays into our offense.

I want to cover our pass protection on the spread offense first. I will go over it against an even defense, and then I will cover it against the odd defense.

Anytime the playside guard is covered, the call is "pin." The right guard makes the call. The guard blocks the down lineman, and the running back is responsible for blocking the A-gap blitz.

If our playside guard is not covered by a down defensive lineman, the call is "lock." The guard calls "lock." The guard blocks down on the noseman. That makes the running back responsible for the B-gap blitz.

We can make a "pin 3 technique" call, and the guard takes the 3-technique tackle, and the tailback looks for the linebacker on the inside blitz (Diagram #1).

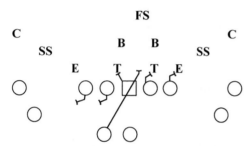

Diagram #1. Pin Call 3 Technique

If we call "lock 1 technique" against the even defense, the center blocks the 3 technique. The onside guard blocks down on the 1 technique (Diagram #2). The running back is responsible for the B-gap blitz by the linebacker.

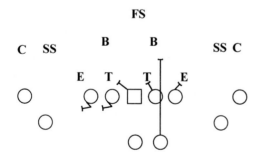

Diagram #2. Lock Call 1 Technique

Against the odd look, the right guard calls "lock zero technique." He is going to block the noseman (Diagram #3). He is going to lock on the zero technique. The running back reads the Mike backer and steps up in the line to take on any blitz in the A gap.

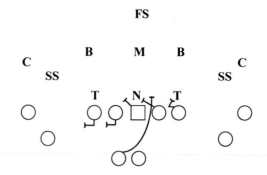

Diagram #3. Lock Call Zero Technique, A gap

Against an odd defense, if the right guard gives a zero technique call, we "lock" on the noseman (Diagram #4). The running back reads the linebacker on his side. He steps up and checks the linebacker. If the linebacker is not coming in the B gap, he steps outside and looks for the first defender to show.

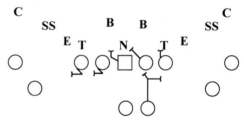

Diagram #4. Lock Call Zero Technique, B gap

The coach who used to coach the offense at the University of Florida was Dan Mullen. He is now the head coach at Mississippi State. He gave me some good information about implementing the spread offense: "Don't use too many formations when you first start out in the spread offense. Let the kids get used to where they line up. Do not play with a fast tempo to start out. Slow things down, and let the players see how the offense looks."

We did not add any formations after we got started. This was especially so in the spring of that year. We only had the basic formations and the plays we were going to run. The more the players became comfortable with the offense, the more we could add to the spread offense. The coaches working with me did not know much about the offense, and I did not know much about the offense. However, when we started to gain knowledge about the spread offense, then we could start adding information.

When we first implemented the offense, we ran twins in the middle of the field and trips to the wideside of the field. That is all we did, rep after rep in practice. We installed the offense in the spring. In Florida, you cannot throw the football during the school year after football. In the summer, you can throw the ball. In addition, in Florida, we have spring football practice. We have 20 days of practice time. We could not have done anything about installing a new offense if we did not have spring football practice. Therefore, we implemented our spread offense in the spring.

The rules permit us to play a game at the end of spring practice. We played a very good team, and they beat the crap out of us. Out of that game, when we looked at the film, we could tell we had a chance to be successful. We sold the kids on the fact that the game did not count against our record. We sold them on the fact we were implementing an offense that was new. No one complained. We got them through the summer, and we will work on getting better.

We did not using many formations. In the middle of the field, we ran a double twins look. To the boundary, we ran our trips set. We were mostly in a one-back set. I knew if we could use two backs, we could run an option game. It is a great thing to think about doing. However, when you are limited with the number of coaches on your staff, it may not be a good thought.

We did end up running some two-back sets, and we use nothing but isolation plays and some quarterback-sweep plays. We practiced the option, but we did not run it very much in a game. It may have been due to the fact we did not have confidence in it as coaches, or our players did not understand it very well. We did not do a very good job on it, and it was a matter of wasting practice time.

Coach Dan Mullen of Mississippi State also told our staff that if we were going to run the spread offense, we needed to have a plan to attack the wideside of the field, a plan to attack the boundary. He told us we had to practice like that. This was not hard because I had been working with the same two or three assistants for several years. We always scripted our practices. Everyone knew the play we were running on offense. We worked our offensive reps like clockwork. We did it with the I formation, and we did the same thing with the spread offense. We feel this saves a lot of practice time. It does not take that long to do. We have been doing this for 35 years. When we go on the practice field, everyone knows what play comes next.

Next, we tried to develop a plan for the middle of the field. We had a plan to attack the wideside of the field and the boundary. Now, we came up with a plan for the middle of the field. We went with double slots on both sides of the formation. That was with one-back set. Then, we ran twins open with two backs. That was our plan to start the season.

When the ball is on the boundary to the wideside, we used multiple principles. Into the boundary, we will always send a receiver into the boundary, or motion a man into the boundary and use that extra man as a blocker.

When we were talking with teams about the spread offense, everyone told me to get two quarterbacks ready to play in the games. I had never gotten two quarterbacks ready to play. I would get the first quarterback ready and get someone who could go in for a play or two. Usually, the second-string quarterback played JV for us. Again, I was an I-formation coach. All the quarterback had to do was to hand the ball off to the tailback. He did run the sprint draw a few times. We just did not ask the quarterback to run the football. At the time we implemented the spread offense, we did not think that mattered too much. We made a mistake.

I will show you what we did on offense. When the ball was in the middle of the field, we were in double slots with one back and the quarterback in the backfield. The quarterback was a good athlete. He was a junior that first year. He is going to be a senior this year. He was athletic, he could run, he could throw, and he could throw on the run. He is a winner.

In the first year we went to the spread, we did not call the formation. The kids knew we wanted to run double twins to both sides. As the season progressed, we started to put one of the slotbacks in motion. We ended up going into trips in the middle of the field if we brought the motion man all the way across the formation.

To the wideside of the field, we were in trips 90 percent of the time in the first five games. That is what we ran with the one back. If we were in the two-back set, we were in the middle of the field.

How did we line them up in the double slots? We used the hash marks and the numbers. We used the numbers on the field for the widest receiver and the hash marks for the inside receivers. You cannot practice if you do not have the hash marks and numbers painted on the field. You need to give the receivers a landmark where they are supposed to go. The shortside of the field was easy. We were mostly in two-backs with trips to the field. We would put someone in motion to get an extra blocker or to run play-action back the other way.

That is what we did for the first five games. We lost eight players to major surgery. Before that, I had not had eight surgeries in five years. I could not believe it. Every time we turned around, someone was getting hurt. We were struggling as a football team. People starting asking me why we did not go back to the I-formation offense. My brother Jeff is one of my defensive coaches. He asked me the same question. I assured him we were going to stay with the spread offense.

In the second half of the season, we felt it was important for us to increase the 60 percent that we were running the ball. Because of the injuries, we felt we could cut down on some of the injuries if we ran the ball more and shortened the games by running the clock. At this point of the season, we had several players playing both offense and defense because we had so many players get hurt. We had players playing two positions, one on offense and one on defense.

One of the first things we did was to insert an offensive tight end. I took a defensive tackle who was 6'3" and 275 pounds and made him my tight end. It was obvious what we were going to try to do with that big tight end in the lineup. It dictated the front the defense was going to play. The defense had to play a 9 technique on top of our tight end. We knew our tight end could dominate the 9 technique. He is a good football player, and this gave us a better running game.

We wanted to make sure we kept our defense off the field as much as possible. We wanted to make sure we could use the tight end when we ran our two-back set. We wanted to be able to run a power play with the two backs and the tight end that we had run out of the I formation. We were trying to keep the defense off the field as much as possible because we had so many players hurt and we had several players going both ways. It took longer to practice because we had players going both ways. We did more 11-on-11 and 7-on-7 drills. There were more people moving around in less time than ever before.

There were not as many small groups because we were trying to double-teach both defense and offense. There was no free time built into practice. We had more people working and less people standing around during practice.

I had our Booster Club buy a lot of the software to break down our game films. We bought an editing system that enabled us to get everything we needed to know about our team and the opponents. My son coaches with me, and he was able to use the system to break down our offense. It was not so much the plays we were running, but he broke down the formations we were running, and where on the field were we running each formation. It helped us very much to formulate our practice sessions with all of the information from the computers. That computer would let us know how many reps we were running to the wideside of the field, and how many times we ran motion. It gave us everything about our offense that we asked for.

When we started putting in the game plan for the next week, we looked at the formation chart. We were running six plays, but running them from a different formation. We would take the six plays and try to come up with a plan to make the defense react to what we did with those six plays. It was amazing how that helped us on offense. Again, I used the same system that Coach Dan Mullen showed our staff. We had a plan for the middle of the field, the wideside of the field, and the shortside of the field. We practiced in those situations. We scripted out our practice sessions. We write everything down.

I use a chart I make up for each game. I take these two or three plays and practice them in special situations. I practice against those special situations during the week. The kids know if we had a third down and two to go, they knew the play we were going to run. We practiced using two or three plays in each situation all week long. We practiced the formation we were going to run the plays out of, and the situation, and the plays we were going to run in each situation.

We practiced those plays in each situation on our goal line and on the opponent's goal line. We did the drill when we were two minutes behind in the game, and two minutes when we were ahead in the game. We practiced the plays two minutes before the first half.

Butch Davis, who now coaches at North Carolina, talked with me about the turnovers. He told me I needed to add the turnover situation to my list of plays we practice during the week. "What plays are you going to call when you recover a fumble on the opponent's 15-yard line?" When that happens, the assistant coaches and players are jumping up and down with excitement. Now, you have a chance to win the game. You must practice those plays that you plan on running in that situation so your players will know what to do when everyone else is involved in the excitement of the game.

What play are you going to call when you block a punt and you have the ball on the opponent's four-yard line? You need to prepare for that situation.

The first year we installed the spread offense in the spring, we emphasized pass protection. In the summer practices, we emphasized fundamentals.

We did speed training. It was important to our offense.

We had two tailbacks who we were counting on that first year. One of them was playing basketball and tore his knee up. The other tailback moved to another school two days before practice started. We did not have much returning after those two tailbacks. We had to use our quarterback as a runner. He improved over the summer because he was in a speed-training program. He really improved after running the spread offense for one year.

The last season, we added one play for the quarterback, and I could not believe how much it helped us win games that second year. We would motion to a trips set and run the quarterback on a power play. We had a tight end, and we called the play "empty tight." We had a tight end and a wingback on one side, a split end and two wideouts on the other side. The quarterback was in the backfield without any backs. We could check either one or both of the backs into the backfield if we wanted. We could bring any one of them across the formation. It was amazing how much that formation helped us that second year.

Here are the six plays we ran when we started with in the fall practice. The first play was our dropback pass. I told you we wanted to throw the ball 40 percent of the time. We ran the dropback passing game. That was the first play.

We added a quarterback-draw play (Diagram #5). We ran a dropback passing game, and we added the draw play as our first running play. I told you he was a runner. He was not afraid to run. He was not afraid, and he could take a hit. It was a lot of fun coaching him. We led the one running back on the linebacker.

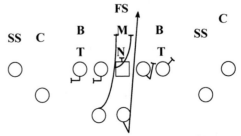

Diagram #5. Quarterback Draw

We could run it either way with the halfback on either side of the quarterback, leading the way on the linebacker.

We ran the inside zone play (Diagram #6). Everyone who runs the spread offense runs this play. So we run it also. We block it the same as everyone else does.

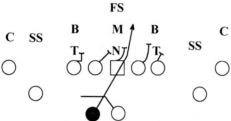

Diagram #6. Inside Zone Right

We double-team blocked the 5-technique tackle. The onside guard steps toward the 5-technique tackle, reading the linebacker. The center and backside guard blocked the nose and Mike backer. The backside tackle filed inside up to the backside backer.

We ran the jet sweep (Diagram #7). It was not an unusual play. We could run it with either back and we could run it either way.

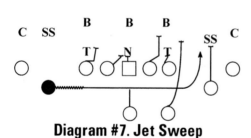

Diagram #7. Jet Sweep

Off the jet sweep, we ran a quarterback power play (Diagram #8). We had the slot faking the jet sweep, and the quarterback kept the ball on the power play with the running back leading the play.

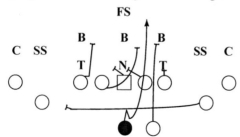

Diagram #8. Quarterback Power

Because the jet play was so good and we had so much speed in the jet runners, we started faking the ball to the slotback on the jet sweep. We made the fake, and then we ran a quarterback trap play (Diagram #9). The backside guard pulled and trapped the tackle. The running back led the play and cleaned up anyone in the hole.

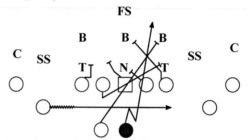

Diagram #9. Quarterback Trap

We started out with those six things on offense. We concentrated on those plays at the start of the season. The formations were constantly changing from week to week. The computer would give us a breakdown on where we were running those plays from on the field. It helped us in running the different formations. I did not care about the plays we ran. All I wanted to know was the formation we should be using each week on the plays.

I cannot count the numbers of times we ran an empty tight from the middle of the field. I only wanted to know how many times we were in that particular formation. In the next game, I made sure we were running the same play but from a different formation. We ran the same plays, but we kept changing the formations.

Our empty tight was a big play for us, but it gave us much more than just that one play. Teams started scouting us, and every time they saw our big number 90 come on the field on offense, they knew he was going to be the tight end. He would line up on the right side of the formation with the two running backs. The defense started sending in their run-support players when we sent in our number 90 tackle. We started switching numbers with different players so the defense could not tell if number 90 was the tight end or just another player.

After a few games, we decided to run a wrinkle in the play. We added empty over to our offense

(Diagram #10). We took the left tackle and switched him over to the tight-end side on the right side of the formation. We put our tight end on the shortside of the formation.

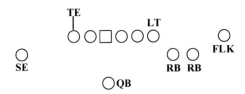

Diagram #10. Empty Over Formation

Now, we had a tackle eligible–type play. The first time we ran it, we scored a touchdown (Diagram #11). The other team was telling the officials it was an illegal play, but they were wrong.

I want to show these plays to you on film. You will see we were not very good at the first of the year. We did get better as the season went on.

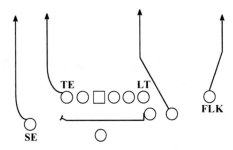

Diagram #11. Empty Over 90 Pass Tackle Eligible Play

Men, it has been an honor to visit with you today. If I can ever help you, send me an email. I do want you to know this. I will never go back to coaching the I formation. If you are a high school football coach and you have limited talent, and limited offensive linemen, this is a great package for you. I am still learning about the offense. Thank you for your time, and good luck next year.

TEAM CONCEPTS AND KICKING GAME TIPS

Saint Xavier High School, Kentucky

We are going to give you a couple of ideas here today. Earl gave us a topic of old and new team concepts. I guess he did it because my brother Bill is older and I am younger. I always kid Bill about that. You can call him the *old* Coach Glaser and me the *young* Coach Glaser.

I am going to talk about team concepts because it is a big thing for our team. Anyone that is a head coach needs to understand team concepts. I believe *teams* win championships. You must keep this in mind. The bottom line is this: We have won seven state championships, we have been in the championship game 11 times, and we have had four state runner-ups. Each one of those teams were special because they were strongly close together. Every good team we have ever had has had that team concept. I think this is important, and I feel comfortable talking on this topic.

When you look at building a football program, and Bill and I will both talk about this, you look at what makes a *strong* football program. Everyone should want to be a head coach. Everyone on your staff should want to be a head coach. I have 17 coaches on my staff, and I look at them as 17 head coaches. The reason I feel this way is because they will not really be a good coach unless they want to be the one in charge. They need to see what kinds of needs there are, and they will really try to meet them. We need the take-charge kind of coaches and not have just one coach doing it.

We have four or five things that we need to talk about. The first step is to develop a philosophy. I have five points on developing a philosophy, in addition to the team concept, that you have to build into your program.

DEVELOP A PHILOSOPHY

- A strong off-season
  - ✓ Three phases: Winter, spring, summer
- Defense
  - ✓ Stop the run first
  - ✓ Great tacklers
  - ✓ Pressure from everywhere
  - ✓ Multiple fronts
- Offense
  - ✓ Run first
  - ✓ Set pace
  - ✓ Be physical
- Kicking game
  - ✓ Practice it
  - ✓ Find: A long snapper, punter, and kicker
  - ✓ Short yardage
  - ✓ Practice it everyday

Number one, you have to have a *strong off-season program*. We make a T-shirt up every year. I am sure you guys have done the same thing. It has St. X on the front, and on the back it says, *This Is Where Champions Are Made*.

The great thing about the off-season is that you can build a great football player. You can take a bunch of raw, young talent and turn them into some good football players if you have a good off-season program. You can make them bigger, faster, and stronger with a lot of hard work. That is basically what we do. I can remember starting out as a head coach. We did not have a guy in our backfield that could run under a 5.0 40-yard dash. I think it was seven years before we got one. Once we started winning and won some state championships, we have gotten some better talent. We have some guys that can flat out fly. That makes it a lot easier to coach. Nevertheless, the bottom line is you can *build* football players.

We like to hit the weight room. We have a few main lifts, and they are the only ones I ever care about doing. We are doing *cleans* and we are doing squats. That is where football players are developed. We also do a lot of *bench press* and a lot of *incline bench press*. Those are the four main lifts we do. The bench, incline, clean, and squat are all you really need to focus on. I do not think you need other stuff. Some people say you need plyometrics. If you are doing squats and you are exploding and putting some good heavy weights on there, you can build some good players.

In the winter program, we have them come in at 6 a.m. It is tough on them. They have to decide how to get there. They may have to stay at each other's houses. Mom and Dad have to commit also. Mothers hate it, but the bottom line is everyone has to be committed to being a St. X football player. No one is excused from these workouts. We do all of this during the winter phase of our program.

Then, we go to our spring phase. We send them all to spring sports, but we still have lifting three days a week. We also give them a running program for the off days.

Our summer phase is three days a week of lifting, running, and doing a lot of other drills. The summer phase is a clinic talk in itself. The reason is because it is vital to your program. You can have all the X's and O's you want, but the players have to be physically strong and sound.

It does not matter how you draw up your diagrams, it will be good if you have studied it, you know it, and you believe in it. No one at any level does the exact same thing as the next team. Everyone is a little different with a wrinkle here and there. If your players are sound, you will have a chance for success, regardless of how you draw up the plays. There is no question that the off-season program is vital to your program's success.

Our second philosophy relates to *defense*. I have seen a lot of coaches that pick up a point or two on a Saturday or Sunday afternoon. We try to never do that. We might get a tip or two, but we never try to change our defensive philosophy very much. I go to clinics and get some ideas on how to improve and how to build on *my* philosophy, but we do not change who we are as a team.

On defense, we believe you have to stop the run first. All the great passing teams that have beaten us have done it with the running game. They spread you out and then run the ball at your defense. If we can stop the run, we feel pretty good about our chances of winning games. Even if they are a great passing team, we want them to throw the football. If they can run it on us, we are in trouble. You cannot defend the whole field. We predicate our defense on stopping the run first.

The second thing is to be *great tacklers*. We tackle every day. We played 15 games and two scrimmages, and we tackled every single day. In 1988, we went 6-5. It was the only time in my head coaching career that we did not go to the playoffs. That next January, we started an off-season program in our basement. We tackled every day without equipment. We bloodied noses and everything else. Moreover, we have been doing it ever since.

We want our tackling to be *sound*. We want it to be *fundamental*. In addition, we want it to be nasty. We want to make you pay for catching the football against us. You may catch it, but we want to let you know it will come at a cost. It is the same for the running backs. That back has the thing that we want—the football. We have to get that ball back.

Offensively, we are a run first football team. You know why? Because today I am the only coach that wants to run the football anymore. Now our coaches want to put us in a one-back and a no-back set. I say I do not like it, and then we run the football. Our offensive coordinator does a great job, but he is the one that calls all of those passes. I am not going to lie to you. I have not called any passes except I tell them to throw it deep. I like throwing it deep and I like some of the tricky plays, but basically we are going to run the football.

We feel if we establish the running game, it will open up our passing game. In the running game, we just have some simple concepts. We have some bread-and-butter plays for our offense. We are going to run the sweep. We are going to run it out of split-back, I-back, and single-back formations. We are going to run the sweep. What is the first play we are going to run inside the 10 yard line? The *sweep*. We tell everyone we play, and they all know they have to stop our sweep. They start to key on our sweep. Our players are telling me, "Coach, they are yelling out sweep, sweep." I say, "You are darn right, but that is all right because we are going to run a bootleg off of it." On the other hand, we will have another way of countering the defense.

Another play we love is the power play off-tackle out of our split backs. We have put in a counter play off split back that has also been good for us. When our opponents see us in split backs, they feel like we are probably running the outside veer or sweep. We have our counter play to hit them when they overpursue. I think that play averaged 12 yards per run for us last year. We run it out of other sets as well. We run it about seven times per game.

As I said, my coaches wanted to throw the football, so we got into a one-back look. We ran the four vertical routes. Our opponents started taking players out of the box. Therefore, we developed a little counter trey out of our one-back set. That has helped us as well. In 2009, we outscored our opponents 225 to 67.

POINT TOWARD THE PLAYOFFS (THREE PHASES)

Another philosophy that I believe in is breaking your season down into three parts or phases. Your emphasis is pointing toward the playoffs and in having your team peaking at the right time.

Games: 1-5

- Establish fundamentals
- Base offense and defense
- Find your players and what they do well

Games: 6-10

- Develop depth
- Develop wrinkles to offense and defense
- Work companion plays and special plays
- Hold special plays if possible

Playoffs: Five Games

- Now use what you need to win
- Play your best football

In the first five games, teach your players the fundamentals of your offense and defense. Games 6 through 10 you need to try to develop some depth. Get your second stringers into the games. Once you reach the playoffs, hopefully, you are ready to play your best football. After our sixth game, we started putting in some special plays and we practiced them every week. However, we wanted to hold those special plays for when we really needed them. One of our big plays in the state championship game this year came off of our sprint action—a throwback screen. We had worked on it for 10 weeks. Our kids would say, "Coach, when are we going to run the screen?" Save your special plays for the playoffs. Use them when you need them. That is a great concept. I think you need to buy into this concept. Do not use special plays just to look good.

TEAM CONCEPT

Football *teams* win championships. I honestly believe that. Following are some things I think will help develop and strengthen your team concept.

Love Your Players

- "They do not care how much you know until they know how much you care."

Sometimes you have to drop the X's and O's, and find a way to show your kids you care about them. Because when times get tough, those kids will fight even harder for you if you have shown them you care. That is the best thing you can do. After all, that is what we are supposed to be doing all of this for anyway—the kids—not our own personal glory. If you care enough about them, the championships will come. I have had kids say, "Coach, I want to win this championship for you." I tell them, "I have my championship, do it for *you*." Nevertheless, you see my point. The kids will rally behind you. It is not enough to talk, but you have to show them. You have to find ways to do things that let them know you care. Let them know you will go the extra mile to help them. In this day and age, they need you.

Have Trademark Themes

- A band of brothers
- *We* and *us* is a must
- We need a lot of good men, not a few great ones

Develop some trademark themes, ones that your kids hear all the time. Kids will listen to you. You need to repeat yourself often. Eventually, they will all understand. One of the greatest words in the English language is *again*. How do you teach your offense and defense? You run plays again and again. Repeating your themes and making them ones the players can relate to is important. Talk and live your themes every day.

Build a Brand

- The helmet—"A Tradition Unequaled"

I love to use the helmet to help build our brand. The reason is simple. Football is really the only sport that lets you have a helmet like this. We put our decal on our helmets, and we tell our players that it symbolizes something special. Our helmets have looked the same for many years. It is a tradition, and it will never change. We do not believe in any spirit or award decals. We have never really done anything like that. We try to keep our team philosophy. This year, we did do one thing. When we won our first playoff game, all 94 guys got a little *x*

to put on the back of their helmet. When we won the second playoff game, all 94 guys got another little *x*, and so on. They ended up with five little *x*'s on the backs of their helmets when they finished with the state game. That is the only time we have done that. We put our helmet on every shirt, sweatshirt, shorts, sweats, etc. that we can. We want to brand our image. When someone sees our helmet, they think *Louisville* St. X. It makes a difference.

More Team Building Ideas

- Do everything together
  - ✓ Weight room
  - ✓ Running
  - ✓ Doughnut days
  - ✓ Locker room alignment
  - ✓ Chapel service
- The team meeting
  - ✓ Time
  - ✓ Place
  - ✓ Tone
- Team functions
  - ✓ YMCA run
  - ✓ Church picnics
  - ✓ Project Warm
  - ✓ Other sports
  - ✓ Team picnic
  - ✓ Picture day

We do everything together. There are no senior privileges on our football team. Everyone carries their own equipment. We stretch together at the start of practice, and we come back together at the end of practice to do our conditioning. When the team comes up and takes a knee at the end of practice, we make sure all of the assistant coaches are there. I ask the staff if they have anything to say. The kids notice those things.

Do not talk to your team if they are looking down. Write this down—"If you look, you listen twice." That is the truth. If your kids are looking at you when you are speaking, they are going to get your message. Tell that to your football team because if they are not looking then they are not paying attention. That is a classroom technique. If a kid comes up after your meeting and asks you a question about something you covered in the meeting, tell them you covered it in the meeting. Do not do yourself a disservice and let them off the hook. Make them learn they have to pay attention.

There are a lot of other team functions we have done. I have listed them for you. One good one is to organize a team bus and go watch another school play a game. We have had so many good responses from families and the kids themselves. They really appreciate and notice your effort and commitment to support them. There are several other ways to involve your team and the school community as well.

Later, Coach Bill Glaser is going to talk about our kicking game and short-yardage philosophies. We believe in those two important areas. Thanks, guys, for being here. I will now turn it over to Coach Bill.

COACH BILL GLASER

As a coach, I believe you have to sell your players on everything you do. Know why you do something. Know your strengths and weaknesses. Then, you have to sell your players on wanting to be a part of your program. Most guys play football to be around you, the coach. Sell yourself and your program to your players.

Selling your players on the importance of short-yardage situations is very important. We have a few philosophies on the short-yardage game that have worked for us. I want to share them with you.

SHORT-YARDAGE PHILOSOPHY

- Beat your opponent physically
- Better conditioning
- Aggressive—No fear
- Consistency—100% every play
- Enthusiasm—Contagious
- Pressure
- Goal line charge—New line of scrimmage

- Attack the tight end
- Defend inside out
- Sneak, iso, power, option, sweep
- Pursuit is imperative
- Best on best

Do not worry about a long snap count. If you jump offside on your one yard line, they get half a yard. If they jump offside, they lose five yards. So let them try the hard counts and the long snap counts. Just get ready to attack.

Make sure you have your best 11 players on the field. It is not a time for razzle-dazzle. Find out who is going to give 100 percent effort on every play. You cannot afford to take one play off.

Be balanced as far as the number of men on each side of the ball. Have five-and-a-half players on each side of the ball. If you are not balanced, then they will get you with the stretch play.

We put our bigger players on the inside of our defense and our faster kids on the outside. You have to be able to stop the inside power running game. You cannot do this with your smaller or less physical players.

After you win the short-yardage battle, then you go into special teams. If you have a small staff, you will have a tough time having enough practice time to get to all of your offense, defense, and kicking game. Nevertheless, you have to practice the kicking game. Sell your players on the importance of the kicking game.

The kicking game starts each half of every game. Quite often, a good return or a bad return can set the tone for the upcoming series. Plays in the kicking game can determine the outcome of the games in the closing seconds of the game. One out of every six plays occurs in the kicking game. Go back and look at your film. Count your plays and you will find this to be true. It could be as low as five plays.

If you win the kicking game, you will win the ball game a lot times against better teams because of field position. They will have to gain 80 yards every time for a touchdown. Your team only has to go 50 yards on average each time. We all know what the usual outcome of that scenario is.

You can protect the PAT any way you want. However, we have found that you have to have the same holder and snapper because when the kicker gets that timing down, it becomes a rhythm. If you can get a snapper that does not play all of the time, that is an ideal situation. There is less of a chance for him to get hurt during another part of the game. Therefore, you get more continuity out of the long snapper position, which only helps the kicker.

The holder needs to have good hands. He does not have to be lightning fast to get to the corner. However, he must have good hands. I really believe it is not a good idea to have your starting quarterback as the holder. Too many things can go wrong. You would be sick if your quarterback went down on a play like that. We like to look for a second-string quarterback or a wide receiver. It is a great way for them to get on the field. They take pride in this. It is their chance to contribute.

On the PAT and field-goal block, you can pressure from wherever you like—inside, outside, or both. However, you must have contain and coverage. You cannot be just selling out and inviting people to run the ball around the corner. You must have contain and coverage in your scheme. The other guys can rush like crazy. I do not think you can send all 11 guys on the rush and be sound.

The punt team is the only team that plays both offense and defense. Think about that for a minute. This is very important. If you cannot punt well, you cannot win. If you cannot protect the punter, you cannot win. There will be times when your great offense gets stopped. It hurts when you average 15 yards per punt—same thing if you have every third punt blocked.

Make sure your punt team knows they are playing both offense and defense. They have to be sound in their protection schemes. They have to be sound in their blocking techniques. The first responsibility is to protect the punter. Have guys call out whom they have in protection. If guys move around, they could change responsibilities. Only after getting the kick away can you go down and cover.

To cover the punt, you have to be able to run. The reason is that you are going to have to cover the whole field. Now, you may have a punter that can consistently punt it to one side of the field or the other. However, for the most part, your players have to be able to run and tackle.

The personal protector needs to be your best decision maker. Find your most reliable guy. He is going to have to make split-second decisions. He cannot always be on the inside because two guys may come, and the outside guy is the one who is the immediate threat. He has to make that judgment. Find a good decision maker.

Once you have stopped your opponent's offense, you can really set the tone with your punt rush and return team. Make sure they send the punt team on the field. Have the same alignment on every punt return. That way you will not tip your hand. But, you always want to threaten them with the block. You will block more punts than you think you can if you work on it. Sell your coaches and kids on it.

Your kids have to *see the ball*. The punt team will call out some dummy calls. We cannot jump offside. Once you see the movement of the ball, you have to get off like a rocket. As your player approaches the punter and goes to extend his arms to block the kick, he should cross his arms. A lot of times, the ball will go between his arms if he does not cross them. This is what we have found over the years. Your player's eyes will take his hands to the ball. He should not look at the punter. If he will focus on the ball, you will have more success. Make sure the kid runs through the ball. Do not have him lay out. If you are running to first base, you do not lay out and slide if there is a close play—you keep running through the bag. The reason is that you are faster running a half step than you are doing a slide. The same thing applies when blocking punts. We tell them to never jump or leave their feet. When you jump, you get bumped into the punter and that causes a roughing penalty.

Some kids will never block punts. They are afraid they will break a finger or be kicked by the punter. Get those kids off the team. You need fearless and aggressive attackers.

Make sure your kids know what happens if a punt is partially blocked. When you see that a punt is partially blocked, have everyone yell, "Peter" or some special word to let the other teammates know it is blocked. It is important your kids know the rules regarding these types of plays.

Kickoff coverage requires a *flying start*. The first day in August, we practice the flying starts. We only go 10 yards. They have to time this up with the kicker. It is better to be a foot behind the kicker than an inch offside. So we practice this with them full speed. This can also be a conditioning drill if you want to use it that way.

We divide the field up into zones. The first 20 yards is the *speed zone*. They want to get through it as fast as they can. The second 20 yards is the *avoid zone*. Try to avoid engaging in any blocks. If they do avoid one, they must get back in their lane. The last 20 yards is the *kick zone*. They need to come under control and find the return man. They need to keep their shoulders square as they squeeze down to the returner. The returner will take you to the football.

On kickoff returns, we do not want our guys to back up. That is our rule, *never back up*. This really helps with the pooch kick. Make sure the other team kicks the football deep. It happened in the Super Bowl this year. The receiving team did not watch with their eyes and turned before the ball was actually kicked. The kicking team recovered an onside kick to start the second half, and it really set the tone and tilted all of the momentum to the Saints.

Communication between your players is vitally important. Make sure they know who has the final authority when calling for a punt. This is another area where our rule of not backing up to catch a punt helps us. We tell our kids, "If you have to take one step back to catch it, let it go to the next guy."

Men, I appreciate your attention. Thank you.

THE 3-5-3 DEFENSIVE FRONTS AND STUNTS

Beauregard High School, Alabama

First, I want to give you a little bit about my background. I coached junior high football for 10 years in Montgomery. I figured that was probably all I would do as a football coach. Then, a friend of mine got a coaching job at Opelika High School and it just hit me— I wanted to be a high school football coach. I called him and said, "I am calling you to ask that if you let me come up there and be a volunteer coach for one year, I will quit my job, and you do not even have to pay me. If I do a good job, I want you to hire me full time."

I told him that is what I wanted to do. I know he thought I was crazy, and my whole family thought I was crazy. He said, "Okay, come on up here. I will take you." I coached the defensive line for a year and he hired me. Two years later, he gave me the coordinator's job. I was the defensive coordinator for five years. We were a shade 50 team and played a cover-2 secondary, and we played seven men in the box. We had seven studs and we would beat your butt with seven people—it did not matter what you did. I learned a lot about coaching and coaching techniques from him.

Let me give you some advice. Do not always take the first opportunity to be a head coach. I took a job at a small country high school in Alabama that did not have much money and they had not had much success. I wanted to be a head coach, so I figured it was time to do it. In a lot of ways, it was a great experience. I learned a great deal. I learned it is tough to coach at a school that does not have much football experience.

I went from Opelika High School, with great facilities and a lot of great support, to a school that had to pay for coaching supplements out of the gate receipts. We had no money. We went 5-5 that first year, but we did a good coaching job.

Next, the opening at Beauregard came up, which is closer to where I am from. It was a similar situation in that they were a down program and never had a tradition of winning. The resources were a lot better there, and it was a better situation in the community.

I have been at Beauregard High School now for four years, and we have evolved into the 3-3 defense. I have taken the shade 50 defense with me everywhere I have been. We still use it some each year. However, we play the 3-3 defense most of the time, and that is what I want to talk to you about today.

In Alabama, we get 10 days of spring practice. Two years ago, I was in my office looking at spring practice tape of our 50 shade defense, and I realized we were not very good. Our defensive linemen were small, and we did not do a very good job of reading on defense. I called in my defensive coordinator. He was teaching P.E. and I told him, "We are going to go to the 3-3 defense today." He said, "Let's wait until after we get through spring practice, then we can put it in over the summer." We had a scrimmage scheduled the next week. I said, "No, we are going to do it now."

We had some DVDs on the 3-3 defense from Georgia Military College. We do the same thing that the Georgia Military does and we use the same terminology. The defensive coordinator and I sat in my office, and he let his P.E. class run wild while we figured out the base stuff. At 4 p.m., we put the whole team in the weight room with the offensive coaches while I met with the defensive coaches. In about 45 minutes, we put a practice plan together for that day. We went out and installed the 3-3 defense, and we completed it in four days of practice. We played the scrimmage and we actually played pretty well.

What that is telling you is that this defense is simple. It is not that complicated. If your kids are not real smart on the defensive line, it is a good defense for them. The defensive line only has to remember about four things. It is a little more difficult for the linebackers and defensive secondary because they have to know what the defensive line is doing. The defensive linemen have to know four defensive stunts. They have to know open, closed, pinch, and jacks—that is it. If they can learn those four things, they can play the defensive line.

I will start with our position names and fronts. Our mascot is the Hornets, so we call our outside linebackers Hornets.

Position Names

E = End (4 technique)

N = Nose

H = Hornet (outside backers)

B = Bat (stack backers)

M = Mike (middle backer)

Defensive Fronts

• Base
• Solid
• Tough
• Under
• G

We do not rush only three or four defenders very often. We like to put pressure on the opponents with five or more rushers. My defensive coordinator is also a baseball coach. You probably know that baseball coaches like to call a lot of hand signals. He likes to signal in a lot of moves, so we run stunts all of the time.

The first year we did not make the playoffs because we were a small 4A squad that had moved up to 5A. We played in a tough league and went 6-4 and 4-3 in the region. However, we did not get into the playoffs.

We had 106 tackles for loss in 10 games, plus 21 sacks. We were averaging at least 12 negative plays per game. Our turnovers were not as good as we wanted them to be, so we worked hard on that in the off-season. We got those turnovers a little better this year. In addition, our sack totals went up. We get a lot of negative plays from this defense.

We are in our *base front* most of the time (Diagram #1). We also run a solid front, which is our four-man front. Our under front is also a four-man front. When we run our under front, we usually change personnel at the Hornet position. It will be more like a shade 50.

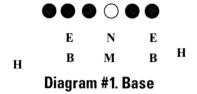

Diagram #1. Base

If we are in cover 3, our Hornets are going to be at three yards and three yards off the edge. They are outside three yards and back off the line three yards. We want them showing blitz and making it look as if they are coming on a blitz every time. Sometimes we will jockey those guys back and forth to make the offense think we are coming. We are always coming with someone. However, we are trying to confuse the offense on *who* is coming. That is our base alignment.

In our solid, we will move some players (Diagram #2). We do not make a strong right or a strong left call to the strength of the offense. Our linebackers make a closed or open call, depending on the formation and the position of the tight end. In this situation, the Mike linebacker will call, "Closed left, closed left." We are going to move to this front. We will be in our base defense with our stack.

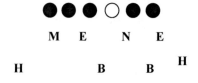

Diagram #2. Solid

We move our defense after the quarterback puts his hands under the center, or we move when the quarterback gives his leg kick when he is in the shotgun. We are going to move away from the strength. The nose will go from a 0 technique to a 1 technique on the weakside. The left end then will drop down to a 3 technique, and the Mike comes up to play a 7 technique. If there's not a tight end, then he is in a 5 technique.

I am not going to talk about our stunt package out of every front. Once you see our stunt package, you can match the same stunt out of any of the fronts. It all works together, and that is why it is so simple.

In our under front, we are going to move to the strength (Diagram #3). Mike is still going to make a closed left call. The nose is going to move to a shade on the strongside. Our 4-technique end will move to a 5 technique, and our backside 4 technique would drop down to a 3 technique. We don't flip-flop anybody. If you play on that side, then that is your side. We want to be able to line up and play. We do not want to have to worry about where to line up.

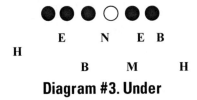

Diagram #3. Under

Here is the difference between G and under (Diagram #4). In the under look, the nose is in a 1 technique. In the G look, he is in a 3 technique to the strongside.

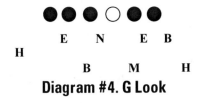

Diagram #4. G Look

In this defense, you have to have a noseguard that demands a double-team because he is going to be double-teamed every snap. He has to be able to handle the double-team. If the offense knows the noseguard is going to slant every time, one way or another, they are going to double-team him every play.

Our ends were too small to play 5A football in Alabama, but they could run and that is what we

were looking for. Our linebackers are not big, but all of our linebackers can run and they are intelligent kids. We want to put as much speed on the field as we can. That is another reason why we went to this defense.

We play five defensive backs. Our Hornets are hard-nosed defensive backs. They may not be able to cover your best receiver in space as a corner, but they are defensive backs. The free safety needs to be the smartest kid on the field. He has to make the checks, give our coverages, and set everything up. He has to be a physical guy that will run and make a lot of tackles for you.

Defensive Line

Stance: Three-point stance (balanced, comfortable); must be able to move either direction.

Aiming Point: Near hip of the offensive lineman he is moving toward.

Assignments: Control the gap you are moving toward and run to the ball.

We want our defensive lineman in a three-point stance—no more than a heel-toe alignment because they are stepping in one direction or the other 90 percent of the time. The aiming point is going to be the hip of the lineman that they are slanting toward, and they have to read that guy. We have to work hard when we are slanting. We do not want forced out of position on the blocks because we are going to get a lot of down blocks and a lot of back blocks.

They have to realize that when they feel that pressure and they are slanting in one direction, they cannot keep going in that direction and let that offensive guy wash him out. If you do not coach that up, he will be knocked out of the gap. On the other hand, they will be so concerned about it that they will not get across the face of the offensive lineman and they will not be in the gap you need. There is a fine line those guys have to play.

We do a lot of drills with them stepping just a half a step with the correct foot. They need to step at a 45-degree angle with that near foot. A lot of kids will have one direction that they are not good at. It is real important that you work hard on those steps with the defensive line. We do not want them upfield once they get in that gap. We want them flat down the line of scrimmage, chasing.

These are the calls the defensive linemen have to know. They need to know the open, closed, pinch, and jack calls.

The defensive linemen only have to listen to the first word of the call. If we call *open*, it means the linemen are slanting away from the strength, or away from the call (Diagram #5).

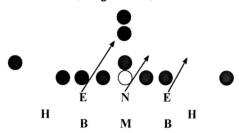

Diagram #5. Open

If we call *closed*, they are slanting to the strength, to the call, or toward the tight end (Diagram #6). We call strength to the tight end side, then to the side with the most receivers, then to the side of the back. If everything is balanced, we will call strength to the field.

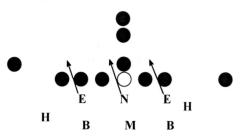

Diagram #6. Closed

If we call *pinch*, our 4-technique ends are slanting to the inside and going to the hip of the guard (Diagram #7). Our noseguard could go either way and we give him a choice. It really does not matter to us but the Mike has to know, so they work together. We give our kids a lot of freedom, which gives them ownership in the defense.

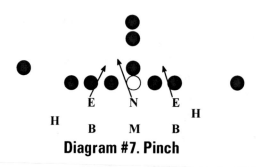

Diagram #7. Pinch

If we call *jacks,* our ends must control the C gaps (Diagram #8). Our nose controls the strongside A gap.

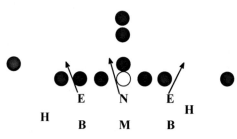

Diagram #8. Jacks

Linebackers

Stance: Shoulder over your knees, knees over your toes, weight on the inside balls of your feet.

Keys: Near running back to pulling lineman.

Drills: Key drill, blitzing, get off blocks, pass drops.

The linebackers' stance is the same stance that everybody else has with their heels at five yards. The linebackers are going to key through the line to the near running back. If we are in man coverage, they really want to key the running back to get an idea of where the play is going. We coach just as everyone else does on getting off blocks. We are going to use our hands. We are going to lock out the same as what everybody does.

We expect our linebackers to be our best players. They have got to run and make plays for you. You want to put your smartest guy at Mike, and you want to put your most athletic guys at the Bats. It is very important that they understand their fit. Because this defense is so simple, you can get by with playing some guys that are not seasoned. The

Mike linebacker is the key to the whole thing. He has to understand his fit, especially because of all the stunting we do. If we get two in the same gap, we are going to have an issue.

There are four frontside keys for our Bats. We base our keys off of cover 3. If they are in cover 3, they can really see through the linemen better.

If the onside guard blocks down, the Bat fills the B gap. If the onside guard and tackle both block down, he fills outside the tackle in the C gap. If the onside guard pulls, the Bat comes outside the C gap and plays the pulling guard. If the onside guard and tackle reach block, the Bat fills outside of the tackle in the C gap.

There are two backside keys for the Bats. If the guard pulls, the Bat goes with the pulling guard. If the guard and tackle scoop block, the Bat plays through the block of the guard over the center.

If we are playing a veer team, we will not stunt as much. We will play a little bit more read so we can squeeze. I do not recommend that you stunt very much out of this defense if you play against an option team.

Hornets

Stance: Shoulders over your knees. If on the right side, the left foot is up and the right foot is back. If on the left side, the right foot is up and the left foot is back.

Keys: Read the *V* between the quarterback and deepest back and the end man on the line of scrimmage.

Drills: Key drill, blitzing, man-to-man, pass drops.

If the tackle blocks down and the near back kicks out, the Hornet comes up and takes on the near back. If the tackle reach blocks and the near back shows fast flow outside, the Hornet comes outside and covers the near back on the fast flow. If the tackle reach blocks and the near back shows inside flow, the Hornet reads the back. He can stay inside, or he can cover outside. If the tackle shows pass, the Hornet drops outside to his pass responsibility.

We expect the Hornets to be our hardest players to block, and they have to work their tails off to get to the ball because we stunt them a lot. We would like to have guys that can play good man coverage on a good slot receiver. Our defensive backs these past couple of years have been the shortest in the history of football. I do not think we had a defensive back over 5'7", other than our free safety.

Here is our philosophy. The ball has to come out in 2.5 seconds. If we can do that, then we can survive with those guys. They have to play hard against those receivers and we want hard-nosed kids at those positions. They are going to have to give up their bodies a lot, and they are going to have to be able to make some tackles. They are midget linebackers. They have their inside foot up and their weight on their front foot so we give them a look that they are coming every time. We expect them to be willing to go up and take out a fullback—that is what we expect.

Coverages

Cover 1: We bring four- or five-man pressure in man coverage (Diagram #9). Either one or two inside linebackers blitz. The free safety is free, our corners have the #1 receiver, and the Hornets have the #2 receivers. The remaining inside linebacker either has #3 or is a low-hole player.

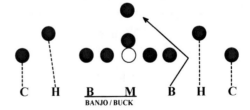

F
Diagram #9. Cover 1

If we are running cover 1, that means we are stunting and bringing four or five people and it is an inside linebacker stunt. Depending on what the offense is showing us, we can check into cover 1 depending on the formation.

Cover Black: We bring four- or five-man pressure in man coverage—either one Hornet or both a Hornet and a Bat blitz (Diagram #10). The free safety has #2 to the blitzside. The Hornet away from the blitz has #2. The corners have #1, and the remaining inside linebacker either has #3 or is a low-hole player.

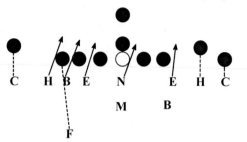

Diagram #10. Cover Black

Our black coverage means we are bringing one of the Hornets. When we play black coverage, the free safety is going to have #2 to the flipside in man coverage, and we are in cover zero. We do not ever ask our stack backers to cover a wide receiver. They are always going to be on a running back. That way, we don't have a bad match-up with a real good wide receiver. Everyone else is man-up. The way we work our inside linebackers is that the backers that are not stunting have the running backs in the backfield. If there is one running back, then we banjo. In other words, if he comes to me, I have him. The other backer away from the flow of the running back is the low-hole player to watch for crossing routes.

Cover White: We bring five-man pressure in man coverage—both Hornets blitz (Diagram #11). The free safety has #2 to the side that he calls (he calls out, "I am left" or "I am right"). The corners have #1, and the inside backers banjo the #3 receiver away from the free safety. The remaining inside linebacker is a low-hole player.

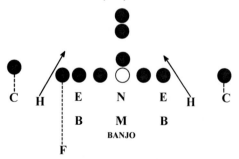

Diagram #11. Cover White

We run white coverage when we are blitzing both outside guys. The free safety is going to take #2 on one side or the other. The Hornets are listening for an "I am left," or "I am right," call from the safety, so he can still stunt. If he does not get the call from the safety, he cannot blitz.

Cover Blue: We bring six-man pressure—all three inside linebackers blitz (Diagram #12). The corners have #1, the Hornets have #2, and the free safety has #3.

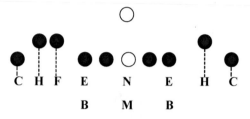

Diagram #12. Cover Blue

Three Deep: We bring five-man pressure in the fire-zone concept. The two inside backers blitz, and the remaining inside backer has the middle-hook zone. Both Hornets have the curl/flat area. Corners are deep outside one-third, and the free safety has the middle third.

If we get an empty look in the backfield, our check is *zoo blue.* That means we are bringing all six and we are in cover zero.

We run our cover 3 and cover 1 against trips. The corners have the #1 receiver counting from the outside to the inside. The Hornet has the #2 to the #3 wide receiver side. The backside Hornet always gets a spin call and replaces the free safety. The Bats banjo the running back. If the back comes to his side, he takes him. If the back goes away from him, he low holes the play.

On cover 3 against double slots, the corners have the outside one-thirds. The Hornets play curl/flat. The Bats play hook/curl to their side. The free safety has the deep middle one-third.

Pressure Packages—Four-Man Rush

Bat open/closed right/left 1/3
Mike strong/weak 1/3
Bob open/closed right/left 1/3
Bam open/closed right/left 1/3
Buc open/closed right/left 1/3
Hornet open/closed right/left black

The linebackers and secondary must know where the down linemen are going on the pressure packages. They must know which gap they are responsible for when they are stunting. The linemen only need to know closed/left or open/right.

We never huddle. Everyone looks to the sideline to get the defensive signal. On our Bat open right, we send the strongside Bat in the A gap (Diagram #13). The secondary plays cover 1 or cover 3.

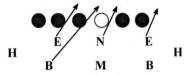

Diagram #13. Bat Open Right 1/3

The opposite of that call is our Bat closed left (Diagram #14). We send the linemen toward the tight end and the backside Bat stunts through the A gap on the weakside.

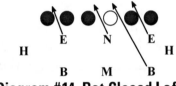

Diagram #14. Bat Closed Left 1/3

Pressure Packages—Five-Man Rush
Zoo strong/weak 1/3
Mash strong/weak 1/3
Double Buc pinch 1/3
Double Hornet pinch white
Jacks blast 1/3
Open/closed boom—Right/left black
Mob open/closed 1/3
Lightning weak black

On zoo strong, we are sending five rushers. The ends have the C gap, and the noseman has the A gap strong. The strongside Bat has the B gap, and the Mike has the strongside B gap. We play cover 1 or cover 3.

On zoo weak, we are sending five rushers. The ends have the C gap, and the noseman has the A gap weak. The backside Bat has the weakside B gap, and the Mike has the weakside B gap. We play cover 1 or cover 3.

Pressure Packages—Six-Man Rush

Zoo blue
Pinch special white
Bat open Bob Hornet black
Bat open Bam Hornet black

On a zoo blue call, we send six men on the blitz. The ends have the C gaps. The nose has the backside A gap. The Bats have the B gaps on each side. The Mike has the strongside A gap.

Pressure Packages—Seven-Man Rush—Pinch Mike Double Hornet White

If white is the call, if a Hornet has two receivers to his side and the free safety is gone, he must check to Buc. We are sending the ends in the B gaps. The nose and Mike play games in the two A gaps. One goes to one side, and the other man goes opposite.

You can see all of the different combinations you can come up with in this defense. You can name the stunts the way your players will remember them. The big thing is that it does not take long to add a stunt once you have the basic system installed.

I know I have given you a lot and I have gone fast. If you want our entire package, drop me a note. Thank you for your time.

THE COMPLETE 3-3-5 DEFENSIVE PACKAGE

Alta High School, Utah

It is a pleasure to be here. I am the head football coach at Alta High School in Sandy, Utah. I am fortunate to be the head coach of one of the best high schools in the country. It is a phenomenal school. We have 2,600 kids in the upper three grades. We are in south Salt Lake. We are a big school. We have over 1,000 Little League kids that feed into our school. We have seven teams for the 9th grade teams that feed into our one sophomore team. We are very blessed in our program. We have great players, great athletes, and we turn out a lot of kids that go on to Division I colleges.

We could probably line up in any defense and do well with it. We do feel that the 3-3 defense is a big part of our success, and it has enabled us to win championships. We have played some good teams in Utah and outside of the state. We have played some good teams out of the state the last few years—Clovis East High School out of Fresno, Grant High School out of Sacramento, and Rainier Beach High School out of Seattle. We look forward to playing other good teams in the future.

We are not trying to reinvent the wheel. I am from Petaluma High School in northern California. My high school coach just retired after 28 years at Petaluma High School. He taught me one thing when I became a head coach. That point has stayed with me over the years. He said, "Don't get caught up in the X's and O's of football. It is about being able to tackle and being fundamentally sound in blocking."

When I took this job five years ago, I sat down with my defensive coordinator and talked about what we wanted to do on defense. We decided we would run the 3-3-5 defense. We felt this defense was going to give us some advantages because of the personnel that we had coming up. Here are other factors we considered in picking the 3-3-5 defense.

Why Run the 3-3-5 Defense?

- Best fits our personnel
- Minimal adjustments from double wing to empty
- Allows us to platoon
- Attacking, disrupting, pressure defense
- Our players love to play it; our coaches love to coach it

If you can pick up a point or two here today from what we do, I hope it will help you with your defense. I will cover what we look for at positions later.

The type of personnel we get at Alta High School is the long and lengthy type of athlete. Our big competition in Utah is Bingham High School. They have a lot of Samoan kids. They get a lot of linemen that, at times, will weigh over 280 pounds. They have some Division I caliber linemen. They always have a 220-pound fullback, and a tight end that is 6'4" and 240 pounds. They have some good wide receivers that are 6'4" and can run. We felt, that to match up with Bingham High School athletes, we needed to play a defense that best fit our personnel.

In Utah high school football, we see all types of teams. We may see a double-wing team one week, and the next week we may face a team that plays with five wide receivers. Jordan High School in Utah is in our league. Their quarterback led the nation in passing last year. He threw for almost 5,000 yards. We see the spread offense, and we see the wishbone attack, and we see all of the different offensive schemes. We felt the 3-3-5 defense would allow us to adjust week by week with a minimal amount of adjustments.

We are a big high school in Utah. We start at the sophomore level of two platooning our kids. They play either offense or defense. I have coaches in the small schools. If I am in a small school, I am going to at least platoon my linemen. This gives us a chance to use a different type of athlete on the offensive and defensive linemen.

When we look for a defensive end, we want long and lanky, basketball type of players. They look like tight ends. We are going to play those types of kids at our defensive end positions. We may use an undersized noseguard just to create penetration. This allows us to keep our big linemen on the offensive side of the ball. For us, being able to platoon is a huge advantage, especially in the fourth quarter.

In 2008, when we won the 5A state championship, we outscored our opponents in the third and fourth quarter by 100 points. If you can just give the big guys a breather and keep them fresh, it will help in the fourth quarter. This system enables you to use different types of athletes on your offense and defense.

This defense is designed as an attacking, pressure, and disruptive defense. If you want to sit in one defensive look, and challenge the defense to drive the ball the distance without making a mistake, that is up to you. I know it is tough for the offense to drive the ball without a mistake. That does not fit the mentality of our program. We are going to get after it and make things happen. You must decide what you want to do on defense. You must answer some important questions if you want to run this defense.

- Is the 3-3-5 right for your program?
- Will you make your defense your number one priority?
- Will your defensive staff put in the preparation time?
- Will you schedule the needed practice time?
- Will you provide the defense with the best athletes in the program?
- Are you willing to develop defensive backs that can play man coverage?
- Are you willing to play cover zero when you are up 21-17 with two minutes to go in the championship game?

Our colors are the Oakland Raiders' colors. When our kids come out on the field, they think they are the bad guys in the state of Utah. We are going to pressure, and we are going to attack the offense. This is our defensive philosophy.

Defensive Philosophy

- We will outhit our opponent.
- We will be relentless to the ball.
- We will pursue to the ball and take good angles. Do not follow the same jersey.
- We will hit the ballcarrier and blockers violently.
- Every position will dominate their opponent.
- Visualize yourself forcing your facemask into the ball while driving your cleats into the grass, squeezing cloth and skin, knocking him backward with a violent strike.
- No YAC (yardage after contact).
- Be the one that makes the big play.
- Don't wait for someone to make a big play—you make the big play.
- Be stingy—no first downs, no scores. (Our defense is ticked off when they give up a first down.)
- Inside the red zone—bleed to keep our opponent from scoring.
- Know your steps every down—excuses.

There is a lot of reading involved in this defense. We spend a lot of time with linebackers and defensive backs running read drills. We read offensive linemen. We have a pass read, pull read, and down read. We work a lot on footwork.

- Know the down-and-distance.
- Pre-read your key.
- Eyes on your key.
- Take your read steps.
- React on run or pass with no hesitation.
- Pursue to the ball or drop into your coverage and never lose your footing. (We only played two games on real grass last year.)

- Tackle violently; make the big play; no YAC. (We want to intimidate the teams we play.)
- Always think three-and-out.
- Win.

We want to be able to determine what the play is after one-half of a second after the ball is snapped. Our free safety defensive ends will be our best pass rushers. We want to determine in a split second if the play is a run or a pass. We expect our safety to make plays at three yards. We line him up at eight yards, and we do not want him backing up on a run after the ball is snapped.

Defense Wins Championships

Our defense is the number one priority in our program. We run the option read offense, but defense is where our priorities are. Other than the quarterback and center, the defense gets first choice of all the other players. If we did not platoon, we would make sure our best athletes were spending most of their time on the defensive side of the ball.

Our defense comes on the field and they are coming after the offense. They do not care who you are, they are going to come after you. They love to practice defense, and our coaches love the defense—it is exciting football. We call it *organized chaos* because we still must be fundamentally sound. We cannot give up the gaps. We are fundamentally sound—it just looks like a mess. Our players buy into the defense every day.

We do not feel you can sit back in a 3-3 defense and play cover 2 and win. You must blitz and move people around. You must apply pressure on the offense. You must put in time in the film room. Your defensive staff must spend the time to make sure you are going to cover everything that can come up in a game. I do not think you can sit in the base 3-3 defense and be successful. A great deal of this defense depends on movement and moving linebackers. You must spend the time to know what you need to know on defense in each game.

These are our defensive goals. I am not going to spend a lot of time on them, but this is what our defense is trying to accomplish.

Defensive Goals

- Win
- 13 points or less
- No big plays
  - ✓ No run plays over 20 yards
  - ✓ No pass plays over 25 yards
- Hold opponent to less than 220 yards of total offense
- Three takeaways
- One defensive score
- Three sacks
- Eight series' of three-and-outs
- No fourth-down conversions
- Less than four yards gained on sudden change
- Three knocked-down or tipped balls
- Set up one score
- 11 Hawks to the ball every play (three-yard area) before the whistle blows
- Three momentum changes; big hit; goal line or fourth-down stand; interceptions, etc.
- Defense wins championships

This past year we gave up an average of just under 17 points per game. We lost in the state semi-finals. For us at Alta High School, if we do not win the state championship, it is not a successful season. That is okay. That is a good standard to have. To us, 17 points per game on defense is unacceptable. To win a championship, I think you must give up under 13 points per game.

Main Teaching Points

We start with the *stance*. You need to make sure your position coaches teach the proper stance. That will most benefit the player to get to his read steps and get off on movement. We stress balance, quickness, and force.

The *alignment* for our defense is very important. Each position has a gap responsibility. On the varsity level we will stem (move) around, but we will get back to our gap responsibility with proper alignment. We utilize the same terminology on alignment.

The *key* is the opposing player that each defender reads to see if the play is going to be a run or pass. The defender reads the player on his read steps. Then, he reacts to the run if the lineman (key) shows run block. He reacts to pass when he sees his lineman (key) pass set.

The defensive line keys the offensive lineman they line up on and by pressure. The Hawks are our alley players, and they key the first down offensive lineman for pass or run. The Stud and Will key the guard. The Mike keys through the quarterback to the near running back. The corners key the tackles. The free safety keys the guard.

You take your read off your key. You do this during your first two read steps. If you read run, you react to the ball, making sure that you first take care of your gap then pursue to the ballcarrier using proper pursuit angles.

Angles of pursuit need to be practiced. You need to know where the sidelines are. The sideline is the twelfth man. If the ballcarrier crosses the line of scrimmage, we need to take a good angle down the field to where the ballcarrier will be. Make sure to never follow the same colored jersey and never give up. When the ballcarrier has to change direction or slow down, you will be there for the tackle.

Points We Stress on Defense

Force: Everyone must know where the force is coming from on each play. This is a gap-control defense, and everyone has a responsibility.

Tackling: This is about attitude. We teach our defensive backs how to tackle low. I do not want my 150-pound defensive back trying to take on a 220-pound tailback on a head-on tackle. He will get his butt run over. We teach our defensive backs how to tackle low. We teach them how to take ballcarriers down. We have some great open field tacklers. We make sure we have tackling practice for them where they tackle below the thigh pads. We want them to wrap up and to get the runners on the ground. We have been very good with our defensive backs coming up and tackling runners below the waist.

Footwork: We practice our footwork and we perfect it. During the off-season, we have players that jump rope and go to the gym and work on their footwork. They want to be ready when we start up in the spring.

Get off Blocks: We teach them how to get off blocks. We have been blessed with Division I linebackers in our program. However, it is a catch-22. We teach our linebackers how to get off blocks. We teach them hand drills to help them get off blocks and to pursue to the ball.

Keep Your Feet: We never want to be on the ground. You cannot play if you are lying down on the ground.

Run Responsibilities

I am not going to spend a lot of time on this because I want to get to the meat of the defense.

DE: On jacks and slant away from the center you have the C gap, and you have the quarterback on option. When slanting to the center, you have the B gap and dive.

N: A gap. Feel pressure. When slanting, you have the A gap. You are slanting, feeling the center's pressure. Try to get to the guard's hip when he pulls.

S/W: You need to know what gap the defensive linemen are slanting to. If your defensive end slants to the B gap, you have the C gap to the quarterback on option. If he slants to the C gap, you have the B gap to dive, but only after you read your guard.

M: You need to know what way the nose is slanting when you have the other A gap. Read through the center to the near back.

Hawks: On option, you have the pitch. On flow away, look for the boot, cutback, or reverse. Help on powers to the C gap, and if the running back bounces, you will be there for a great hit.

C: Help on run support only after you are sure it is a run.

F: You are the last level of defense—no one gets by you.

Pass Responsibilities

DE: Contain quarterback and pass rush when on jacks or slanting to the C gap. Be relentless. If the running back crosses your face, follow for the screen. When slanting to the B gap and you read pass, stay in your lane and get to the quarterback. Get your hands up. Feel pressure or lack thereof, and read the screen or draw.

N: On a pass rush, stay in your lane and feel for the screen or draw.

S/W: On a blitz, stay in lanes and get to the quarterback. You also need to read for the screen or draw. If not on a blitz, drop into your coverage and redirect receivers.

M: You are a run stopper. If you read pass, get to the middle of the field and knock out anyone running crossing routes.

Hawks: On a blitz, contain the quarterback; in man, contain the #2 receivers.

C: #1 on man coverage.

F: Deeper than the deepest, read the quarterback's eyes.

Our Personnel

We have five defensive backs:

- *Corners:* Confidant; technically sound; quick cover guy. On an island most of the time. Does not have to run a 4.5. Our best ever was a 6'0", 155-pound, 4.9.
- *Hawk:* Aggressive; good open field tackler; good cover guy.
- *Safeties:* Center fielder; great open field tackler. Can read the offense. Has led our team in tackles every year.

We have three linebackers:

- *Mike:* Quarterback of the defense. Understands scheme, offensive formations, autos, and alignments.
- *Will:* Quick and aggressive. Can be undersized but must be a solid open field tackler and good at avoiding blockers.

- *Stud:* Generally, our strongest and most athletic linebacker.

We have three down linemen (two ends and a nose man):

- *Defensive Ends:* Long, aggressive, basketball player or tight end type of kids. Good lateral movement; good hands.
- *Nose man:* The most explosive lineman or quick penetrator. He is a linebacker type. You are in business if you have a two-gap player.

I want to talk about defensive line stunts. This is what we call *jacks* (Diagram #1). This simply means the defensive ends are going to penetrate to the outside shoulder of the tackle. We line up every time in a 4 technique head-up with the tackle. We have one variation, and I will cover that later. The nose is in a 0 technique on the center. These are our line stunts. If the defensive line does not receive a special call, they are in jacks. That is our base defense.

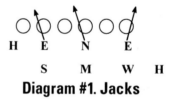

Diagram #1. Jacks

We want them to penetrate one yard into the backfield. Now, they must be able to read the offense. If they are not blocked by this time, they must know there is a pulling lineman coming out after them. If the quarterback goes away, they have the bootleg play and the reverse back to their side. You must go over those plays with the ends. We do not want our defensive ends four yards up the field.

We use jacks the most, and then we use pinch next. I only tell coaches at clinics about the diagram on the *pinch* (Diagram #2). We show them in a 4 technique pinching inside. The diagram shows we are going through the inside of the offensive tackle. That is not the true angle. We are pinching on the outside hip of the guard. We pinch hard to the hip of the guard and one-yard penetration. We want him to find the ball or to find out why he is not being blocked.

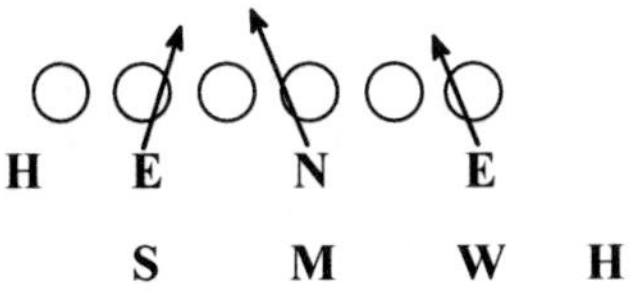

Diagram #2. Pinch

On *open,* we are slanting toward the weakside (Diagram #3).

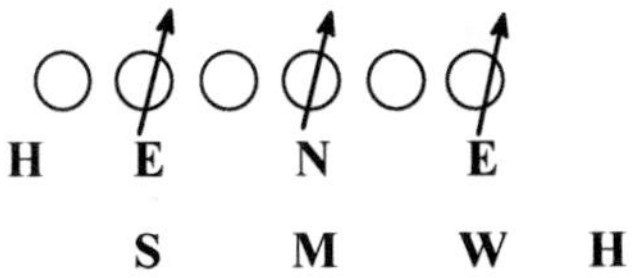

Diagram #3. Open

On *close,* we are slanting to the strongside (Diagram #4).

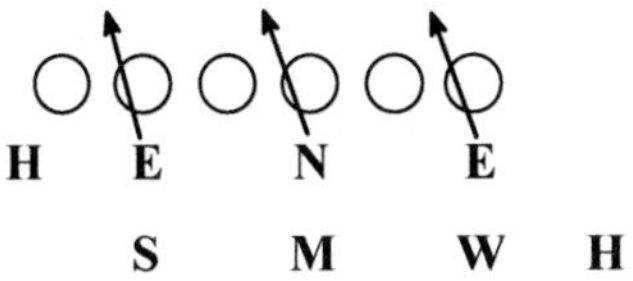

Diagram #4. Close

Those are our four basic alignments and stunts for the three down linemen. The only variation is the *force* (Diagram #5). It is similar to pinch, but we are bringing the ends down into the 2 techniques. That is all we do as far as the defensive line goes.

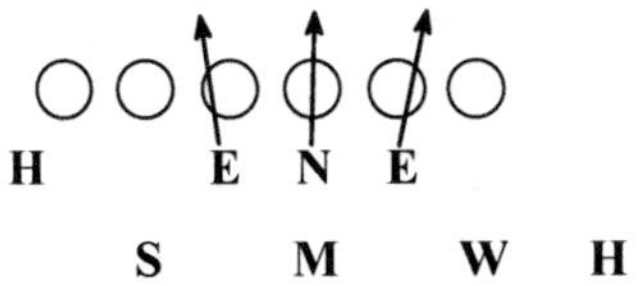

Diagram #5. Force

Linebacker stunts include the following. Here are some of our one-man blitzes. We rarely blitz our Mike backer. He is our least blitzing linebacker. He is our best reader, so we rarely blitz him. If we want Mike to go to the tight end, we call *Mike strong* (Diagram #6).

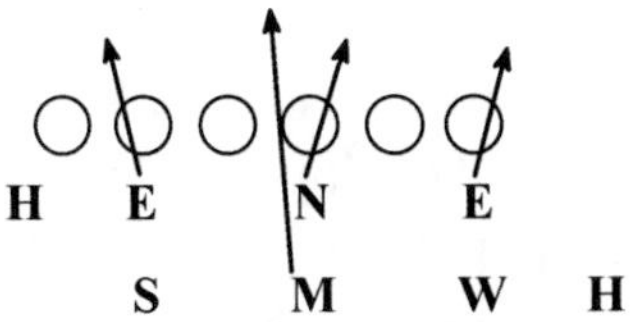

Diagram #6. Mike Strong

If we want him to blitz to the backside, we call *Mike weak* (Diagram #7).

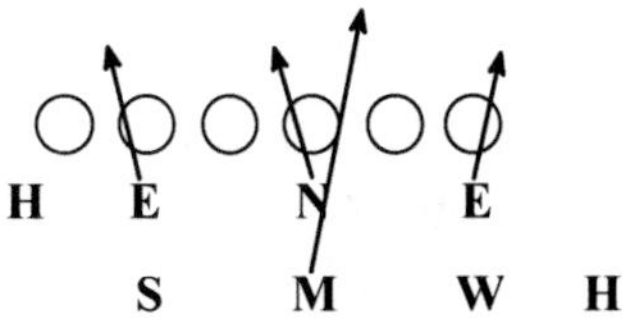

Diagram #7. Mike Weak

These are our most common blitzes. In *open Will,* we slant the line to the weakside and blitz Will in the B gap (Diagram #8).

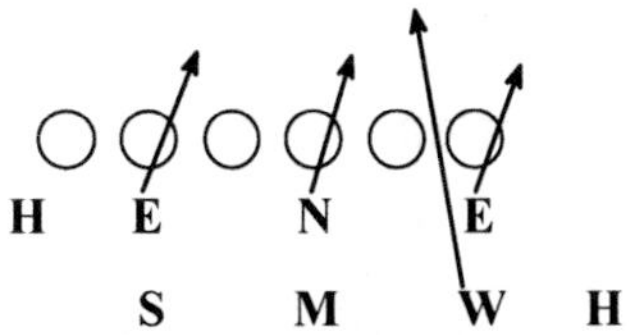

Diagram #8. Open Will

If we want to slant to the strongside, Will is going to blitz the backside A gap (Diagram #9).

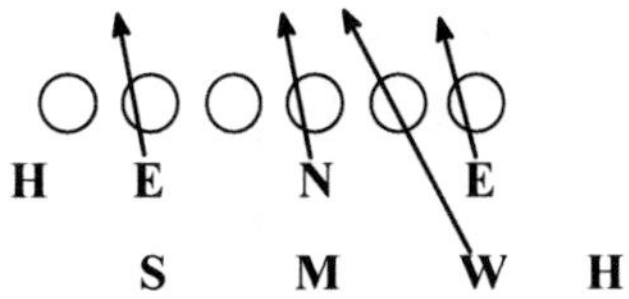

Diagram #9. Close Will

Next, we use the same concept but we are slanting away from the tight end and bringing our Stud linebacker (Diagram #10). The Stud has the onside A gap.

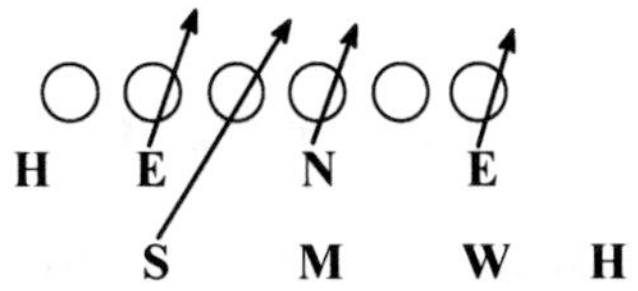

Diagram #10. Open Stud

If we slant to the tight end, the Stud has the onside B gap (Diagram #11).

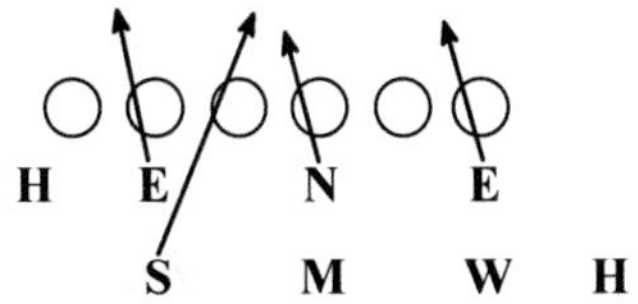

Diagram #11. Close Stud

We must spend the time to make sure the players know they must get to the gaps they are assigned. If they do not get to their gaps, we have a breakdown in the defense.

If we are playing an option team, we like to run the *open stick stunt* (Diagram #12). The end has the dive, and the Stud has the quarterback on the option. They must understand who has the dive, who has the quarterback, and who has the pitch.

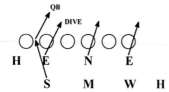

Diagram #12. Open Stick

Closed whack is the same stunt to the backside against the option (Diagram #13). The end has the dive and the Will has the quarterback.

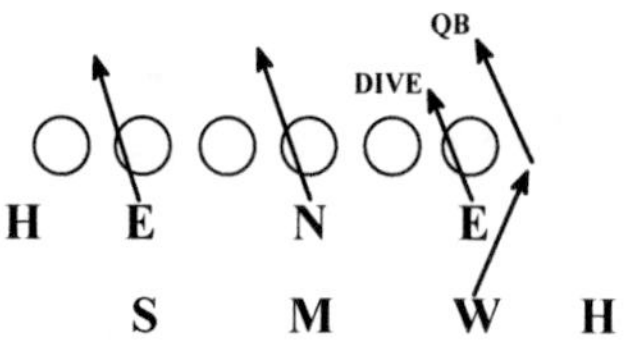

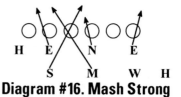

Diagram #13. Closed Whack

If we want to run the stunt to both sides, we call our *pinch stick whack* (Diagram #14). The nose slants to the tight end A gap.

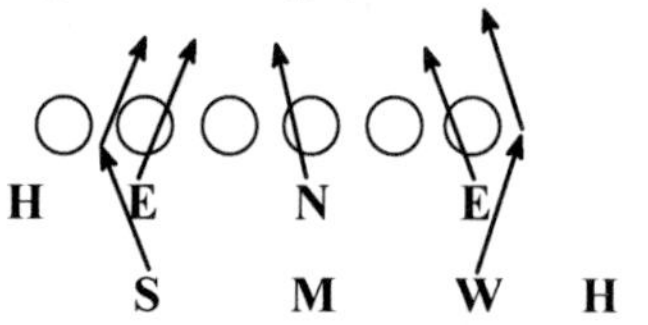

Diagram #14. Pinch Stick Whack

Blast is one of our most often-used stunts (Diagram #15). These stunts are not rocket science. The ends go outside and the Will and Stud go inside. The nose slants to the tight end A gap.

Diagram #15. Blast

Our next most often-used stunt is the *mash.* In mash strong (Diagram #16), the ends slant outside and the nose slants to the tight end A gap. The Mike and Stud linebackers cross. The Mike blitzes in the B gap to the strongside, and the Stud comes through the strong guard.

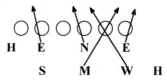

Diagram #16. Mash Strong

The *mash weak* is to the split end side (Diagram #17). Mike goes in the B gap, and the Will backer comes through the backside guard.

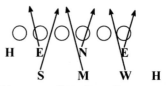

Diagram #17. Mash Weak

If we want to send all three linebackers, we call *zoo strong* (Diagram #18). Now, all three linebackers blitz to the tight end side or the strongside of the formation.

Diagram #18. Zoo Strong

If we want to send the linebackers to the split end side or the weakside, we call *zoo weak* (Diagram #19). All three linebackers blitz toward the split end side.

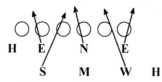

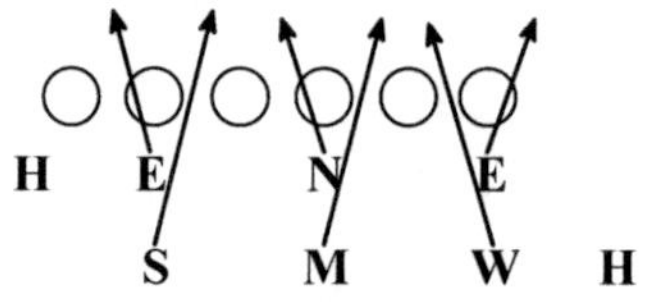

Diagram #19. Zoo Weak

Now, we want to get our defensive backs involved in the blitz game. We run linebacker and defensive backs combination stunts. We have open Hawk, closed Hawk, pinch double Hawk, open boom strong, close boom weak, open boom strong, and closed boom weak. Now, we start to bring combinations of alley players and linebackers on the stunts. We bring the alley players off the edge. Our linebacker/defensive backs combo stunts include the following.

If we call *open Hawk,* the Hawk on the tight end side comes up and blitzes over the tight end

(Diagram #20). He comes over the 9 technique. The line is slanting away from the tight end.

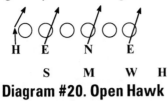

Diagram #20. Open Hawk

By now, you can see how we are calling our stunts. When we call the *close Hawk,* we bring the Hawk up on the split end side and send him on the blitz (Diagram #21). Again, the line is slanting away from the Hawk toward the tight end.

Diagram #21. Close Hawk

If we call pinch double Hawk, we are sending both Hawks (Diagram #22). The ends slant inside, and the nose slants toward the tight end in the A gap.

Diagram #22. Pinch Double Hawk

We add the Hawks to the stunt to get our *open boom strong.* The line and Stud run their open stunt (Diagram #23), and the Hawk on the tight end side runs his stunt over the tight end.

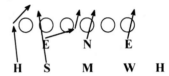

Diagram #23. Open Boom Strong

To run the same stunt to the backside, we call our *close boom weak* (Diagram #24). The Will and the defensive line run the open stunt, and the Hawk to the split end runs his stunt. The Will comes inside off the tackle, and the Hawk comes outside, where the end would be up in a tight end set. The Will is coming hard over the tackle, and the Hawk is outside.

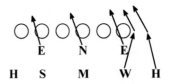

Diagram #24. Close Boom Weak

On the *bang stunt,* we bring one of the ends from the 4 technique down inside to the A gap. On open bang strong, the strongside defensive end slants from the tackle down inside to the A gap (Diagram #25). The nose and weakside end slant toward the split end. The Stud and Hawk on the tight end side run their stunt and blitz the C gap and outside the tight end.

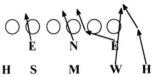

Diagram #25. Open Bang Strong

On *close bang weak,* we are running the same stunt to the weakside or to the split end side (Diagram #26). The end on the split end side slants from the head-up position on the tackle down inside to the A gap.

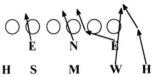

Diagram #26. Close Bang Weak

In wrapping this up, you must decide as a staff to be dedicated to put your best players on defense. You have to put the time and effort into the defense. You must develop confidence in the secondary players that they can play man coverage. I am not telling you that you have to run as much man coverage as we do, but they need to be confident that they can cover man to man. This will allow you to overload the box to stop the run. We do not mind if teams throw the fade route on us—we love it. We know they will be lucky to hit 1 out of 10 of those passes. Our success has been better than 1 out of 10 plays against the fade route.

Make sure your kids are good open field tacklers. Teach the backs to tackle low. Don't try to be a hero. Make sure the defenders never follow a player of the same colored jersey. Then, you need to cultivate the attitude where your defense is ticked off when the opponents get a first down.

Again, this is not rocket science, and we are not reinventing the wheel. We feel this defense gives us an opportunity to defeat some of the teams that we do not match up against talentwise. It gives us a chance to do what we do week after week without a lot of changes. I hope you can find a few points that may help you with your defense. I will be around if you want to talk about the things we do in our program.

Coaches ask me what my number one job is at Alta High School. I tell our assistants this, and I tell those that ask me that question—My number one job is to *develop young men.* As a byproduct of what we are trying to do, we are teaching our young men to make good decisions.

We have been fortunate to win some games, and we have had some great athletes. The number one responsibility we have as coaches is to develop young men in our culture. I think this is something that is going by the wayside. We need to teach young men how to make good decisions on and off the field. We need to teach them to have integrity and discipline and how to become good citizens. We hope they will make good fathers someday. This is our number one responsibility.

It has been my pleasure to spend time with you today. If you have questions, I will be here until noon tomorrow. Feel free to visit with me. Thank you.

Mark Iammarino

SPREAD RUN AND PASS OFFENSE

Chagrin Falls High School, Ohio

It is an honor for me to be here. This is my first opportunity to speak at the Pittsburg clinic. I hope to say a few things that will make sense to you, and to give you something to think about. It is an honor to be asked to represent Northeast Ohio and speak at this great clinic.

The thing we are proudest about at Chagrin Falls is we get a chance to coach real student athletes. Of the 61 tenth-, eleventh-, and twelfth-graders, 42 of them made the honor roll. That included the grading period before the state finals. We have some solid kids in the classroom, and that transfers over to the football field.

Today, I want to talk about the run and pass opportunities that we use out of the spread offense. I first started coaching in Texas. When I was coaching in Texas, everyone ran the veer option. I do want you to know I am originally from Ohio. When I came back to coach in Ohio, the school I went to was a true I-formation, power off-tackle, Ohio State–type football team. That is what I was used to coaching. However, if you did not have the classic big I-back tailback and his backup, or the classic big fullback and his backup, you could not win big. If we had better personnel, we won games. When we went up against teams that were a challenge, we could not get the job done.

I wanted to come up with something that would give us a chance against those types of teams. I wanted something that we could use year after year and make the best of the talent we had. That is how we migrated to the spread offense.

We play in a league in Northeastern Ohio. It is a conference with 18 schools, and we are split into three divisions. We play in the largest division. In the last two years, a representative of our conference has played in the state championship finals game. Unfortunately, we did not get the job done this year and lost in the state finals.

I am going to talk about our transition to the spread offense. There are some important things in offensive football. We are going to talk about tempo, personnel groupings, formations and motions, and some of our base plays.

In our transition to the spread, we had to identify what we wanted to accomplish. We had to understand our philosophy. We decided we wanted to spread the field. Last night, we were in Cleveland and we listened to Jeff Mullen, the offensive coordinator at West Virginia University lecture. He talked about defending 54 yards from sideline to sideline. He talked about having a give, read, and pitch on every play. Listening to him, we are headed in the right direction. We are not there yet, but we are improving.

We want to use as many players as we can. We do that for two reasons. When I played in high school, we had a Stud fullback. We were a small school. The Stud fullback also played Stud linebacker. He was hit hard on both sides of the ball. By midseason, he couldn't remember all the days of the week. It takes a toll on players.

The last two years, we have had two good linebackers. The assistant coaches wanted to play them at fullback or at guard. I told them if we did, they would not be as effective at linebacker. Our good linebacker is going to be the Stud linebacker. He will play defensive specialties and will be the goal-line fullback. Playing a lot of players give us the opportunity to spread the responsibility to a lot of different players. We have had to work hard at making it easy for us and hard for the opponent.

If you were to come watch us play, you would think we were very confusing and complicated. It is not. We want the defensive coordinator to be under pressure to prepare for us. We want them to be thinking about more things than getting ready to play. We think this gives us an advantage. The shotgun has been good for us because it allows our quarterback more time and vision to make plays.

In 10 years, we have had one quarterback who has been the 6'3" big prototype quarterback. Most of our quarterbacks are in the 5'11" range. It is difficult for them to see over your front. We try to move the pocket and get them on the edge. That has been beneficial for us. Another thing we have been able to do is call a play or change a play late. If you have a quarterback who can check off, that is great. Sometimes, we have that and other years we do not. I would rather put the pressure on myself as an offensive play caller to change the play. We are able to do that.

I make the letter "G" is very important. You must have a "go-to" scheme when times are tough and you have to call something. That is what the offenses and your players hang their hat on. A perfect example happened in the state semifinal game. With the score tied 14-14 with six minutes to go in the game, we had the ball after holding on downs at our own 22-yard line. This is what everyone dreams about happening in a big game. It was our chance to make the final drive to get us to the big dance. We ran the same play six out of eight times. It was not the same ballcarrier, but it was the same scheme. We took the ball down and scored using our go-to scheme.

That was one of my concerns when we went to the spread. What was our go-to scheme going to be? If you are Texas Tech, their go-to scheme is to throw the ball. If you are West Virginia, you run the outside stretch with the quarterback carrying the ball. We had to come up with the go-to scheme, and we will talk about it today.

The quarterback has to get the ball off quickly and throw a high percentage. High schools are not always blessed to have a rocket-armed quarterback.

We have to do it with timing and getting the ball out quickly. It is great to throw a quick bubble pass and have the back runs for 30 yards. In the paper the next day, the paper states it was a 32-yard touchdown pass. People think you have a big-time quarterback, when it was a five-yard throw and 32-yard run.

When you are in the spread offense, regardless of the score, you are never out of the game. You may be down by three touchdowns in the first half. You are not out of the game because of the style you play. If you are a wing-T team, you are forced to do something you do not normally do.

This year, we were a spread team, but when we had to, we could control the ball and the clock. We could slow the game down and milk the clock. We could get the tough yards running off-tackle. It was different personnel. We used our linebackers and those types of players to control the ball.

We developed our philosophy of what we wanted to do and took the next step. We found out who ran the offense and did it well. When we found them, we went to see them to let them teach us. We talked to the coaches that did the things we liked. We talked to high school coaches and college coaches. We went to a Division II college in Painesville, Ohio by the name of Lake Erie College. They had an interesting scheme of how to get the ball to their players. We talked to Matt Campbell, the offensive coordinator at the University of Toledo. He was at Mount Union College for some time. That is where we go to summer camp every year, and we are able to pick his brain.

We talk to the guys who did the things we wanted to do. We had to be sure it was consistent with things we wanted to do. You may hear some good ideas that are not consistent with what you want to do or what your players can do. The spread offense lets us think outside the box. When the defense's X's are bigger and faster than your O's, you have to be creative.

You have to implement the scheme at the sub-varsity level. There are too many things for a quarterback to handle from the get-go. You have to develop him.

Another thing that helped us was allowing our cadence to assist in our play calling or adjustments. I was one of those coaches who had a cadence that seemed to be endless when you were trying to get off the play. We still say a bunch of stuff, but it is not part of the cadence. We have the ability to snap the ball on the first sound. All automatics are not part of our cadence.

Tempos play an important part of making it easy for us and hard for them. Two years ago, Ohio State played Texas in a bowl game. Texas was going so fast, Ohio State could not get lined up. I thought to myself that was hard to defend. You cannot get the defensive call into the game.

I talked to Tim Beckman, the head coach at Toledo. He came from Oklahoma State. He told me when Oklahoma goes to their speed-up tempo, they tell their wide receiver not to block. They simple take two to three steps down the field and find the place the ball is going to be marked so they are ready for the next play. That shows the importance of tempo.

We came up with some tempos that we wanted to use. We do not use all six of these tempos all the time. We pick and choose what fits in for certain games, opponents, and situations.

TEMPO

- Memory plays: Snapped between 7 and 10 seconds after the ball is marked ready to play.
- Signal: Formation and play run between 15 and 20 seconds.
- Look: Formation and play look to sideline to run the play or change it.
- Freeze: Just give a formation, and then decide after the defense declares third down or short yardage.
- Huddle: Late in a game or half to control the clock.
- Package: Put two plays in a row for the week.

In a memory play, you have a word or signal that identifies a play for each week. Everyone goes to the line of scrimmage and runs that play. It does not have to be a fancy play. It can be something as simple as an inside zone play. Sometimes, it is better if it is not fancy. If the defense cannot get their defensive call in, they have to play a "base dummy" call. We could be forcing the defense to get into a base call on a big play. The best time to go with the memory play is after a big run and a first down. We get to the line and run the play in 7 to 10 seconds.

Most of what we do is signal tempo. I call the play with input from everyone. I can get a different point of view and talk to the assistants before we call the play. The quarterback does not look at me. They look at the signal caller, who is signaling the formations and motion. When the play is over, the receivers look immediately to the sideline to get the formation for the next play. They are the ones who have to travel the most distance to get to their alignment. The linemen love it. They have to find the ball and get on it.

In the look tempo, we signal in a formation and play. We get to the line of scrimmage quickly as if we were going to snap the ball. The quarterback gives a dummy call and looks to the sidelines. If we like the call, we give him the okay, and he runs the play. If we do not like the play, we give him the new play, and we run that one.

We use the freeze on third-down or short-yardage plays. We do not give them a play. We give them a formation and tell them to get to the line of scrimmage. The defense does not know if we are going to snap the ball and must align. That keeps them from substituting, and it prevents defensive calls. It gives us a chance to read the defense and decide what to run.

The weakness of a spread team is their ability to run the ball. Spread teams are soft. What does the offense do when they are up by two scores? We made a special point to change our personnel and huddle. This allows us to take time off the clock and run for the tough yards when the defense knows you are going to run the ball. When we go into the huddle, we take out the little players and put in the bigger players.

The last thing we did not do much. It is a good idea, and we should do it more. You package two plays together for the week. We give the signal, and the offense runs a play into the boundary, comes back to the line, and immediately runs a play into the field. You can pick any combination of plays you want to package.

PERSONNEL GROUPS

- Take advantage of players' skills.
- Give multiple players a chance to play.
- Stay with some offensive plays, different formations.
- Adjust practice prep and coaching responsibilities for specialists.
- You will need two players at the same position for the season.
- Focus on most of your players contributing one-and-a-half ways

We want to take advantage of what our players do best. In the spread, it gives multiple players a chance to play. If you coach high school football with 60 players on the team, you want team chemistry. If most of those 60 players feel they are contributing to the success of the program, that makes for a happy locker room. It also makes good practices and competition. If you have 60 players on the team, and 38 of them know that Friday night they are not going to play, it makes for a bad situation. They do not practice well and are not motivated. If they know the only time they are going to get in the game is mop-up time, they will not try as hard. We try to give multiple players a chance to play.

We run the same offensive plays from different formations and tempo. We had to adjust our practice preparation as well as our coaching responsibilities to make sure we have a good positive, productive practice and could coach all our players. When we are practicing the outside zone play, what happens to the defensive specialist who plays in your I-formation plays? We have to make sure we have someone to work with them specifically. The same thing is true of the slot receivers when we work goal-line situations. We have to make someone responsible for coaching

them. If we have 60 players, I hate to have anyone standing around doing nothing.

We have a rule on our practice field during scrimmages. It is the 3x5 rule. The players are not allowed to have anyone within a 3x5-yard area. We do not want them standing around talking to one another. If they are supposed to be in the scrimmage, we want them in it. If they are gabbing with their best friend, talking about what happened in school today, they forget to go into the game and are not paying attention to what they are supposed to do.

You want to have two players at the same position for the duration of the season. You do not want to develop the entire offense around one player. If he gets hurt, you are out of luck. One will be better than the other will, but you have to back him up with someone. If you are fortunate to have two players that you can interchange, you are in great shape.

We want to focus on most of the players contributing in one-and-a-half ways. That means we will play them one way on offense or defense, and they will spot someone in game situations on the other side of the ball. The starting linebacker is the short-yardage specialist. You cannot afford to take some players off the field because they are talented.

FORMATIONS AND MOTIONS

- Remember formations and motions are the key to successful diversity.
- Expand and contract formations, and change tempos.
- Limit the number of plays (do not let the linemen think).
- Be aware of what is tough for your defense to defend.
- Practice formations, motions, groupings, and tempos from day one.

If your plays are going to be simple, your attack should be diversified. I believe in expanding and contracting the formations. Do not let the cornerback know someone will be at the top of the numbers all the time. While you are expanding your formation, make sure to adjust your tempos. We want to make it easy for us and difficult for them. I used to coach the offensive line. I told them I did not want them to think. I wanted them to play. We want to simplify everything for the linemen.

I ask our defensive staff what causes them problems defending our sets. This is the most important point. From day one, you need to practice these formations, motions, groupings, and tempos.

We use a perfect pass and run drill to practice those things. It is also a conditioning drill. We have three groups. They begin at the 40-yard line with a formation and play. They make all the checks at the line. They snap the ball, and sprint 20, 30, or 40 yards. The second group goes, and then the third group goes. We come back from the other side with the first group and repeat the drill. We want perfect execution. If something goes wrong in a play, it does not count.

BASE RUN GAME

- Inside zone
- Power off-tackle
- Counter/reverse
- Outside edge play

This year, we were successful because we were able to run the football a number of different ways. An old coach told me a simple philosophy for play selection. He told me that you can run the football up the middle, off-tackle, around the end, and have some kind of counter or reverse. We run the inside zone up the middle. We run the power off-tackle, which I cannot give up. We had to tweak it to make it fit with the offense we run. We have a reverse to trick them and an outside edge play. That is our base offense for the run game.

My background had been power football with the double-team kick-out mentality. I was leery of the full-fledged zone scheme. How can a small guard block a huge 3 technique? We talked to people who were good at the play and adopted their scheme.

INSIDE ZONE

- Cutback, read play, slow to the hole and fast through it, read the backside A gap.
- Double-team on line of scrimmage to assigned linebacker. Stress security on the first level, then coming off in the second level when the gap is threatened.
- Covered lineman gets help from the uncovered linemen.
- Backside defensive end is unblocked for the quarterback to read.

This is a cutback and/or read play. It is not designed to go wide. The quarterback funnels the ball inside toward the center (Diagram #1). The back reads the backside A gap. I like to run the ball to an A-gap player. That will ensure we have double-teams across the line. I want double-teams at the point of attack so we can dent the defensive line. I do not want single blocks all over the place. The running back is slow to the hole but fast through it. If we run the play to the left, the back aligns behind the right tackle with his toes on the quarterback's toes.

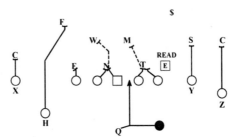

Diagram #1. Inside Zone

The back takes two shuffle steps to the quarterback because I want his shoulders square to the line. He cannot read the backside A gap if his shoulders are pointed to the sidelines. The quarterback keys the backside defensive end and walks over the handoff to the running back.

We want double-teams on the line of scrimmage. In this defense, the playside guard has a 3 technique aligned on him. The frontside guard and tackle are responsible for the 3 technique and the linebacker playing in the A gap. The block starts out as a double-team on the 3 technique. The guard and tackle want to be leg-to-leg and hip-to-hip square on the 3 technique. If they are not square, they will not see the run-through of the linebacker. They punch the respective number to their side of the 3-technique defender and drive. The guard wants his inside arm free, and the tackle wants the outside arm free. We want to get vertical movement back in to the linebacker. If the linebacker runs through either side of the double-team, that blocker comes off to block him.

The mistake the linemen make is to try to get off on the linebacker. We want to secure the down lineman and not think about the linebacker. We stay on the double-team and do not leave until the linebacker threatens the gap. It is the back's responsibility to move the linebacker so we have a fighting chance when he goes for the cutback. This play has a timing factor with it. It is essential the linemen talk. We make calls on every play. Some are dummy calls, and others are live. That is why we snap the ball on the first sound because of all the talk at the line of scrimmage.

The inside zone gives you two possible plays with one call. The center and backside guard have the same scheme for the nose and backside linebacker. On the play, the backside tackle blocks the defensive end. The frontside slot blocks the Sam linebacker because the quarterback can pull the ball and get on the edge right up his butt.

There are adjustments we would make to the way some teams play their defense, but this is the concept of the play. We see the 4-3, 3-4, and 3-3. Blocking the 3-3 presents some problems. The scheme may involve bringing someone in motion to block a box player.

POWER OFF-TACKLE

- Similar to I play
- Playside linemen use a "down-block scheme" we can adjust to fronts.
- Center blocks "on to back."
- Backside guard pulls for the kick-out.
- Backside tackle pulls through the hole for frontside linebacker.

- Back reads the end defenders on the line of scrimmage.

I am an Ohio State fan and always have been. That is why we run this play. Even when we went to the spread, I kept this play as part of the offense (Diagram #2).

In the spread, the blocking back with two backs lines up behind the offensive tackle and does not have an angle to kick out the defensive end. The play will end up bouncing, particularly if the end is a spill player. We decided to use the offensive guard to kick out the end. The down scheme is to identify the first defender on or outside the playside guard. That is the point of the semi-block. We use the term "semi" so the linemen do not get it confused with the inside zone double-team. It is the same block except it goes to the backside linebacker instead to the frontside linebacker. We double-team that defender to the backside linebacker.

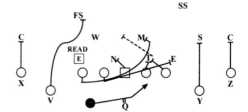

Diagram #2. Power Off-Tackle

We say the backside linebacker, but we are looking for any color crossing that line. If the playside linebacker runs through that gap, the guard comes off and blocks him. If we block it straight, the guard or tackle comes off for the backside linebacker. The backside guard pulls and kicks out on the defensive end. The offensive tackle opens, puts his hand on the guard hip, and turns up when the guard kicks out. He is looking for the frontside linebacker or the first color he sees. We control the backside end with the quarterback. The quarterback can pull the ball if the backside defensive end is in a chase mode on the running back. Again, we get two plays with one call.

This is a gap scheme. We run this play when we find teams that like to blitz a lot. We get down blocking and kickout blocks. If we get an odd-front defense, the playside guard is coming down on the nose with the center chipping and blocking the backside A gap. We either adjust with a tight end to double with the playside tackle to the backside linebacker, or zone release the tackle inside for whoever is playing the B gap. We use that scheme with the 3-3.

We run a quarterback counter off this play (Diagram #3). We fake the power, and the quarterback runs the ball to other way after he rides the running back. We run the power blocking away from the backfield action. If we are going to run the play to the left, the running back runs the power to the right. The linemen block the play to the left. The right guard and tackle pull. The running back makes the fake and fills for the pulling tackle on the defensive end. We hope the end will tackle him. If he does not, the back blocks him.

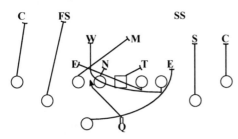

Diagram #3. Quarterback Counter

The counter and power was a great combination scheme for us. When we ran the I formation, the offense was 10 against 11 every time. If the quarterback handed the ball off, it was 9 against 11. In the spread with the quarterback carrying the ball, we stack up better. In the spread, you have to account for the quarterback as a ballcarrier.

OUTSIDE EDGE PLAY

- Use the pitch to quickly get to the outside (long handoff).
- It allows you to use more running backs instead of your main back.
- Emphasize speed.

If you are in the I formation, to get to the edge you have to run a toss sweep or some kind of dive option. We have other players on our team we like to get the ball on the edge. This is consistent with

our philosophy, and it challenges the defense to defend you horizontally. Our tailback was All-Ohio. Teams concentrated on him and the quarterback. We had two little slot players who ran this play and ran it well. This is a pitchout play.

We do not run the jet series because the line has to reach block on that play. We want to get to the edge immediately, and we pull linemen. We pull the playside guard. We do not block a 2-technique or a 3-technique defender. On the pitch play, the back receives the ball outside the playside tackle. On the jet play, the back receives the ball behind the center. This has been more successful for us to get the ball to the edge. We got this concept from Lake Erie College.

This is a speed play to the outside. We want the ball to get to the sidelines (Diagram #4). It does not matter how many yards he gains. When he goes in motion, someone on the defense is moving in that direction. That is when we can run the ball away from the motion or we use play-action passing. The hard block is the reach block on the defensive end. The X-receiver has to block the corner and force him to the inside. He wants to get his butt toward the sidelines. The slot receiver stalks the free safety. The playside guard pulls outside and looks inside. He looks for the linebacker or the safety in run support.

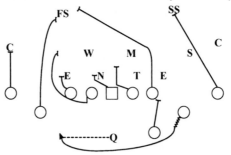

Diagram #4. Pitch Play

The center and the backside guard are responsible for the nose and backside linebacker. We tell them to use whatever technique they need to use. We describe the block of the playside tackle as "getting run over slowly." It does not have to be a pancake or anything drastic. He has to get in the way. He has to hold up the defensive end from getting down the line too quickly.

The back receiving the ball runs with uncontrolled speed through the heels of the quarterback. That means he runs as fast as he can. We snap the ball as the back reaches the quarterback. Once the back passes the quarterback, he turns and looks for the pitch. When he does that, it will take him automatically downhill and on an angle to get to the edge. The quarterback catches the snap, takes three steps toward the motion back, and pitches the ball as far as he can. If the play is going left, he steps with his left foot, right foot, and pitches the ball off his left foot. The slot can run the play as well as the running back. We tell the backs to challenge the quarterback to pitch the ball wide. We want them to receive the ball as wide as possible.

This is a good philosophy for us. We have what we want to do. We have an inside run, an outside run, a power play, and a counter. Those are our base running plays from the spread offense. With the running game, you must have a play-action pass. The pitch play is a great play-action pass for us. The quarterback takes his three steps and fakes the pitch, steps back, and throws the ball. The safety sees the motion and starts down for the quick pitch. The slotback can run past him.

In the spread offense, we did not want to lose the value of the three-step pass in the shotgun. That is an important pass for us. We wanted to make sure we could incorporate the play-action pass with the offense.

BASE PASSING GAME

- Quick passing game and base route and protection are quarterback-friendly.
- Still can develop play-action off base runs.
- Boot/waggle pulls the backside guard.
- Move pocket to set up different launch points.
  ✓ Full sprint
  ✓ Semi-roll
  ✓ Boot/waggle
- Do not be afraid to go empty.
  ✓ Five receivers? Hot receiver

✓ Routes appropriate for protection
✓ Does the quarterback need to read?
- Vertically and horizontally stretch on defense.
  ✓ Throw four verticals once a quarter
  ✓ Side to side, deep to short
- Back and receiver screens
  ✓ Bubbles
  ✓ Jailbreak

When you run this offense, you cannot be afraid to go into an empty set. When you run empty, you must have hot receivers built into the scheme. The routes we run from the empty set are appropriate for the protection we run. If the tailback is a receiver, you have one less blocker. The routes cannot be long because the ball is coming out quick. The main strategy for the defense against an empty is to blitz the quarterback.

Your quarterback cannot read five receivers. We give our quarterback one read. He read high to low or inside to outside. He is 17 years old and cannot handle reading five receivers in the time he will have to throw the ball. Even though we have five receivers in the pattern, we are not reading all five.

We try to throw four vertical patterns a game. We want to throw one a quarter. Even if the play is incomplete, we do it. We run it out of bunch, doubles, or triples, but we want to drop back and chunk the ball downfield. First down is not a bad time to throw something deep.

We throw receiver screens. We throw the bubble and jailbreak screen. They are high percentage pass, and it allows you to get the ball in the hands of the athletes. Those passes are simple and look good at the end of the season on the quarterback's stat sheet.

The play-action pass we like is a high-low triangle (Diagram #5). The X-receiver runs a slant corner, the V-receiver runs a flat pattern, and the backside slot runs a crossing pattern behind the linebackers. We tell the quarterback to throw the ball to the flat until they take it away. With two-high safeties, he will have to look for the cross pattern because it will be some kind of cover 2, man, or quarters coverage. We read high to low on the pattern.

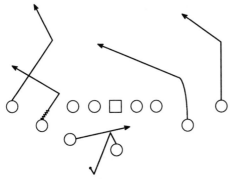

Diagram #5. High-Low Triangle

We like the bunch routes from the play-action pass. My favorite pattern from the bunch is this route (Diagram #6). The receiver on the line runs the corner route. The inside receiver runs an arrow route to the flat. The outside receiver runs a roll route off the linebacker. He finds the linebacker, comes down, pivots off of him, and sprints away from him. The corner stretches the defense vertically, and the arrow stretches them horizontally.

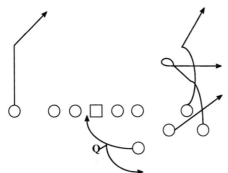

Diagram #6. Bunch

If you scouted us you would think cover 2 would be a good coverage to play because we attack the flat so much. We threw this pattern this year to attack the middle of the field (Diagram #7). We took

the tight end or slot receiver and started him down the middle of the field. He stopped his pattern over the ball at 10 yards and settled in between the linebackers. The inside receiver from the backside ran the crossing route in front of the linebackers. This gave us a high-low read in the middle of the field.

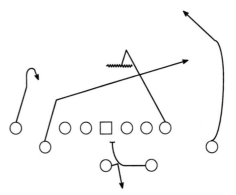

Diagram #7. Middle Route

This is one point I want to leave you with today. We have a play analysis of our offense. We do this week to week during the season. We have one of our freshmen quarterbacks chart the plays we call during a game and the results of that play. We chart the total yards gained on each play, average yards per play, and the percentage of plays considered successful. A successful play was one that gained four yards or more. If it got more than 10 yards, we considered it a big play.

We had a comment section for each play. If the play went for a touchdown, we wrote "TD." If there was a penalty, we recorded what type of penalty it was. This is a good way to look at what you are doing and how successful you are. This helps you learn from your mistakes and reinforces what you are doing well.

I want to thank you, and it is an honor to talk football with you.

ORGANIZATION USING MULTIPLE QUARTERBACKS

Webster Groves High School, Missouri

I am going to talk about the spread offense today. The angle I am going to talk about in the spread offense is the use of multiple quarterbacks in the spread offense. We have played multiple quarterbacks in three out of the last five years. We are talking about playing different quarterbacks in the same game. We are not playing two players at quarterback at one time—I want to clear that point up first. I am going to talk about how we coach all of our quarterbacks and how we practice them. I want to give you some background of what we do.

Gun Spread Offense

- Gun 95 percent of snaps
- 51 percent run (2,322 yards)/49 percent pass (2281 yards) by yardage; 65 percent run (448)/35 percent pass (243) by play selection
- Power run game; quarterback heavily involved; quarterback 58 percent carries (202); running back/wide receiver 42 percent carries (186)
- Diverse pass game
- Distribution of all to all positions

The only time we are under the center is in short yardage. We like to be 50/50 in the run to pass balance. In the past, we have been more of a passing team, but this year we ran the ball more. From a yardage standpoint, we were 50/50 in our run to pass percentages. However, in our play selection we were 65 percent run and 35 percent pass.

We were a power running team this year with the quarterback heavily involved in our running attack. The quarterback carried the ball 58 percent of the time. This year, we played with three quarterbacks. In the preceding season, we rotated quarterbacks. We had our two starters back from the previous year and had a transfer from North Carolina that played as well. I do not think anyone felt sorry for us trying to coach three quarterbacks.

We are very diverse in the passing game. We run the quick game and bubble screen package. We throw vertical routes and the crossing game. We also have a screen and draw package we use.

General Play List

Run (QB and RB)

- Inside zone
- Trap and GAT (guard and tackle trap)
- Isolation and power
- Stretch (jet)
- Stretch option
- Sweep
- Draw

Pass

- Quick game
- Vertical
- Shallow intermediate cross
- Screens
- Play-action and boot

We run the inside zone. We use the trap and the GAT, which is the *guard and tackle trap* with the counter trey play. The isolation and power play is generally our quarterback running the ball. However, we will get into a set, bring the H-back in motion, and hand the ball to him. The stretch is our outside zone play. We also run a little stretch option. We get the outside receiver involved with the jet in the outside zone scheme. We run the toss sweep and draw plays.

In the pass game, we run the quick game and bubble. We are a big vertical team. We send four verticals as part of our passing game. We run screens to our running backs and the jailbreak screens to the wide receivers.

We have been fortunate to have great players at the quarterback position.

Multiple Quarterbacks

- We have a very rich quarterback history at Webster.
- The first two gun quarterbacks (2001 to 2003) were not normal human beings. Since then, we have had more typical, athletic, basketball player types.
- We have played multiple quarterbacks three of the last five years. In 2005 and 2008, we played two quarterbacks, and in 2009, we played three quarterbacks.
- We fell into this system; we did not go multiple quarterbacks by design.

The first two years, we had quarterbacks that were big and athletic and could throw the ball 70 yards. They were 240-pound running backs that were playing quarterback. Since then, our quarterbacks have been more the typical quarterback. They look more like basketball players. They are the type of player the opposing coaches think they can get physical with and knock them out of the game. We were worried about that and began to develop depth at that position.

In 2005, we fell into the multiple-quarterback scheme. We had a senior returning from the previous year. He was 6'3" and 185 pounds. We wanted to move him to quarterback. He did not want to play quarterback but we talked him into it. The first couple of games that year he did a great job. He got into some discipline problems and could not play in the third game. We had to play a less talented sophomore in his place. The first game he played, he threw for over 300 yards. We started him the next week against a team that was as talented as we were. They had a huge blitz package and pressurized the young quarterback.

We brought in the senior and he stabilized the situation with his running. When we brought the sophomore back into the game, he was more relaxed. We rolled them in and out of the game and took advantage of the strengths of the two players.

The two years that followed that season, we had a sophomore at quarterback. He had offers to go to the Air Force Academy, but we did not have a capable backup. The two years we played him, we were not a very talented football team. We could not run the football because we did not have the talent in the offensive line.

The season that followed that year, we had a sophomore and a junior. The junior was tall and threw the ball well but could not run it. The sophomore was a good runner. He had a strong arm but was not very accurate. We played them both and felt good about the way they played.

We felt good with both of them returning, and then the North Carolina kid showed up. We had a lot of talent at the quarterback position and were able to roll them into and out of the game in situational times. Our senior quarterback, who was the starter, hurt his knee in a summer AAU basketball tournament and was not going to be available until four games into the season. We pushed the other two along early so they could take over if the senior could not make it through the season. It turned out to be a good situation for us.

Personnel Description

- We are not a two-platoon team.
- The offensive line gets rest on defense; linebackers get rest on offense.
- We are usually going to be as athletic or better than our opponent.
- This season, we were exceptionally deep at more than just the quarterback position.
- We played 16 different skill position players per game on offense: Three quarterbacks, three running backs, four tight ends, three outside receivers, and three inside receivers.

We are not a two-platoon team. We do not have the numbers or talent to play that way. We try to play as many players as we can and roll them in and out of the game to give them rest. We play probably a team and a half as far as the 22 positions are concerned.

In our games, we usually are as athletic as our opponent. In most games, we have more talent. We had a lot of options when it came to the skill positions and played 16 different players at those positions.

Practice Organization

- Typical practice is 2.5 hours: One hour offense, one hour defense, 30 minutes individual stretching, special teams, and conditioning.
- Offense split into three 20-minute segments of individual, group, and team.
- Quarterbacks get a lot of fundamentals in individual stretch and often work with receivers or running backs during part of the individual period.

Typically, we practice for two-and-a-half hours daily. That could differ as we get deep into the season. We always start out with individual stretching. We are fortunate to have 13 coaches in grades 9 through 12. On the varsity level, we have seven coaches. Those seven coaches have been together for a long time and do an excellent job. When I send the players to their position coaches, the job is going to be done.

After the stretch period, we go to 20 minutes of individual work with the position coaches. The next 20 minutes is group drills. That is where we run 7-on-7 and drills of that nature. The last 20 minutes is a team-oriented drill.

We work a lot of the fundamental drills with the quarterbacks during the individual stretch period. That work is finished before we start the one-hour clock for the offensive segment of practice. They work with receivers and running backs during that time. We get on the field at 3:15 for our individual stretch period. At 3:30, we start practice. During that period, the quarterbacks work with receivers on release drills and the running backs on draws and screens.

Individual Offense Period

- Pre-season we will do more straight individual fundamental work with the quarterbacks in this 20-minute period.
- As we get out of doubles, we use individual stretch as getting the arm loose and footwork in the passing game. We also use our 20-minute time as a combination of one quarterback with the running backs in *mesh* and one quarterback with receivers in *hookup* and rotate quarterbacks at the 10-minute mark.
- Fundamental time means position specifics and individual could be shared time among two positions.
- Ball positioning, high release, and drops are the main thing we work on with the quarterbacks in fundamental time.
- Mesh and hookup are used for timing with running backs and receivers.
- Besides mesh/hookup, we will rotate quarterbacks during the running back drills and work with receivers in combo drills or 1-on-1.

Early in the year, we work more fundamentals in the individual periods. I am going to talk a lot about mesh and hookup. We have a line of running backs and wide receivers working on the mesh point and handoff with one quarterback. When we install the offense, we start from the inside and work out with the plays. We start with inside zone, trap, and work out to the outside zone and sweep. Early in the season, we do receiver hookups every day.

The biggest thing we do is go through the aiming points to the receivers. We go through that with all the drops the quarterback has. He has to know the aiming point on the three-step, five-step, and sprint-out games. We do that daily. The mesh/hookup is how we do option tracking with our backs and receivers.

Our base formation is a 2x2 formation with doubles on each side of the formation. We have double slots, and sometimes there will be a tight end in one of those positions. We start working from the left side to the right side. In 8 to 10 minutes, we can work every pattern in our playbook. We snap the ball and the quarterback throws a hitch to the wide receiver on the left side. As he is coming back, the ball is snapped and the slot receiver runs a quick out. We work across the board to all receivers and it is a continuous drill. This year, the drill did not run as smoothly as in the past because we were too young at the receiver position.

As we went from the individual period to the group period, we ran the entire playbook every day in practice. In the group period, we went 7-on-7 and 9-on-8. With the hookup drill in individual period and the group period, quarterbacks and receivers got a tremendous amount of reps. You do not do all this from the very beginning of the season.

We split the quarterback's time between passing and running skills. We send the quarterback who excels in the run to the mesh drill to begin with. The better passing quarterback starts with the hookup drill. They work for 10 minutes in their drill and rotate to the other drill.

If we are extremely young, the passing game may be one-, two-, or three-man combo drills. The one, two, and three refer to the number of defenders in the drill. If we start with a double or triple set, we put one defender in the drill to represent a read key for the quarterback and receiver. We stand behind the quarterback and tell the defender what to do. The quarterback has to go through his drop and read what the defender is doing. He could be playing cover 3, cover 2, man-to-man or whatever technique we want.

We progress to two and three defenders in the drill. In the three-man combo, we usually have a corner, safety, and linebacker as the defenders. We do this type of drill when we are young at the quarterback and/or receiver position. We also rotate the running backs into this drill.

During pre-season, we will send the quarterback down to the running backs coach. If the quarterback's primary skill is running the football,

we put him through the same drills the running backs go through. They get training on ball security and cutting drills.

With three quarterbacks, we had to have a practice schedule to deal with that. It was easier and preferable to schedule two quarterbacks.

In the *one-quarterback schedule*, the quarterback gets his fundamental work during individual stretch and then splits time between the running backs and receivers. He does 10 minutes in the mesh drill with the running backs while the receivers do individual drills. He does 10 minutes with the receivers while the running backs do individual drills. The running backs and receivers in this schedule will have an extra 10 minutes of individual drills.

Most of us are in the same boat. We do not have two good quarterbacks. You have the starter and the junior varsity quarterback to back him up. You hope he never gets hurt. Even in years where we have only had one starter at quarterback, we will bring the JV quarterback up with our varsity practice. When we go out, we start with varsity offense first and the JV team will start with defense.

The JV quarterback works the individual stretch, individual period, and group period with the varsity. After the varsity group period, the JV quarterback goes back to the JV team. That way, he is there when the JV offense segment begins. The JVs start their offense practice while the varsity works on the defensive side of the ball.

The *two-quarterbacks schedule* is the easiest and simplest to organize. We send one quarterback to the mesh drill with the running backs and the other quarterback to the hookup drill with the receivers. They are there for 10 minutes and they switch. It is very simple.

The *three-quarterbacks schedule* was a headache, and we thought about it for a long time. We put two quarterbacks together in one of the groups. We put two quarterbacks in the hookup drill. One quarterback threw to the right-side receivers, and the other threw to the left-side receivers. The quarterbacks switched back and forth from left side to right side. We ran the two hookup drills at the same time. We did that on Wednesday and Thursday.

Later on during the season, we created a third group with the tight ends and running backs. We worked on play-action routes we were specifically going to throw in a game during the mesh and hookup period. Our junior quarterback and the North Carolina player worked with the play-action and mesh period, and the senior quarterback spent most of his time with the hookup drill.

Group Offense

- Typically will be 7-on-7 and 9-on-8 with quarterbacks, running backs, tight ends, and slot receivers rotating at the 10-minute mark.
- We used 11 formations this year and divided our personnel into two groups: flex and heavy. Flex started in 7-on-7; heavy started in 9-on-8. This year, only one quarterback moved at the 10-minute mark.

We use a lot of formations. We were blessed with talented players this year. We ran 11 formations and ran the same plays from all the 11 formations. We divided our personnel into *flex* and *heavy* personnel. In our flex personnel, we did have one tight end. He was a tight end, but we sent him with the flex personnel. He caught most of our passes this year. He was okay as a blocker at tight end, but his asset was catching passes.

Our starting quarterback stayed in the 7-on-7 drill, and the other two quarterbacks went to the 9-on-8 running drill. The strong receivers and the tight end went to the 9-on-8 drill first. After 10 minutes, the heavy receivers went to the 7-on-7 passing drill, and the slot receivers came to the 9-on-8 running segment. Since we have been sending our slot receivers to the 9-on-8 drill, their ability to block has gotten better. One thing that has made our running game is the receiver's ability to block. We work hard with the slot receivers in this drill.

We use the slot receivers in our option game as pitchbacks and blockers. This drill gives them a better understanding of the play and helps them

with their pitch relationship with the quarterback. This year, with the three-quarterbacks situation, we did not get as much work for the slot receivers in the running drill. We had to keep them with the additional quarterback in the 7-on-7 drill.

At the 10-minute rotation, we sent the Carolina kid up to 7-on-7 and switched the tight end in the flex group with a tight end in the running game.

On Wednesday and Thursday, we had our running back working on blitz protection with our linemen. The quarterback who threw the ball most of the time was down in the end zone working on red zone hookup. The third quarterback went with the tight ends and receivers and worked on quick game and play-action vertical routes.

When we got to the middle of the season, we felt our starting quarterback was going to make it through the season. We took the other two quarterbacks and they worked on the running game almost exclusively. The only reason they threw the ball was to keep defenses honest.

The good thing about what we did this year was our ability to run the football. When teams put seven or eight defenders in the box, we had success lining up and running the football. We were not good enough to kick somebody's butt, but we were as good as the defense. It forced defenses to commit defenders to the box and opened up our slot receivers on the vertical routes.

Realistically, the slot receivers were going to get two or three passes thrown to them a game. We wanted those patterns to be the vertical routes. If our starting quarterback would have gotten hurt, we would have gone to the two-quarterbacks rotation.

Team Offense

- Rotate personnel packages during team.
- Must prep scout team defense and keep personnel consistent during the week. Use the same players from group during team.
- Coordinate team script with group script. Early in the year the same; as season progresses cover more.

We talked about playing 16 skilled players and rolling quarterbacks in and out of the game. If we had one quarterback and were exclusively a running team or spread offense team, we would spend a lot more time in the group period. This year, we were rotating so many people in and out of the game, we needed to keep our 20-minute team period to work on personnel.

If we were going to call a trap play, the quarterback called, *gun right 832 trap*. The first number in the call is the formation. The second number is the back receiving the ball, and the third number is the hole he runs. If it is a pass, he calls *gun right 853 slant*. The first number is the formation. The second number is a drop-back pass, and the third number is a designated receiver. In practice, we grouped our personnel groups on the sideline. We had a double tight A, tight slot A, flex B, or regular B. Those formations come from one formation package. We practiced substituting with the personnel groups.

Our players did a good job of getting in and out of the game. We did not have too many instances where we had to take a time-out or where we received a penalty for taking too much time. You will always have the wrong personnel on the field at some point during the season, but we try to minimize those times.

One thing that helps our offense in practice is to have the scout team prepped so they know what to do. It is also important to have the same defensive people in the 7-on-7 drill be the defensive people in the team period. We want the scout team linebackers that played in the 9-on-8 drill to be the linebackers in the team period. We want the defensive backs that played in the 7-on-7 drill to be the backs in the team period. It helps our offense if the adjustments made by the defense are the correct ones. We do not want to reteach personnel to get them aligned in a team drill. That takes time away from the offense and slows everything down. The quarterback has to see the picture we have told him he will see. If they are supposed to adjust a certain way to an empty set, it has to happen.

Early in the season, we will run the same plays in-group drills as we run in team. We are still installing plays, and everything is repetition. As we progress in the season, our group drill plays will not be the same plays we run in the team period. We will cover more plays in the team period.

I am going to show you some game film and try to tie that into what we do as far as practice is concerned. The first formation is a trips formation with the tight end to the trips side. The quarterback in the film is the senior with the knee injury. He was our passing quarterback. He ran the ball 66 times during the season, and most of them were not called runs—they were situations where he was going to throw the football or hand it off to the running back. We did not use him in our 9-on-8 period. He stayed in the 7-on-7 drill. The route is a double slant, which he would throw every day in practice in the hookup drill. We would throw it in a 7-on-7 drill but probably not throw it in the team drill. It is a timing pattern we throw based on the way the defense plays us.

The next play is from the same formation, but we run the counter trey. The quarterback did not play in the 9-on-8 drill and did not go to the mesh drill very often. His ballhandling reflects that.

In the next play, there is motion across the formation from the slot. When we practice motion, we do most of it in the mesh period. We do not work him on his blocking assignments. We work on the timing of the motion to the mesh. In the mesh period, we work on the motion with the fly sweep. We use the slotbacks as motion backs. They come in jet motion and run the stretch sweep play.

The next play is a draw off a sprint action. On Wednesday and Thursday during the season, we have a draw, screen, and protection period. We work on the scheme with the offensive line in those periods.

My time is up. If you have any questions or need anything, give me a call. I have enjoyed the opportunity to talk to you. Thank you very much.

INSIDE ZONE READS VS. 3 AND 4 TECHNIQUES

Middletown High School, Ohio

Thank you. For years, I have heard stories about a great football clinic in Louisville. I heard a lot of stories about the Louisville Nike Clinic, and how much fun coaches have at this clinic. It is an honor to be here today to speak with you.

For a few years, we have run the inside zone, but now we have developed a twist on it in the last two years to where we read an inside technique. In an even front, we are going to read a 3 technique. In an odd front, we are going to read the 4 technique. What we were really trying to do is to develop a running game that can compete against much larger schools than we are.

Why do we think we need this? It is best explained in our philosophy.

Philosophy

• We do less better. Allows us to play fast.
• Simple scheme to even the playing field. Match-ups.
• Block one less man; make him decide.
• Athletic quarterback is a threat with his feet/speed.
• Attacks traditional defensive schemes to stop the zone.

In the past two years, we have had three run schemes. We run inside zone, outside zone, and the inside zone read which we call "razor." We do run several variations of those plays. The key is to keep it simple for the guys up front.

This allows us to play fast. Middletown high school has been the Ohio state champions in track and field a few years. We have guys who can run. That is what we are best at right now so we want to play fast. With those three schemes, over the past two seasons, we have led our league in yards per game. We averaged 373 yards per game. We averaged 189 rushing and 184 passing. We averaged 40.1 points per game, which also led our league. That tells you right there that the schemes we are using are working.

I grew up understanding the K.I.S.S. method ("Keep It Simple, Stupid!"). We believe in that. We want our kids to be able to understand things and play fast in their head. If they are taking time to think and wonder how things are supposed to be working, we feel like they play on their heels and play slow.

We felt like our interior match-ups were not good in the past. Six of the 10 largest schools in the state of Ohio are in our league. We aren't one of those six. We are the smallest team in our league. Typically, up front we are smaller in stature than our opponent is. This scheme helps our match-ups. We count guys in the box. With this, we have one less guy that we have to deal with now, and usually that is a bigger guy. We don't have to block him because we let him chase and make a decision. I hope that our quarterback can make the right decision on our end, and things go well for us.

The key to our offense is our quarterback. We have been fortunate to have a good one for the past two years. He is now going to Bowling Green State University. We have also been fortunate that our kids could throw the football. In the spread scheme, you want your best athlete with his hands on the ball every down. Our guy has to be a threat with his feet, and he has to have speed.

This scheme attacks traditional defensive schemes created to stop zones. We run the inside zone like a lot of people do. We are in the gun.

Defensive coaches started to develop schemes with somebody staying at home to take on the quarterback. They have to put somebody on the quarterback if your quarterback is any good and know that he is going to pull the ball. We like to pull the ball. Defensive teams started to leave someone assigned to our quarterback. We developed this as a way to attack that type of defensive scheme. We block out on that outside guy, and we read the inside guy.

Counter Look/Misdirection (back goes one way; the quarterback goes the other)

- Ride the mesh
- Express
- Hits fast, problem for second-level defender
- Simplifies the quarterback's read and alleviates indecision

The other thing we like about this scheme is it provides us a counter look. Whenever you give that defense a flow look in one direction with the back across the defense's face, the quarterback has an opportunity to go the other way. That is a counter look or misdirection. This is a counter scheme for us.

There are some important pieces to this. Our quarterback runs this every day in practice. You have to ride the mesh. We tell the quarterback to get the ball back to the running back as fast as he can. We like to have the defense see that mesh all the way across the line of scrimmage. When that happens, it forces the defense to commit. The longer we ride that mesh and sell it, the more the defense has to commit. The defense cannot sit and wait. The defense starts to play slow. Our back is about a yard-and-a-half deep and about a yard-and-a-half outside. His aiming point is the inside leg of the tackle. We practice it every day. It is monotonous and tedious, but the quarterback got better at it as the year went on, and it is vital.

Once the ball is handed off to the back, the quarterback must carry out the fake as if he has the football. We call it expression. It's just option football out of the gun. The quarterback has to make the defense worry that he has the football. The quarterback sometimes wants to just hand off the football and watch. We had to harp on that every single day throughout the year up until the playoffs. Until then he really struggled with it and he is a good quarterback.

This play hits more vertically than our other inside zone play, which hits more lateral. This play hits inside, fast, and hard. It does not give the defense much time to react, change direction, and try to run you down. On this play, with the quick vertical hit and because of the misdirection, we are running past guys with their backs turned to us.

The last thing is we think it simplifies the quarterbacks read. Some of the teams we played against started to bring two guys off the backside edge. Our quarterback did not know which guy to read. In this scheme, he is reading the B-gap defender. Whomever they bring to the B gap, he is the guy we are reading. This eliminated a lot of our mistakes. The read that we give him when he reads the inside technique is done in three words: shoulder, sink, and soft.

If the 3 technique is going to give his outside shoulder to you, then you know that you are going to pull the football. If he is sinking down into the A gap, we are going to outrun him to the B gap. Most 4-technique players are trained when they get a down block, they are going to play inside run. We are going to go where they just left. If he plays soft, we are going to give the ball.

Read

- Versus even front: Read 3 technique for give or keep decision
  ✓ Tried 1 technique, too fast on mesh
- Versus odd front: Read 4 technique for give or keep decision
- Versus bear front: Read 3 technique for give or keep decision
- Versus any front: Read the first technique outside the guard's nose. Tackle BOBs the C-gap defender.
- Stack: Week to week

In the even front, the frontside blocking assignments are inside zone. The two guys that need to be involved in this scheme are the backside guard and tackle. When they have a 3 technique on their side, the guard is thinking we are going to go down inside and work toward the backer. We confirm the 3 technique through cadence. We tell the guard he is going to veer that 3 technique and then to work to the backer and square up on him. He does not know if the ball was given to the back, or if the quarterback kept it. When we get to him, we play with leverage.

We tell the tackle that he is going to block out. We say "BOB" him. BOB means "big-on-big." We are going big-on-big on that guy in the 5 technique. Usually, that guy wants to rush upfield so that makes it an easy block for us. It just creates a big running lane for us.

Versus the odd front, we are going to read a 4 technique. We see a lot of this type of front, and some of the teams are real good at it. Now, the center has a head-up noseman on him. It makes it a little more intense for that guy, and he has more on his plate, so to speak. By rule, we are going to read that B-gap defender, and we are going to BOB out to the C-gap defender. We tell the guard that he has zone-stepping, and to make sure that there is no return by the noseman, and work up to the backer.

In a Bear front, where they have a 3 technique and a head-up nose, we read the 3 technique. If the nose goes away, we try to work up to the backer. If they are a man-cover team, we like to formation them to try to get the advantage for us. We are a big formation team. We try to get the defenses put in places, as we want them to be, for our success.

In any front we get, the key for our guys is understanding the gaps. We are going to read the guy in the B gap. It might be a backer, or it may not. It might be a tackle slanting. If he is not going to be a threat to tackle the zone, we are going to go ahead and give it. If that backer is a threat to tackle that zone, we are going to pull it. The B gap and C gap are keys for us. It is a lot like midline but in the gun. This gives the quarterback a little more time to see things and to react.

We are seeing more and more of the stack defense. We run it ourselves, and we practice against it daily. We feel like we had better get the bandit out of the box. If we don't, we are in trouble. We try to get him out of the box by using our "formations" to get him out of the box.

We like to go trips. If they don't take him out of the box, then we are going to attack by throwing the bubble outside, and we are not going to run the ball. The rules have to stay the same. It is the B gap and the C gap. In the stack, you don't know where they are going. You have to still maintain your rules. The number-one rule for our quarterback is: indecision, you have to give it. You can see the reads in our film. If you have questions, feel free to get my attention.

I want to thank you guys for your attentiveness. What a thrill it has been for me to be able to speak to you today. Thank you.

THE BASE MULTIPLE OPTION SCHEMES

Chantilly High School, Virginia

Thank you. It is an honor for me to speak at such a great clinic as this. It is a special deal to me to speak here with Western Pennsylvania being such a great haven for football. I have been in the Pittsburgh area a few times, and I know how good football is up here. It is indeed an honor to speak with you today.

I was a walk-on at the University of Notre Dame in the late 1980s and early 1990s. I played for Coach Lou Holtz. At that time, we ran the option offense from the I formation. I learned the offense from him. What we run now is so old it is now new again in our area. I coach at a Division VI school in Virginia. Chantilly High School has between 2,600 and 2,700 students. Most of the teams in our area used to run the wing-T offense. They moved to running the midline veer offense. From there, they went to the spread offense. There are still two or three schools in our conference that use a tight end–type offense.

I will go through what we do on offense. I know nothing we are doing is new to many of you. I hope that some of you can gain something from this lecture.

Why do we run the option offense?

- Increases the opponent's defensive prep
- Forces the opponent's defense to be disciplined
- Allows a smaller team to block effectively
- Has basic blocking rules for flexibility and multiplicity
- Is excellent in short yardage and goal line
- Allows athletes to get to the edge
- Gets more athletes involved as threats

We can run several types of option in our offense. We run a zone-read scheme, but we can run the dive option, veer option, speed option, or the inside veer option, and we do not have to change anything. We have a simple blocking scheme from multiple formations. Unless it is a dive play, we preach for the running backs to get to the sideline. We do not like the pitch to go to the running back, and he cuts back to the inside when he is behind the line. We tell the back that is not an option. We want to get our athletes to the edge on the option.

In coaching option football there is one thing I have learned. It is important to stress the following points if you are going to run the option:

- Must make a commitment to the option
- Practice plans must represent that commitment
- Must have offense each day
- Sample practice plans
- Option period (10 minutes)
- Sample option period

In the first year that I was a head coach, I would run offense one day and defense the next day, and then we would stress special teams another day. We do not do that anymore. You need to run the option every day so you can get the timing down on the plays.

Every day we have a team option period. We have a period of offense and defense each day. If you are going to run the option, you need to factor in time during each day where you have a team option period. It is like most things in football. You need to work on them every day to become good at what you are doing.

In our practices, I have 20 plays, 10 left and 10 rights, scripted into the session. We run the plays 10 yards down the field. We do this on air until we get into pads, and then we do have a dummy defense lined up. I call the plays out. I may call split right 34 veer. I call the play out loud, and the players line up and go on the snap count.

#	Formation	Play
1	Split Left	25 Veer
2	Split Right	34 Veer
3	Left	33 Veer
4	Right	32 Veer
5	Left	33 Dive
6	Right	32 Dive
7	Left	19 Dive
8	Right	18 Dive
9	Spread Left G	27 Read Power GT
10	Spread Right G	26 Read Power GT
11	K Left	19 Spread
12	K Right	18 Spread
13	Split Left G	30 Read
14	Split Right G	21 Read
15	Split Left G	19 Shovel
16	Split Right G	18 Shovel
17	Bunch Left	19 Spread
18	Bunch Right	18 Spread
19	Double Left	19 Spread
20	Double Right	18 Spread

We are trying to get those 10 plays to each side completed in that 10-minute period. We may run the first unit four plays, and then run the second unit two plays, and then we bring the first unit back, and they run four more plays. For the entire period, I am calling out the plays we are going to run. We run those plays as fast as we can.

The goal for the drill is to gain reps. We try to do some teaching and coaching at that time, but we are working for reps. If we can film this session, it helps a great deal. We feel we have to run this drill each day. We got a lot of this drill from Elliot Uzelac who used to coach at Colorado when Cordell Stewart was the quarterback. He was later the head coach at Western Michigan and Navy. He coached at Michigan and Ohio State as well. He used to call out the plays when Stewart was the quarterback, and he could run the offense. However, we did not have a quarterback that fast, so the drill

was not as good as it was when Stewart was running the drill.

We say the option begins and ends with the quarterback. Consider the following points with the quarterback and what he does with the option:
- Speed of play
- Execution of play
- Quarterback fundamentals
- Stance
- Six inches apart
- Quarterback on his toes
- Weight on drive foot
- Purpose
- Allows quarterback to cover more distance
- Allows quarterback to attack pitch key

He dictates the speed of the play. You do not need to have a fast quarterback, but you do need a quick quarterback. He must be agile on his feet. His discipline will dictate the execution of the play as well.

The first thing we do differently relates to our stance. We teach our quarterbacks to have a narrow stance. We only want the feet six to eight inches apart. The reason for this is because we feel the quarterback can gain ground from that stance. We run the outside veer. If we run it right, it is tough. We have a running back lined up behind the guard, and he is going to run as fast as he can to the outside leg of the tackle. The quarterback has to get the snap and get down the line to make the mesh. That can be tough for the quarterback. If your feet are wide apart, and your first step is a little step, versus being in tight, it makes a big difference.

My quarterback coach will tell you it is better for passing if he has a narrow stance. If he wants to drop back, the first step is the momentum step. He can gain more ground on the first step. I am not here to try to convince you how to coach the quarterback, but this is how we do it. If the quarterback can get the ball to the dive back without having to stretch out so far, that is one reason we want him to be able to move on his first step. In the film, you will see our quarterback reaching out at times.

Quarterback Fundamentals

- Seat the ball
- Two hands
- Ball at chest
- Ball held vertical with hands vertical
- Reach and ride
- Extend arms out and back
- Don't look back at the running back.
- Eyes on key

Seating the ball is a big thing for us. We take the ball with both hands, and we want it chest high. We want to lock the ball in our hands vertical to the line. We want the quarterback to extend his arm and not to reach back. He has his hands and elbows locked in. This will help protect the ball when defenders hit him from the side. This allows us to give the ball or to pitch the ball when we get to that point.

The outside veer is a strict read, and we do not get as much of a ride on the play. When we reach the dive man, we want to ride him as long as possible with our eyes on the key for the quarterback. By doing this, we can really sell the play. He must run the play every day in practice so he will have the confidence that someone will be there on the pitch and he will not have to look for him every time.

Other quarterback fundamentals include the following. The pitch is vital. We teach the quarterback to set and flip the ball on the pitch. It is almost like a basketball pass. We feel we have more control of the ball with the basketball-type pitch.

Pitch

- Basketball pass
- Push with fingers
- Snap wrist

We teach the quarterback to take the path to the inside shoulder of the pitch key. We do this so we can run right by him.

- Attack the inside shoulder of pitch key
- Maintain angle to sidelines

- Defeats slow play technique
- Makes the play faster

Speed is the key to the play. We want to attack the line of scrimmage. If it is not fast, it will not press the defense. We want to get under the defensive end, where we can fake him and keep the ball, or fake the keep and pitch the ball.

Here is the assignment for our quarterback on a typical play. It is our 32 dive play.

With feet narrow together under center and on the toes, the ball comes to the cradle from the snap. From under center, takes one step down the line to the right with the right foot at a 45-degree angle. Eyes go directly to what would be the pitch key if we were running option. Extends the ball with both hands for the handoff, as he gathers his left foot. Eyes remain on the imaginary pitch key. Executes the handoff, and carries out the option fake by taking a straight line to the inside shoulder of the imaginary pitch key and running full speed.

A few years ago, we were very fortunate in that we got to the state final game. We were 0-10 in 2004, and in 2006 we made it to the finals. The biggest difference was the fact we had bigger and better athletes all the way around in 2006. I was the assistant coach in 2004 and moved up after that. The number-one reason we were better in 2005 when I became the head coach was our fullback. He ended up being a 1,000-yard rusher. He really became a factor for us on the inside game. Here is want we want from our fullback and tailback.

Fullback

- Three-point stance
- Four yards deep, "heels at four"
- Must take proper line
- Dive option
  - ✓ Butt crack of guard
- Veer option
  - ✓ Outside leg of tackle
- Inside veer option:
  - ✓ Outside leg of guard

- Steps are vital for the play's success
- Inside running sets everything else up

Our target on the dive option is the butt crack of the offensive guard. We tell the dive back he is not to cut off that path until he is one yard past the line of scrimmage on the dive give. They will see a crackback toward the center, and they cut inside. They run into the quarterback, and the whole play is a bust. We tell them they must maintain that line until they get across the line of scrimmage. On the veer option, our target is the outside leg of the offensive tackle. That is the pre-snap target. The outside veer is the hard play to execute for us because it is not a natural play for the quarterback. We rep the play over and over to get the play consistent.

One of the reasons the outside veer is tough to run is because we do not block the defensive end. The good part about this is the fact that the defensive end may tackle the quarterback and then the dive back goes for a long run on the play.

If we run the inside veer, we have to offset the fullback to run the play. He lines up behind the guard. On our 32 veer, we run to the outside leg of our offensive guard. We stay in the traditional I formation most of the time. We can run the triple read on the inside veer because we have more time to run the play. The inside game can set the outside game up, but the inside veer must be a true play every time. When someone deviates off the path, that is when the quarterback starts looking around and everything starts breaking down.

Our tailback is similar to the fullback on the stance.

Tailback

- Two-point stance
- Hands on knees
- Thumbs in, fingers out
- Pitch relationship with quarterback
  - ✓ Four yards deep
  - ✓ One yard in front
  - ✓ Maintain relationship across line of scrimmage
- Says "Pitch, pitch, pitch" when in position.

- Lets the quarterback know the tailback is ready for the pitch
- Allows the quarterback to keep his eyes on his key

The pitch relationship for the tailback with the quarterback is four yards deep and one yard in front of the quarterback. He wants to catch the pitch going downhill. The pitch is almost a forward lateral. We want the ball pitched outside so the tailback is catching the ball when running toward the line of scrimmage. He wants to be attacking the line of scrimmage when the ball is pitched. If he is too deep, the play will not work as well.

We do several drills to teach the quarterback his steps on the option. Most of you know these drills, so I will not spend a lot of time here. We start on the footwork drills first on the hose, and we do them slowly. We use the bag drills and incorporate the pitch with the drill. We know we are going to have defensive linemen coming inside to try to knock the ball out of the quarterback's hands.

- Footwork on air with hose
  - ✓ Rep footwork slowly without running back
  - ✓ Allows for better teaching
- Bag drill and pitch
  - ✓ High-step over bags, and pitch to coach
  - ✓ Coaching points
    - ❏ Being on your toes
    - ❏ Step and pitch
- Pitch drill
  - ✓ Down the line, sideline to sideline, five yards apart
  - ✓ We run half speed, and three-quarters speed, and then full speed
  - ✓ Every three to five steps, the quarterback pitches the ball

Our running back drills are as follows. First is the train track drill. This is just getting on the hose and running the lines. In running the veer offense, it is so important to be on line with the quarterback. We will paint the marks on the field in the early part of the year to make sure we get the proper relationship for the veer.

- One half-speed, three-quarters speed, and full-speed progression
- Two lines in three-point stances
- Go through the veer and dive line.
- Switch lines to do it both ways.

We have to practice catching bad pitches on the option. You must work on this. I have lost games because of a bad pitch on the option. We work on the pitch drill early in the season and try to work on it as much as we feel we need to during the season.

Pitch Drill: Good, High, Low, and Behind

- While in pitch relationship and running
- Quarterback or running back pitch in variety of locations

Hand-Eye Drill: Practice Catching Pitch

- Five yards from coach or player turned around
- On command, turn and catch the pitch.
- Variety of locations

We work on group drills with the quarterback and the running back. We include a center in the drill. We run the arch hose, where the quarterback can go down inside when he rides the back and goes down the line of scrimmage. We want him to go forward down the line toward the read key. This emphasizes attacking the line of scrimmage and the pitch key. The target for the quarterback is the inside shoulder of his key. We run these drills along with the arch hose drill.

- On air with hose
- Add pitch reads
- Add pitch reads with shields/bags
- Film

Group Running Back, Quarterback, and Center on Hose Drill

- Arch hose
  - ✓ It emphasizes attacking the line of scrimmage and pitch key.
  - ✓ Quarterback target is the inside shoulder of the key.
  - ✓ It emphasizes attacking the line of scrimmage and pitch key.

- ✓ Quarterback target is the inside shoulder of the key.
- On air with hose
- Add pitch reads
- Add pitch reads with shields/bags
- Film
- Basic rules
  - ✓ Option the end man on the line of scrimmage.
  - ✓ Inside veer
  - ✓ Option the last two men
  - ✓ Block anyone who crosses your face

Let me get to the X's and O's. This is our blocking scheme for our dive play. From the I formation, we call the play 32 dive (Diagram #1). We want the quarterback to go downhill on the play and carry out the fake to the pitchman. This is our basic blocking scheme.

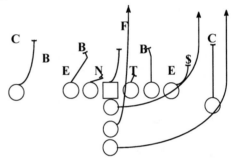

Diagram #1. Base Blocking Scheme

We want to run the ball with a one-back set so we can go either way with the deep back. This is our blocking scheme out of the one-back set (Diagram #2). The quarterback is reading the end on the play. That is his key. The tailback runs the arc, looking for the pitch.

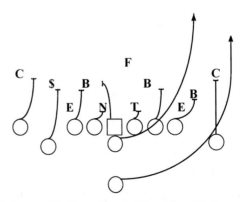

Diagram #2. One-Back Blocking Scheme

We do have an option pass off the dive play (Diagram #3). It is a play-action pass with the tight end running an outside release down the middle of the field. The wide receiver runs the takeoff route deep.

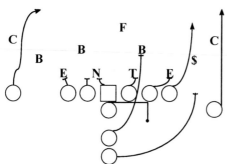

Diagram #3. 32 Dive Play-Action Pass

We can run the play to both sides and from different formations. We can release the tailback out into the flat to flood the zone. The quarterback must sell the run before he drops back and looks for the open receiver.

We can run the counter option play off the dive play. The quarterback turns away from the direction of the play and fakes the dive to the fullback (Diagram #4). We block the end man on the line on the counter option. If the quarterback has his back to the end, we want to protect him on the counter moves. The tailback takes a good counter step to the opposite side the play is going. The ride to the fullback should hold the linebackers. The quarterback counters after the fake to the tailback and runs the option to the backside with the tailback as the pitchman.

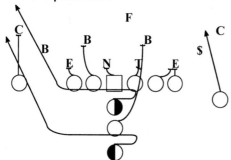

Diagram #4. Counter Option

What happened a lot on this play is the quarterback ends up keeping the ball up inside. If the defensive end goes outside, he can cut up off the tackle and pick up some yardage.

We can come back with the option reverse play off the dive play. The play starts out as the dive option (Diagram #5). We fake the fullback inside, and come out on the option. The quarterback comes off the line and pitches the ball to the slotback coming the opposite way. It takes timing to make the play work. We have to work on the pitch and making good fakes on the play.

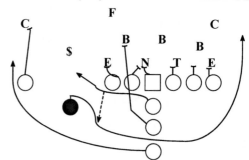

Diagram #5. Option Reverse

We can pull the guard and have him lead us on the option. We tell our tailback to get into a 5x1 alignment instead of his normal 4x1 alignment. The reverse man comes inside at four yards. He wants to catch the pitch on stride and gets around the edge.

We like to run the reverse out of a slot formation. Another thing that will help is to tighten the flanker down inside. If he is too wide, the play develops too slowly. We normally line up on the numbers, but he can cheat inside on this play. We try to get the pitch to happen in the defensive end area, where the slot is going back the other way on the reverse. We do not want him outside wide because the pitch comes to him to slow.

Against a Bear front Defense, we want to run toward the weakside. We want to attack the D gap because the man covering that gap is the free safety. The D gap is the area we attack against that defense.

We do have other plays that we run that are not a part of our option package. We do run a trap off the option, and we have other plays off the option. I have given you a few of the plays we use on our base option scheme. I hope you can take something from this lecture.

I appreciate your attention, and thank you for coming to hear this lecture.

HOW TO REDUCE THIRD DOWN CONVERSIONS

Woodruff High School, South Carolina

I want to thank Nike for inviting me to speak here. I am going to be talking on secondary play and how to reduce third-down conversions. I am an offensive-minded coach, but you must know how to coach defense as well.

First, I want to talk briefly about our coaching philosophy at Woodruff High School. To understand why and how we do things to make our secondary better, it will help if you know how we go about coaching in general. When we meet as a staff just before the season starts, we talk about our coaching philosophy. We are responsible for the product we put on the field. In that first meeting, I stress these points:

- We (the coaches) are accountable.
- We must have a great attitude.
- We are indivisible as a staff.
- We are great innovators and teachers.
- We have excellent player/coach relationships.
- We want to be the best in all we do.
- We want our players to be good citizens/students.
- We will coach our athletes to work harder and play harder than our opponents.
- We will be ethical in all we do to be the best.
- Our team will be prepared every game we play.

When we are in coaching meetings, we do not complain about our lack of talent. We have to play with what we have. I talk with the staff about having a positive attitude. What the coaches bring to the practice field is what the kids are going to mimic. If you are having an off day and you take that to the practice field, your kids are going to have an off day. If you are excited at practice, it will make the young kids excited, and they know how to make us old guys get excited.

In our staff meeting, we may talk about the problems of the world. We talk about the problems we have with our players and the problems the players may have. We may disagree on some of these situations. However, when we go on the field, we have no conflict in front of the players. I want the players to see us as a staff. I want them to see us together—eating together and doing things together as a staff.

We try to create an atmosphere that will allow us to have good relationships with our players. It does not matter what area of the country you coach, you are going to have players that have aspects of their lives missing. I talk to our staff about being that missing link—that father image the players may not have. The coaches have to build relationships with the players.

We want our staff and players to know we want the best in all that we do. We want the best cheerleaders, band, equipment, uniforms, and stadium. We focus on being the best in all that we do.

My job as the head coach is to get the team ready to play in every game. That is what I do as the head coach. That is the foundation of our program.

DEFENSIVE PHILOSOPHY

I want to move on to our defensive philosophy. This is what we believe in as a staff on defense. I love the 3-3-5 concept. However, we do not always have the athletes to play that defense. We have to adjust our defense so much because the league we play in is so diverse. One week we may play a spread team, and the next week we have to play a power I formation team. We know we cannot run a 3-3 defense against that offense. They will find the bubbles in the defense, and they will beat you to death.

We have to be multiple in our defense, and we must be able to adjust on the fly out of the defense. To accomplish that ability to adjust, this is how we think on defense.

• Determine the abilities of our defense (defensive line, linebackers, and defensive backs). Get our 11 best athletes on the field.
• Do the little things right—maximize our repetitions.
• Limit our blitz package.
• Categorize coverages into run/pass coverages and blitzes into run/pass blitzes.
• Simplicity, execution, consistency, and discipline are vital to the success of our defense (2009 third-down conversion: 33 of 137 = 24 percent)

I will ask the assistant coaches to list the best 15 players on the team, regardless of their position. I try to get our 11 best athletes on the field on defense. We do not put them on offense first. We try to get our offensive staff to understand this philosophy.

We want to maximize our reps. We do not stand around a lot talking in practice. I do not want a lot of talking on the field when we are practicing. All of the talking needs to be done in pre-practice. When we are on the field, we run the plays and coach on the fly. We tell the player what he did wrong on a play. I tell the staff we are not passive coaches. I want the players coached. If you are a passive coach, I will help the assistant coach, but I want them coached. We do not have any problems in this area, as our coaches do a good job of coaching the players on the little things.

The 3-3 defense is a good defense to run a lot blitzes and stunts. However, what I have learned is this. If we limit our blitzes, our kids play faster. In the last two years, we have won 22 games and lost four games. Limiting our blitzes and making sure our kids know what to do on defense has helped tremendously.

We have categorized our coverages into run/pass coverages and our blitzes into run/pass blitzes. If we are going to blitz to try to control the run, we may assign the Sam or Will backers to the running back. If the defense pulls a guard, they are in the hole now as quickly as possible keying that running back. We try to mix things up between our blitzes and our coverages.

Last year, on third-down conversions, we were right at 24 percent. We want simplicity and execution on defense. Our offense averaged 25.0 points per game. The consistency of our defense helped our offense because we got them the ball more in a game.

One thing that helped our defense and made us more consistent is the fact that we think outside the box. This may not seem simple to you—it may sound crazy, but we did it and it worked for us, and I have said this before.

First, we actually named the third down. We gave the third down a special name—we call it our "money down." We did not allow anyone to mess with the money down. This let the kids know this is the time to give their best if they want to win the game.

• Think outside of the box.
• Give third down a name—money down.
• During home games, our announcer plays the same theme song right before every third down.
• Brainwash players to think third down stops are turnovers.
• Practice situations—don't just run plays.

Our announcer is a former DJ. He plays the theme song just before each third down. It is a verse with church bells in it and then it is Young Jeezy singing, *I Put on for My City*.

This actually helps me during the games. I am working on offense when the defense is on the field. If I am talking to the offensive line and I hear those bells ringing, I realize it is third down so I need to focus on the defense again. I know it is third down. I know this helps us on defense. The crowd gets into the game. The kids hear the bells and they start shouting out, "It is third down. What is the distance?" They know when they hear, *I Put on for My City*, it is third-down time and it is money down.

One thing about coaching is that kids are easy to brainwash. What we want to do is to get the kids to believe what is important. I always tell them not to believe what they hear and read in a newspaper. It does not matter if it is good or bad. We talk about this all of the time. What we want to brainwash the kids into believing is that third down is the same as a turnover.

We also award the players for third-down stops. Our reward system is based on stopping the opponents three out of four times on third down. That means we are striving to hold the offense to less than 25 percent success on third down.

We always practice situations. We do not run plays just for the sake of running plays. Have plays with a purpose. We want to visualize the game situation as much as possible on the practice field. We want to create pressure in game-type situations in practice.

The types of game situations we work on in practice include the following:
• Normal first and 10: Runs, play-action, and bootlegs
• Third and long (seven or more yards): Drop-back passes and screen passes
• Second and long (eight or more yards): Drop-back passes and draw plays
• Third and short: Runs and some passes mixed
• Red zone: Runs and passes
• Two minutes: Passes, draws, and screen plays

There are some points I look at when I am evaluating a defensive back. We all know that some players may look good in uniform, but they do not meet the criteria when it comes to game-time football. As coaches, we must put them under pressure in game-type situations to find out how they react under pressure. Still, there are some special indications that will help in selecting defensive backs.

Evaluating a Defensive Back

• Football intelligence
• Mental and physical toughness (Put them in no-win situations; follow drill)
• Quickness
• Speed
• Strong work ethic

We try to teach some of the fundamentals in drills that are basic but important.

• Design drills that focus on specifics, for example, stance. We cannot teach stance, start, backpedal, and sprint all in one drill.
• Break down the position in individual parts, then put it all together.
• Technique training begins with stance: Weight on his front foot, his foot ahead of his nose, shoulders ahead leaning toward front foot.
• Start by pushing off front foot, stepping back with his back foot; allow shoulders to come up naturally and arms to move normally.

Once the players have mastered the fundamentals, we put them into drills that are more involved.

• Backpedal: All defensive backs must master this to have success.
• Defensive back pushes with front foot and steps/reaches backward with back foot, keeping his shoulders in front of his hips.
• Don't be in a hurry to raise your shoulders.
• Fault step: Back foot comes forward on your first step (you will lose two steps in coverage and have to come out of your backpedal much sooner).
• While running backward the DB should not push with his feet but should reach back with each step and pull his body over his feet, as if he were running forward.
• He must keep a slight forward lean with shoulders and keep arms moving normal.

I want to mention a few drills we use. Some of you may want to use these drills and some of you may not. We call this one the M drill (Diagram #1). We like drills where we can get a lot of players involved. I do not like kids standing around during drills in practice. We are working on the stance and the backpedal. We line up on the sideline and on the coach's ball movement, the players backpedal. On the second movement of the ball by the coach, the players break it off and come back toward the direction the ballcarrier is going.

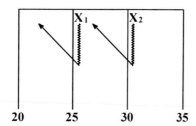

Diagram #1. The M Drill

Another drill we use is our three-cones drill (Diagram #2). You can make it a one-cone, two-cone, or three-cone drill. It is a start, stop, and start again reaction drill.

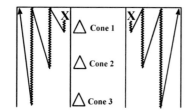

Diagram #2. Three-Cones Drill

This next drill we use to work against corner routes, our out route, or the hitch route. When they reach the third cone, they know they are going to roll their hips and break to stop the corner route. You can do different drills once you have the kids understand what you are doing on the cone drill.

The next drill we teach is a shuffle, backpedal, and speed drill (Diagram #3). We have a four-cone box set up. The defender lines up with his back to the first cone and shuffles to the next cone. Then, he backpedals to the third cone. He turns and sprints to the fourth cone. Now, he turns and backpedals to the first cone. From there, he goes diagonally into the box looking for the ball. He tries to make the interception and sprints through and out of the box.

This is a combination of all the techniques taught on the backpedal and the intercept drills. This is putting everything into one drill. You can do the drill half speed, and after they are comfortable in the drill, you can run it full speed.

Let's talk about our man-to-man defense. We are a 2A school with about 900 kids. We do not have

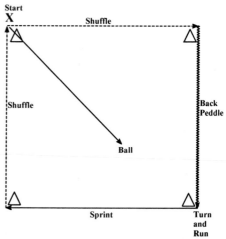

Diagram #3. Shuffle, Backpedal, and Speed Drill

a lot of athletes, but we go into some games where we feel our athletes are better than your athletes are. We are going to play man coverage against you. The thing I try to get our players to understand is to know our priorities when we are in man-to-man coverage. Psychologically, they must know and accept these priorities:

- Force an incompletion (top priority).
- Never miss a tackle in space.
- Remember that third-down completions that don't gain a first down are victories.
- Eliminate the long touchdown pass.
- Go for the ball whenever possible.
- Defensive backs must be able to recognize patterns and know the breaking point and interception point.
- He must understand the importance of the cushion.
- He must also know when his teammates are in position to help him and where the help will come from.
- The defensive back must master the elements of a good backpedal: stance, start, sprint, change of direction, and roll to run.
- Then, he must know the basic patterns that receivers and running backs can run.

Outside Receiver Routes

- Quick out
- Hitch
- Slant
- Deep out

- Cadillac (cross)
- Comeback
- Hook
- Curl
- Post
- Go

We have found we can have our offensive people make a video of these routes. Then, we can get the defensive backs together and show them the film of these routes so they can understand where the receiver is going to break on each route. You can quiz them on the breaking point for each route. You can play the video back and forth, pause it, or show them any phase of each route. It is a great teaching aid. Men are visual learners. We learn by seeing the different routes. As coaches, we want to make it visual so the players can see what we are trying to teach them.

Slot Receiver Routes

- Quick out
- Hitch
- Slant
- Deep out
- Cadillac (cross)
- Comeback
- Hook
- Curl
- Post
- Go

Offensive Back Routes

- Quick out
- Hitch
- Slant
- Deep out
- Cadillac (cross)
- Comeback
- Hook
- Curl
- Post
- Go

We work on recognition and the intercept point. A defensive back's knowledge of these basic patterns and his ability to recognize them quickly are essential to your secondary's success. Get them some videos so they can see these routes on film. There is nothing like a visual image that they can actually see.

Another important point is the interception point. The interception point is usually six yards in front of the receiver when the defensive back recognizes the pattern (Diagram #4). Here is the interception point for the slant route.

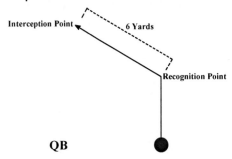

Diagram #4. Slant Route

For the out route, it is the same thing. It is six yards in front of the receiver when the defensive back recognizes the pattern (Diagram #5).

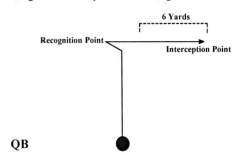

Diagram #5. Out Route

The same is true with the post route (Diagram #6). The defensive back who cannot recognize the

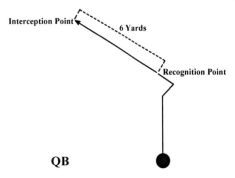

Diagram #6. Post Route

interception point will always be a follower on patterns that he should be able to cover.

In a zone defense, the ball will take the defender to the receiver. In the man defense, it is just the opposite—the receiver is going to take you to the ball. If you are in man-to-man, you follow the ball because that is where the ball is coming. These are points we try to get our pass defenders to understand.

We do a drill we call the redirect drill (Diagram #7). We try to watch the shoulders on the drill. It is a drill where we want the same arm and same shoulder to redirect the receiver's route.

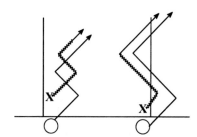

Diagram #7. Redirect Drill

We do a backpedal-and-leverage drill (Diagram #8). This drill is more of a press man-to-man type coverage drill. You are backing up but you are keeping leverage on the receiver.

The next drill is a pass breakup drill (Diagram #9). You can do the drill without anyone to receive the ball. It is a drill that goes quickly, and you need

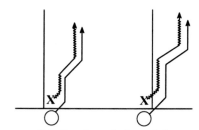

Diagram #8. Backpedal-and-Leverage Drill

someone to retrieve the balls for the coach. The coach is going to toss the ball underhanded toward the receiver on the command, "Ball." The defender comes up to knock the pass down or intercept the ball. It is a low toss by the coach, so the defender must plant the back foot and come back up on the ball and knock it down.

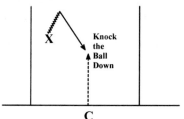

Diagram #9. Pass Breakup Drill

We must remember the incompletion is our main goal on this drill. We start backward, and then come up on the ball call, and try to get our hands on the ball.

This is all of the time I have. If you have questions, let me hear from you. Thank you.

THE SPREAD OFFENSE FROM DAY ONE

Saguaro High School, Arizona

Our offense is called the west gun. I have some experience with the spread option. When I was at Cal Berkeley, Al Borges was the offensive coordinator. We also run some single-wing football with the quarterback in the shotgun formation. If you mix all those things together, that is what our offense is.

If we have a tight end, we use some more of the West Coast scheme. We had a Division I tight end two years ago, and we ran the West Coast offense. If we have no tight end, we get more into the spread option. I have been there three years. The first year I was there, we had the perfect quarterback to run the spread option. He threw for 2000 yards and rushed for 2000 yards. That year, he was the "Gatorade Player of the Year."

The second year I was there, our quarterback was a 6'5" "look like Tarzan, play like Jane" type of player. We had to hide him a little more. In 2008, we had a tailback who gained 2000 yards. He is now at the University of Utah. We are a running team. Because we run the ball so well, it allows us to do some other things well.

When I do a lecture, I like to start with what I hope to achieve today. I want to expose you to an efficient offense system. It is by no means the best. It is not for everyone, but we have found it to be efficient. We have had several types of players be successful in the system.

Let's Begin From the End

- Exposure to an efficient offensive system.
- Plant ideas that you could use in your current system

- Mastery of the fundamentals and creativity can co-exist.
- Have a clear plan for the practice and communication.
- Answers to common hurdles of a no-huddle offense

In our terminology, we have two things that denote what we do:

- Chunking: Refers to a strategy for making more efficient use of short-term memory by recoding information (states = run schemes).
- Word association: The connection and production of other words in response to a given word (Houston starts with letter "H," which means all-hitch).

Chunking and word association are psychology terms. I was a psychology major, and I use those words to make people think I am smart. In our offense, if the player hears a state, that is a run scheme for us. That is an example of the chunking part. Houston is part word association. Houston is not a state, so it is not a run. It is a city, and that falls within the passing-game concepts. The city routes are designed to beat a one-high safety in the middle of the field.

We have a play pool we use every year. Some coaches may refer to it as a play menu. We use the plays in the play pool that are good for our personnel. We have the same problems that everyone else has. We have the same players for four years, and then they are gone. You have to continue to tinker with the offense to fit the personnel you have.

That was the inspiration behind the no-huddle offense we run.

PERSONNEL GROUPS

Animals/Birds

- 10, 20: Bird (Eagle, Falcon)
- 11, 12: Four-legged animal (Bear, Stallion)
- Panther: Non-quarterback taking snap

A 10 personnel grouping is no tight ends and one back with three wide receivers. The 20 personnel group is no tight ends, two backs, and three receivers. If there is a personnel set that does not have a tight end, it is a "bird" call. That is a way we get the right players on the field. If we call "Falcon" or "Eagle," that is the personnel group with no tight end. It can be any bird. If you are playing with a formation that has a tight end, they are given four-legged animal names. The Panther for us is the formation with someone other than the quarterback taking the snap.

FORMATION BASICS

- Royalty formations: 2x2
- "TR" formations: 3x1
- Number-tagged formation: Empty

Examples

- Kings, queens, jacks, jokers, jester
- Trips, trax, treo, trigger
- 5 trips, 2 kings, 7 Joker

If we are in the middle of the field, we are a 2x2 team. We refer to those sets as the royalty formations. Royalty is kings, queens, jacks, jokers, and jester. Those are the 2x2 sets. To change the formation, we adjust the splits of the inside receivers, or we invert them and bring players to the inside.

A formation that starts with "TR" is a 3x1 formation. If we are on the hash marks, chances are you will see a 3x1 formation. Words we use in these formations are trips, trax, treo, and trigger.

We do not add formations at all. If we want to go to an empty set, we do it with numbers (Diagram #1). We have alignment spots in the formations. If we tag a number to the formation, we want that

player to start in the backfield with the quarterback and motion out to that spot. It does not matter if it is a running back or wide receiver. He starts in the backfield and motions to the designated spot.

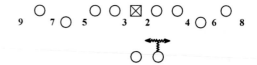

Diagram #1. Empty Alignment Spots

The even numbers are to the right and the odd numbers are to the left. The spots are the same on both sides. The #2 is an up back position behind the right guard. He does not motion to that position; he aligns there. The #4 is a wing set outside the tackle. The #6 is midway between the slot receiver and the split end. The #8 spot is outside the split end. The numbers 3, 5, 7, and 9 correspond to those spots going to the left. In a kings set, if we add the number 7 in front of the kings, after the motion we are in trips set to the left. The motion back motions to the 7 spot between the split end and slot receiver.

NO-HUDDLE RUN BASICS

Blocking Schemes Have Their Own Category of Terms (States)

- Arizona: Inside zone
- Florida: Fold scheme
- Utah, UConn, UMass, UTEP: Counter schemes
- Ohio, Oregon: Outside zone
- Wyoming: Wrap scheme

Arizona is an inside-zone read play for us. The "zon" in Arizona is the key to the play (Diagram #2). I am not going to get into the X's and O's of the play. We call the plays 2/3 with 2 to the right and 3 to the left. We read the backside end on this play.

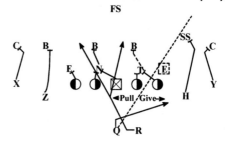

Diagram #2. Arizona

The Florida plays are our fold scheme (Diagram #3). Florida is a state, which designates a running play. It starts with an "F," which tell our players it is the fold-blocking scheme. We fold on the 1-technique defender. We will fold the center on certain defensive fronts. We always run the fold scheme against the 1-technique defender.

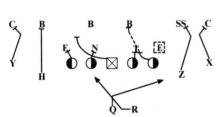

Diagram #3. Florida

If we ran 3-Florida and the nose was to the right of the center, the center blocks back on the 1 technique, and the guard pulls around for the frontside linebacker.

The linemen become keenly aware when they hear a call with the letter "U." Utah is a pulling scheme (Diagram #4). The U scheme is one of our favorite plays. If we are in a two-back set, the R-back goes first, and the H-back jab-steps and runs the ball. It is a power-O play for us. The play in Diagram #4 is 5-Utah. The companion play is 4-Utah.

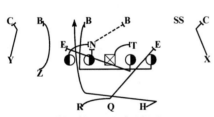

Diagram #4. Utah

The "O" lettered states stands for our outside zone plays. They are 8/9 hole plays. If we call "Ohio," that is a running play because it is a state (Diagram #5). It starts with the letter "O," which is the outside zone scheme. We have two outside zone schemes. One is Ohio and the other is Oregon. The difference between the two plays is a read on the tackle. If we run Oregon, we read the tackle. We do not block him. If he comes up the field, we hand the ball off. If he takes the back, we pull the ball. The play in Diagram #5 is Ohio.

Diagram #5. Ohio

We read the backside end on this play. If he comes down the line and tries to make a play on the running back, the quarterback pulls the ball and runs where the defender left. If the end comes up the field or stays on the line of scrimmage, we hand the ball off.

Wyoming is a tackle trap. It correlates with the wrap scheme that Urban Meyer runs at Florida (Diagram #6). That is how we get the players to understand it.

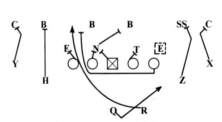

Diagram #6. Wyoming

This is a way we can become creative with a base set of offensive schemes. We add letter tags to the plays to alter the play somewhat.

Backfield Tags

- K tag: Keep after mesh
- Q tag: Straight quarterback run
- T tag: Makes the blocking scheme a triple option, and builds in appropriate motion
- S tag: Makes the play a speed option. Blocking scheme designates the pitch player.
- H tag: H Player is the ballcarrier.

If we add a "K" to the front of a play, that tells the quarterback to mesh with the running back and keep the ball. We never tell the running back where to go in the formation. He goes where it is appropriate for him to play. He knows if we run a K play, he aligns opposite, and we fake the ball to him.

A "Q" tag is a catch and run by the quarterback. There is no faking or anything else. He takes the shotgun-snap and runs with the ball. If the call is "Q8-Ohio," the running back knows he aligns to the side of the play and becomes a lead blocker on the play. If it were 8-Ohio, he aligns to the left of the quarterback and runs the ball to the 8 hole right.

The "T" tells the H-back to go in motion and become the pitch player on an option play. The H-back is the hybrid back. He is not quite good enough to be the R-back, but is on the field because he is the second running back. If we call "3T-Arizona," we run the inside zone scheme into the 3 hole (Diagram #7). The T tag tells the H-back, aligned in the left slot to come in motion behind the position of the quarterback. If the quarterback were to pull the ball, he becomes the pitchback on an option play to the right.

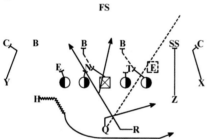

Diagram #7. 3T-Arizona

If we call "3K-Florida," that is the inside zone play in the 3 hole with fold blocking (Diagram #8). The R-back aligns opposite of where he would normally align. He knows the quarterback will keep the ball and run into the 3 hole. We fake the ball to the R-back running through the 2 hole. We hope the linebacker to that side will tackle him. If he does not, the R-back is assigned to block him. The quarterback fakes to the R-back, and he becomes the running back in the 3 hole.

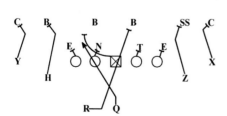

Diagram #8. 3K-Florida

If we call 5-Utah with an H tag, we tell the H-back he is the back carrying the ball (Diagram #9). The R-back knows he is not the ballcarrier and does what he generally does on the Utah play. He cuts off the backside of the play. The H-back at the snap of the ball adjusts himself, comes underneath the quarterback, and takes the ball. The offensive linemen do not care about the letter tags. They are blocking the play called. In this case, they block 5-Utah.

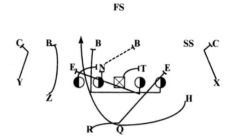

Diagram #9. 5H-Utah

If we call 8Q-Ohio, the quarterback catches the ball and runs the outside zone play to the 8 hole (Diagram #10). The R-back who normally carries the ball on this play sets to the right and becomes the blocking back on this play. This is a good play to have a running back or wide receiver at the quarterback position. If we want that to happen, we call "Panther." The line blocks the outside zone play.

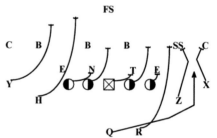

Diagram #10. 8Q-Ohio

If we tag K onto Wyoming, it becomes the same type of quarterback wrap that Florida runs (Diagram #11). The R-back runs the fake across the ball and tries to influence the backside end. We want to try to hold him because the tackle is pulling, and we do not want him in the play. If we call "5K-Wyoming," the quarterback fakes the ball to the R-back and follows the pulling tackle into the hole.

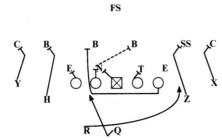

Diagram #11. 5K-Wyoming

We organize our passing game in a similar fashion as the running game. When we prepare for an opponent, I want to know the theme of their defense. The spread offense will force a defense to react some way. We feel if they are a one-high safety team, we want to run plays that beat the one-high safety. They will play cover 3 or cover 1. If the theme of their defense is two-high safeties, they will try to run that coverage. If they play man-to-man defense and load the box with defenders, that is what I want to know. If a team plays one-high safety and will change up with no high safety, you have to prepare for that.

If we play a team that plays one-high safety, we do not practice our two-high safety beaters in practice that week. We do not rep "car" routes that week. The players know the routes, but we do not rep them in practice. If the team totally changed their defense for us, we can always go back to the two-high beaters. The only drawback is we did not rep them in practice that week.

Organization of Passing Game

- One-high beaters: City routes
- Two-high beaters: Mascot routes
- Zero high beaters: Car routes
- Play-action pass: Act 2/3
- Pocket movement: Dash, boot, naked
- Running back screens: 60 slip
- Wide receiver bubbles: Alpha, Bravo, Charlie

Our two-high beaters are "mascots" routes. The zero-high beaters are "cars" routes. Men drive cars, and all our "car" routes have wheels associated with them. That is the last thing a linebacker playing over a slot receiver wants to see. He does not want to play a wheel route.

In our pass game, we have play-action passes. We have schemes to move the pocket. We have bootlegs, dash plays, sprint-outs, and naked. We have slow running back screens and wide receiver screens.

In our pass-protection scheme, we put the slide protection and play-action pass protection together. They are the same target for the linemen and running backs. The running back in the play-action has to fake and block the end man. In the slide protection, he does the same thing except he does not pass the quarterback in the slide-protection scheme. He is opposite his blocking assignment in the play-action pass. We can block big-on-big, and we can move the pocket and protect it.

As a receiver coach, I became frustrated because of the adjustments the receiver had to make in their routes in pre-snap or during the play. There were times we would run plays that were not good against one-high teams, but we were trying to force them in against them. That is when we went to the system we now use.

Our one-high beaters are Houston, Wichita, Chicago, and Omaha. These are the city routes. Houston is an all-hitch route. Wichita is hitch-seam routes. Chicago is curl-out routes, and Omaha is fade-out routes. All these patterns are mirrored routes to the frontside and backside of the pattern.

In the Houston scheme, the interior hitches are three yards deeper than the outside receivers are (Diagram #12). The quarterback is taught to read the buzz defenders and throw opposite of what he does. If he stays inside, we throw outside, and if he buzzes to the outside, we throw inside.

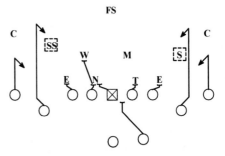

Diagram #12. Houston All-Hitch

In the 3x1 formation, the inside slot has a read key to take care of the blitz off the edge by the defender aligned on him. If the defender blitzes, the quarterback goes to the #3 receiver immediately. Everything else is the same.

The Wichita is a hitch-seam route. We started to work a bend into the seam route (Diagram #13). The reads are the same for the quarterback. He reads the buzz defender. If the defender goes outside, we throw inside. On the inside, we have started to teach the receiver to bend into the open area.

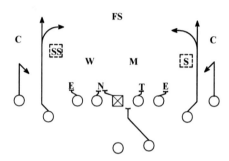

Diagram #13. Wichita Hitch-Seam

In the 3x1 route, the #3 receiver has to get to the opposite hash mark to get up the seam. We never want two seam routes next to one another. In addition, as he releases inside, he becomes a blitz beater as he goes across the field to the opposite hash. The two players up the seams put the one-high safety in a bind. The single receiver runs a hitch.

The Chicago pattern is a curl-out pattern. The "C" in Chicago means curl, and the "O" in Chicago means out (Diagram #14). The read is the same for the quarterback. The outside receiver run the curls, and the inside receivers run the outs.

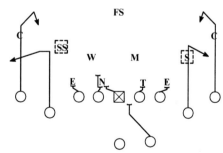

Diagram #14. Chicago Curl-Out

We have the same concept in a 3x1 formation. The #3 receiver has a read seam and is the hot

receiver on the blitz. The single receiver runs the curl route.

The Omaha call is a fade-out pattern (Diagram #15). The outside receiver runs the fade routes, and inside receiver runs the out routes. We want the quarterback to take the out if he can get the ball there.

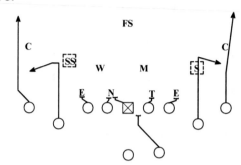

Diagram #15. Omaha Fade-Out

In the 3x1 formation, the outside receivers run the fade, the #2 receiver runs the out, and the #3 receiver to the trips side runs the seam-read pattern. We always want the quarterback to read the blitz coming off the edge. He faces that way and can see it coming. We protect his blind side.

The two-high beaters are "mascot" routes. As well as we run the ball, we have found the two-high teams cannot stay in that coverage too long. We rush the ball for 250 yards a game on a routine basic. We play teams that are worried more about stopping the run than they are about the pass.

The first two-high beater is Cowboy. That is the smash route concept from West Coast offense (Diagram #16). The outside receivers run a hitch route, and the inside receivers run a corner or a short corner.

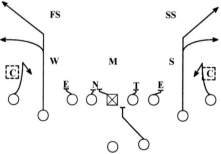

Diagram #16. Cowboy Smash

When we go to the empty set, this is our favorite play (Diagram #17). Our players call this play our touchdown route. We run the double smash routes on the outside, and the #3 receiver runs a vertical route up the middle of the football field. He is the hot receiver on a blitz off his edge.

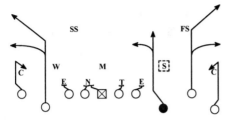

Diagram #17. Cowboy From Empty

We run a shallow cross concept, which I got from the University of Kentucky when Hal Mumme was there. We call it Spartan/Warrior (Diagram #18). The concept side runs a shallow cross and the deep dig pattern. The opposite patterns are two vertical patterns trying to get the safety out of the middle of the field. If we call "Spartan," the strongside has the concept. If we call "Warrior," the weakside has the concept.

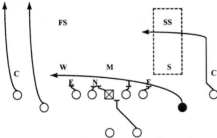

Diagram #18. Spartan/Warrior

We call quarter coverage a man concept. Man and quarters coverage are the same to us. We run "car" routes against them. These are man-beater routes. All the names and play concepts are named after cars. Corvette starts with a "C." The receivers in this pattern are running a curl and wheel route. Suzuki is a slant-wheel concept. Porsche starts with a "P." The patterns in that route are the post and wheel. If we tag the work "red" to any of the cars, we break off the route and run a wheel-stop pattern. If we add "turbo" to any of the routes, it doubles the outside routes and the wheel route run by the #3 receiver.

In the Corvette route, the outside receivers run the curl route (Diagram #19). The inside receivers run the wheel routes. This route presents some

problems for the defender covering the wheel and the free safety.

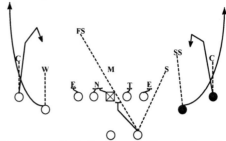

Diagram #19. Corvette Curl-Wheel

The Suzuki uses a slant route by the outside receivers and a wheel route by the inside receivers (Diagram #20). An adjustment we could use with this route is to start the slant inside and come back to the outside.

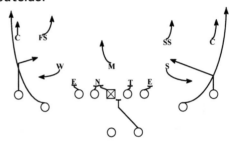

Diagram #20. Suzuki Slant-Wheel

I want to show you the Porsche from a trips formation (Diagram #21). Porsche is a post-wheel combination. The single receiver runs a post. The two outside receivers to the trips side run the post-wheel combination, and the #3 receiver in the trips set runs the read-seam down the middle of the field.

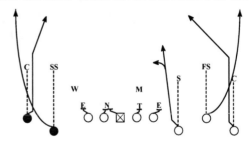

Diagram #21. Porsche Post-Wheel

If we tag the term "red" to any of the cars, we run a wheel-stop pattern (Diagram #22). The pattern is Ferrari, and we run it from the trips formation. The outside receivers run a fade route. The #2 receiver to the trips side runs a wheel-stop, and the #3 receiver runs the seam-read patter.

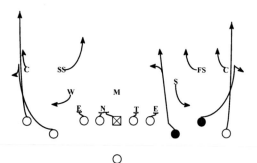

Diagram #22. Red Ferrari

The last one I want to show you is Suzuki with a "turbo" tag added (Diagram #23). This is from the trips set. On this pattern, the #1 and #2 receivers run the double slant to the inside. The backside single receiver runs a slant. The #3 receiver in the trips set runs the wheel route up the sidelines.

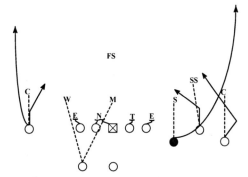

Diagram #23. Turbo Suzuki

Before I close, I want to cover quickly some of the things we do with quarterback communication. We work off a wristband. The cards for the wristband are color-coded so those like formations are grouped together by color. We divide the card into runs, pass, specials, and others divisions. We feel the colors keep the quarterback from making a big mistake by misreading the card. If he calls play 21 instead of play 22, it will be from the same personnel group and formation. It will be a good call, but not the one I wanted. However, if he reads a play from two different colors, it is a disaster. That is the reason for the colors. That does not happen very often. The coach and quarterback have the same card. That way, we are on the same page.

On the back of my sheet are situational call scripts, which we write out prior to the game. The things I have listed are opening plays from the middle and hash marks. I have plays for sudden change, goal line, beat the blitz, backed up, last six plays, final three plays, turtle, and wind-down plays. I have plays listed for all those situations. Turtle plays are when we want to slow the tempo of the game and run out the clock. Wind-down plays are the ones we use to center the ball in the field for a field-goal attempt. If I get those situations, I call the plays listed on the sheet.

The last thing I have listed on the sheet is when to go for a two-point conversion. If we are up by 1, 4, 5, 11, 12, 19, 22, or 25 points, we go for two. If we are down by 2, 5, 10, 16, 17, 18, 21, 25, 26, or 28, we go for two.

I am not saying the way we do things are the best way but it has been efficient for us. If you have any questions, we are going to the breakout room. Thank you for your attention.

IMPLEMENTING THE 3-4 DEFENSE

F. J. Reitz High School, Indiana

I want to thank the Nike Clinic for having us on the clinic today. First, I want to talk for a moment about our school. We are a member of the Southern Indiana Conference. Our enrollment is just under 1,500 students. We are in Class 4A in Indiana, which has five classes, with 5A the highest. We won the 4A State Championship in 2007 when John Hart was the head coach. Our record that year was 15-0. I was an assistant coach at Reitz from 2001 until the 2008 season, when I took over for John Hart, who moved on to Warren Central High School in Indianapolis.

We had a great year in 2009 by winning the 4A State Championship again, with a record of 15-0. A big reason we were undefeated and state champs was the play of our defense.

Our defense was a big factor in our success. We played 15 games and our defense did an outstanding job in all of the games. We ran a lot of stunts from our 3-4 base defensive fronts. We did a lot of angling when the ball was snapped. Here is how we stacked up stat-wise with our defense:

Team Statistics Defense (15 Games)

- Total points: 130
- Points per game: 8.7
- Rushing yards per game: 101
- Passing yards per game: 100
- Forced turnovers: 41

Today, we want to share some of the things we do on defense. I hope you will be able to pick up one or two points that may help you in your program. I am going to ask our defensive coordinator, Coach Tolly McClatchy, to talk about the X's and O's with you.

COACH TOLLY MCCLATCHY

Thanks Tony. First, I am going to talk about defensive implementation. We play a toolbox system at our school. Anytime you have a carpenter, he has to have a toolbox to get things done. He does not need everything in the toolbox every day. However, he does not leave the toolbox at home. He brings all of his tools every day, so he can handle any situation. In football, you better have a couple of other tools in your toolbox. If you like to run a certain scheme, and you are not having any success with it in a ballgame, you need to have some other things ready you can use.

One of the tools we use is a defensive numbering system. We want to be able to communicate to our kids where to line up, and where to go when they snap the ball. You need to be able to communicate that. It cannot be some big long verbal sentence. It has to be quick, to the point, and meaningful.

I read a book by Bear Bryant back when I first started coaching in 1971. In that book, he used a defensive numbering system. My head coach at the time actually used that same numbering system. He only used the even numbers, and did not use the odd numbers. We only worked on the defense for three days before the first game. It was all offense with him. That is how he coached defense in those days. We did not do a lot on defense. We just lined up and played hard-nose football.

We use the defensive numbering system. We have fronts that we start in, and we angle when the ball is snapped. We were not very big on defense this year. We had one defensive end that weighed 212 pounds. Our noseman weighed 193 pounds, and the other end weighed 196 pounds. They could run, but they were not very big.

We have to be able to indicate the way we are going to stunt. We have fronts that we start in and we angle when they snap the ball. We have to be able to communicate how we are going to line up and how we are going to be able to stunt. Sometimes, we will stunt from the huddle call, or we may have communicated something before the game that we will use a certain defense if they come out in a certain formation. We will stunt in a certain way with the defense we have called.

We are a four spoke secondary. We are in two high safeties. What we play is mainly quarter coverage. However, we will have different guys that will come off the edge that have the run support. They will be the primary force to that side.

The outside linebackers and safeties are the guys that make the adjustments. You need to be able to understand that. When I started coaching in 1971, on offense it was either a full house backfield or the wing-T. You do not have to make many adjustments to those formations because everyone is in so tight. However, today, if you are to be competitive, you have to be able to adjust, because they line up so many people outside the tackles.

This is how our numbering system works (Diagram #1). I am sure most of you are familiar with this system and I know many of you use something similar.

9 8i   7 6i   5 4i   3 2i   1 1   2i 3   4i 5   6i 7   8i 9
9 ⑧ 7 ⑥ 5 ④ 3 ② 1 ⊠ 1 ② 3 ④ 5 ⑥ 7 ⑧ 9

Diagram #1. Numbering System

The following technique chart is what we use. This enables us to communicate with our players, so they know what we are talking about when are working with them.

Position	Head-up	Outside shoulder	Inside shoulder
Center	0	1	
1st man past center	2	3	2i
2nd man past center	4	5	4i
3rd man past center	6	7	6i
4th man past center	8	9	8i

- The front 7 use the defensive numbering system in Diagram #1 to properly align, angle, slant, and stunt versus an offensive formation.
- Offensive players are numbered 0, 2, 4, 6, 8 from the center out.
- Offensive gaps are numbered 1, 3, 5, 7, 9 from the center out.
- Outside shoulder alignments are numbered 1, 3, 5, 7, 9 from the center out.
- Inside shoulder alignments are numbered 2i, 4i, 6i, 8i from the guard out.

First, we number the offensive players using even numbers. We number the center 0. The first man past the center is 2. The second man past the center is 4, etc. In addition, we talk about helmets, rather than using the terms "guard" or "tackle." We say, "Line up on the first helmet outside the center." That is how we line up. We do not talk about getting on the guard or getting on the tackle.

The next thing we do is number the gaps. The gaps are the odd numbers. We use 1-3-5-7-9. That tells us where we are going to angle toward. The outside shoulder alignments are odd numbers. We use that a lot on the scout team. We tell a kid to get into the 3-technique when we are in practice and he knows where I want him to line up. If I say, "Get in the 3-gap," he knows where to line up. When I call a 31-defense, they know exactly where to line up. We have a 3-technique and a 1-technique.

The inside shoulder alignments are simple. We just add an "i" to the number we want them to align on. We would say 2i, 4i, from the guard to the outside.

We have multiple 3-4 base fronts. Our base defense is our odd call (Diagram #2). We call it in the huddle by simply saying, "Odd." When we get to the line of scrimmage, our middle linebacker gives a right or left call, and that tells us the direction we are going to angle. We tell them which way to slant at the snap, either right or left. We want to get off on the snap and get through the gap. Most of the time, we are not trying to get a hand on anyone, but rather, we are trying to get penetration into the backfield and cause a disruption. We want to penetrate first and then try to read and react.

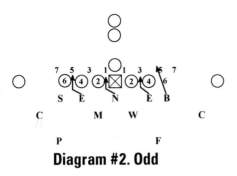

Diagram #2. Odd

We put in a special defense for the Trips Formation. We call it Bozo Odd (Diagram #3). If the offense does not come out in trips, we are going to stay in our odd alignment. Our linebacker will make the call "trips," and put the Bozo to the strength of the formation, then we angle away from the trips set. This gives us a defender coming off the edge.

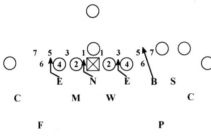

Diagram #3. Bozo Odd

Again, this is something we put in for the trips formation. If it is not trips, then we will stay in odd. However, if we do get trips, we have to adjust.

We start both defenses in a 4-0-4 front with our two ends and noseman. That means we have a man on both of the second helmets outside the center and a man head-up on the center. A nice thing about our 3-4 defense is that we do not have a lot of people moving around before the snap. When we played the 4-3 defense, it was like a fire drill with our guys trying to adjust to the formations.

The next stunt is part of an old 3-3 stack defense. In an odd stack, we angle back away from the tight end, so we have a guy on each side (Diagram #4). When you do that, you wind up in a 4-3 alignment. However, we just start it from an odd front look.

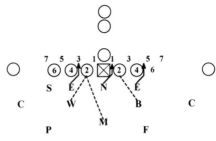

Diagram #4. Odd Stack

On the even stack, we slide away from the tight end (Diagram #5). The linebackers make the call and we angle back away from the call. If the linebacker calls "left," we move over to a 6-2-2 alignment, and angle back to the right.

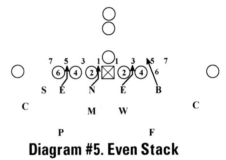

Diagram #5. Even Stack

We did use a gap stack on occasion this year (Diagram #6). We used this against double tight end teams and teams that took big splits with their line. We got into the gaps to force the offense to tighten their splits up. Our line started in a 4-1-3 alignment up front. We angled to the gap according to the directional call by the Mike backer.

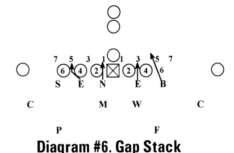

Diagram #6. Gap Stack

In an Eagle look, we just bring one side down to a 2-technique, so we have a 4-0-2 (Diagram #7). The linebacker will make a call to tell them which way to slant.

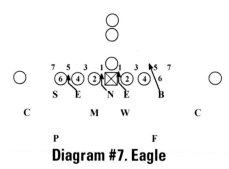

Diagram #7. Eagle

In a double Eagle, we start in a 2-0-2 (Diagram #8). Again, our Mike linebacker will make the call, left or right.

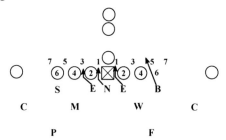

Diagram #8. Double Eagle

Our goal line defense is called "pride" (Diagram #9). It is no more than the double-Eagle stunt. This is what we call it when we get down on the goal line. We tell them it is time to button down the hatches. We work eight minutes every day on our goal line defense.

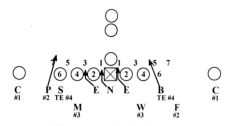

Diagram #9. Pride

Coaching points:
- AZ: tells the defenders that we are playing all zone.
- The corners are AZ on #1.
- The safeties are AZ on #2; versus a quad set, the safety comes over and is AZ on #4.
- The inside linebackers are AZ on #3.
- The outside linebackers are man on a tight end or AZ on #4 versus a no-tight-end set.
- The tight ends are not counted as #1, #2, #3, or #4.

- Versus a tight end set, the defender is responsible for the running back.
- The Will runs blitz off the edge.

Our goal line defense paid off for us in the state championship game, where we made a big goal line stand. I bet we worked more on goal line defense this year than in any other year I have coached. It really paid off for us and it is something we are going to continue to work hard on. I think you get distracted with those other things, but do not forget about how important this can be.

A two-digit number may be added to a defensive call to adjust where the defensive linemen go at the snap. The first digit tells the strong defensive end where to go and the second digit tells the weak defensive end and noseman where to go. Odd 52 (Diagram #10) is an example.

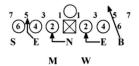

Diagram #10. Odd 52

The weakside end is going to a 2-technique. The strong end goes to a 5-technique, and the nose goes to a 2-technique. It is a fact, the total numbers of the backside end and nose will be 4. If both of the called numbers are the same, for example odd 33, then the nose goes to zero.

You may ask why we have all of these different stunts and calls. I think it is like a socket wrench. A big socket will fit over everything, but a little socket will not always get the job done. We want to have a socket that will fit every situation we come across.

We draw up our stunts using a color system. Each backer gets a color. The Mike backer is red; he is the strong linebacker. The Will backer is blue; he is the weak linebacker. The bandit or weak outside backer is yellow. Black is the strong, or Sam, linebacker.

If we want to send more than one linebacker, we can do it one of two ways. We can just combine the colors or just say both colors. Alternatively, you may designate another color, such as brown, that may be sending three linebackers on a blitz. One color can send multiple people. You could use green, which would send your Will backer and the bandit on the weak side. The kids pick this up quickly.

We use our guts stunt when we want to cross two linebackers (Diagram #11). We can cross a lot of different combinations. You can use the colors to identify the players involved. For example, we can call "purple guts strong," which is a cross stunt between the red linebacker and the blue linebacker with the nose angling weak to the 2-technique.

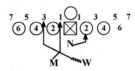

Diagram #11. Purple Guts Strong

We can call "green guts weak," which is a cross stunt between the blue linebacker and the yellow linebacker. The nose angles strong to a 1-technique.

We also use some numbers in our defensive system (Diagram #12). If we call a loop stunt, it means the outside man will go first. We also call a number for this reason. When we call "strong" or "weak," it also tells the noseman to go the opposite way. For example, if we call a "7 stunt," the outside backer is coming down hard through the 5-gap off the tail of the tackle, and the end is looping outside.

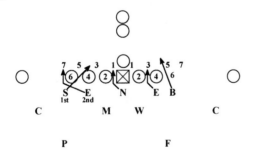

Diagram #12. Odd 73

We use this stunt against teams that run the outside veer. I can remember when a lot of teams ran the play and we were effective using this call.

The defenders involved in this call need to communicate on what is going on with the call. It takes a lot of communication between the end and outside linebacker. As the season progressed, we added some other numbers to the toolbox. We wanted to make sure we had our basics installed first. However, we did add to the system as we progressed on defense. We did use the 8 stunt a few times this year, but we did not run the 9 stunt. It is in the toolbox if we need it. We end up in a zone blitz with the numbers. We tell our defenders not to give up any yardage after the catch by the receivers. We are not telling them to get to the receiver and knock the ball down. We are just telling them to get to the receiver.

As I said earlier, we use a four spoke secondary. It starts out as a nine-man front. We do not know which way we will have to adjust. On passing plays, it ends up being a seven-man front with 4 deep. On running plays, it ends up as an eight-man front with 3 deep. The defense is designed to outflank the offense and be strong in the off-tackle hole.

When I was at Murray State University my senior year, I took a football class. Our offensive coordinator taught the class. I remember Coach Carl Oakley saying, "The team that wins the off-tackle hole, is the team that is going to win the football game." I still believe that statement is true. It does not matter whether it is on offense or defense. I still believe that holds true today. That is the reason the 3-4 puts a body in the off-tackle hole, while the 4-3 has a Sam backer on a bubble in the off-tackle hole.

We are a quarter's team. All our defensive backs are keying the quarterback. We do not key the receiver off the line of scrimmage. You say, "Why not coach?" My answer is this: Have you ever played an option football team? The tight end is the man our defensive back is reading. The end is going to arc release to block the force player on an option play every time. Tell me how is our defensive back going to figure out if the tight end is arc releasing to block, or if he is arc releasing to go out for a pass? You cannot read this. That is the reason we read the ball. If we get a pass read, we are going to go to quarter's coverage and then we will match up with the receivers.

Let me list the 4-spoke secondary coverages. We can play the different defenses with the coverages to match up with the formations we face.

- Cover 2 = 4 deep 1/4 coverage
- Cover 3 = 3 deep 1/3 coverage
- Cover 4 = 4 deep 1/4 coverage
- Cover 5 = 3 deep 1/4, 1/4, 1/2 coverage
- Cover 6 = 3 deep 1/3 coverage
- Cover 7 = 3 deep 1/3 coverage

If it is a run in cover 4, we are going to be in sky run support (Diagram #13). This means the safety is in the run support. Our cover-4 allows us to have run support from the safety (sky) or the corner (cloud).

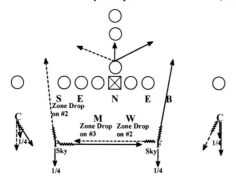

Diagram #13. Cover 4

If we run cover 2, it is still the same pass read. The only difference is we are simply dictating that we have cloud run support.

Our cover 3 means we are going to be in one-third deep with 4 men under versus the pass. If it is a running play, we have sky support to the strong side and cloud support to the weak side.

We have rules for adjustments. We have the following adjustment rules to cover teams that like to spread the field with multiple formations:

- Two men out rule coaching point: The outside linebacker aligns halfway out on the #2 receiver, and 3 to 5 yards off the #2 receiver (Diagram #14).
- Three men out rule coaching point: The outside linebacker aligns on the #3 receiver, 3 to 5 yards off the #3 receiver, and at the snap of the ball or just prior to the snap, he slides halfway out on the #2 receiver.

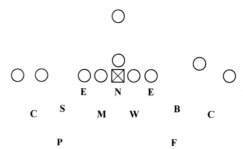

Diagram #14. Two Men Out Rule

- Four men out rule coaching point: When the offense aligns in a quads set, one outside linebacker aligns on the #3 receiver, 3 to 5 yards off the #3 receiver. At the snap of the ball or just prior to the snap, he slides halfway out on the #2 receiver. The other linebacker aligns on the #4 receiver 3 to 5 yards off #4, and at the snap or just prior to the snap, he slides halfway out on the #3 receiver.
- Inside rule coaching point: The outside linebacker's inside rule tells him when the coach makes an inside call, he does not move outside until outflanked by three offensive men.
- Polecat rule coaching points: Count backs as the #2 Receiver. We cover the receiver with our defenders in this order. We count from the outside to the inside (Diagram #15).
  - ✓ #1 – Corner
  - ✓ #2 – Safeties
  - ✓ #3 – Outside linebacker
  - ✓ #4 – Defensive end
  - ✓ #5 – Inside linebacker
  - ✓ #6 – Nose tackle

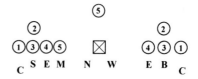

Diagram #15. Polecat Rule

We start working on this phase of the defense in our pre-game for our first game of the year. We always have it in our toolbox. We work on it every week. You may not need it every week, but I will guarantee you that you will see it sometime during the season.

This year in the playoffs, we went to the eastern part of Indiana to play a game. In the middle of the second quarter, the opponent started running the polecat offense from the middle of the field. Our kids did not react at first. They just looked to the sideline for help. They looked like a deer in the headlights. Finally, one of our defensive coaches yelled out, "polecat rule." Then, the players settled down because they all knew what to do because we had it in our toolbox. Terminology and being able to communicate paid off for us in that situation.

We have a two men out rule. If two guys outflank our outside backers, they are going to play halfway between the second helmet from the sideline and the third helmet from the sideline. The tighter that offensive guy aligns, the closer we are going to get to the line of scrimmage. We do not want the offensive guy to get under us. Our help is behind us not under us. We have to be aware of the drag routes.

We also have a three men out rule. If the offense outflanked our linebacker by three receivers, he splits the difference between the second helmet and the third helmet. However, he will start on the third helmet, and on the snap, he will slide outside. His rule is player #2. The backer has #3.

On our four men out rule, we have a bozo call. The backer comes over and we will slide over right before the snap.

We also have an inside rule. If you are playing a running team that tries to split you out and get another man out of the box, we just tell our players to stay inside, unless they get three men outside of them.

You may not need all of these rules each and every game. Terminology and being able to communicate is extremely important. Load up your toolbox with schemes that will allow you to handle different types of offenses.

I have enjoyed spending time with you today. Please do not hesitate to contact us if you have any questions. Thanks for coming to the Nike Coach of the Year Clinic.

DEVELOPING A DEFENSIVE GAME PLAN

Middletown High School, Maryland

It is quite an honor to be here. Middletown High School is a 2A school with an enrollment of about 1300 students. We were blessed to have had a good year. I would like to share some lessons I have learned about life and coaching. The first thing I have learned is that you are not your own and that it is not about "me."

Whether you are the head coach, an assistant coach, or simply the water boy, each of us is just a part of the overall system. Throughout my coaching career, every year I have learned that lesson better, and it has become more relevant to me as I get older.

The most important part of coaching to me however, is just helping people. Football gives us a wonderful opportunity to help people. For whatever reason I was put into the game, I firmly believe my major purpose is not to do the X's and O's. I try to learn as much as I can about the game, but the best thing I can do in football is to care about the people I work with.

Finally, I think that gratitude is a virtue, and we should be thankful when we are not doing well just as we should be thankful when things are going our way. We should all be thankful for the people who have made a difference in our lives. There are certainly many to whom I am grateful.

In preparing for this lecture, I came up with *seven steps* in the way we develop our defensive plans. Those seven steps will provide the topics for my presentation here.

The first thing is philosophy. I think you have to *begin with the end in mind.* Then, before laying down your own plans, *seek first to understand your opponent.* Learn as much as possible about the various offensive schemes you will face.

The next step is to *gather and organize information* relative to your own plans. After you gather the information, you need to *synergize.* Get with your staff, share information, get their input, and develop your game plan. Only then are you ready to *implement the plan*, and by that I mean in practice, in meetings, and on the field.

After the plan is implemented, you take it into the game on Friday night and *make game-time adjustments*. The final step then would be to *debrief the results* and make a "lessons learned" binder to use the following year.

Those are my seven steps. To give you a better idea of how each one provides a foundation for the next, I prepared a pyramid (Diagram #1). It provides a visual expression of the sequential nature of the steps. It makes it clear how defensive preparation starts with a philosophy at its foundation and works through a logical process that ends with results.

Diagram #1. Maturity Pyramid of Defensive Coordinator Success

Philosophy—Begin With the End In Mind

- Attacking, aggressive, together—We want to be known for this

- Play hard and fast—We coach this hard and get our kids to believe in our scheme

- Great tackling—The first fundamental of defense that we do each day
- Communication—We will call out all recognitions and adjustments before each snap
- Odd front (want to cover the center)—We believe in it, and it fits our kids
- Zone coverage—It is what we know and what we believe in
- Gap control/read keys—We emphasize techniques, reads, and advantage
- Less is better/keep it simple—Do a few things, do them well, build confidence
- Blitz only when necessary—We believe in the soundness of base defenses
- Winners adjust philosophy (improvise, adapt, overcome)—When conditions change, we will change

Seek First to Understand Your Opponent

- Know your opponent's offensive system/philosophy—Understand what is important to your opponent
- Study and learn all types of offenses—It is essential to stay current
- Prior game films/films from other years—Technology makes it easy to archive and select
- Read the papers/previews—Get additional information, get valuable insights

Gather and Organize Information

- Scout films (relevant films)—Start early in the week, gather data, appreciate style
- Digital scout/computer software—Turn play-by-play information into empirical data
- Formation tendency hit chart—Draw each formation, put hits and frequency in each hole
- Draw up and analyze all plays—Taken off of film, but drawn against our defense
- Down-and-distance chart—Develop this from computer printouts, key to situational plans
- Develop a gut feeling for what they are doing—Comes from time spent compiling data
- Internet/web pages/stats—Additional source of information on our opponents

Synergize (Create a Plan)

- Staff input—Get all points of view before decision making begins
- Scout films to all coaches—Every assistant breaks down every opponent
- Stress assistant coaches being proactive—Take initiative in making a contribution to the plan
- Let coaches break it down with their style—Get a clearer interpretation of data that way
- Phone conferences—Staff networking during film work at home
- Friday postgame/Sunday night meetings—Come together as a staff
- Look for tips to help: stance, signals, alignments, motion—Often overlooked valuable source of information
- Rough draft plan ready before meeting—Have a general idea to use as a starting point
- Draw up each formation and decide how to: front alignment, coverage, autos, etc.—Build the plan
- Motion: How to adjust versus each formation—Motion changes everything—Must be ready
- Be fundamentally sound with front, alignment, assignment, match-up evenly with numbers—(Don't be outflanked)—One entire session of practice devoted to formation adjustment

Implement the Plan

- Detailed practice plan—Putting the plan into place, organized by periods
- Watch film with team daily—25 minutes before each practice
- Instill belief in the plan with players—Has to come from the entire staff
- Simulate offense with key team—One assistant must take responsibility
- Practice situations: goal line, two minute, third and long, field position, etc.—Prepare for each play in the context of the game situation
- Debrief daily with staff and players—Get feedback from everyone involved
- Adjust plan when flaws are exposed—Initial plans are refined during the week

- Listen to player input—Sometimes more insightful than staff input
- Fundamentals: Tackling, pursuit, double whistle, etc.—Sharpening skills is always part of the plan

Make Game-Time Adjustments

- Watch pre-game warm-ups—Two assistants assigned to scout opponent pre-game
- Box coaches recognize formations and make sure we are lining up correctly
- Relay and adjust to new information/play—See what they have changed for us
- Have formations and alignments in your view on the sideline—Can make sideline notes
- Recognize and fix any weakness discovered (open routes, mismatches, unbalanced formations, etc.)—Game management and game adjustment is difference maker

Debrief the Results (Lessons Learned)

- Friday night postgame meeting—Grade the game film on hustle, performance, and technique
- Performance grades—Make available to players, gets them bought in
- Statistical review—An empirical measure of team productivity
- Performance in crunch time—Isolate and evaluate key situations
- Determine if issues were personnel or scheme related—Determine causes of breakdowns
- Vote on players' awards if earned: player of the week, hit of the week, black knight—A tradition that means something to players

- Team binder/file: Lessons learned, adjustments, notes, and all game planning materials used that week—Always complete this before starting preparations for the next game

Now, I want to discuss some samples of the charts, diagrams, and plans that we prepare and use throughout the week. However, I do not have time to go into details with them.

- Formation hit chart, showing every formation with plays run and tally marks for play frequency
- Plays drawn up through the eyes of the offense to be numbered and used by the scout team in practice
- A digital scout printout showing down-and-distance formation breakdown by percentage
- A digital scout printout showing passing zones attacked by percentage
- A copy of our actual defensive game plan by diagram, which is given to the players
- A copy of our practice plan, broken into five-minute periods, which are signaled by air horn

I want to finish by showing you some film on the demo system we have. It allows me to navigate through the film using a remote control and to get to plays I need to emphasize. I can show tendencies quicker, make meetings more efficient, and get the players out of meetings and on the field.

If you have any questions, I will be around for the rest of the clinic. Thank you.

DEFENSE WINS CHAMPIONSHIPS

Detroit Catholic Central High School, Michigan

It is a pleasure to be here. I had more fun coaching football this year than I can remember. I have had a good long career. This year, we had a real good group of young men to work with—they love the game of football and they love to play football. They came to practice every day ready to go. They showed a lot of enthusiasm and spirit. We really had a great group to work with this year.

Our staff did a great job this year. It was a magical year that I hope everyone in this room has an opportunity to experience at some time in their life as a coach.

I hope I can give you a few ideas about coaching. If I can suggest just one little thing that will make you a better coach, I will be happy. This is the attitude I always take going to a clinic. If I learn one or two things back and put them into our program it will be a big benefit to our program. We are going to talk about defense today. If we can help you with your defense, we would be glad to visit with you. Our staff will be around if you want to visit with them.

We do not have all of the answers. In fact, our fans in the stands tell me I do not know what the hell I am doing. Our offense is basic, but it is effective. Our defense has gone through some changes over the last few years. We go after it real hard on defense.

The best thing I can tell you as a coach is this: It really does not matter what you think is important, it is what the kids think are important. It is important to communicate the message we want our kids to receive.

I was a 5-2 defensive coach for 30 years. With the introduction of the spread offense, we found ourselves taking our defensive end and moving him outside. We had to adjust our defense to the spread

so much, we had a hard time covering in the secondary with our 5-2, 3 deep concept. Because we had to make so many adjustments, we decided to switch our defense to the 4-3 scheme. That is where we are now, and we have made the adjustments we needed to make.

Thank goodness Dan Anderson is on our staff. He has done a good job of converting us from the 5-2 to the 4-3 defense. We can still play the 5-2 if necessary.

We are going to talk about the 4-3 scheme that we have evolved to today. Our 4-3 defense may not be much different from the 4-3 defense you use today. It is the way we approach our defense that makes our defense different.

Before we get to the Xs and Os, I want to leave you with a couple of ideas. As I get older, I get a little more philosophical in my approach to football and to coaching. I understand that winning is important, however, it is not the most important thing. What we teach the kids is the most important thing in coaching. We have won the state championship before. Every year that we have won it, we had a banner year. What we want to do is to give those young men something they can think about for the rest of their life.

I think it is important for us to teach young men to believe in themselves. It is an important thing that a coach can do. We always coach in a positive vein. We want to help the young men to believe in themselves individually and as future successes. It is important for coaches to teach young men how to be successful. If you run a good program, and have discipline and a tough program, you are teaching the players lessons for life, and not just in football. It is important to win football games because we get kids' attention that way. At the same time, we feel it is important for them to learn how to be successful, and to believe in themselves as individuals. If we can teach them these two points, I think we are successful as coaches.

Players do well on the points that coaches do a good job of emphasizing in practice. If the players are not doing things the way we want them to do it, it may be because we did not emphasize those points enough with the players. In that case, it is not the fault of the players. It is the fault of the coach for not spending more time on the situation to start with.

Right now, we are in our morning workouts. I am retired from teaching, which is great for me. I can just concentrate on football. I am getting up at 4:30 AM because we meet at 6:29 in the morning. We go from 6:29 AM to 7:29 AM for four days a week. Next week, we will only have two more days of morning workouts.

In these sessions, we teach the players what we want them to know for the rest of the year. We include our theme, the belief, and the concepts. You talk about commitment! I am driving to school that early in the morning, and I keep thinking this is a dedicated commitment on my part. However, for those players to get up and get ready for school, and to make it to the morning workouts—*that* is a commitment. They line up and are ready to go at 6:29 AM.

We run at what we call the toughest hour in Michigan. We go from 6:29 AM to 7:29 AM and we are moving. We open the gym doors and get after it. On Monday, we did 80 down-ups. With the doors open, the players are yelling motivation chants and other expressions of pride. With the doors open, everyone coming into the school can hear them. Kids coming to school will look in the doors and ask, "What is going on?"

We have 125 players in that gym working out. This is a great scene of pride for the team. The principal comes down to the gym to see how we are doing. Teachers come down to see the kids working out. Everyone wants to come in to see just what is going on. This is great for the school. It lets everyone

at school know that we work hard. We want the players to know we are going to make them a success one way or the other.

We finished the 80 up-downs the other day and I yelled out, "overtime." They did not know what to think. I asked them, "How are you going to win the overtime, if we do not work on it?" We had to start all over again and work the up-downs again. We won the overtime, and then they had to rush to get to their classes on time.

We want to teach them what we want them to be able to do during the season. We teach them what we want in the morning. Players will do what you emphasize. I am positive when I call out "overtime" again in our morning workouts, we will get a big reaction from the team. They will be excited, because they know they have to work to win that overtime.

I believe a person's attitude is the greatest asset to becoming successful. Just being here today for this clinic is an attitude. You want to learn something new, and you want to be successful. It is the same for our kids. We tell them, "Now that you are in the weight room, do something that is going to help you become a better player." Have an attitude. Our theme for the team this year was, "Attitude Makes a Difference." That is what we started with in our morning workouts last year—attitude makes a difference.

We had a sub theme as well this past year. "Destiny is not a matter of chance; it is a matter of choice." We won the state championship this past season. However, I think we won the state back in January in our indoor program. The team came together in the weight room and they busted their rear ends off. They worked from the time they got here until they left the workout.

We went to March Madness with the same type of attitude and the same type of spirit for our workouts. They won in their heads in January and followed it through all the way through the year. That was the type of kids we had and, as a group, they were a team. The coaching staff did not have to say anything to them to get them to work. I did not have a member of the staff who did not tell me they had fun coaching this year. It was fun to be around these young men. That is a something good to see. When you have such a class group as we had this year, it makes it hard not to want to continue. What that group accomplished is what coaching is all about. It was fun, and I hope all of you can have a year as we had this past year.

In 1976, we had to establish the program. We emphasized three main concepts. First, was the mental approach. We talked about visualization. This has always been one of our major themes. "What the mind sees, the body can achieve." We have used this saying for 34 years. "If you can see it in your mind, you can achieve it with your body." You are not going to achieve it unless you can see it. This is where we talk about visualization. You need to see yourself doing it before the job is right.

We believe the mind is four to one to the body. We feel we need to work on the mind with concepts, such as the March Madness indoor program and in the weight room. You have to work on the mind before practice, during practice, and after practice.

The next approach is the physical approach. This is where the toughness comes into play. If you are tough, you can have a good football team. We could run the spread offense, but I do not think you build toughness when you run the spread offense. You can have fun, and it is fun to watch. Nevertheless, you do not build toughness by running the spread offense. I think getting after each other is what makes a football team tough. Three yards is a real battle or a war. You can win the war in the end, but you are going to battle for every yard. You are going to make the other team battle for every yard. You must be tough.

We talk about two types of toughness. We talk about mental toughness. "The job has to be done, when it needs to be done." We may tell the team we need a first down in the first quarter. That is okay, and it is big, but it is not that tough. We know we have to do that to win games. If the ball is on the one-yard line, and you have time for one play, and you have to get the touchdown to win the state, that is when it is tough. You have to get that score to win the game. That is toughness.

The next point we stress is strategic approach. We can sum this up in three words—*Defense Wins Championships*. That is what I told our first group in 1976 when we sat down in the gym to start our program. You can have all of the fun everywhere else, but if you want to win a championship, you better play hard-nose tough defense.

We put a lot of emphasis on our defensive coordinator. I am running the offense, and I know that offense does not win championships. Defense wins championships.

We play in a tough league. Four teams from our conference were in the semifinals this year. We play good opponents. We held all of our opponents to 148.8 yards per game. We gave up 75 points in 14 games. That comes out to 5.4 points per game. That makes my job a lot easier as the offensive coordinator. I only had to score one touchdown per game to win.

We had 18 interceptions. We had a great group of guys that went to the football. We recovered six fumbles. I thought our defense this year was one of the best we have had in our 34 years. The kids did a great job. Our coaches are to be commended for the job they did. They really coached hard.

A lot of the credit goes to coach Dan Anderson, our defensive coordinator. We let Dan know what we think we should do for the upcoming game. We get out of the office around 11:00 p.m. The next morning, Dan comes in and he has the game play for every formation we are going to face in the next game. We know he did not get much sleep on Monday night, but he had it ready to go. He did that for 14 weeks in a row. On Tuesday, we tell him he has a great plan. I will let him tell you what we do on defense. Coach Dan Anderson.

DAN ANDERSON, DEFENSIVE COORDINATOR

As Coach Mach said, we had a great group of kids this year. It was a lot of fun going to practice every day. We were lucky in that we had the same players for two years. At linebacker, I had the same three players for two years straight. They loved to play football.

One thing that helped our defense is the fact that our offense is a ball-control style offense. Time of possession is a great thing for a defensive coordinator. Our offense runs the ball a lot, and we do not throw the ball that much. Time just ticks away when we are on offense. That is a great thing for our defense.

Our base defense has changed over the last three years. We are in a 4-3 base alignment as our base defense (Diagram #1). We do a number of different things out of this base alignment. Ultimately, in our base defense, we have a 3-technique toward the tight end. We have Mike, shamrock, and Will linebackers.

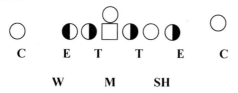

Diagram #1. 4-3 Base Defense

We also run a 50 look base defense (Diagram #2). The big thing for us is the fact our shamrock linebacker is the type of player who can play the defensive end for us. He is an outside linebacker, but he is also a defensive end who can play up on the line in a 9-technique. We just kick the front down if we want to get into our 52 defense.

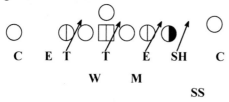

Diagram #2. 50 Base Defense

Today we want to go over our philosophy, what we do on defense, what we do in practice, and I will talk about our linebackers. Then, Coach Roy Dudas will talk about the defensive line, ends, and tackles. Coach Justin Cesante will talk about the defensive backs.

As far as gasp and alignment go, I am sure we run what is similar to what other people run. We letter the gaps, and we number the shoulders of the linemen with one on the inside and seven on the outside Diagram #3). We have calls for a head-up alignment. When we make a 50 call, the players know where to adjust their head-up alignment. The head-up is not on the diagram, because it is a call.

Diagram #3. Gaps

Our defensive philosophy centers on a foundation of stopping the run. An effective run-stopping defense must form a *tough* mental and physical presence. We expect our defensive players to play hard to the whistle, have a relentless pursuit, and gang tackle.

One of my favorite quotes came from Coach Jack Ward, one of my high school coaches:

We may not all be smart and we may not all be fast, but we can all control how hard we play.

I think I heard this every day of my life when I was in high school. I believe in this quote and I use it as well. It is a matter of mental attitude.

The key to our defense is discipline. This is where we start with our defense. We are going to keep our defense simple for the players. This is how we see our program and the intangibles that make us a good defense:

• Discipline/simplicity/execution = success
• Consistency/confidence = success
• Great demand/great effort = success

For every position on our defense, we start with these points: stance, alignment, key, and responsibility. We spend a lot of time getting to know our opponents. We use films and scouting reports to learn about our opponents.

We also study our weaknesses. It is important to know our weaknesses. We study our films a great deal. We film our practices. After practice, I go in and look at the films. The coaches and players can come in and watch the film with me. This year our players were in there after every practice. They love to watch the films. Normally, I just let the films run. If the kids want to ask questions, they can. We had a lot of questions asked this year. We ran the films back and forth more this year. One of the things we look for is the opponent's pre-snap read. We look for what the opponents are giving away, and where they are giving the plays away.

On Monday night, I go home and put together a scouting report. I list the formations, what we are going to do defensively against each formation, and then I draw every play they run out of that formation. In addition, Coach Cesante does a scouting report. He lists all of the formations and draws each pass pattern used from that formation. It is amazing to me, but our kids are so excited to get those scouting reports on Tuesday morning. Before I can get to my classroom, I have kids asking me if I have the scouting report ready. We give the scouting report to them on Tuesday morning. I have not heard of a player abusing the other classes to review the scouting report, but I am sure they are looking at the scouting report as soon as they can.

Leave little to chance as possible.
Preparation is the key to success.
—Paul Brown

We are an attacking defense. We are not blitz happy. We do not have a ton of blitzes. We try to play good, solid, base defense. We want to play on their side of the ball. We are not getting over penetration. We want to get just past the butts of the offensive linemen. We want to find the ball and react to the ball.

In talking about the gaps, we always tell the kids they have to do their job. When you are talking about the 4-3 defense, you are talking about gap control. They must control their gaps. They must do their job. If they are a contain player, they must contain. On the backside, we tell our ends and linebackers to slow play all plays away from them. We want to pursue the football and we want to gang tackle. We talk about 11 people to the ball all of the time. We use a two-whistle drill to emphasize this. The first whistle is to end all hitting on the ballcarrier. On tThe second whistle, all 11 players must be on the ball. We want them to the ball. We want gang tackling and to get on the ball on that second whistle.

We use the "*kiss*" principle. We all know about that. We may look at different adjustments on defense. However, when we get down to what we want to do, we come back to our base defense, or some variations thereof. We want to keep it simple—*do what we do.*

Dick Vermeil said it best regarding the time spent in those long Monday meetings. I use this quote with the players and with the defensive staff:

If you don't invest very much, losing
won't hurt too much and winning
won't be very exciting.

I want to talk about goals. Theoretical goals are those that would happen every day in a perfect world. They would allow you to accomplish what you wanted to happen. Things would be great. The following is what I am referring to on theoretical goals.

DEFENSIVE THEORETICAL GOALS

- Read keys, pursue to the ball, tackle.
- Stop the run.
- Gain possession of the ball.
- Hold your opponents scoreless.
- Score on defense.

I know Coach Mach mentioned the shutouts we had this year. I do not put a lot of emphasizes on shutouts. In some of the other places I have coached, we did emphasize shutouts. If a team scores, it knocks the wind out of you if you are concerned about shutouts. I did not emphasize the shutouts for that reason.

DEFENSIVE GAME GOALS

- Win the game.
- Hold your opponents under 12 points.

- Hold your opponents under 100 yards of rushing and passing.
- No big plays: Runs over 15 yards/passes over 15 yards.
- Force at least three turnovers.
- Have at least five three and outs.
- Score on defense.
- Have no mental penalties.
- Make all "big play" opportunities.
- Win third and fourth down percentage.

One thing we do in practice that I like is this: When we are in-group or team drills and the offensive team fumbles, or we make an interception, our defensive players take the ball back for a touchdown. It may take a few minutes out of practice, but we feel it is worth it and will pay off in a game. The rest of our defense is leading the player who makes the play to the end zone. They are cheering and having fun.

I like the following quote by Bob Stoops of the University of Oklahoma:

A defensive player's value to the team can and will be measured by his distance from the ball at the end of the play.

I want to touch on our practice plan for each practice, and talk about the key points. As a coaching staff, we place our players through routines on a daily basis. The objective behind those routines is to create confidence in each individual, so they can play with the greatest possible speed on the field. One thing I say in practice is this: "If you think, you stink!" Both players and coaches must come to practice prepared to build confidence.

At every practice, our coaches stress fundamentals. We work on the following points of emphasis during every defensive practice:
- Mental toughness
- Make plays
- 11 people to the ball
- Create turnovers
- Play together with enthusiasm; team goal

We want to do the common things, uncommonly well.
—Unknown

I will move on to the individual period. As linebackers, we get 10 minutes to cram in as much as we can. This is how we break it down: The defensive backs get 30 minutes of individual work, and the defensive line gets 30 minutes individual. The linebackers only get 10 minutes. The rest of the individual period for the linebackers is covered in groups, and in group backs. We always do footwork to start every individual period. We do a number of footwork drills through the bags. We may do step-overs and ladders through the bags.

From there, we go to tackling. We tackle in every practice, as well as every individual practice. We always see a film at the beginning of the year. It is on tackling and is called "see what you hit." In the film, a young man makes a tackle the wrong way, is injured, and becomes paralyzed. We stress to the kids to do things the right way. We really stress technique on tackling.

We do the tackling stations:
- Form tackle
- Bag drill—form tackle
- Shuffle and attack tackle
- Defeat the block and angle tackle
- Weenie sled—one-man sled used to form tackle

We try to get in two stations each day. We want to do as much tackling as we can in the individual period.

We do the pass drop, passing tree, and reaction drills. On the passing tree drill, I find out the pass routes that the opponents run and we work against those routes.

We do the line and back reads. Then, we do half line reads and reaction drills. They are pre-snap reads. We do group run for 20 minutes with our front seven live. We run every run play both directions. We do this from all formations that the opponents run.

We run our group pass drill for 20 minutes with the linebackers and defensive backs. Every coach has a script of what we are doing in all of the drills. We have a bomber's scout team and they run the plays against our defense. It is real quick and we go through the runs and the passes we expect to see in the next game. We rotate the players in the drill. The first group gets five plays, and then the second group is in for five plays.

This is what we look for in our linebackers. We want them to be leaders on the field and off the field. The linebacker should:

• Be the best and surest tacklers
• Be aggressive
• Know assignments
• Know the defense
• Know the situations:
  ✓ Down and distance
  ✓ Field position
  ✓ Quarter and time remaining
  ✓ Opponent's tendencies
• Special situations

This is how Will, Mike, and shamrock linebackers line up in our base defense (Diagram #4). The Will and shamrock are similar, and the Mike is different. The difference in the Will and the shamrock is the fact we move up the shamrock when we run our 5-2 defense.

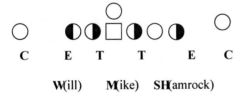

Diagram #4. Linebackers

Stance/alignment/key/responsibility
• Will (weakside)
• Stance: Feet shoulder-width apart
• Weight on the balls of the feet (see air under the heels)
• Hands slightly up
• Knees bent in a good football position

Alignment: Five yards deep
• Based on formation
• Key: offensive lineman to the backfield
• Find the ball
• Read and react
• Pre-snap read

Responsibility: option/pitch
• Gap responsibility: inside or out
• Slow play plays away
• Pass drop responsibilities

COACH JUSTIN CESANTE, DEFENSIVE BACKS

I was fortunate to have played for Coach Mach back in 1997 and 1998. He teaches players to visualize, organize, and he motivates them to work hard. It shows in the players today, as it did back when I played for him.

The type of player we look for as a defensive back is a good athlete and one who has confidence in his ability. It is a difficult position to play, because the defensive backs end up playing against the opponent's best athletes and they must be able to make individual plays. Everyone knows it when a defensive back makes a mistake. Because of the nature of the game, we need great athletes who have confidence and are leaders in the defensive back positions. If they make a mistake, they must be able to bounce back. They have to be able to "play the next play."

We want defensive backs who love contact. We stress being physical. We feel that defensive backs are a different breed of athletes. We look for playmakers, and players who are smart. We want them to be students of the game. This is how we line up in our base defense.

We feel that we must allow the defensive backs to feel comfortable with their coach. We want them to have the confidence to play fast and to make plays. That comes from being smart and confident.

In order to play fast, you must develop this in the drills. You must have good quality drills during the individual, group, and team drills. Let me focus on the drills.

Individual Stations: All drills start on ball movement. We do lateral movement drills, quick hips, and range of motion drills. We work on the backpedal W drill with 45-degree angles and three breaks. We concentrate on the drills during the individual stations.

- Ball skills
- Strip techniques
- Attack at highest point
- Eye/hand coordination drills
- Tackling drills
- See what you hit
- Breaking feet down in open field
- Weenie sled (run your feet)
- Angle tackling

Our staff feels that the individual period should be the most intense period of the day. We want players working hard and fast, and we want quality work. We expect great technique. We think the ability to pay attention to details is important. If we find the players are not paying attention, we will start the drill over.

We have three steps from all of our defensive backs. Our first responsibility is on the pass. We want them into position for the pass before they come up for the run. We like to start our individual drills from moving lateral drills, to backward drills, to moving forward drills.

The lateral drill we use is for foot quickness and hitting. It is for range of motion in the hips. In the backpedal drill, we use the W drill. It is a drill to teach the players to break out of their stance. We set up cones in a zigzag pattern real close to each other. We have them back up as quickly as possible, getting the feet working. Then, we run drills where they open and accelerate. This is where we see the vertical routes.

Our corners line up four to seven yards deep, depending on the down and distance. At times, we were pressing at three yards, and sometimes we were as deep as eight yards. We want them lined up on the outside eye of the receiver. We do not want a team to stretch out defense.

Our safeties play a traditional stance with the inside foot up, and the outside foot back. They line up 9 to 11 yards deep, depending on down, distance, and the situation. The safety on the strongside is our better tackler. We call him our monster back. He is a hard hitter.

COACH ROY DUDAS, DEFENSIVE LINE

Our job as the defensive line is to build a wall that the offense cannot run through. We do not want them to be able to get around our wall. We build that wall with gap responsibility. The first thing we do to teach the young men how to do their job is to show them their stance.

Tackles

I want to talk about our tackles. To save time, I will list the points we stress with the defensive line, starting with the tackles. The following is how we line up on our base defense:

Stance: We use the loaded stance and we use what we call the jet stance. On the load stance, we have a wide base with our feet. We stagger it and put our weight on one hand. We have a lean toward the direction we are headed in. In the jet stance, we call from the sideline. We narrow our feet on our stance and get in more of a sprinter's stance. We are thinking of rushing the passer from this stance. We are forgoing our run responsibility. We are trying to get after the passer.

We are in a 3 or 4 point stance, with the feet parallel or inside foot back (heel to toe). The shoulders are parallel to the ground, and the arms are straight down from the shoulders. The back is flat, the buttocks is slightly up, and the knees are bent, ready to uncoil. Get the weight on the hands and the balls of the feet.

Alignment: 2, 3, or 50 technique. We want to crowd the ball, getting as close to the ball as possible. Our first step: Concentrate on the offensive lineman; move on his movement, and lead with the hands to the landmark.

Responsibilities: First, fill the tackle-guard gap or center-guard gap and hold on double-teams, at all cost. Second, when the ball goes away, pursue two holes, and then pursuit angle.

Pass: Contain the football and rush in your lane. In a 2-technique, have the draw responsibility and rush your lane. Keep the quarterback to the front and to the inside.

Keys: Feel the guard and anticipate the tackle. Feel the guard and read the tackle.

Defensive Ends

Let me talk about defensive ends. Their alignment is on the outside shoulder of the last man on the line of scrimmage on his side of the line of scrimmage. If we have a tight end, we have our defensive end outside the tight end. The other end to the split end side is lined up outside the offensive tackle. We line up on the crotch of the offensive man we are facing. We play half the man and cover the gap. The other half is free.

Stance: Play a 2-point stance for the end that will not be moving into the defensive tackle position. A 2-point stance: The back is straight, bend at waist, the buttock is dropped, with the knees bent. The weight is on the balls of your feet. The hands are in front of the belt, ready to deliver a hand shiver.

Play a 3-point or 4-point stance, if moving to the defensive tackle position. The feet are parallel or the inside foot is back (heel to toe).

Alignment: On offensive lineman: Split his crotch as close to the line of scrimmage as possible.

First step: Concentrate on the offensive lineman and move on his movement. Lead with the hands, jamming your landmark, then take a 45-degree lead step with the outside foot.

Keys: Tight end or near back, fullback, pulling guard, and then find the ball.

We do not want the linemen going around a block. They must defeat the blocker first by fighting across his face. If they go around blocks, they are going to be chasing the ball from behind. We are building the wall across the line of scrimmage and reinforcing it to get to the football.

I see our time is up. We want to thank you for coming and good luck next year.

Wayne Maxwell

THE 4-3 SHADE DEFENSIVE SCHEME

Woodinville High School, Washington

What I am going to talk about today is our 4-3 defensive system. I want to talk about my upbringing on the defensive side of the ball. I played for John Zamberlin at Washington State. He is now at Idaho State. I learned from John Graham. He is the defensive coordinator at Eastern Washington. What I know about the 4-3 defense comes from those two coaches.

What I will focus on today is the shade front. Back in the day, they called it an Eagle front. We get into this front by walking the Sam linebacker down on the tight end. We were enjoying success in the package we were playing, but we gave up too many yards especially against one-back teams. We made the adjustment, and it helped us tremendously. It is an easy adjustment to make.

We play fast physical football and our players fly around and hit you. We have had a lot of success running this scheme. We like to keep it simple, and it is easy to teach.

Defensive Philosophy

- Keep it simple
- Tackle
- Mentality
- Takeaways

We want to keep the scheme simple so our players can play fast and get to the football. In high school football, the coaches have to play a juggling act. We have offense and defense to handle. That is too much. There are great schemes and packages that you can add to your package or scheme. There is a fine line you have to walk as to what is too much. We will margin on the error so we can be simple and our players can play fast.

You cannot be a good defensive team unless you can tackle. Everyone has to tackle out of the base front. The mental aspect of the game is important. I feel our coaches do a good job of coaching our players up with respect to the mentality of the games. You have to practice the mental things in practice to get better at those things. We coach as much of the mental aspects of the game into our practices as possible.

The last big aspect of our philosophy is takeaways. Takeaways are one of the biggest things that coaches look at in the success of a defense. If you win the turnover battle, you have a chance to win the game.

In our under front, we walk the Sam linebacker down on the tight end. We feel our players can be master technicians. We will be good at what we do. We rep the techniques so much, we become good at gap-control defense. We read off the blocks and play our keys. We feel through repetition and becoming so good at what we do, we become an attacking defense. We play fast and run to the ball. We go wall-to-wall from the snap to the whistle on every play.

The coaches teach concepts so the players understand the big picture of what we are trying to do. I want to show you a simple pursuit drill. We do the pursuit drills to warm players up and for conditioning. We have a philosophy about drills. We do not want to do drills that do not relate to Friday night. We also want to condition during a football drill. We do not want to run for the sake of conditioning. We want to run to prepare for what we do in the games.

When we set the drill up, we have three teams of defensive players (Diagram #1). We have a group of rabbits on each hash mark. One of our coaches runs the scout quarterback as he goes through the cadence. We make a defensive call, which has line movements or blitzes in them. The defense has to recognize the set and adjusts to the formation. The quarterback calls the cadence and fakes a pitch to one of the rabbits aligned on the hash mark. He runs to the outside of the cones, and the defense pursues in the proper angle and gets into their run fits.

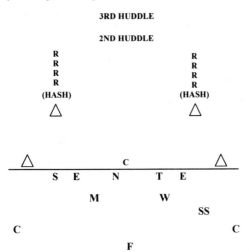

Diagram #1. Pursuit Drill

The reason we do not toss the ball is the tempo of the drill. If the quarterback pitches the ball and the rabbit drops it, we have a wasted play. Everything in this drill is about fast tempo. The defense goes through their stunts and pursues the ball. Everyone gets to the ball, breaks down, and breaks to the area behind the coach. The second group sprints up to the ball, and gets the call. We adjust to the offense, run the defense, and pursue the football.

This is a good way to warm up for practice, and you are not wasting time. We do another pursuit drill with the cones lined up on the sidelines. We assign each player a cone. This gives the players an aiming point in their pursuit angles. The problem with this drill is it takes longer to run.

Mentality

- Attitude: "Dark side"
- Pride in our end zone
- Takeaways

We try to develop the "dark side" image. We want to have fun with it and get our players fired up. We have to toughen up our players. We play the "dark side" music and wear black jerseys. We use music many times in our meetings and at practice to project the image. We want the players to think about that image we want to project. We use music before practice and during the pre-practice sessions. That is one of the things we do to fire up our players. The players buy into to it, take ownership, and run with it. You need something to build a mental swagger in the players. This is a fun thing that draws them together.

Your players must take pride in their end zone. They have to take pride not to let teams into the end zone. We have to implement that attitude in practice. When we get into our red-zone defense, it becomes a competition. The offense is not going to score. The defensive coaches are pumping up their players and working on protecting our end zone.

The offensive coaches are doing the same thing with the offensive players. There is friendly fire going on between the offensive and defensive players. We keep track of the number of times the offense scores and the number of times the defense stops the offense. Sometimes the players get mad, but that is good. They have a lot on the line. The coaches must have enthusiasm in a drill like this. If they do, the players will feed off that.

Defensive Goals

- No touchdowns allowed
- Two-plus (two or more takeaways)
- Hold the opponent under 100 yards rushing
- Hold the opponent under 125 yards passing
- Stop the opponent 75 percent on third- and fourth-down conversions
- No assignment errors
- No touchdowns after sudden change
- No missed tackles

You have to talk about these things, and then back them up in practice. If you do not do that, it will not become a habit. That is the attitude it takes to keep the opponent out of the end zone. We want a minimum of two takeaways a game. I am not a big stats coach, especially with yardage stats. The third- and fourth-down goals are important because it gets your offense back on the field.

The thing about goals is you cannot only talk about them. You have to make them happen in practice. You have to script the third- and fourth-down situations in practice and keep track of how the defense reacts. No assignment errors and no missed tackles never actually happens in a football game. That is coaching. We want to challenge the players and work them *toward* those goals. We want to develop the mentality reflected in our goals.

The coaches have these goals on the board. The players hear and see them every week. That eventually sinks in as to how important those goals are. The sudden-change aspect of defense occurs in practice. In our offense practices, we script a sudden change in the offense session. Play number 7 (as an example) on the script will be a sudden-change play. The defense has to run on the field and allow no touchdowns after the sudden change. It is like a fire drill for the defense. That prepares the defense for what that situation is like.

The defense holds a team on downs, and the offense goes to the field. Two plays into the series, there is a turnover. We want the defense prepared for those moments. We do not want them to run around, looking for the helmets. They have to be prepared for those things in a game.

We do the same thing with our special teams. We could be working on any period of practice when this happens. We stop the practice and yell for the field-goal team. They have to hustle from all parts of the field to line up for a field goal. It teaches them to be ready to get on the field at any moment. This teaches them to execute in a tight situation.

Takeaways

- Two-plus
- Practice: Keep score
- Takeaway drills during conditioning

During our practices, we have a coach who keeps track of the takeaways that occur in practice. If there are no turnovers or less than two, they hear about it. We carry that over to the offensive side with ball security. We keep track of the takeaways and ball security. We do this so the players are aware of takeaways and work on them. We do not like to condition after practice. We want our players to condition during practice by going full-speed all the time. We do a takeaway circuit as part of our conditioning.

In the takeaway circuit, we teach punching the ball out, clubbing over the top on tackles, intercept drills, and fumble drills. We also incorporate some a special-teams drill on blocking punts and kicks. We cover angles to the ball and taking the ball off the foot. To get takeaways, you must practice them; they will not occur in the game unless you make them happen.

Base Scheme

- Eagle (over-under)
- Cover 3
- Gap-control read defense (attack)

We are base 4-3 over-under defensive front. We start out playing cover 3 with the strong safety up in his alignment. We are a gap-control read defense, but play faster because we are very competent in our reads. Our alignment scheme is different from the traditional style used by college teams. We try to put ourselves into the minds of our players and make it as simple for them as we can. The difference is the techniques assigned to the tight end. His inside shoulder is a 6i technique. The head-up position is a 6 technique, and the outside shoulder alignment is a 7-technique.

That gives us a standard sequence from the inside to the outside. The head-up positions on the guard, tackle, and tight end are 2, 4, and 6 techniques. The inside positions are "i" numbers. The inside shoulder of the guard, tackle, and tight end are 2i, 4i, and 6i techniques. The outside-shoulder positions on the guard, tackle, and tight end are 3, 5, and 7 techniques. That means we number sequentially from the inside to the outside. The players have one less thing to focus on.

In the 4-3 under front, we can call the reduced side to any number of situations (Diagram #2). We can align according to the alignment of the tight end, run or pass strength, field, or boundary. We cover the situations during the practice week and put our players in the best situation to win. To the tight-end side, the Sam linebacker plays a 7 technique. The end and nose to that side respectively play a 5 technique and shade strong technique on the center. To the weakside the end plays a 5 technique, and the tackle plays a 3 technique.

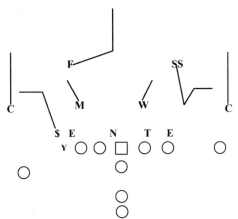

Diagram #2. Base 4-3 Under

The linebackers align in a 30 technique, and the strong safety is five yards outside and five yards deep from the openside tackle. We play cover 3 in the secondary with the corner aligned at six to seven yards deep. The free safety aligns in the middle at 10 yards off the ball.

The techniques of our defense start with the defensive line. We want them to get off the ball. We teach that in a takeoff drill. We want them controlling their gaps and penetrating to the heels of the offensive linemen's feet. They want to destroy everything in their path to their destination. The goal for our defensive line coach is to kick the offensive lineman's butt. We do not worry about the reach block. We want to get penetration. We want to establish a new line of scrimmage and keep the down linemen off the linebackers.

We teach our players concepts of the defense. We can slow things down and increase the speed of the defensive linemen if they understand what likely will happen to them. We must know what teams will run to the reduced 3 technique to the weakside of the defense. We must know how teams will attack the bubble on the strongside of the defense. We have mastery of our scheme, and we want to be the master of the opponent's scheme.

The nose, strongside end, Mike, and Sam linebackers travel together. The tackle, weakside end, Will linebacker, and strong safety travel together. We flip-flop the defense to the strength or call of the defense.

We want all the down linemen to make plays, but typically we want our best defensive lineman at the 3-technique tackle position. He is the B-gap defender, and in some techniques he plays the C gap. He will have one-on-one match-ups on the offensive guard and can make things happen.

The nose is a space-eater. He has responsibility in the A gap. He wants the offense to double-team him. If the defensive ends are not equal in ability, we like to play the smaller, more athletic end to the openside of the formation. He plays the C gap, and on occasion he plays the B gap. We would rather be undersized to that side as opposed to the tight-end side. You can adapt the under front to the 3-4 defense easily.

The Sam linebacker walks down and plays a 7 technique on the tight end. He is a D-gap defender. He plays a tough technique with his inside foot up, and his hands read to shoot on the tight end. He takes a six-inch power step and cannot let the tight end reach him, in our base coverage scheme. He is our force defender. If you play a second-line player in a back-up role, he needs to widen his alignment to keep from being reached. He may have to align at a 2x2-yard alignment. The more talented and skilled the player, the tighter he can align to the tight end. If we change the coverage to a cover 4, we take the force responsibility away from the Sam linebacker and he can play tighter.

In this defensive scheme, everyone spills the ball to the force defenders. The Sam linebacker and strong safety are similar players. The strong safety has to be more athletic. He has to play in the two-high inverted look in the secondary. We ask a lot out of this player. He has to be the brains of the secondary as far as alignment and coverage. He has to be able to blitz and play man coverage.

The Will linebacker can be a strong safety–type. He is covered by the 3 technique on the Eagle side and does not have to take on a guard. He is an A-gap player. He does not have to be the typical inside linebacker. He can run and make plays. We tell him if he sees daylight, he can shoot the gap and make a play.

The Mike linebacker plays in the bubble to the tight-end side. He has to be more of the plugger type of linebacker. He is the B-gap defender. He gets the zone, dive releases from the guard, and has to match up on the guard. He has to play a box technique and attack the outside shoulder of the guard. He forces the ball back into the Will linebacker. He has to be the physical linebacker.

From the start of practice, we teach the players the strength and weakness of the defense. In our cover 3, we play four-under and three-deep in our scheme. In the defense, there is a weakness in the deep seams and the quick flat. When we start practice, we coach the strong safety and Sam linebacker on their techniques on rerouting the #2 receivers. The corners have to play the #1 receiver going deep, but he has to be aware of the #2 receiver in the seam and be ready to leverage his route.

We teach the corner to get into a controlled backpedal and read the three-step drop of the quarterback. That way, they can get a jump and drive back to the receiver. We also teach the slant-flat and quick-out concepts from the first day of practice. The offense wants to make the flat defenders commit to the arrow or slant. We want to take the slant window away, sit on the curl, and push to the flat. We will rally and break on the flat route from the inside-out and the outside-in with the flat defender and corner. We hammer that in from day one.

Other Possibilities

- Getting into multiple fronts
- Multiple coverages

We are essentially an Eagle team, and that is what we want to play. We want to stop the run. However, we can easily get into other fronts. We can play the over front, which we call Falcon (Diagram #3).

Diagram #3. Over Front

We can play two variations of the G front (Diagram #4). We move the nose from the shade on the center to a 2i alignment on the strongside guard in the G front. If we want to run a Tiger G, we move the backside tackle into a 2i alignment also.

Diagram #4. G Front

We can get into the Bear front (Diagram #5). The Bear is the double Eagle for us. We move the strongside defensive end into the 3-technique alignment on the strongside guard. This allows us to control the A gaps.

Diagram #5. Bear Front

The last front is a Tiger front (Diagram #6). The Tiger front moves the 3-technique tackle into the 2i technique on the weakside guard. If we want to move the nose over to the 2i technique on the strongside guard, we call "Tiger G." The G call moves the nose, and the Tiger call moves the 3-technique tackle. If we put the defenses together, we move both defenders.

Diagram #6. Tiger

Defenses do not set in the base 4-3. They are moving into multiple fronts to confuse the offense or play offensive tendencies. These are simple adjustments, but they are very hard on high school offensive linemen. We have had much success moving our fronts.

Instead of getting in lines and doing warm-ups, we do football-related warm-ups. That way, we do not waste time in a stretching drill. We do the pursuit drill and work on pursuit paths, screen, reverses, and things of that nature. They are loosening up and getting the body warm in these running drills. We work lateral, forward, and backward movements. One of our concepts is not to do non-football related activities at practice.

We are not driving at full speed in these drills. We are warming the body slowly, but we are conditioning and working on the mental aspects of the practice. As the players begin to warm up, we increase the tempo of practice accordingly. This is the time we play the music and work on our player's mentality of what we are teaching.

We have multiple coverage schemes we use. We start our disguise in a two-high-safety look. When we play cover 3, the strong safety drops down in the 5x5-yard alignment, and we play three-deep.

We can stay in that alignment and play cover 2 (Diagram #7). In this coverage, we roll both corners down into the flat areas. The Sam and Will linebackers become the hook/curl players and wall the #2 receivers to the outside. The Mike linebacker is the middle hook player.

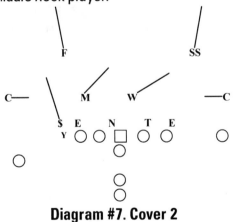

Diagram #7. Cover 2

From that two-deep shell, we play quarter-quarter-half coverage. We can also play five-under man coverage, when we get into some of our blitz schemes.

I am not going to spend a lot of time on tackling, but I do want to touch on the progression of tackling.

Tackling Progressions

• Fundamentals: Demonstration/warning label
• Teaching progressions: Closed to open environment
• Attitude: Be physical, and take pride

The first slide I showed you was about being simple and focusing on fundamentals. We start from a close environment. We start down on the knees and snap the hips. All we want to teach is what it feels like to snap the hips. I think it is important for all the coaches to use the same terminology when teaching tackling. I think the players start to relate to the terms we use.

One of the terms I like in an open-environment tackling drill is "shimmy." That term takes the place of breakdown. When you approach a tackle in the open field, the tackler has to come to balance and chop his feet. Instead of breakdown, we say to "shimmy down." Another comparative term we use is "Step on his toes." That means the tackler is too far away from the ballcarrier. He has to move closer and step on his toes. Instead of "Grab cloth", we say, "Clamp."

Anytime we do a tag drill instead of a tackle, we teach a particular method. When we tag off on the ballcarrier, I want the tackles to tag with their palms. To tag with the palms, the tackler has to lower his hips to make the tag. To tag with two hands, he has to turn his hands over and comes from the bottom up to get the palms on the ballcarrier. This makes him get closer and forces him to lower his hips.

Tackling Progression Drills

• Knee progression drill: Snapping the hips, head, and arm and hands
• Two-step form tackle drill: Adds in the feet, and adds lowering the hips
• Head-up tackling drill: Increase tempo, in close proximity

- Sideline tackling drill: Leverage working inside-out through the ballcarrier
- Open field tackling: Create an angle, do not square up.
- Defeat a block and tackle drill: Multiple skills used
- Agility and tackle drill: Work on agility and tackling.
- Small group setting: Old-school Oklahoma drill
- Inside run: Reads and multiple skills
- Team setting: Open environment (Tempo: tag off, thud and wrap-up, live)

We want to make our players fast in their defensive action. We do that with confidence. If the player is not confident, he will not play fast for you. In the first two days of spring practice install, we do not do anything on defense. We work individual drills on defense, but there are no team activities on defense. When we teach, we have a scope and sequence we use:

- Individual technique
- Straight flow/drop back
- Split flow (misdirection)
- Scrolling coverage
- Formations
- Motions
- Flow screens and draws
- Trades/shifts
- Trick plays

The first thing we do is work individual techniques and build the confidence in the players.

We teach straight flow and drop-back passing to begin with. When the players become confident, in those flows and directions, we move forward and teach split flow and misdirection plays.

From the drop-back scheme, we scroll the coverage and teach different schemes and movement. We add formation adjustments and motions within those schemes. We work on shifts and trade positioning of the tight end. Finally, after we have taught all the fronts and coverages against the multiple sets and formations, we cover the trick plays. Defending trick plays requires a player's total understanding of his technique. If he understands his technique and plays it to the letter, the offense will not fool him.

You must have a plan for installation of the defense. You have to be prepared and have a plan for how you progress. That development allows your players to play fast. You must progress only when the confidence grows in the players. You cannot add too much at any one time. You have to make sure the players get the reps to do what you are going to ask them to do. You have to incorporate that into your practice plan and the in-season plan.

It is fun to talk football. The 4-3 Eagle has many options. Your players have to be physical and fly around and make plays. It is simple, and we have had success playing it. We have created an identity for our program. We have learned how to play fast and do many great things. I hope you have fun during the rest of the clinic. Thanks for your attention.

MAKING SPECIAL TEAMS SPECIAL

Solon High School, Ohio

Through the 36 years I have coached, I have benefited from many people that have helped me. I see that as a responsibility to you coaches. I will tell you all I know about all I know. If there is anything that you find interesting and would like to know more about it, I will help you. That is my responsibility.

I want to make mention how I came to be at a clinic in Michigan, when I am an Ohio guy. A year ago on Easter, I was on vacation in Florida. I was sitting on Siesta Keys beach in Sarasota. A young fellow came over and began a conversation with me. I came to find out he was a young football coach from Michigan. He was more interested in talking to my son than he was interested in talking with me. My son Josh is the head coach of the Denver Broncos, and my youngest son Ben is the quarterback coach there. I think he was using me to get to know Josh, and that was okay.

We did a lot of X's and O's on the beach during the week. He asked me if I had any interest in doing clinics. He asked me if I would be interested in speaking at a clinic in Michigan. He passed my name along to Mary, and here I am.

I am going to talk about making special teams special. That is the first key about being good at special teams. We have young kids when they are little who want to grow up to be quarterbacks. They want to be wide receivers. They even want to grow up to be offensive linemen. However, no one, when they are young, wants to grow up and be the safety on the kickoff team or the wing on the extra-point team.

It is essential that we make special teams important. If you make it important for them, you have a chance to be good on special teams.

Very quickly, I want to talk about our philosophy that relates to special teams. I think the approach and philosophy you have about playing special teams is critical:

- One of every five plays in a game is a kick of some kind; it is important
- Opportunity to gain field position: 100 yards of field position equals six points
- Opportunity to score
- Opportunity to prevent a score
- Opportunity to keep or change the momentum of a game
- We see special teams as a one-play series; make it count
- Our structure of special teams is basic and simplistic; that lets us play hard and utilize our talent
- Players must know the rules, play smart, and be aware of situations; they must be coached

If one of every five plays in a game is a kick of some kind, that is important. That is 20 percent of the plays in a game. Field position is important in any game, and the last time I checked, 100 yards equaled six points. If we can gain field position through our special teams, that gives us an opportunity to accumulate points.

When teams punt the ball or kick the ball off, that is an opportunity to score. When a team lines up for an extra point or field goal, that is an opportunity to score. If you have ever lost or won by one point, you know how critical that can be.

If we are doing the kicking, it is an opportunity to prevent a score. If the other team feels the way we do about the special teams, they are looking to score.

The special teams are a way to change or keep the momentum of a game. We feel if we can get a big hit on a kickoff, that can change momentum and affect our entire sidelines. If we can light someone up in a kickoff situation, it has an impact on us. If you block a punt or a kick, those are momentum-changing plays and can affect the outcome of the game.

We see special teams as a one-play series. If the offense goes on the field and scores, it is good for our team. If the defense stops the offense, we have gained an advantage. We feel the same way about special teams. It is a one-play series, which could lead to a score or prevent one. It is just as important as what the offense and defense did. Players have to think about it that way and make it count.

The structure of our special teams is basic and simplistic. We are not exotic when it comes to schemes. That lets our players play fast. They can master what they are trying to do better. We are not going to have two or three kick returns. We only have one return.

I have coached for 36 years as a head coach, and as an assistant. I can remember putting in walled punt returns to the left and right. We spent countless hours on teaching those wall returns. We very seldom used them in the games. You cannot set up a wall and get a great return unless you have great punting. We do not see many good punters anymore. We do not teach the wall return anymore.

Our approach to that part of the game is very basic. That allows the players to play hard and fast, and we can utilize the speed we have on the field. They have to know the rules, play smart, and be aware of the situations. That is where the coach comes in. They have to cover and review the variety of situations that happen during the special-teams play. Those situations are different from penalties on offense or defense. We have a whole list of situations that we work through before the season. We want to have rehearsed all situations before we get to the first game.

We hope that carries over to the games. We have to know the rules and communicate them to the players. We have to get them to play smart and be aware of the situations. That way, we down the punt that is rolling toward the goal line instead of letting it roll into the end zone.

Our Approach Trumps Our Scheme

- It is the first thing we practice each day
- 25 to 40 minutes each day: It is a priority.
- Special teams during summer camp and conditioning days
- Best personnel available: Guys who can run and hit
- Individual, group, and team: practice organization
- Special-teams coordinator: All coaches assigned
- Evaluation: Individual and team performance
- Preach special-teams musts
- Chart impact plays and special teams by the numbers.
- Pre-game introductions, POWs, and helmet awards
- Preceding game day practice plan

The first thing we practice each day is the special teams. We are not going to tack it on at the end of practice. We work on the special teams with the players fresh and not tired. We assign 25 to 40 minutes of practice time to special teams every day. It is not an afterthought, and I am not giving lip service to it. It is absolute the first thing we do, and we spend the time on it. We make it important by putting it first and spending the appropriate amount of time on it.

In Ohio, we have 10 days from June 1 through July 31 where we can use the football and actually coach our players. They call it camp days. You cannot use any gear, but you can use the ball and coach all facets of the game. Too many people spend all that time getting ready for the 7-on-7 camps. That, to me, is not real football. We do that too, but we spend some of the time installing our special teams. We install the drills we use on our special teams in those practices.

We use the best personnel available. I want players who can run and hit. I do not care if he is a sophomore. If he can run, hit, and be responsible, he is going to play. I do not care if it is a two-way starter. If he is the best and we need him, he plays special teams. If we have a young player who can play and not diminish the play, we pull the starter off that team. We will use anybody who can run and hit. Those are the only requirements outside of the extra-point and field-goal teams. In those situations, we want big bodies.

We practice teams at the individual, group, and team levels. When I started coaching in 1972, we did all the special teams on Thursday night before we played the game on Friday. Even at that, it was all team drills. Now, within the 40-minute period, we have individual, group, and team special-teams periods. We coach the special teams the same way we coach offense and defense.

We have an offensive and defensive coordinator, and we have a special-teams coordinator. You need to find a coach on your staff who has a keen interest in and is excited about special teams. It is a way to elevate him and get more responsibility. You may have to coach him up and teach him, but he can help you in that area.

Even though we have a special-teams coordinator, all of our coaches are assigned in the coaching of special teams. If we are working on the field-goal team, there is a coach assigned to the snapper. We have a coach assigned to the right guard, tackle, end, and wing. We have another coach assigned to the other side. There is a coach assigned to the holder and kicker. We assign coaches to the special teams and other coaches to the scout teams to make sure we get the look we want. It is every coach's responsibility to coach special teams.

We evaluate all our special teams. After 25 years as a head coach, this past season I was an assistant coach. It was a great experience for me. We did the same evaluations we did for the offense and defense. We also posted those grades. I know that all grading is subjective to some extent. A two in our grading system means you were technically and fundamentally right and got a good result. A one means your techniques and fundamentals were right, but the result was not good. It could also mean that you got good results but your techniques and fundamentals were bad. That means you found a way to get the job done. A zero means you did not do anything we wanted. We got no technical or fundamental work, and the results were bad. That is how we grade special teams and offense.

We grade defense differently because we look for production. We have players get twos and never make any tackles. We want some different results, so we grade differently. We have a team grade for each special team. We take the 10 players on the punt team, average their individual grades, and get a team grade.

We have special-teams musts that we preach. If we did these things and did not accomplish anything else, we would be all right. We are in pursuit of many things, but these particular things are not negotiable. We have to accomplish these four things while we are trying to accomplish some other things. I will show those to you in a second.

We chart impact plays. We keep track of all the impact plays we have each week against that opponent. We also chart how many impact plays the opponent had against us. We keep a running total throughout the season. I will show you a slide in a second that will illustrate that point. If we talk about making an impact in the special teams, we have to recognize what an impact play is. It is important to see we are generating more impact plays than our opponent is.

We are also going to chart certain special-teams situations by the numbers. This is our part in making this part of the game important.

In pre-game introduction, instead of introducing the offense, we introduce the punt team. Instead of introducing the defense, we introduce the kickoff team. We have at one time or another introduced every one of our special teams. It might seem like a little thing, but we have players who only play special teams. It is a small thing, but it matters and makes it more important.

We have a special-teams POW (Player of the Week) award. All we do is say their name in the team meeting and clap our hands. They do not get a week in Hawaii or a free car. We recognize outstanding special-teams play. The unit earns the helmet awards. If our offense achieves its goal, everyone on the offense gets an award. The tailback may have run for 260 yards and five scores, but if the offense did not achieve their goals, he does not get an award. None of our decals has to do with individual accomplishment. They have to do with unit accomplishment.

We have a day-before-the-game practice routine. I will show that to you because we will hit a variety of special-teams situations. In that practice, we need to get the movement of the units on and off the field. We kick off and send the defense out. We make three defensive calls and play defense. After that, the punt-rush team comes on the field. We do that because that is the way it happens on game night.

Special Teams Musts

- 100 percent personnel sure
- 100 percent penalty-free
- 100 percent ball security
- 100 percent great effort

We do not need 12 players on the field when we are supposed to have 11, or worse have 10 players when we need 11. That is an absolute requirement. We want to be penalty-free. If these were the only things you did in the kicking game, you would be satisfactory in the kicking game. When we return the ball, we have to make sure we secure the football. You can measure the first three things. The great effort comes from knowing your players. We can tell if a player is not giving 100 percent.

We know all the goals we set for our teams will be hard to meet against good competition. However, these things are more in our control than anything else is.

Impact Plays

- Net punt over 35 yards
- Opponent net punt under 15 yards
- Kickoff return past the 50-yard line
- Opponent kickoff return inside the 20-yard line
- Converted field-goal attempt
- Get a turnover
- Block a kick or punt
- Recover an onside kick
- Score

We chart our impact plays, and we chart the opponent's impact plays. If we do not attempt to onside kick the ball and get the ball, it is a turnover, not an onside kick recovery. We chart these on a weekly basic and a cumulative total for the year. We post these things on the bulletin board. Our players come in on Monday and go straight to the bulletin board where all of these grades and results appear. This is another way to make it important.

Special Teams by the Numbers

- Starting position after punt versus opponent
- Starting position after kickoff versus opponent
- PAT/field goal versus opponent
- Impact plays versus opponent

Must Win All Four Phases To Beat the Best Opponents

If our starting position after a punt is the minus 37-yard line and the opponent's is the minus 17-yard line, that is our advantage. That is 20 yards of field position we had we gained on the opponent. The win or lose does not come down to just offense or defense. It comes down to the special teams in these areas. If you want to beat the best, you must win all four of those phases of the game.

We play in the big school division in the state of Ohio. When we play the best people in the state, we will not outplay them offensively, and it will be tough to outplay them defensively. If we can break even in those areas and win the kicking game, that may be the area that wins the game.

Special-Teams Priorities: Practice Time

- Punt: 50 percent
- Kickoff: 25 percent
- Punt return: 20 percent
- Kickoff return: 5 percent
- PAT/field goal: Every day in some capacity

The numbers in the chart are general in relationship to the time spent. We added up the special teams' practice times during the week and looked at the results. Of that total, 50 percent of it should be in punting. Twenty-five percent of the time would be practicing our kickoff. Anytime we give the ball away, we do not want any long returns coming back at us. We work extra hard in those facets because those are the opportunities for the other team to score. We work on the punt return 20 percent of the time and the kickoff return 5 percent of the time. I hope we do not receive many kickoffs. If we play great defense, we will not receive many kickoffs. I want to do some kind of field goal/PAT in some kind of capacity every day.

In the 25 to 40 minutes in the special-teams period, we may not do field goal and PAT. That may be the last play of the team offensive period. We run the final play and down the ball at the 27-yard line. We call out the field-goal team and try to convert. We may practice the long snapper and not do punt or extra point. The long snapper will snap, and the holder will hold. We do some form of PAT or field every day in some period.

Special Teams Practice: Week #1 Practice #2

- Individual: 8 minutes
  - ✓ Punters, snappers, punter returns
  - ✓ Three-station kickoff drill
- Team punt: 10 minutes
  - ✓ Two red punts: One each group
  - ✓ Six black punts: Three each group
- Team kickoff: 7 minutes
  - ✓ Six kickoffs: Three each group
  - ✓ Two surprise onside: One each group

This is a practice schedule from the second practice of week one. The individual period is eight minutes long. We have punter, snapper, and punter returns working. If the players were not a snapper, punter, or returner, they went through a three-station kickoff drill. They rotated through the three drills. Anyone not on a special team got extra work with their position coach. That, generally, was the offensive or defensive linemen.

For 10 minutes, we go to team punt. Red and black are schemes, which is insignificant in this lecture. We use two units. Each one of them will get a one red punt. The black punt is a punt block. Each unit gets three of those apiece. We always time the snapper and the kicker, and we may not cover every kick. If we did that, the drill would end up a conditioning period. We do not need to cover every punt every day. It is not that critical.

We get seven minutes of team kickoff. We work two units in this period. We have six kickoffs, which is three with each group. In that period, we will have two surprise onside kicks. That is one for each team. You use an onside kick when everyone in the stadium knows you have to do it. There is also an onside kick, which is truly a surprise. We do not line up in an onside kick formation as we do not to give it away. That is how we spent our 25 minutes that day.

Special Teams Practice Organization

- Scout teams posted with coaches assigned.
- Groups assigned specific areas of practice field.
- Special teams coaches' responsibilities posted.
- Players not involved use that time for individual position skill work.

When we have our special-teams period, we post the scout teams with the coaches assigned to that period. The players had better know they are on a particular scout team. When we have scout-team members involved in a drill, we coach them just like the other side. If you do not do it this way, you waste time. You wait for bodies to show up and get their scrimmage vests on. Do not get on the field and say, "Give me 11 people over here." Some players do not care, and others do not want to help. We do not ask for volunteers; we tell them by listing them on the scout team.

All the areas on our practice field are designated areas. We always have the punt drill in a particular area. We always have the kickoff drill in a certain area. We do not want to waste time by having people looking for their area. We have many players and a lot of land to practice on.

I have a job description for assistant coaches. In that description is his practice day, game day, and off-the-field duties. If he checks the weight chart every day to make sure players are weighting in and out, that is an example of off-the-field duties. We explain, identify, and post the duties of the assistant coaches. We do it for the players and coaches.

Anyone who is not involved in the special-teams period steals some extra time for individual instruction. That could be the situation of my quarterback. If he does not punt or have a special-teams responsibility, he works on drops or some other techniques. Many times, our quarterbacks are a holder for the placements and are involved. The offensive linemen do specific position skill work. We try to free up the offensive line coach to handle those players. He has the line on field goal and extra points but not many other special-teams duties.

- Weekly scouting report: Special teams section
- Weekly special teams individual and team grades
- Weekly and cumulative special-teams-by-the-numbers report
- Preceding game day practice plan
- Kickoff team drills

We have a weekly scouting report we pass out. In that scouting report, we have one full page devoted to special teams. We identify the returns and diagram them if it is unique or we have to make a special adjustment. This is another way to convince the players we are very serious about special teams.

We condition after practice, especially early in the season. At two of the places I was head coach, we played many Saturday games. That was great because I scouted everyone on Friday night, and it gave us another day of practice. If we played Saturday, we conditioned Monday, Tuesday, and Wednesday. If we played Friday, we conditioned Monday and Tuesday.

There were times that the amount of conditioning and kind of conditioning was the results of a question I asked after practice before we conditioned. I asked special-teams players questions about the scouting report. If I got a right answer, that had a direct bearing on how much we conditioned.

I told you we grade our special teams. If you are getting what you want from nine players on the unit, we probably have made a mistake. It may not be the tenth player's fault. It is my fault because I put the wrong player out there. If it was a replacement added to the team, we give him another chance.

The people on special teams who grade below everyone else become the topic in our coaches meeting. We have to decide if it is the coaching or the players. We may need to drill the deficient players more or even change the drill. We may need to explain ourselves and ask what they do not understand. The players with lower grades, we coach more and try to improve their performances. The players scoring the lowest by far, we replace.

The extra-point team graded out at 96 percent. We have one player who did not grade that high. That tells me that is where the defense brought the pressure. The wing on the extra point has a tough job. He has to prevent anyone from coming to the inside, but at the same time, he has to get a bump on anyone going outside. The wing on the field-goal team has two gaps of responsibility. He cannot let anyone come inside, but we would like to get a reroute on the defender coming off the edge. What we read into those figures is that he had a tough assignment and the defense focused the pressure to his side.

We post these charts on the bulletin board. Sometimes, we do not have to say anything to the players who graded out low. His teammates do all the talking for us. They ride him out to the point he has to improve. We take these charts down on Monday. That is the previous game, and we want it behind us. It is up on Monday, but we take them down as they go out to practice on Monday. The previous game is over, and I want to focus on correcting the mistakes and getting ready for the next game. We have to go out and fix the problems. We are going to make sure they know how they played and how we feel about how they played.

When we chart our special teams by the numbers, it proves what we have tried to tell them about the importance of special teams. You cannot simple tell your players; you have to show them the proof. In this cumulative sheet for the year, we had 92 impact plays, and the opponents for 10 games had 22 impact plays. That means if we can play to a draw on offense and defense, we should win the game. That is what charting, posting, and monitoring our progress help within the program.

I have a few drills that I will talk about briefly with you. These are drills for kickoff coverage. The first drill is a kickoff coverage defender and a blocker with a bag (Diagram #1). We tell our coverage people they have to beat the first attempt to block them with speed. We want to avoid the first player attempting to block us. We do the drill from the sideline to the hash mark. The first bag is between the sideline and the hash mark, and the second bag holder is at the hash mark. We sprint, avoid the bag, and get back in our lanes. When we get to the second bag, we attack it with our hands and stay square on the ballcarrier coming from behind the second bag. The coverage player sheds the bag and breaks down on the football.

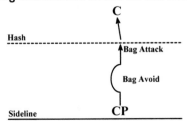

Diagram #1. Avoid and Rip

The second drill is a four-station kick coverage drill (Diagram #2). We send four coverage players at a time. We use the big stand-up dummy and place them close together. We have eight bags and holders for the four coverage players. The dummies represent wedge blockers. When we attack a wedge, we do not take one defender for one blocker. We attack the wedge in the seam of the blocker and take at least two blockers out of the wedge. When the coverage player hits the seam of the wedge, he wants to get skinny and get through or at least occupy two blockers. The ballcarrier comes up the middle. If the coverage players get through the dummies, they attack the ballcarrier. They rip, get skinny, and find the ballcarrier. The ball does not have to stay in the middle. It can move to the right or the left. That makes the tacklers find the ball and converge on it.

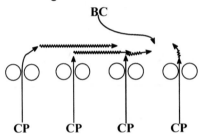

Diagram #2. Four-Station Kick Coverage

We do these drills when the punters are punting in that eight-minute portion of our individual drill.

The next drill is a takeoff drill. We have a kicker and four kick-coverage players. The kicker times out his steps to the ball. He approaches the ball, and he may kick it or he may not kick it. The coverage players are timing their run to the ball. When we hit the 40-yard line, we want them to be at full speed and onsides. We have four players going at once, but we may have four players in lines behind them ready to go next. We practice this so they know what we want.

There was a time that all the coverage players lined at the same place. They all started together and covered the kick. We do not do that because of the speed differences in players. One player may start at the 30-yard line in his run to the ball, while the player next to him starts at the 32-yard line.

The only thing that concerns us is for them to be at full speed when they hit the 40-yard line. I do not care where they start as long as they hit the 40-yard line when the kicker hits it and they are at full speed.

This is the avoid drill (Diagram #3). The player avoids and gets back in the coverage lane. We run this drill from the hash mark to the sideline and from the 30-yard line to the goal line. We do not cover huge amounts of distance to get a concept taught. We bring three coverage players down and have two blockers with bags. The blockers lock two of the three coverage people.

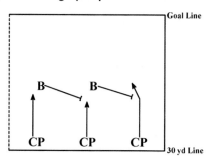

Diagram #3. Avoid Drill

The coverage player has to be aware of what blocker is going to block him. When he avoids the first blocker, he has to know who that will be. If he has an idea of who is going to block him, he stands a better chance of avoiding him. He has to recognize who is attempting to block him, and he must get to the football.

We are concerned about lane integrity. When a seam opens up, someone is out of his lane. When that happens, the football gods punish you, and that is where the opponents return the ball. We practice these drills in individual drills before we put them in the team scenario. A good takeoff is essential to good coverage. The players should be running full speed when we kick the ball. We want to squeeze the ball, keeping the returner inside and in front and never allow the returner to cross our face.

We divide our kick coverage into zones. We have a sprint zone, avoid zone, and contact zone. The sprint zone is from the 40-yard line to the 40-yard line. That is a 20-yard sprint. We have to convince our players that is how to beat the first blocker. That is especially true of teams that cross block in the middle. The next zone is the area we have to avoid blockers and get back in our lanes. That zone is from the 40-yard line to around the 30-yard line. The last zone is the collision or contact zone. That is from the 30-yard line to around the 20- to 25-yard line. It is the area you take on wedges and blocks.

On our kickoff team, we have fast players. When we kick the ball, we kick from the hash mark and place the ball on the numbers between the hash marks and the sidelines. We want to pen the returner in the corner of the field.

I thank you for your time. If I can help, please call.

A YEAR-ROUND CHAMPIONSHIP PROGRAM

Highlands High School, Kentucky

It is an honor to be here today to represent Highlands High School. I am here to help you in any way possible. I want to give you an overview of the things we do in our program that we think are good. I want to give you a general view of our year-round program. We will look at our whole season, and we will look at a few areas where we think we do something special. I am not going to be talking about individual plays but rather more of an overview of our program.

There are really two areas where we think we are better than our competition. The first is in motivation. The second area is how we run our off-season program. We develop our players on a year-round basis.

Motivation comes from realizing what a great profession we are in as high school football coaches. There may be a better profession out there, but I do not know what it is. We are taking young men and helping them develop their lives.

Men can go one of two ways. When you look at the great leaders in communities all across the country, they are oftentimes men who played high school football. By the same token, you go to the jails and look at all the inmates, and they, too, are oftentimes men who have played high school football. After these men leave your program, they will go in one of these two directions or somewhere in between. We are dealing with those men that are tough guys and are more likely to go to the top or to the bottom. The influence we have on them is probably bigger than any other influence they have in their lives. Our influence can make the difference for them. What we are doing is extremely important. That motivates us as high school football coaches.

We have to be completely crazy and passionate about what we are doing. We all are going to want to win. We all want to win. Really, for me, if I was just winning and I was not having any influence on my players' lives at all, it would still be fun. Winning is fun. However, it is the phenomenal influence we have on our young men that is special to me.

When I was growing up my parents were divorced. My high school freshman football coach had such a tremendous influence on my life. My varsity high school head coach and all of the assistants were influential as well. I try to have that same influence on my players. My assistant coaches are involved as well. That is really, what it is about.

I am going to talk about our philosophy. I am not much of a reader. I am so tired when I get home at night. Nevertheless, I did read one book recently. It was about a former pro football player. I can't remember his name. He was an assistant coach now in the pros. The book just followed their season. However, one thing stood out to me. People would ask the coaches what kind of team they thought they were going to have. Most of the responses were something like this. The coaches did not know. They would not know for 30 years. It would take that much time to find out what kind of men the players really are. You will know in 30 years if their wives can count on them. Can their children count on them? Are they a blessing to their community?

That really stuck with me and has become our major goal. I want to make sure, when I look at my players in 30 years, the answer to all of those questions is yes. I can accomplish this goal through my influence. I say that to our guys on a regular basis. We want them to know what we are trying to do for them. It is extremely motivating to them when they know their coaches have their best interests and their future in mind. To our players, it is not about winning games—that is just a part of it. It is also about becoming the kind of man each player has the potential to be. That is our foundation.

We think there are some things that men are supposed to do. Men are expected to be workers. Working is good. Guys that are trying to get out of work are not being men. We believe men are destined to work—coaches are destined to work and players are destined to work. When we have them working hard, we are doing a great thing for them. We are giving them a bigger gift than they could get if they won a million dollars in the lottery. The ability to work is the most important thing you can develop as a man.

In addition, men have a vision for their lives. I am a day-to-day liver. I am not a big dreamer. If I have a vacation planned next weekend, I am not thinking about it today. I am just thinking about what I am going to do today. Overall, men have a vision for their lives. They have an overall picture of what they want to do.

Men also are protectors. Good men are not brought up to be wimpy people that just slide around through life. Men are developed to be protectors.

Good men have developed to be a loyal part of a group. I see a Marine standing in the back of the room. I just appreciate those guys so much. It is because of them that we are sitting in here completely free to do what we want. We do not have to worry about people shooting us. We are able to live our lives in a great country at peace. And the military of our country are the kind of men I am talking about. Those guys work very hard. They are protectors. They are part of a loyal group that has a vision for their lives. That is what I would like to see with our football team. We are trying to get our kids to become superpsycho, dedicated football players.

On the first day of our off-season weight program, we absolutely kill them. We have players throwing up. They finish the first day of training and can barely walk. On the second day of our indoor program and weights, I look at them and say, "Are you guys crazy? You showed up again? We are going to do the same thing we did to you yesterday again today. You guys are psycho." At times, I think they are. That is what we are trying to motivate our players to become. We want them to become unbelievably dedicated people.

Motivation can be both positive and negative. We want someone who is doing something because it is coming from his heart and soul. We do not want someone that is going to be upset if he gets yelled at if he does something wrong. We look to motivate guys in any positive way we can.

Our defensive coordinator read somewhere that it takes nine positive things to forget one negative thing. I do not know if that is true or not, but we really believe that you have to say positive things to your players.

Not all positive reinforcement works with everyone. As anyone who has worked with people knows, all people are different. If my wife is always positive with me, I do not take out the trash or do the dishes. She occasionally says some negative things to me, and that motivates me, actually.

We may say some negative things to our guys at times. We will yell and scream at them, especially if they are doing something substantially wrong. We do not get very upset if they miss a block or drop a pass. We do get upset if they make the mistake because they are not working hard or not trying.

We believe motivation begins as soon as we can have contact with our players. We have a junior league that starts at the third-grade level. We try to motivate those young guys. We have a camp at the start of the summer. We break it down into two groups. Kids that are going into the second through fourth grades are in one group. The other group is for kids going into the fifth through eighth grades. The whole goal of our camp is to get these kids jacked up about playing football. We do not care how many football skills we teach them at the camp. We show them football skills and drills. That gets them fired up when they see they are improving. However, the focus is to get them excited about playing football.

Their freshman year is the year we really want to try to peak a young man's desire to play football. We get freshman just like everyone else does. They may be young and unsure of themselves. They may roll their eyes sometimes when you are coaching them. Nevertheless, we continue to motivate these kids on a daily basis.

Then, we get them to their sophomore year. This is when we say that guys drink the Kool-Aid®. This is about the time we feel they become these super-obsessed guys that we have been talking about. They are willing to do anything we tell them to do all year long.

One of my favorite movies is *The Karate Kid*. You have a little skinny kid that continues to get beat up. He goes to the wise, old man and asks him to teach him karate. The first thing the old man says is, "You have to do everything I tell you to do." He has him waxing his car and painting his house, etc. The kid gets mad and is not going to do it anymore. He says to the old man, "You are not teaching me karate, I am leaving." The teacher attempts to hit the student. He yells, "Wax on," and the student reaches up and blocks the punch. Now the student sees that he *is* learning karate. The instructor reminds him that the first thing he told him was that he must do everything he tells him to do.

Players are coached to be fired up when we tell them to do something. If we tell them, "Today we are going to do sets of 20 on the squats," their response is an expected, fired-up, "Yeah," because they are supposed to be excited. If I tell them we are going to do 35 stations today and each one is going to be a war, the player's response needs to be one with excitement. They are supposed to be fired up every day of the year.

We are looking for ways to motivate our guys all the time. We want them to work hard, and we have to motivate them to do that. When the game starts on Friday night, as coaches, we have to stand on the sideline. It is the players that go out and fight the battles. It is all about the players. If they do not get better, you are not going to have success.

I have a cell phone and I put all my players' numbers in my contacts by class. I put all of the sophomores together, etc. If I want to send out a text, I can send it to all the sophomores. I can send it to the entire team if I want. I am sending them texts all the time.

Every day before we practice, we say something to motivate the guys. I really believe that is the biggest key to having a successful team. It is a bunch of individual players being highly motivated.

We do not say much to our players on game day. If we get to game day and our players are not fired up, we might as well throw in the towel. You only have 15 games—at max—to play in a season. You are doing all the other things during the off-season and in the summer for those games. You better be motivated and fired up for the games. Guys should just naturally be excited and motivated on game days. We are looking for ways to motivate them on the other days as well.

We tell them our philosophy about being a man every single day. Our junior-league program is set up to develop a love for football. We want guys to get to us as freshmen. We do not care how good they are in second through eighth grades. Some of our best players were not stars in the junior leagues. That is all right because we can develop both skills and strength. The kids grow so much between the 9th and 12th grades. A lot of times, we look at our seniors and think back to their freshmen year. We are just amazed. They are not the same people that came to our program in the 9th grade. Some of them you do not even recognize because they have developed so much physically. We do not worry about winning as much in junior high. We just want to get them to us at the high school level.

One thing that I hear a lot about is developing self-esteem. One way to do it is by telling someone they are doing a good job, even if they are not. That is the worst thing you can do for somebody. High self-esteem is not that great of a thing. There are murderers in jail today that have a high self-esteem. They are strutting around thinking they are just cool people, but they are not.

Our goal is not to develop our guys' self-esteem. We feel men develop their own high self-esteem by working hard and accomplishing their goals. If you work hard, you are going to develop self-esteem. Nevertheless, and way more important, you will develop *character*. This means being the kind of man that people can count on. When we have a guy who develops character, then he will be the kind of guy we can count on.

One of the last points of our philosophy is that we have to become people that overcome adversity. My talk at our banquet this year was about what a rotten year it was and how we had to overcome adversity to make it a great year. We had a phenomenal year, but it was really all about overcoming adversity.

Here is an example of what I was talking about. Our best player really could have been in the running for Kentucky's Mr. Football, but I did not push him for the award. I did not give him the ball enough to build up the big stats. When we were winning big, I was not going to give him the ball and let other teams hit him and increase his chances of getting hurt. He had a frustrating year. I took away his chance of being Kentucky's Mr. Football. He had to overcome that and still go on to be the leader of our team.

None of our running backs or wide receivers got the ball as much as they would have liked. Not every single guy on our team got the playing time that he wanted. All of our players are overcoming adversity every day. All of us have to overcome adversity. I have times when I am upset about something. I have to overcome whatever it is that I am upset about.

We have one of the worst weight rooms in the state. We could whine and moan about that for the entire year. Instead, we take it as another chance to overcome adversity. The ability to overcome adversity is vital to success, both in life and on the gridiron.

Your entire staff must be one unit. If one of your assistant coaches says he cannot get something done because the head coach does not completely believe in it, then that is nonsense. You have to make it work as one group. Every single coach on the staff is extremely important. Every coach has a role to play.

In the same way that players work, coaches have to work. If you are not willing to work, it is hard to be in the greatest profession there is. We believe being a high school football coach and being associated with the players is a 12-month-a-year job. There is no off time for any single coach. In addition, if your staff does not believe in that, then you are missing out completely. If you have a strength coach and he runs the off-season program by himself, you are cheating everyone in your program. The season is only four months long. That means the off-season is eight months long, or twice as long as the football season. If you are only coaching four months, you are not going to be successful. You have double the time in the off-season to make your kids better. Every coach should coach football 12 months a year. You may not always be teaching football skills. Nevertheless, there are always things you can do that will make a dramatic difference in your players and your program. That is not to say that a football coach who is also the track coach cannot be the track coach. There are things that kids can learn from other sports that translate over to football. We try to coach football 100 percent of the time. For kids who are in spring sports, we try to have them attend as many off-season workouts as possible.

In the same way that we expect our players to have a vision for their lives, to work hard to achieve those goals, and to be part of a loyal group, we also expect the same thing out of our coaching staff. Coaches may disagree on personnel or play calling, but that should never be an issue in front of the players. My offensive coordinator may play a certain kid over another. I may not know all of his reasons. However, if someone asks me about my offensive coordinator's decision, I will respond by saying, "I knew what my offensive coordinator was thinking and I support him 100 percent." That is exactly what I would do.

I am the athletic director as well as the head football coach. If a basketball player's parent came up to me and said their son should be playing point guard, I would not say, "Gee, I cannot overrule the basketball coach." I would instead reply, "Hey, the object of this is to win, and they are playing the other player over your son because the other player is better. If you want your son to play more, he needs to know he has to be a better player than the player in front of him." I think it is important to be a loyal group. That is what real men are—they are loyal people. This is why we are the country we are. Loyal men have protected our country and they have done their duty.

In the season, which is only four months long, we probably do not do any one thing better than anyone else. Here are a couple of things that we believe in that I think have been very helpful to us.

First, in your schemes, decide what you know best and teach those schemes. I do not know how to run the option. We have had guys that may have been good option players, but I do not know the option game. I cannot coach the option, and we are not going to run the option.

However, we do run the counter well. We pull the guard and lead the tackle. I know how to coach that. We are going to do the things that we know how to coach and we believe in. We are going to keep that same concept from year to year. Our guys are going to be four-year experts at running the counter. We like to throw the fade. Our guys will become four-year experts on blocking, throwing, and catching the fade. Find out what you do the best, what you know the best, and what you believe in and make that the focus of your coaching.

I do not think high school football is a smaller version of the NFL or even college football. I think it is a waste of time to see what college or pro coaches do and then try to emulate that in your program. We are playing a different game. In the NFL, there is no linebacker than can cover better than any corner. You try to get a match-up where you get a receiver on that linebacker because the receiver will be able to get open. However, in high school, your best cover guy might be your middle linebacker because in high school your middle linebacker is going to be one of your best athletes.

Your middle linebacker may be going to college at the University of Kentucky, and your corner has no shot of playing college football at any level. This is completely different from what happens in college and the pros.

Today, everyone is running the zone play on offense. In high school, to me, the zone play only means you do not block the linebackers. In college and the NFL, they practice this play repeatedly. They are able to learn how to get up on those linebackers. However, in high school, it is hard for our kids to figure that out. Most zone blocking teams I see just never get to the linebacker.

Take what scheme you know and work with it. We are a shotgun, two-point stance team. We can run the ball out of this formation. We won the state championship two years ago, and we ran 95 percent of our running plays out of the shotgun from a two-point stance. A lot of times, we were just snapping it to our quarterback and he just ran it right from there.

We really feel like we get a better block from a two-point stance versus a three-point stance. First, we can see things a whole lot better. Moreover, we do not want to get to the block so quickly. Instead of having to making a block for 1.7 seconds, we may only have to make a block for 0.8 seconds because we do not get to the blocker so soon. We get to you right as the ballcarrier is getting to you, and we feel like that is more effective for us. Maybe that is not the best way to go, but that is what we believe in and know.

A lot of times on defense, we can tell where the ball is going or what type of play they are running based on the alignment and stance of the offensive linemen. It is hard for a kid to get in the same stance every time because one time he is going straight ahead, another play he is pulling, and another play he may be pass blocking. We feel like we can tell what is happening in a play from the stance. In our two-point stance, you cannot tell what we are going to do.

My whole point is to do what you believe in. We are a 3-3 stack defense. We may change where we line up. However, our reads stay consistent from week to week and year to year. Everyone has a scheme on offense and defense. We feel it is important to do your thing.

Player organization is very important. Probably most of you play some or all of your players both ways. Most of us teach our kids both offensive and defensive positions. If you can make your players one-way players only, it will be an advantage for you. You have to have enough players to do this. We are really trying to get to that point. We try to make as many guys as possible just one-way players.

If you have a soft guy who catches the ball really well but shies away from contact, he is a one-way player. Our quarterbacks are one-way guys. They practice their techniques all day long. Sometimes we have offensive linemen that are not real aggressive. We make those guys strictly offensive linemen and do not put them on the defensive line. They will get good at being offensive linemen because they can focus and practice on this one thing.

We may have a tough, aggressive kid but he has a hard time remembering where to go and who to block on offense. This kid can be a great defensive lineman, and we do not worry about trying to teach him how to play offense. He is a defensive lineman all the time. We have guys who will really hit you but they cannot catch a pass. These are our one-way defensive backs. I think you see my point.

You also have to have coaches to do this. We can only have a certain number of paid coaches on our staff. We have volunteer coaches. They are coaches that want to coach football. We just do not have money to pay them. They may have another full-time job and they cannot be there every day. You have to have some of those types of coaches. Those guys are obviously motivated to be there because they are not doing it for the money because there is none.

This year in spring football, for the first time, we are going to completely split up. Spring football only lasts 10 days. We are going to split up and tell each player, "You are going to offense," or "You are going

to defense." We may have a few that end up working both sides of the ball, but it will be as few as possible. We are going to practice that position all 10 days and get better at it. During prior spring practices, we have tried to teach both offense and defense to each player, and we really feel like that was one of our weaknesses in our spring practice. Therefore, this year, they are only going to be on offense or defense.

When we have practice in-season, Monday through Wednesday, the first thing we do is get taped. It can take a long time to get all of these players taped. It is at this time that we may break up into groups and go over things with our players. During the specialty period, if you are not a kicker, holder, returner, or snapper, you are working on improving your techniques.

Then we have the first part of our practice toward offense. If we have a player who is our starting middle linebacker and is also our backup right guard, this is the time he is getting some reps at right guard. He will not get as many as the starter, but we want him to have some idea of what he needs to do on each play. He will not be as good as our starter because of the lack of reps, but if he had to go into a game, he would have a fighting chance.

We gear the second part of our practice toward the defense and the opposite thinking applies. If my starting right guard is my backup nose man, then this is the time to try to get him some reps. The more we can go with the whole time spent focusing on one side of the football, the better off we will be as a team.

Practice time is very valuable. Plan each practice with detail. It always upsets me when I see players waiting around on the coaches. We are out there to maximize their time. They are the kings. We are there to make them as good as we can. Therefore, if we have a drill, we want to make sure it is all set and ready to go. We design a practice schedule. However, it does not mean we have to stick to it exactly. If we are in an inside drill period and we are playing a team that likes to run inside, we may get into something that takes me a little longer to teach than I allotted for. We will practice as long as it takes to get it right. We are not done with a drill just because we allotted eight minutes and our eight minutes are up. We are going to do the drill until we get it right. Only then will we move on to the next thing.

We are looking to motivate players. We are looking for players that are willing to work hard and are loyal to the team. If you have a weight program, all the coaches should be there. If you do not have everyone there, then your program is not going as well as it could go. I am giving this speech at 2 p.m. so I can get back to my school for our off-season workouts. How can you tell a player he cannot miss if you, as a coach, can miss? We are there every day. We are intense every day.

In the eight months of the off-season, you can make twice the improvements. You do not have to rest for the games on Fridays. You can push your players five days a week. Once the season starts, your football skills improve, but you do not improve as an athlete.

We have a couple of things that we do not believe to be true. The first thing is that you cannot teach speed. That is complete nonsense. You can make players dramatically faster and much quicker.

Another one is this: "If they do not bite as a puppy, they will never bite." Again, this is nonsense. We have to coach them to make them hitters. We are developing them physically so they will be hitters.

Men, you are welcome to come visit us at any time. You do not even need to call me to tell me you are coming. I hope that you can learn something from this lecture today that you can apply to your program. Thanks for coming to the Nike Coach of the Year Clinic.

Jeremy Plaa

AIR RAID OFFENSE PRACTICE ORGANIZATION

Thomas Downey High School, California

Thank you. I want to talk to you about the practice structure of our air raid offense at Thomas Downey High School. In addition, I want to tell you how we utilize the Hudl® software program. You may have heard about it, and you may be using it yourself. With the Hudl program, I can take this presentation that I will be making for you and show it to my whole team in a meeting, or I can share it with them individually if they have an Internet connection. So, this presentation is something that my kids will have, with the exception of some of the slides I inserted specifically for this clinic. I am going to show how we install our practice structure using this and using video. Hudl is a great deal for us.

Within an hour after practice or after a game, it is on the Internet, and the kids, and especially my assistant coaches, can watch film any time on Saturday after a game, or within an hour after practice. The coaches can go on there and type in notes in real time. It is simple to use.

Hudl has an exhibit at the clinic here, and Kim Burnham is one of the Hudl reps. She is great to work with so definitely pay a visit to her exhibit booth before you leave.

Men, we have a great staff of coaches at Downey High. If it were not for our offensive-minded coaches, we would not be throwing the ball for almost 400 yards a game. We are located in Modesto, Northern California, in a school much as you probably have here. We would be considered an inner-city school, with a large number of minority players who come from disadvantaged backgrounds and broken homes.

We do not have many big kids. We only had six kids on a 55-man roster this year who weighed over 200 pounds. That is okay for the spread offense, but it is not very good for defense. Because of that, even though we had great numbers on offense this year, every game was a shootout, and it did not bode too well for our record.

I have won 12 games in three years of trying to rebuild this varsity program, so you are going to get an ego-free coach up here. If you want to talk to me at any time, I am more than willing. We are doing some great things on offense, while our defense still needs a lot of work. I will be attending some defensive sessions today.

We are a two-platoon team for the most part. Some of our special athletes go both ways, but for the most part these kids are practicing on one side of the ball for the majority of practice. Our practices run no more than two hours long, and we try to get as many reps as possible. As I get into the practice presentation, you will see how we do that.

Our quarterback was statistically rated number one in California through 10 games this year, and our receivers were rated number one and number two. The main reason they had so many catches was that we lacked a running game. It was not that we loved throwing it so much. It was more that we found ourselves behind in games because we lacked talent on defense. Our screen game and our short passing game served as our running game. We threw the ball 78 percent of the time.

Tempo

We are a tempo team, and a hurry-up team. We are going to go as fast as we can. We run a "fire alarm" kind of offense, where we call two plays, run the first one, get back on the line and run the second play as fast as we can. We will do that maybe four or five times a game.

One of our favorite things to do is a play called "do it." When a play is over, we say, "Do it! Do it! Do it!" and we line up in five wideouts, and snap the ball on "go," and all five receivers run five-step stop routes. We put our three-receiver set to the wideside with both of our outside receivers on the numbers, inside guys on the hash, and the third guy to the wideside splits the hashes. The quarterback just finds the easiest completion and throws it. We were 93 percent on that play this year, for what is usually a six-yard gain. We like it as a second-down play.

On top of "do it," we also have a fire alarm play called Cobra, which is just like "do it" except instead of stopping at five steps, they all go deep. Next year, we will change it a little and have our middle guy go shallow across the field. We only ran Cobra about five times last year toward the end of the season as a complement to "do it," and we hit it twice for touchdowns.

We run simple plays. Each of our plays are one-name words, and we signal everything to our players. Our four-vertical pattern is "viper," and our comeback route is "bench." We have funny signals for every play we run. We give our kids 100-percent ownership over coming up with those signals. One play we run is an action pass, so the kids named it "rap." Of course, our offensive coordinator's signal had to be a little sideline dance.

Practice Structure

I am not going to go over many X's and O's with you today. I am going to discuss practice structure. One of the things we did is run our plays on landmarks once we got inside the 40-yard line, and that made a huge difference. We did not have a play for every yard line, but we did have two plays for every five-yard line. We had a main play and an answer for that play.

In practice on Mondays, we are a left-hash team. On Tuesdays, we are a right-hash team, and on Wednesdays, we are a center-of-the-field team. We were 88 percent hash plays this year, and 12 percent center-of-the-field plays. We want to use the field as much as we can.

We have three basic formations. We line up either in spread, trips, or empty sets, and we always set our best route runner, who is our Z-receiver, to the wideside of the field. We always set our two outside receivers, X and Y, on the numbers, and they never switch sides. Finally, our A-receiver, who is as a do-it-all H-back, is the one who adjusts to spread or trips. He could be a receiver or a blocker. If spread, he is on the shortside, and if in trips, he is on the wideside. We actually just yell the formation from the sideline, and the kids line up in it right away.

Running our practice this way has had a big effect because in practice every Monday we will get on the left hash and go from the 40 down to the goal line. After we get inside the 10, we have a play for every two yards.

We practice like that every day. On Tuesdays, we go down the right hash and Wednesdays we run our center-of-the-field plays and our special plays. Doing it like that, we get repetition and our kids get comfortable with our play calls. With comfort comes success, so as we go through that, we get better and better and our efficiency goes way up.

One key to having a good offense is having good play callers who understand defensive structure. More than that, I think is repetition in practice. Another key is positive feedback, which we do through video. We will film everything we can. We once filmed off of a 12-foot ladder set up behind the offense, but now we have one of those nice end-zone cameras that we use for both practice and games.

The other thing I brought with me today is a little flip camera that you can use from a ladder or any other way you like in practice. I just went on their website and found out that, if you are a teacher, they have a deal of two for 150 bucks. It is just a little one-hour hard drive video camera with a three times zoom, but that is enough.

The picture is clear enough that you can film any segment of practice, plug it into the USB port, save it as a video file, and upload it to Hudl. The kids can then go into Hudl and watch right away. The coaches can make notes and send them e-mails on the films. Our wide receivers and quarterback coaches are doing drill tapes with it right now. I understand that Hudl is coming out with a texting feature, so as soon as you upload something it automatically sends a text to the players' phones, telling them that there is new film up on Hudl. The kids get on it, they watch it, and that is way more than we did a year ago. It is a good deal.

Now, before I get on with our practice structure, if you are interested in this presentation, and you are on Hudl, I can literally escrow this to you. That is, if you e-mail me, and you are on Hudl, I can send you this presentation just as I would send it to one of our players.

The First 25 Minutes

I want to talk about the first 25 minutes of practice. To me, this is the most crucial thing. Our offensive coordinator this year was new. As he saw what I did, I honestly think he might have had some doubts at first. Though he never said it, I think he wondered why we did the same thing every single day, but at the end of the season, he said he totally agreed with the plan. It is about repetition and comfort. It is not necessarily about play calling on Friday night.

Downey Football

First, we want to set up all of our drills to compete against ourselves. A drill is not going to be fully effective unless you incorporate some sort of competition that goes along with it. We want to focus on doing it right, doing it quickly, and having some competition in the process.

The best way to motivate kids is time. If we have a kid who has bad grades, we bring him in for "Monday Lunch Club." We are taking his personal time away from him. If we want to motivate them in practice, we have a five-minute break following the first 25-minute period, which we can lengthen if they did well and shorten if they did not. We want to go fast in that first 25-minute period, but we do not want to sacrifice quality.

We get at least 10 receptions per minute of practice, and usually more. We are also going to

score right around 200 touchdowns in that 25-minute period. Two years ago, we did not score 200 touchdowns in a week. You want to practice scoring touchdowns. This is all in your handout.

As soon as we start practice, we will run our "stops" play as our warm-up (Diagram #1). Our goal is to have 90 percent completions versus air.

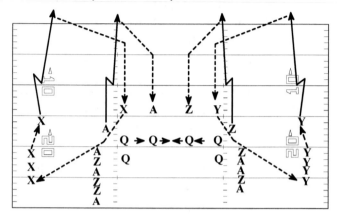

Diagram #1. Stops Warm-Up

You can see here how the landmarks are important. We will have our guys run five-step stops, and we will start with them running about 50 percent. We want to make sure they get a good first step with no false stepping. We coach that hard all spring and summer and all through the fall

Then, we want to make sure they catch the ball right around the six-yard mark. That way the quarterback knows where they are going to be. We also want to see them get a good base. When the ball is in the air, they start to set up their feet so as they catch it, they can do something with it. They might only be going half speed, but they can still be doing it correctly.

The rule for us in practice is that the receivers are going to go through two lines at the same speed, or they are going to score a touchdown. I say two lines because some of our routes on air have some guys going deep and some guys going short, so to keep the drill going fast, we say, "Two lines or score" every single time. Two lines for us is 20 yards. Whatever it is, you want to see them burst after the catch.

Our goal is 90 percent or we want 30 completions. Once we get into August and September, this drill takes about two-and-a-half minutes. When we start to teach this on May 12, when we get all of our spring sport athletes out, we may spend a full 45 minutes on this drill. We are going to make sure on day one that they understand everything there is about this drill, from what they do to why they do it.

Quarterback Focus

Our quarterbacks each bring three footballs to the drill. We want them to spread out from hash to hash. Remember, this is a warm-up drill, and they probably have not thrown a ball yet, so this is just a 12- to 15-yard throw. They will take the ball and throw nice and easy, with good technique, working up to normal velocity.

Every time we have an "all-ball" catch, meaning all four guys catch the ball, or all five if it is a five-man route, the quarterbacks will recognize this and alert the receivers with a call of, "All ball, give me three!" Everyone claps three times together, and it gets them going. You get four or five "all balls" during a 25-minute period, and you are ready to go, ready to keep scoring touchdowns. We want to push the reps and eliminate down time.

Receiver Focus

Our receiver focus is the same thing. We take a one-half- to three-quarter-speed warm-up, and after two-and-a-half minutes, we are up to speed. We do not stretch before practice. We go out and start running drills. We want to use the noose, thumbs, and fingers, tuck the ball, and burst two lines. If the receiver does not run through two lines, which is 10 yards, we count that as a drop in this drill. Starting this year, we will have our receivers bring the ball back, get down on one knee, and simulate a shotgun snap to the quarterbacks for their next throw. Then, they go to the back of the line and rest.

We only gave up nine sacks this past year in 470 pass attempts. Part of the reason is that we screen a lot and we throw a lot of short passes. As a result, teams stop blitzing us as much. They try to play five across on us, or they will play four high and play it safe.

For all of our practice we are on a segment timer. If you do not have one, get a kid with a stopwatch, but it is important to me that we stay on time. You can use a horn or megaphone, but our segment timer is set up to time our sessions. It was worth the thousand dollars we spent on it. We take it out every practice, plug it in, hit the start button, and we go on and run our drills.

I want to show you how we keep track of completions in practice. We have a typed-out form, which we laminate, put on a clipboard, and keep in the ball bag. Our goal is to be 90 percent or better catching the ball and finishing the play. We want 30 completions in the first two-and-a-half minutes, so this sheet has a row of numbers from 30 down to 1. A manager or injured player stands behind the drill and crosses off every catch. Any time we have an incompletion or a drop, he puts a tally mark there. At the end of the drill, as soon as we get this all the way down to zero, we are done, so we just go on to the next drill, which is our viper versus air drill. The manager keeping the stat sheet just goes on to the next row of numbers to record the catches there.

He can take however many tally marks he had in each drill, add it to 30, and put it right there on the sheet. At the end of practice, we can see if we met our goal or not. Maybe early in the season, we will have to adjust our time so we are getting more reps, so keeping track of completions tells us what we need to do.

Viper Four High

We do the same thing for our viper four high drill. We go 10 reps from the center of the field, 15 from the hash in spread, and 15 from the hash in trips. I will go over all of that, but nothing changes here. This is how our routes on air run. We have this form with Mondays on one side and Tuesdays on the other. It is laminated, and we use a dry erase pen on it. At the end of the week, we can just wipe it off so we can use it again.

Our players are competing against themselves for more time. As soon as they get to 30 completions, we go on to the next drill. As soon as we get to 30 completions in viper versus air, we go to the next drill (Diagram #2). As soon as we get 40 in viper four high, we go to the next drill. There have been times when they have had a seven- or eight minute-water break, and there have been times when they only have a minute or two to get a quick washout and then get back to business.

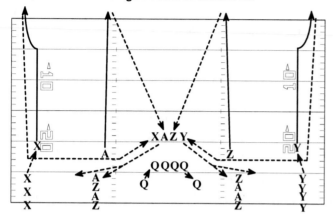

Diagram #2. Viper on Air

Viper air is our four vertical route. The objective here is to finish our warm-up and go from 75 percent to full speed. We still want to be 90 percent complete, and we still want 30 completions in two-and-a-half minutes. The drill does not change.

The techniques are a little bit different. Our X's and Y's are our fastest guys or maybe our tallest guys if they are borderline speed. Our Z-receiver is our best route runner. He has to make all the adjustments. He is the player who is usually open. Our A-receiver can be a little slower mainly because he usually works the shortside of the field.

Our A-receiver has to be a good route runner too, but is usually not as talented as our Z-receiver is. Our A-receiver this year had very average talent, but was a great kid who was very smart and did the things asked of him. He maybe ran a 5.0 40 and had marginal hands. By contrast, our Z-receiver caught 103 balls and the Y-receiver caught about the same, while our A-receiver caught about 50.

Quarterback Focus

For our quarterback focus, we teach "rocker, plant, and throw" if throwing outside. For us, that means you are taking a rocker step as you receive the ball, you plant, and you throw the ball with some air to the outside. We want to complete that outside throw within 30 yards to the outside bucket or the outside window.

If we are throwing inside, we play action on viper if we are going to throw the seams. If we see one-high, we are throwing the seam. We will give a little ride, plant, and complete the seam at 20 yards on the hash. We will keep our eyes downfield and watch the safety while we are faking the ball. We want to see which way he turns his hips and which way he commits. If he inverts, you know the other corner is probably inverting, and if he inverts we want to pick up the far wide receiver.

Outside Receiver Focus

Our outside receivers run down the numbers. We want to stay on the numbers as long as we can. As the ball is released, we want to keep that six-yard window open between the numbers and the sideline. The quarterback is told to throw the ball to our outside shoulder, which gives us three or four yards to work with easily. At the last second, we want to adjust out, have our pinkies together, and snap our eyes to our hands as the ball comes in. This is a key for the receiver. It made a big difference for us.

In addition, our coaches or managers will get the little shields and in this drill, only we will jump out in front of these receivers and try to jam them up. We want them to learn to restack that defender. Every year there is one team that will play press coverage on us and bring six or seven on the rush every single time. We have to be ready for that, so we can lick our shops and hit the home run.

Restacking means that when the defender jams us, we want to get around him, get back on our landmark within 5 to 10 yards, and get him on our back hip. That way the quarterback knows where we are going to be, and we can slow down if we need to in order to catch the ball, or draw a pass-interference call.

Inside Receiver Focus

For our inside receiver focus, we want to run down the hashes, speed release, and snap the eyes to the hands. For our inside guys, it is okay to catch the ball palms up in the noose, but they can catch with pinkies together as well.

Lack of effort in this drill means 10 pushups. We want to hustle back and give the quarterback a snap. We can check all these things on film, make notes on Hudl, and let all the kids see them.

After these two drills, we have five minutes done. The first period is half stops and half viper versus air. Period two is a five-minute period. To us, four vertical is our best play. We only completed it about 40 percent of the time this year but we averaged twelve yards per attempt.

On four verticals, we want to run landmarks. The Z-receiver has the option to bend it, on the wideside of the field, if the center of the field opens up. He can bend it into a skinny post, expect to catch the ball at 20 yards, and take a hit from the far safety. All the other receivers have the option to shut it down, but not until they cross 10 yards, and only if the defensive back is still stuck in a backpedal over the top.

We saw a lot of four-high this year. People just stayed in four-high against us because we could not run the ball much. We run the routes as fast as we can, and if the defensive back is still pedaling when we cross 10 yards, we just shut it down. We probably completed 10 shutdowns all year long, but you will see a good example of it on the film I am going to show later.

Quarterback Focus

For our quarterback focus, we want to use the correct inside or outside throw technique. A "two ball" for us is just over the backers with just a little air, while a "three ball" is a lot of air to the outside. We want to make the correct read on the defensive back, so as the quarterback drops, he first looks at the defensive back over the top. If he is reading the inside guy, he is looking at the hash.

Receiver Focus

We want the Z-receiver to bend the seam to the skinny post if the middle of the field "opens" post-

snap. For the X-, Y-, and A-receivers, they run a go route with speed. If the defensive back is still over the top after they cross 10 yards, they should shut down their route. We want them to score or run through two lines. They must hustle back and give the quarterback a simulated snap.

The receivers' focus should now be on going full speed. They are fully warmed-up and they are still scoring touchdowns. We run it from the center of the field first, get 10 catches there, and then move it over. We put four kids out, 10 yards away, simulating defensive backs. We ask them to move in one direction for five yards on the snap, which gives our receivers a good read. Most of the time, we like them to go deep but it is not always going to happen that way. After four or five reps, the defensive kids switch. That way, one kid is not playing defense the whole time.

Any time we run viper and the ball is on the hash, actually, any time the ball is on the hash, the two shortside guys have an automatic switch route (Diagram #3). The outside guy is going to cheat down inside the numbers, and by the time he gets to 10, he will be running up the hash. He cannot run across the hash mark and still be an option for the quarterback because it creates a difficult angle for the throw.

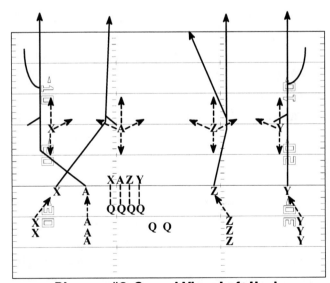

Diagram #3. Spread Viper Left Hash

ROUTES ON AIR

Monday Script: Left Hash

- Trips stretch
- Trips bench
- Trips X-shallow
- Spread mesh
- Cobra
- Do it

Tuesday Script: Right Hash

- Trips stretch
- Trips bench
- Trips Y-shallow
- Spread mesh
- Cobra
- Do it

Wednesday Script: Center of the Field

- Spread smash
- Spread A-shallow
- Spread Z-shallow
- Spread bench (alternate)
- Cobra
- Do it

Our routes-on-air period is 10 minutes long. We have a script that we run, but we do five reps of each play or 15 catches per route, and we run six every day, which is 30 plays max every day. That comes out to be six plays from the left hash on Mondays, six from the right hash on Tuesdays, and six from the center of the field on Wednesdays. That is how we practice that.

Tailbacks sometimes are in the route, and sometimes they are not. If they are not, they are expected to run their play-action fake or run their pass protection. We tell tailbacks to jump out on each other as we do in the four-high viper drill with the receivers, and give each other some work.

We run this thing we call "max screens," where all five receivers are running their type of screen (Diagram #4). For our outside receiver screens,

their screen is an alley screen. On the shortside, they run three steps up, come back, catch the ball inside the numbers, and run straight up the alley. On the wideside, they take one step up the field, catch the ball behind the line of scrimmage, and get into the alley.

It is the same for the Z-receiver. He runs three steps up, comes back and catches, then gets up the field. The A-receiver will fake a block, then slide underneath, catch the ball, and get upfield. Our tailback has two types of screens. He has a swing route, and he has a letter screen, which is a triple screen we can throw left, middle, or right.

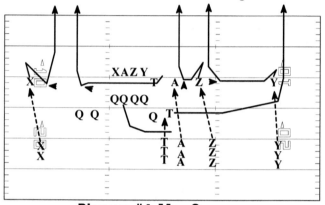

Diagram #4. Max Screens

We are also looking for 50 completions on these as well, the same kind of thing I showed you with that chart earlier. We want to cross them off as we complete them. This goes really fast because we go up to the 10-yard line and we are scoring about 15 or 20 touchdowns a minute here. Because the throws are short, the drill goes even faster.

We want about four reps per minute on this. In routes on air, we want about three reps per minute, in stops about four reps per minute, and on viper versus four-high about three reps per minute.

We have a second part of our max screens that we call "bubble" (Diagram #5). That is a two-in-one concept. We never call bubble; we always call zone. If there is any leverage where the outside backer is inside at all, the quarterback has the freedom to throw the bubble right away. At any time it is zone, these guys are running bubble out here. If it is trips zone, where we only have one receiver, he can run an out, and the quarterback will throw it if it is open.

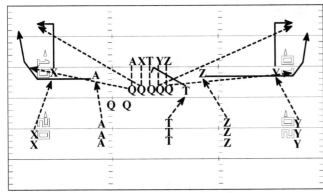

Diagram #5. Max Bubbles Screens

Let me wrap this up by showing you a statistical summary of what we are trying to accomplish in our air raid practice.

Success = Repetition and Feedback

Period	Minutes	Goal	Catch	TDs
1	5	90%	60	60+
2	5	80%	40	20+
3	10	80%	90	40+
4	5	90%	50	50+
Total	25		240	170+

Men, if you are interested in what we do, I am going to be here during the dinner hour. I will be around during the other clinic talks.

If you are not on Hudl, and you are interested in it, you can put in my name, and they will give you 10 percent off. In addition, I always get tons of requests for game film, so I brought some DVDs with me if you are interested. If not, just email me if you are on Hudl, and I will email you whatever I have. I will escrow everything out to you, and you can check it out. I think our success is all about the practice structure. Thank you again for having me.

THE WINNNG EDGE: PUNT RETURN/BLOCK

Ogemaw Heights High School, Michigan

We have three basic principles that we try to live by with special teams. We treat our special teams as a third phase of or third team in our program. I have coached with a lot of coaches who have talked about their offensive and defensive philosophy. I have heard a lot of clinic speeches and coaches talk about their offensive and defensive philosophy. We feel that we have been able to change things in games by what we do with our special teams. We spend as much time in film study of breaking down the opponent's special teams as we do on offense and defense. We feel this is a great way to impact the game. We try to use this to our advantage.

We use our best players on special teams. If you are in a small class D school, you may not have a choice of the players on the special teams. We will use the players best suited for the positions. Special teams is not an area to sneak a kid into the game. Each spot has a talent need and we must find the best kid to fill that spot. For some of these special teams, it may not be the quarterback, and it may not be the stud offensive lineman.

We want to use a relentless attack with our special teams. We will always look to take advantage of a special team's weakness and attack it relentlessly. We will not miss out on an opportunity to change the game.

I want to talk about the practice plan. We spend about 30 to 40 minutes of our practice time each day on special teams. We try to focus on two special teams and we mirror them. We may do kickoff with our varsity team, and we will do kickoff returns with our JV team on our other field. We do not go with our varsity team against the JV team.

We take each segment of the kickoff and break it down into individual drills. We know all coaches spend time with the individuals on the offense and the defense. I have been on teams where we only worked on the punt team. We put the team together, lined up the punt team, and did team drills.

We spend between 10 and 15 minutes on the individual phase of the special teams. We break it down into small chunks before we go into the team situation. I am going to focus on the punt return today. We call it punt return and block. We ended up with seven punts returned this year and we blocked nine punts. We did have a lot of fair catches in between those returns and blocks. We take advantage of some things we do, and we get after the punt.

I want to talk about some of the drills we do with the punt. We go to team camp in the summer. We work with some other teams at the camp, and when we get to team sessions we actually use them to work on special teams. One of the things we do is a lot of fun at camp. The coaches get all of the lawn chairs up and we do a gong show. Each kid who is in our program tries to punt. The coaches give the kids a thumbs up or thumbs down when they punt the ball. We move them all through the lines fast. It is a great way to start the camp. We are going to find the best punter on our team.

The last five punters (we have used only one of them) was a punter in junior high school. We find kids are labeled as non-special team players when they are young and never get a chance to show what they can do as a punter. We can take the time to look at them in the summer camps. It would surprise you to find out that the kid who is the fastest may not be the best at catching a punt. In camp, we give everyone a chance to show what they can do on the different special team positions.

PUNT RETURN AND BLOCK

I want to start with our punt return. First, stance and starts. We are in a sprinter's stance. We want the inside hand down, and the inside foot back. We want the hips high, with the back arm up. We want to explode on the high hip and take a big ground-gaining step. We rip the outside arm hard through the hole. We try to stay low on the push move. In the film, you will see all 10 of the rushers in that stance, and we are coming after the block in that stance. The big coaching point is to make sure they are explosive with the technique.

We are going to play kids with speed on this unit. We do not play a lot of kids who cannot move. Moving kids around and finding kids who can be effective is important.

We set up a wall on the return. We have different types of returns on the punt return. It is the fence concept where we set the fence outside to form a wall.

The wall anchor sets the wall on the numbers and works back to the returnee (Diagram #1). The following players space out five yards apart, slowly working to the middle of the field. Never let a man by you.

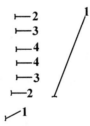

Diagram #1. Punt Return Wall

We number the players involved in the return in the following order. We have the #1 man as the anchor and he sets the wall. Next, comes the 2, 3, 4, 4, 3, 2, and the other number 1 is who we call the leaker. He picks up anyone who leaks through the wall with a knockout block.

We run this repeatedly in practice. We run the drill without a ball, without a set, or without a punt team to go against us. We want to make sure they are set up in the wall with proper spacing. They must understand where they need to go on the return.

We set up punt rush drills that we call weeble-wobble. We call out the player's numbers one at a time and they work out of their stance rushing to the block point (Diagram #2). We want the rush man to take a good angle toward the block point. We want him to be sure to run through the point, keeping his hands over the point as long as possible. We tell him not to leave his feet.

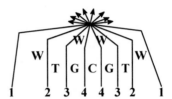

Diagram #2. Rush Drill

Next, we set up weeble-wobbles in the formation of our opponent's punt team with personal protectors on each side, then we work live. We want them to rush upfield until they can no longer be blocked by the inside man.

The first thing we want to know about the opponents' punter is if he is right-footed or left-footed. We found a big difference in the angle you have to take against a right- or left-footed punter.

The next point we look for is the depth of the punter when he lines up to take the long snap. We do not care where he catches the snap. If he catches it at 15 yards or 10 yards, we are not concerned. We want to know where he makes contact when he kicks the ball. That is our block point and that is where we must aim for to block a punt.

We set this up depending on which foot the punter uses, and the depth he kicks the ball at the block point. When we practice against the team during the week, we can tell our punt rush the kicker is right-footed and he makes contact with the punt at a depth of seven yards. That is our aiming point.

To keep teams from running a fake punt on us, we run a drop drill to have players drop out of the rush to protect against the fake punt (Diagram #3). We run a drop drill. Players, one at a time from each side, take one step into their man then drop to over the top of the wing, looking for fakes, then getting to their block. On the first rep, one side gets to the corner, and the other gets to the deep middle of the field for the center's release.

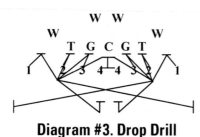

Diagram #3. Drop Drill

This is how we get to where we are going in the wall. We stress to the players that they are going as if they are going to block the kick on every punt. We want to put pressure on the punter that we are coming after every punt.

On the release drill, as a group, each player will step, punch, and sit, waiting for the kick Diagram #4). Our called number will drop to depth. When the kick is away, the players will circle to the wall.

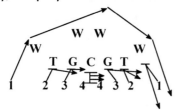

Diagram #4. Release Drill

We line up with an eight-man line, numbered 1 to 4 on each side. We line up on the inside shade.

- #4s play inside shade of the guard (2i).
- #3s play inside shade of the tackle (4i).
- #2s play inside shade of the wing (7).
- #1s line up for a direct path to the block point.
- Corners jam gunners and keep them away from the returnee.

We see a lot of different punt formations. We want to make sure our kids know how to line up on the different looks. We have our basic rules. We make sure the #1's pick up any wide split formations.

If the #1's do go wide with the bullets split outside, our #2's do what the #1 did before they split. Now, the #1's become extra gun protectors.

I will show you our alignments against the different formations we see. First is the spread punt formation with both ends split and a wide slot to each side (Diagram #5).

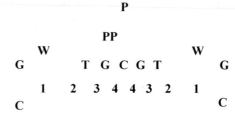

Diagram #5. Spread Punt Formation

Against the tight punt, we line up with the #1's wide and the corners inside over the wings (Diagram #6).

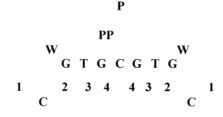

Diagram #6. Tight Punt

We move the interior line inside against the inside slot formation, where the two up backs are in the slots between the guards and the center (Diagram #7).

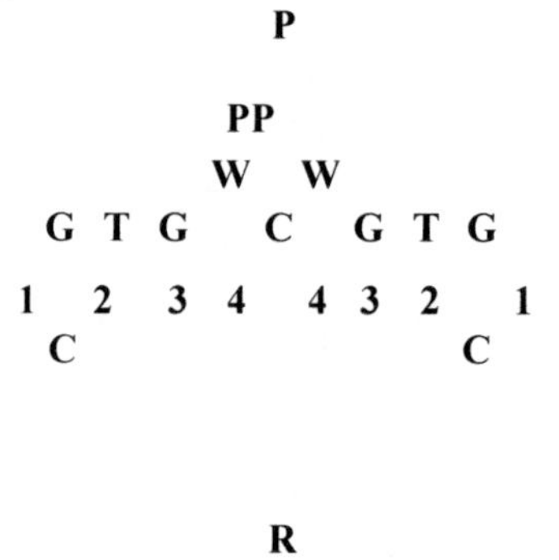

P

PP

W W

G T G   C   G T G

1   2   3   4   4   3   2   1

C   C

R

Diagram #7. Inside Slot Formation

Against the teams that use the three deep protectors, we line up the same way we do against the wing formation punt (Diagram #8).

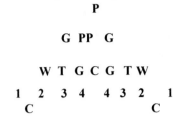

Diagram #8. Three Deep Protectors

Against the trips split punt, we adjust the corner and our #1 and #2 players (Diagram #9). We move the backside #1 over on the outside slot man and the corner has the widest man on the outside.

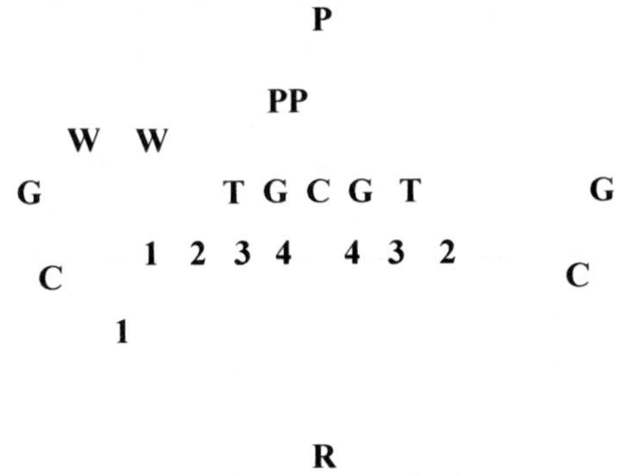

P

           PP

  W W

G   T G C G T   G

  C   1 2 3 4 4 3 2   C

    1

R

Diagram #9. Trips Split

Against the wing spread punt, we move the corner up to cover the outside ends, and bring our #1's outside on the wings (Diagram #10).

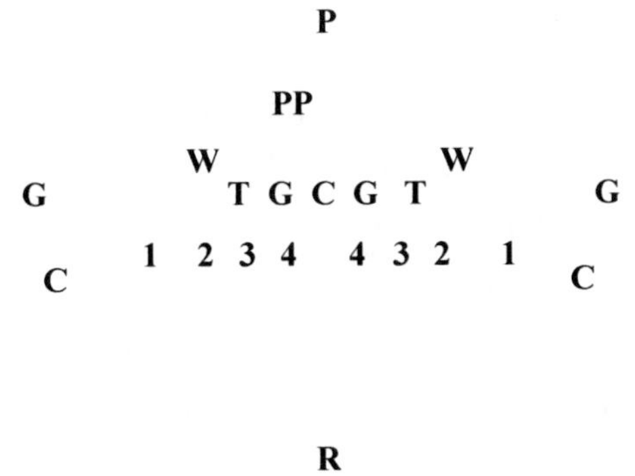

P

      PP

     W   W

G   T G C G T   G

  C   1 2 3 4 4 3 2 1   C

R

Diagram #10. Wing Spread

We make any adjustments from the scouting report and from film study. We want to make sure the kids understand what the opponents do on the punt team, so we can take advantage of it in the punting situations.

Here are the basic assignments for the punt return and block:

- If not on a block, step into the man inside you and hold until the ball is away.
  - ✓ #4s: snapper
  - ✓ #3s: guards
  - ✓ #2s: tackles
  - ✓ #1s: wings
  - ✓ If on a block, rush upfield as far as you can until the man inside cannot block you anymore (about three to five yards).

The rushers come off the ball on the snap. When they become free, they head straight for the block point. If knocked off their course, or if they cannot get through, they automatically go to the wall. We want them to make every effort to get to the wall.

Against the wing set, we line our #1's over the wingback. After the snap of the ball, the following is what we want from those four men to each side of the center:

- #4 steps laterally and waits for the long snapper to pick his head up, then holds him up, not allowing a free release.
- #3 steps right to the guard and engages.
- #2 steps right to the tackle and engages.
- #1 steps over in front of the wing. If the wing releases, he is man-to-man coverage, looking for the fake. If no fake, he continues to run with him and becomes a protector.

We had a hard time getting across the fact that the rushers must be on one side or the other of the punter to block the kick. They go to the aiming point and then get their hands across the ball. We are going to lay out across the body. If the #4 rusher gets free, he wants to stay on the same side of the field that he lined up to rush from. The #3, #2, and #1 are going to cross. The players who cross have a better angle to block the kick and they are less likely to rough the punter coming from an angle.

- When approaching the block point, start to lean out over your toes, as if falling on your face.
- Place your arms up above your head and cross your wrists.
- Twist your upper body in order to keep your hands over the block point as long as possible.

We usually get the pole vault pit out and work on the punt block. This helps the players who are afraid to lay out. I am a big fan of Superman. I want those punt blockers to lay-out as Superman does when he is in the air. The big point we stress is the aiming point. We want the hands crossed when they launch the layout.

We used to say the aiming point is two yards in front of the punter. We do not say that anymore. Now, we tell them their aiming point is seven yards in front of the punter. We set up the drill with the pole vault pit at that distance, so they can get a visual picture of what the aiming point looks like.

The question now becomes how we are going to decide which players will drop out to check for the fake punt. We assign the players numbers for their positions. We stress the fact that players must know their numbers and where they line up on the front line. For example, say we call 32 (Diagram #11). That means our #3 man in from the end inside to the center on the left side, and the #2 man on the right side, are going to be the drop players. This is how we work the calls.

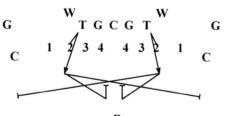

Diagram #11. #32 Drop

- Know your numbers by heart.
- Numbers will be called for players who will drop out and check for fake.
- Numbers could be double digits, triple digits, or quadruple digits. For example, the first number is for the left side, and the second number is for the right side (32).

- When dropping, step into the line of scrimmage, then run out at a 45-degree angle, while looking for the fakes.
- If to the wall side, check fake, then drop to protect the middle of the field (long snapper early release).
- If away from the wall, check, and then help block the gunner to the wall side.

When we first started using this system, we only used double-digit numbers. I let the younger coaches talk me into calling multiple numbers now. We may call no number, one number, two numbers, three numbers, or even four numbers now. Against one team, I was so worried about a fake punt that I called 2-4-4-2. We took both 2's and both 4's out to look for the fake.

We have all eight men walk up on the line of scrimmage on the punt situation. They all take that first step, but we can drop someone out to watch for the fake punt. The technique we use on the drop to look for the fake punt is similar to the drop of a linebacker to the hook/curl zone. A lot of the kids we use on the punt block and return are the linebacker-type kids who have the ability to drop back as they do in the linebacker's position. It could be defensive end-type players as well. In addition, we use some strong safeties in those drop positions.

Typically, we do not drop #1's on the calls. They are the players who have the great angles to block the punt.

When on a block:
- Run upfield until the man inside of you can no longer block you (usually three to five yards).
- When free of a blocker, roll over to the block point and run through it.
- If knocked off course, abort and get to the wall.
- If you are picked up by a blocker, abort the block and get to the wall.
- #4, #3, and #2 must run straight upfield until the man inside of them can no longer block them.
  - ✓ #4: upfield until past the snapper, passing through the personal protector, attacking his inside shoulder

✓ #3: upfield until past the guard, going through the personal protector's outside shoulder

✓ 2 upfield until past the tackle, passing the personal protector outside

- #1 can rush straight through the block point.

If we call 03, it means no one is dropping from the left side. We are only dropping one man to the middle of the field. We are playing a one-linebacker drop. It occurs in a situation where we do not expect the punt team to fake the punt. We put the one man back looking for the fake. If the fake does not come, he has the long snapper.

If the punt team is backed up to their two-yard line we do not think they are going to fake the punt, so we call 00. We sent eight men after the punt. If they fake it, they may end up scoring, unless we get to the ball first. We only have that one return man back to help. We do not do that very often, but we try to take advantage of the situation.

Here is where this gets unique or different to a degree. A few years ago, we went from a numbering system to names for the calls. We did some crazy thing in regard to how we teach the kids to remember these calls. Most of our staff were teachers and we wanted our kids to learn some things differently. One thing we did with our special teams was to give them names. The coach who was running the teams was a science teacher. He was a big geology buff. He enjoyed the study of rocks. He came up with a system to name these calls for our teams. We set the walls with the rock names. These are all rocks:

- Granite and marble are hard rocks and hard to break. On our full returns, we want to build walls that they cannot break through.

- Basalt and quartz are rocks created by heating and cooling processes, making them hard. On our half blocks and half returns, we want to bring the heat and set up a solid wall too.

- Shale is a rock that breaks apart easily, allowing it to fit into cracks. We want to break through the cracks in their protections.

- Magma is our middle return, because it comes from the center of the volcano.

In addition, because there may be some of our players on the field when we run the return team out on the field, we may not have time to huddle. Therefore, we use the rocks for our punt returns. This allows us to change the play on the fly.

- gRanite = Full return right
- marbLe = Full return left
- Shale = Full block
- Magma = Middle return
- feLdspaR = Block left, return right
- hoRnbLende = Block right, return left
- basaLt = Block left, return left
- quaRtz = Block right, return right

You may ask why we would want to do something like this. Sometimes, I wonder the same thing. It gives kids an opportunity to learn something else outside the classroom situation. It forces them to try to understand something different from X's and O's. It does not matter if they ever become a geologist, they have a little better knowledge of the world. It is not a big deal, but it enables us to call out the return we want without just calling out left or right return.

- basaLt = Block left, return left
- quaRtz = Block right, return right

The terms basalt and quartz are heating and cooling rocks, so we made them our half-wall and half-return calls. On basalt, we are going to block right, and return left. We send one-half of the players to block the kick. We send the other half to the other side to set half of a wall to the return side. If the side that goes for the block punt does not get through, they drop off and join in the wall on the opposite side of the field.

We call shale as our all-out full block of the punt. On Magma, we are setting the wall to the middle of the field.

I want to give you a few examples of our calls against the punt formations. First, we call a 43 full return left (Diagram #12). Our #1 away from the wall is going to take an angle to go to block the punt. We have had this call on before when the #1 man has blocked the punt. We are always sending one man to force the punt. He is going hard after the block at the aiming point. He has a good angle on the point. If he does not get through to block the punt, he is going to be the man who filters through the wall and serves as the leak man. He picks up any opposite jersey that penetrates the wall.

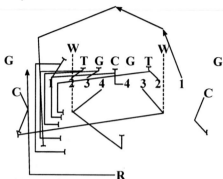

Diagram #12. 43 Full Return Left

We are dropping the #4 man on the left side to pick up the snapper. The offside #3 helps the onside corner on the double-team block. The #1 man on the side of the return is setting the depth of the wall. He must check the wingback before he leaves to set the depth of the wall. The other down men step up and peel off to form the wall, based on the depth the #1 man has set. They space five yards apart on the wall. This is ideally a five-person wall. The corner is blocking the split end on the opposite side. He stays with him all the way down the field. If everyone takes the proper path, we should have the five-person wall. We are not including the #1 end coming from the punt block. He is the cleanup man or the leak man. He picks up the trash coming inside the wall. Our return back wants to start up the field and then cut behind the wall and get down the sideline.

The full block is something that will cause you to get a little nervous. We can still call any numbers. If we are going full block we are all going after the block kick (Diagram #13). If all the offensive linemen block down inside, the #1's should become free to the aiming point of the punt. It forces the personal protector to pick a side.

When a player gets off-course, aborts the block, or misses the block, he circles around in the direction he was going to make a wall in that direction. This will create a double wall return.

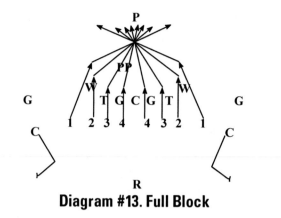

Diagram #13. Full Block

If we abort the full block, we are going to set up the wall. During a game, we can call, "Full block, abort, wall right." If we have seen something in the scouting report or on one of their films, and we think we can block the kick, we will call the full block. During the week, we work on setting the wall to our bench if the opponents make a change from what we are looking for from the scouting report. We can abort the block and run the wall to our bench. We do not want the kids getting confused where half of them run the block, and half of them abort, and they end up running into each other.

We run our middle return a little differently. We do not do this very often. Some of you may call this a "mugger" return. We want to stay with the man and push him to the sideline. The #4 to the side of the personal protector will pick up the personal protector when he releases. We have our return man catch the ball and find the seam and head upfield.

We can run a block right, return right. We do not have to cross on the play (Diagram #14). We still send the right side after the punt. We want them to block the punt if possible. The backside four men have to come across and set the wall. The two corners are blocking inside out on the two wideouts.

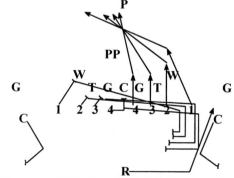

Diagram #14. Block Right, Return Right

One thing I like about this return is that punt teams will see us coming hard from our right side and they assume we are returning the ball to the other side of the formation. We can get a four-person wall with the deep man trying to get down behind the wall and inside the wide out. If we have to abort, we can get five or six players over in the wall.

On block right return left, we can still call the drop-out numbers, or we do not have to call them (Diagram #15). It is a similar concept. If we miss the block, we can fill to the wall. We want to make sure the corners are good athletes and can stay with the wide receivers on the play. In practice, we set up cones to make sure the players know where the hash marks are. We have the gray hats on the field.

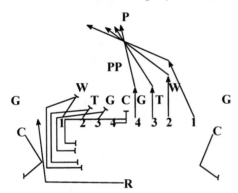

Diagram #15. Block Right, Return Left

The goals we have for our season include the following:
• Block four punts
• One block punt for a touchdown
• No penalties
• No yards given up on a fake
• Return yardage of 15 yards per attempt

We want to block four punts. In a nine-game season, if you can get a punt blocked every other game, that is not bad. It is a good thing. We had nine blocked punts this year. What is great about that is the fact we got six of those blocked punts in the playoffs. In the playoffs, you see different teams that you do not see very often, and it helps. If you play teams year in and year out, it is tough to block

a punt, because the opponents know you are going to be attempting to block the punts.

Another goal is to get one block for a touchdown each year. It could be a block at midfield and we scoop and score on. We had two blocks inside the 10-yard line and fell on the ball in the end zone for touchdowns. One of those came in a conference championship game, and the other came in the state playoffs. Those two plays were big and helped us add two trophies to our trophy cases this year. They can be big momentum changes and can change a game around in a hurry.

We do not want any penalties on the punt block punt return game. It is easy to jump offside when we are looking to block a punt. We want to make sure that we spend as much time on those situations as possible. We go against the no-count in practice to make sure our players are aware of these situations. We spend a lot of time in the summer working on these situations. We cannot wear pads during the early practices, but we can work on the kicking game in this respect.

We do not want to give up any yardage on a fake punt. One thing I was proud of this year was the fact that we did not give up any yardage on a fake punt return. We did give up yardage on two occasions when we had our regular defense on the field in punting situations. We were running our punt safe, where we keep our regular defense on the field. Twice, the opponents gained first downs on fake punts against our regular defense.

We want to average 15 yards per attempt on our punt returns. We averaged 19 yards per return this year. We want to pressure the punter with our rush on punts. We have seen the punting average go way down on their punts because of the pressure we apply on the punt block. It is a big thing for us to put pressure on the punter by going after the aiming point where the punt is going to leave his foot on the punt.

You will be able to recognize our punt return and block on the film. If you have questions, I will be glad to stick around. Thank you for your attention.

Howard Rub

WING-T OPTION OUT OF THE SPREAD OFFENSE

Astoria High School, Oregon

I appreciate you being here. What I am going to do in the next half hour is give you our base running game. Obviously, we do more than what I will show you. If you would like me to elaborate on some of the things we do, I can do that for you. The topic of this lecture is the spread running game. and I want to talk about how we incorporate it into the rest of our running game. If you are thinking about adding some wrinkles with this concept, this will be a worthwhile lecture for you. If you run this scheme already and feel like you are an expert on it, you will not get much from the lecture.

We have found this to be a good deal for us. Like any type of option game, the defense has to play assignment football. The quarterback is a running back, and someone has to account for him. We feel we can easily outnumber the defense. We can shift to an alignment to do that. The defense will want to keep a defender to spy the quarterback. He will probably align on our backside. To the strongside, we have found it relatively easy to outnumber the defense.

The focus of how we implemented this scheme was to have easy blocking adjustment. We did not change our rules or job assignments. We do not have a zone running scheme and do not do any zone blocking. We are in the shotgun and run the backside read option. We did not incorporate any zone scheme with it.

If you are familiar with Oregon High School football, you will know why we did it. One of the reasons we did it was the personnel was suited to take advantage of the system. Jordan Poyer was an outstanding player for us, who just completed his first year at the Oregon State University. He was the 2008 Oregon player of the year on offense and

defense. He was an amazing player. We knew that after his first year we were going to have to do some things to exploit his skill.

To do the things we wanted to do, I felt we needed outside help. I knew Urban Meyer did an outstanding job and one of his assistants landed the head job at University of Nevada, Las Vegas. I took my staff to Vegas, and it was a great trip for us. That is how we implemented the spread system we run. The biggest question we asked was how to teach the quarterback to read the defensive end. The answer we got was very simple. If the quarterback can outrun the defender, pull the ball. If he cannot outrun the defender, leave it with the running back.

We could not imagine that was how they were teaching the quarterback, but it was. We are not the most technical coaches, but we came up with something to tell the quarterback. We ask our quarterback to focus his eyes on the outside shoulder of the read defender. However, we use the same premise: if you can outrun, him pull the ball; if you cannot, do not pull the ball. The type of back we had in Jordan Poyer, this offense was what we needed to run. I would encourage you to incorporate this scheme because it can be affective.

Prior to 2005, we were a wing-T blocking team. We ran all the wing-T plays. We had four basic run schemes and four basic rules about blocking those schemes:

- Playside: Base rule
- Trap: Triangle
- Down
- Double (down)

The playside blocking rules were our base rules. Our linemen count defenders. The center declares the zero-numbered defender. That is his responsibility to block. The guard, tackle, and end determine whom they will block by counting defender from the zero defender. If the center calls the nose as the zero, the guard blocks the #1 defender from that position, and the tackle blocks the #2 defender.

Base Rules

- First steps are always to the direction of the call.
- OIL: Always block *over* or *inside* or *linebacker*.
- When in doubt, never block out.
- Note: Center declares "zero." Count from there.

We base the trap rule on the triangle. The trap rule is for the center and guards. The tackle to that side is blocking OIL. On the inside trap, we have add an "on/off" call to determine who the backside read is going to be.

Inside Trap Scheme

- Play 3-on-3 to the side of the call for the guards and center
- Tackle to the call uses playside rules
- Tackle away from call is either "on" or "off

We use a down blocking scheme. The down scheme means the center will declare the defender over the pulling guard. That defender is the zero defender and everyone else counts according to that man.

Down Scheme

- Center declares he is responsible for the defender aligned over our pulling guard.
- Hence, every defender away from the call must block one defender down.

In the "double" down scheme, the count will start over the tackle.

Double (Down) Scheme

- Center declares he is responsible for the defender aligned over our pulling tackle.

- Same rules apply to the offensive line as if we made a "down" call.

What we have done in the last four seasons in our base run game is all the same rules and blocking. We have not changed anything for the offensive line coach or the five players up front. We still run the base plays. What has changed is what we do on the backside relative to the read scheme. I will share some of the terms we use in the scheme. The previous coach was a wishbone/veer coach, and we kept some of his terminology in the run game. He used the term OIL, which meant over, inside, linebacker. He used the phrase, "When in doubt, never block out."

- Trap with backside read
- Buck with backside read
- Power with backside read
- Counter trap with backside read

By counting, we can eliminate some of our calls. I still use the call when we have our quarterback watch film. They make sure the center is declaring the right number. That is another lecture on how much time we spend with the quarterbacks. They spend a lot of time preparing. Every Monday and Wednesday, they come back to the school after dinner and watch film for an hour-and-a-half. We put a lot on the quarterback's plate.

In terms of counting on the edge, I had not heard these terms until we went to UNLV. We changed our concept from blocking specific people to blocking the most dangerous man. We started counting the defenders on the edge. That is a basic concept, but I must not be one of the sharpest men in the world because I was not doing it.

When we run the speed option, we use the same counting method that we used to the backside. That tells us which defender we will option on the speed option.

If you are not familiar with the spread game and you are looking for some tidbits, there things have been successful for us.

Points of Emphasis

- Two-and-a-half-foot splits for the offensive linebacker.
- Quarterback is at a five-yard depth with the heel of his foot.
- Running backs split the outside leg of the guards at a five-and-a-half-yard depth.
- Offensive linemen count to determine assignments.
- Perimeter count to determine assignments.
- Quarterback will communicate backside assignments:
  - ✓ Route or blocking assignment for slots and split ends
  - ✓ "On" or "off" for backside tackle (if not pulling)

In addition to making an "on" or "off" call, the quarterback can make calls to the receivers to the backside. Instead of blocking the defenders aligned on them, they will exchange assignments and use a fold block. He can also make a call to the slot receiver to make him the pitchman on an option play to that side.

I want to start with the inside trap play (Diagram #1). To the offensive line, it does not matter if we are running the inside trap from 2005 or 2009. They block it the same way. The five offensive linemen are blocking inside trap rules against the box defenders. The center and two guards block the triangle made up of the 1- and 3-technique defenders and the Mike linebacker. The playside tackle uses his base rule and blocks the Sam linebacker. The backside tackle has an "on" and blocks the Will linebacker. The defensive 5 technique is the read man to the backside.

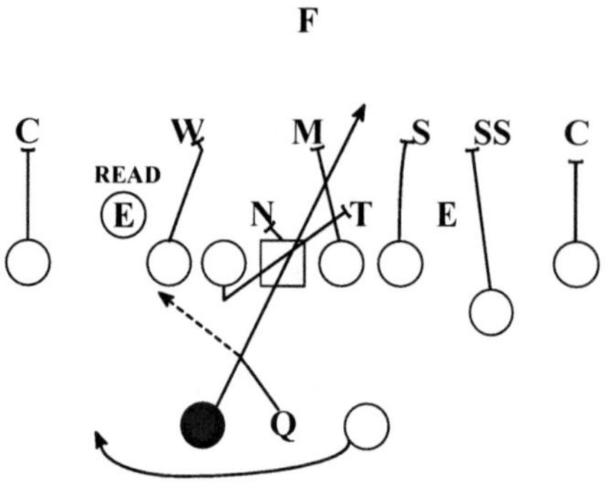

Diagram #1. Inside Trap

The formation is a shotgun set with two backs in the backfield on either side of the quarterback. The play is an inside trap to the right, and the left halfback carries the ball. The right halfback is the pitchman if the quarterback pulls the ball. The point I am trying to make is nothing changes for the offensive line on the inside trap play. They still use their trap rules and execute accordingly.

If the quarterback pulls the ball, he has decided he can outrun the defensive end. The split end has to block the corner. In the past, the split end was on the backside of the play and tried to get across the field to the inside safety. He now may be at the point of attack. He has to aggressive block the corner.

The Buck play means we are going to trap the end instead of someone inside (Diagram #2). It is the same option concept as the inside trap. We are trying to trap the end, but we may end up trapping a linebacker. In the two-back set, the fullback fills for the pulling guard. The center declares the Mike linebacker as the zero defender and blocks him. The guard blocks the #1 defender, which is the 3 technique. The tackle blocks the #2 defender, which is the Sam linebacker. The left guard pulls and blocks the defensive end.

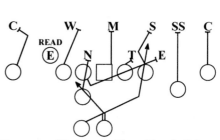

Diagram #2. Buck Two-Back Set

If we go to a one-back set, the blocking scheme becomes a down blocking scheme (Diagram #3). The center declares he is blocking the defender over the pulling guard. To the playside, the guard and tackle scheme the 3 technique and Mike linebacker. The formation is a trips set. The quarterback has to read the box. He has to determine if the Sam linebacker is in the box or out of it. If he determines the Sam linebacker is in the box, the Buck trap may not be a good play. He has the option of pulling the ball and getting out the backside.

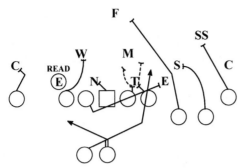

Diagram #3. Buck One-Back Set (Down)

If we were under the center and ran the Buck play the way we did in 2005, we would have had a loss on the play.

If the defense is a 3-3 look, we can use the base call to block the Buck play (Diagram #4). The center blocks the noseguard and declares him as the zero defender. The guard blocks the #1 defender, who is stacked behind the nose. The tackle has the #2 defender. Since he has a stack over him, he releases inside and blocks the B gap. Someone will fill that gap. If the down defender slants inside, the tackle washes him to the inside. If the down defender slants outside and the linebacker comes inside, the tackle inside releases and blocks the linebacker. If the defense plays the stack straight, the tackle goes inside and blocks the Sam linebacker.

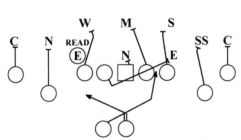

Diagram #4. Buck vs. 3-3 Base Rules

If the quarterback gives the backside tackle an "on" call, that tells the tackle to block the defensive end aligned on him. The quarterback reads the Will linebacker as the read key. The on call means we are blocking the down lineman and reading the linebacker. The off call means the tackle blocks the linebacker, and the quarterback reads the down lineman.

On the counter trap, we pull the tackle and guard from the backside (Diagram #5). In the past,

we would have to cut off the backside defensive end with someone. In the spread scheme, we read him to control him from chasing the running back. If he chases the back, we pull the ball and run the option to the backside. On the counter play, we block a down scheme. The guard kicks out, and the tackle turns up for the playside linebacker. We block the play as if it were the buck play, except the tackle pulls and blocks the linebacker. The playside blocks down.

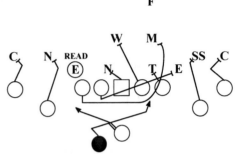

Diagram #5. Counter Trap

The slotback blocking the nickel back on the backside will look lazy as he gets into his block. He wants to get into position to block the defender, but at the same time give the defender time to react to the counter play. The further he goes to the inside, the better chance we have of pinning him to the inside if the quarterback pulls the ball. Because the play will take longer to get to him, he does not start out as aggressively as he will become. With this scheme, we give up the downfield blocking of the backside receivers. In the past, the backside receivers were trying to get to the frontside to block defenders on the second level. In the spread scheme, they hang back as crackback blockers for the quarterback when he pulls the ball.

We get into some physical mismatches on the backside with some 3-3 defenses (Diagram #6). When the defense aligns in a 3-3 defense and walks their outside linebacker up to the line of scrimmage, we end up with a blocking mismatch. We feel mismatched blocking a small slotback on a monster outside linebacker. To combat that problem, we run a dash by the slotback. If the quarterback pulls the ball, the slotback bubbles to the outside. The quarterback forces on the linebacker and throws to the slotback.

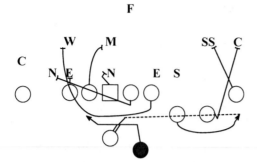

Diagram #6. Counter Trap Dash

The twin receivers outside the slot can run a fold block for the corner and strong safety. The wide receiver cracks on the strong safety, and the outside slot folds outside for the corner. That gives them a better angle to block the outside. We can call this from the sideline, or the quarterback can add it on the field.

We have another wrinkle we can use against the 3-3 defense (Diagram #7). We align in a two-back formation. We run the counter trap with the fullback chipping on the backside defensive end. Since the fullback chips on the defensive end, the center goes to the backside linebacker. We take the angles on the playside and down block on the nose and Mike linebacker with the guard and tackle. The backside guard pulls and kicks out on the defensive end. The backside tackle pulls and turns inside the guard's block for the Sam linebacker.

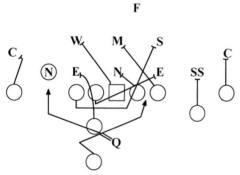

Diagram #7. Counter Trap/Chip Block

We get good numbers to the counter trap side. The slot and wide receivers stalk on the strong safety and corner. The chip block is like an on call for the offensive tackle.

I want to show you the counter trap with the option (Diagram #8). We align in a two-back set. The offensive line blocks the counter trap. We pull both the guard and tackle to the off side. We are going to option away from the counter fake. The fullback runs the counter fake, and the running back becomes the pitchback on the play.

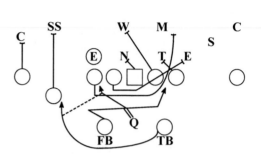

Diagram #8. Counter Trap/Option

The last play is the power off-tackle (Diagram #9). On this play, we pull the backside guard and kick out the defensive end. This is two-back play. The fullback and tailback counter step to the weakside and come back to the strongside. The fullback follows the pulling guard and turns up inside his block. He is looking for the Sam linebacker or the first color to show. On this play, the backside tackle blocks on the defensive end, and the quarterback reads the flow of the Will linebacker. If the linebacker flows to the strongside, the quarterback pulls the ball.

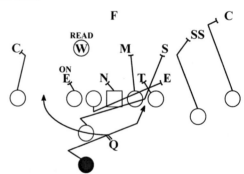

Diagram #9. Power

The purpose of this presentation is to show you that you can use this as part of whatever you are doing. It is a spread formation, but we use conventional plays and add the read option to those plays. You can add this wrinkle to your scheme. You do not have to change what you are doing in the offensive line. It can enhance what you are doing and give you an option out the backside. You do not have to go to a zone scheme to run the option read off the backside. The amount of time you spend on this concept is how much authority you want to give your quarterback.

If you do this as a change-up type of scheme, it will not require a huge amount of time. It can be similar to the wildcat offense everyone uses.

If you want to get into the scheme as part of your offense, you have to turn the reins over to the quarterback. He has to deal with the number of safeties and the defensive balance.

Why Incorporate the Spread Run Into Your Current System?

• Pressures defense to play assignment football.

• Can "outnumber" the defense from all formations.

• Easy blocking adjustments up front and on edge.

• Personnel suited to take advantage of system.

The basic spread concepts can be easily adapted to your basic running game. Depending on how much authority you want to give your quarterback, that will determine the magnitude of your use. This is a brief explanation of what we do. Our blocking techniques are like everyone else's; we do not depend on single blocking through the offense and use combinations and double-team blocking when the opportunity presents itself.

If you would like to see more of what we do, I will be around. I am always willing to talk about football. I appreciate your attention and I hope there was something you could use in your program. Thank you very much. It has been fun.

Devin Rutherford

RUNNING THE OPTION FROM THE SHOTGUN

White Station High School, Tennessee

It is a pleasure to speak to you this morning. I would like to talk to you in some depth about running the option out of the shotgun formation. We run a lot of option, and we run it out of the shotgun. Except for the "goose play" on the one-inch line, we never go under the center. Every other play we run is out of the gun formation.

Why do we run the option out of the shotgun? Assignment football—assignment, assignment! We want to make you blow your assignments. I have heard guys say before we play them, "No matter what happens, stay where you are supposed to be because he is coming back." We may run the dive to one side and have the backside guy do a little hot read. That means we are probably going to catch you sooner or later not paying attention, and we will throw the hot route.

Options are *choices*. It is not necessarily dive, quarterback, or pitch—it is about choices. You do have an option. Do you want a hamburger or a hotdog? That is an option. Do you want a Coke® or a Pepsi®? That is an option. Not all of our options are the traditional triple-option play. We do a lot of different things that you will see in this film that are option plays.

Not every option play ends with a pitch. Not every option play is predicated upon the quarterback reading the end. That is just not all that option football is about.

In addition, by running options out of the gun formation, it allows the offensive line to stay physical. Our offensive line stays physical and does a great job of blocking.

Running options out of the gun formation also eliminates blitzing by the defense. Teams will not blitz you as much if you are an option team. Preparation for defending the option takes up practice time for our opponents. When defenses are preoccupied with who has the dive, who has the jet, and who has the pitch during the entire week of preparation, then they are not doing what they are good at doing. It is something different from what they had to defend the previous week because not everyone runs the option.

When you present option football to a defensive coordinator, you give him the chance to do the one thing you want him to do, and that is to show just how smart he is—that is his chance. He may put in things that they have not run all year. They will be looking at each other and trying to get the new defense down after playing 4-3 cover 2 the entire year. Now, they are asked to do things they have not done before. It really does show just how smart the coordinators are.

Now, I am not saying that we are selling the farm for option football. We have all seen the success of the few option teams in major college football, but a lot of that success comes on first and second downs. Some of those teams do not have good answers for third-down situations.

I will not tell you what to do with your offense, but I cannot sell out one hundred percent to the option. I cannot stomach getting into third-down situations and looking like we have never practiced. I do not want to get into that situation and either get sacked or throw it in the dirt simply because we were not prepared well enough.

You have to have something you can hang your hat on. People are going to get you into those situations, and you have to have answers. I hope you can get one or two ideas from this presentation that you can add to what you do to make your offense more successful in all the situations you will face.

The option is not a meat course—it is more like a vegetable. You know how you get a plate with one big compartment and two little ones. We do not serve up the option in all three spaces. We may serve the option in the big compartment, with the screen in one of the little compartments and our quick game in the other little compartment. That is us in football.

Nevertheless, you want to have some options. As the old man says, "It is not what I am going to do—it is what I *might* do." That is what you have to have. You have to have a "might" in your attack. You have to have a chance, every time the defense plays you, to cause them concern about their option responsibilities. It is not what you can do—it is what you might do.

Now, why use the shotgun? As I said earlier, we are a running team first. When people see us line up, they see four wide receivers and the quarterback in the gun and they think pass. It is only natural. When they see trips, they think it has to be a pass. They think something funny is coming when there are three receivers to one side. The effect becomes more pronounced if we go empty. All of this because the shotgun and the spread sets make you think *pass.*

Next, I believe the quarterback has better vision in the shotgun and his mechanics are simpler. When we run the jet option, he can see the end better, and he does not have to go through all the footwork and mechanics required if he was under center.

You are still able to run your quick game from the gun. There is essentially no footwork in it because the quarterback simply catches and throws. Everybody runs the slant route with the slot receiver running a quick flat, where you read the man over the slot. For us, there is not dropback, crossover, and push off—it is simply catch and throw. You can do that in the gun without all the other stuff.

We run different types of options. We run speed, triple, midline, isolation, and a couple of other plays. I am going to go over four options. I will show you what we do, how we do it, and all the various blocking schemes. Feel free to ask questions as we go along.

SPEED

I will start with the speed option. We mostly see a 4-2 look in the box, which we call *regular,* but we do not assign special names to the defensive personnel. To us, they are just tackles, ends, and backers. If he wears a different color jersey and is trying to tackle our guy, then we are going to either block him or pitch off of him.

Let me draw up the *speed O* (Diagram #1). First, we are going to make the defense cover us two-over-two, or three-over-three If they do not honor our receivers, we will go trips, crack with one receiver, lead with the second one, and throw a one-step hitch pass to the widest man. We are going to make you honor our wide receivers.

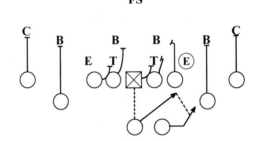

Diagram #1. Speed vs. 4-2

The backside tackle and guard will zone through the playside gaps, working up to the linebacker on that side. We do not think the backside end can run the play down. The center blocks the A gap, working with the playside guard on a double-team on the defensive tackle. Our playside tackle will pound down on the defensive tackle and work up to the linebacker. It obviously becomes an easier block if we can run it to a 1 or 2 technique.

The quarterback catches the snap and runs straight at the defensive end because that forces the end to declare. We do not run the option to get it pitched or to get it kept. We run it to gain yardage, and we keep it as simple as we can.

If the defense is covering us three-over-three, we can stick it to them by going trips bunch and then running the play to the one-receiver side (Diagram #2). Now we have them in a situation where the free safety has to come up to make a play from 12 yards deep.

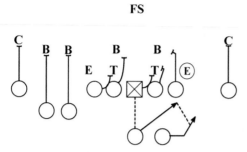

Diagram #2. Speed From Trips

When we make a steady diet of the speed option, defenses will counter by walking the outside linebacker up to the line, making it hard to get him blocked. When we see that, we will make a base call, telling our playside tackle to base block the defensive end, and we will pass the option a man down. This has been a simple, but effective, adjustment for us.

Against the Bear front with man coverage, the speed option is the best play you can run. We will go trips, zone the inside, and run the speed to the split end side. They are a man short. Our backside tackle will zone up to the backside.

Against the 3-3 look, our backside tackle will zone up to the backside linebacker, and our backside guard and center will zone block the stack and tie those guys up (Diagram #3). On the playside, our tackle will drive inside, step up, and then get back out to that outside shoulder. The guard bails and zones the tackle area.

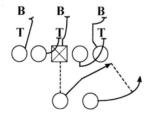

Diagram #3. Speed vs. 3-3

We have tried to reach block with our playside tackle, but when the stacked linebacker reads flow

and flies outside, we are in trouble. On the other hand, if we step in and up to get our release and the tackle tries to cross our face, we can wall him down and let the guard lead up on the stacked backer. If the defensive tackle does not cross our face, we will release in, up, and back out and try to get onto the stacked backer. Finally, if the outside backer walks up, we will go base with our tackle as we did before.

Our back has to be a football player. We are going to try to get in some people's way and get him some running lanes. He has to open his eyes and run because it is probably going to be a quick pitch. If the playside tackle ends up chasing the stacked backer, our back may have to cut it back to help set up the block.

It may look like we are wasting a guy, but we are not. If the guard takes his zone step and the defensive tackle closes, the guard will seal him inside. If the defensive tackle takes himself out of the play, the guard will just work upfield. I will show you a film where our linemen trust their zone steps and end up on defensive backs 20 yards downfield. Now, let us talk about the triple option.

TRIPLE OPTION

The way we run the triple option is different from everybody else in the world (Diagram #4). First, we will put our slot man in orbit motion. We can bring either one of those wideouts in motion with a simple call. The motion man will become the pitchman on this play.

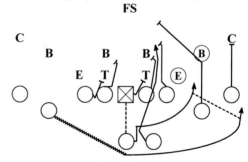

Diagram #4. Triple vs. 4-2

We are going to cut block with our left tackle here and zone upfield with our left guard. The center and right guard double their defensive tackle and work up to the backer. The right tackle goes in and up and forms a wall, just like on the speed option. The slot runs a post and blocks the safety, and the widest receiver blocks the corner.

Our back takes an inside step and meshes with the quarterback. He does not fix his eyes on the A gap because he is going to run to the hole wherever it develops. It may come out the back, go out the front, or develop right in the A gap. We just want him to run hard. Because we are in the gun, he has more time to see things open up.

Our quarterback reads the defensive tackle. If the tackle blows our back up in the backfield, our quarterback will pull the ball and run it until the outside backer gets ready to tackle him. When that happens, he will pitch the ball to the pitchman coming around. This is our way of running the triple option. That is the "White Station triple."

Now, if we see a cover-2 look, our wide receiver would go get the half-field safety and the slot would block the hard corner. It would be the same zone—same blocking on the inside. We still have the alley and we still have the triple. Now, I want to show you our midline.

MIDLINE

We are only going to run the midline against even defenses. If we face a noseguard in the defensive front, we check out of the midline. Some teams have had success with it, but it does not work for us. That being said, I am going to show you how well it sets up against even looks and the great blocking angles we get.

Against the 4-2 defense, the center blocks back on the inside linebacker (Diagram #5). The left guard will influence and turn out on the defensive end. The left tackle comes down on the other inside linebacker, and the right tackle just bases the defensive end.

The right guard pulls and traps the defensive tackle on the left side, and the quarterback reads the defensive tackle on the right. If that tackle follows our guard, as most defensive linemen are coached to do, our quarterback pulls the ball and

runs to the vacated area. If the tackle comes upfield instead, the play becomes a handoff. That is the first option in the play.

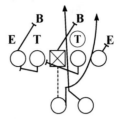

Diagram # 5. Midline vs. 4-2

We are always going to make the defense line up to our wide receivers. If the outside backer cheats in too far, we will check out to the fade. The wideout runs a fade, the slot runs a quick out, and the quarterback reads the corner. If the corner covers the fade, we throw the quick out for at least three yards.

ISOLATION

For the isolation phase of the midline package, the slot on the right lines up in a tight position. The slot on the left goes in orbit motion (Diagram #6). We block it the same way with our offensive line and the right slot leads up for the isolation.

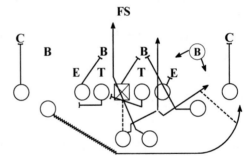

Diagram #6. Isolation Phase

Once the quarterback makes his read on the defensive tackle, his eyes go to the outside linebacker immediately. That is his second read. If the backer goes inside with the slot, the quarterback will run the option and pitch the ball immediately. If the backer stays outside for the pitch, the quarterback keeps the ball and runs the isolation.

In the interest of time, I am going to give you a chance to ask questions at this time. Thank you for your attention.

SECONDARY DRILLS AND TECHNIQUES

Butler High School, North Carolina

I am going to talk to you about the secondary. Mainly, I want to talk about defensive secondary drills. I am going to talk about the basic fundamentals of what I think it takes to be a defensive back.

There are three ways of doing things. There is the right way, the wrong way, and my way. I do not want the defensive backs to have any gray areas in their training. I am going to give them definite rules to play by. When the defensive back is playing, there should not be questions about what he is doing. We want them to play the way we teach it, and there will be no gray area for the player.

The first thing we want to talk about is the stance. If we play zone coverage, we want to align with outside leverage and the outside foot up in the stance. If we play man coverage, we play with inside leverage and the inside foot up. We want bend at the waist, the knees flexed, and the arms relaxed. We want the chest up and the hands relaxed. The problem with the stance in high school is it does you no good to have a great stance if you do not use it.

So many times, we see defensive backs walking around and trying to get lined up, and they never get in their stance. The offense snaps the ball before he gets into his stance. It is very important as a defensive back to challenge the receiver. When the receiver splits, the defensive back wants to hustle to his alignment. He wants to align on the receiver and wants to let him know he is going to cover him and that he will be there all day. We make sure we check the defensive back's stance in every drill he does. We want it sound and done right. We want them in their stance before the ball is snapped.

The first drill is a backpedal into run support. When the defensive back goes into his pedals, 80 percent of the time he has to plant and come back up the field to make a play. It could be a short out or it could be a run, but he has to know how to do that.

We teach the back to pedal, plant, and break and drive. The plant foot is the foot opposite the break (Diagram #1). We teach a 45-degree angle on the plant foot. If the defensive back goes to the right, his left foot is his plant foot. When he plants the left foot, it should be at a 45-degree angle to the line of scrimmage with all the cleats in the ground. We do not want him to crow-hop or bicycle in his footwork. We do not want to push off the toe. We want to drive back with the full foot in the ground.

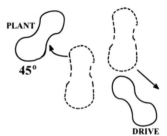

Diagram #1. Plant Foot

When you crow-hop, you have three cleats in the ground. On a wet field, you will have trouble breaking without slipping. This is the way we teach the plant and drive steps.

The other thing we teach off the backpedal is the break to the line of scrimmage (Diagram #2). When we plant and drive back toward the line of scrimmage to support on the run, we drive at a 45-degree angle. If we come straight back, we open up a running lane to the inside. As we come back to the line, we want to squeeze the running lane so we have less ground to cover and the running back has less room to make a move. When we do our drills, we come back at an angle to the line of scrimmage.

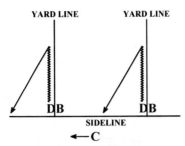

Diagram #2. Attack the Line

What you practice becomes a habit. When we attack back to the line of scrimmage, we get our shoulders square to the line of scrimmage.

This drill incorporates the first two drills together in one drill. We call it the W drill (Diagram #3). On this drill, we start on the sideline and backpedal down the line for five yards. At five yards, we plant and drive to the next yard line on the sideline. When we hit the sideline, we backpedal up the yard line for five yards and drive down to the next yard line. This teaches the backpedal, the plant step at 45 degrees, and the drive back to the line of scrimmage at 45-degree angles.

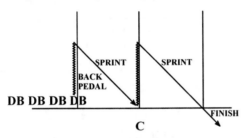

Diagram #3. W Drill

When we do this drill, we want the players to go full-speed the entire way and to finish past the line. This is a good backpedal and change-of-direction drill. Make sure your players always finish the drill. Make them sprint hard past the sideline.

The next drill is a three-step or five-step drill. It takes three minutes to do this drill, but what it teaches the player is to drop recognition. If we are playing man-to-man or zone on a receiver, we are going to look at the quarterback for a key to what is happening. If the quarterback takes a three-step drop, the defensive back knows the pattern is a hitch, slant, or fade. That tells him the ball is coming out quick.

If he sees the three-step drop, he is going to break back on the receiver and stop the slant because that is the number-one pattern he has to stop. Think about all the slants that Jerry Rice caught for touchdowns. He caught the ball and split the safeties. The three-step pass ended up a big play. We are going to stop the slant pattern first. We line up with inside leverage, and that is the number-one pattern we are going to stop.

The defensive back starts his backpedal when the quarterback starts his drop. The quarterback in the three-step drop will carry the ball high so he can deliver quickly. The ball will be above the shoulder in a throwing position. If the quarterback plants on his third step, the defensive back stops his backpedal and comes to balance. He eyeballs the receiver and reacts to the pattern he sees.

In the five-step drop, the quarterback carries the ball low around his chest level. When he hits the fifth step, the ball comes up to the throwing area. The defensive back reads the ball position of the quarterback. Once the quarterback goes past the third step, the defensive back focuses on the receiver. He knows the ball is not coming out until the receivers reach the 10- to 12-yard depth. He focuses on the receiver and reacts to the pattern he runs. This drill conditions the defensive back to read the drop of the quarterback.

If the quarterback aligns in the shotgun, the defensive back reads the ball position the same. In the drop, if the quarterback gets the ball into a high position, the defensive back sits on the three-step pattern. If the quarterback carries the ball low after the shotgun snap, the defensive backs play the five-step drop. That is a little thing, but it will help the defensive back.

For the offense to score on a drive, it takes them 12 to 14 plays. We tell the defensive back not to get upset if they complete a pass or two. However, he cannot give up the big play. If they are going to score, make them drive the ball down the field. Do not help them.

The defensive back wants to carry the receiver down the field. The cushion will start to break down in the 8- to 14-yard area. When we teach the backpedal, we want the feet underneath the defender with the shoulders square to the line of scrimmage. We want to backpedal on the toes, but we want the weight on the toe taking a long stride. We do not want to false step by taking a step forward with the foot before we get into the backpedal. We want to push off the front toe and pull off the back toe.

The feet glide on the grass and are close to the ground. When it comes time to plant, we can do it immediately. We want the feet clipping the grass as he backpedals. We want to stay in the backpedal as long as we can. The receiver is trying to drive at the defender until he gets the defender to turn his hips. When the defender turns his hips, the receiver will break in the opposite direction of the hip turn.

The defender wants to keep his shoulders square in the backpedal as long as he can (Diagram #4). If the receiver stems or breaks to the inside while the defender is in his backpedal, the defender wants to weave inside and not turn his shoulders to the inside. He maintains his leverage position on the receiver but does not come out of his backpedal until the receiver breaks the cushion and tries to run past him. We teach that as a weave drill.

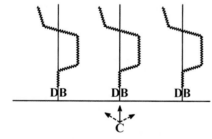

Diagram #4. Weave Drill

The defenders continue their backpedal, but they change direction in the backpedal. All the fundamentals of the backpedal are observed. The shoulders are square to the line, and the feet do not cross as they change direction. This allows the defensive back to maintain his leverage and not commit his shoulders and hips to the receiver.

When the receiver breaks the cushion and threatens the defensive back deep, the defender must turn and run. The next drill is a backpedal and

turn drill (Diagram #5). When we teach this drill, we teach it down a yard line. We backpedal the defender down the line and give him a direction to turn. The defensive back has to make a 180-degree turn with his body. He wants to make the turn without coming off the line. When he throws his head, shoulders, and hips to get the body turned, he wants to accelerate down the line. You should see a burst of speed as the defender turns from the backpedal to the run.

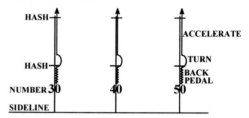

Diagram #5. Backpedal and Turn

The defensive back must turn before the receiver eats up the cushion and gets on top of him. He has to turn and stay in front of the receiver. To do that, he has to accelerate out of the turn. When you do the drill, start the defensive backs on the numbers, backpedal them to the hash mark, turn them at the hash, and make them accelerate through the opposite hash mark.

If the receiver breaks the cushion of the defensive back and threatens the deep pattern, the defender turns and runs. When he turns and runs, his eyes go to the receiver. The defender must be aware that the receiver will probably run a route with a breaking point somewhere between the 10- and 15-yard areas.

We do a drill called "directions." In directions, the defender does an abbreviated backpedal and turn drill. He starts inside the numbers and backpedals for three steps, then turns and runs for two steps. He chops and collects his feet down as if he were mimicking a pattern run by the receiver. The last part of the movement is to plant and return down the line toward the coach as if he were reacting back to a pattern. This drill gives the defensive back the confidence to look at the receiver and play him.

The defensive back has to make two different types of turns. There is the zone turn, where the defender opens his hips to the quarterback and runs in that direction. The other turn is a flip turn (Diagram #6). The flip turn is called a speed turn. If you do a zone turn, the defender has his eyes on the quarterback at all times. To do a zone turn, the defender has to break his momentum to get his hips turned from one direction to the other. When he does a flip turn, the defender turns his head and shoulders away from the quarterback as he turns his body direction. He loses sight of the quarterback shortly, but it is a much faster turn.

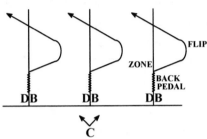

Diagram #6. Flip Turn

If the receiver turns the defender in one direction and breaks in the other, the defender can use the flip turn to get back on the pattern quickly. When you do the drill, turn your players to the post and make them flip turn to the corner and then turn them to the corner and make them flip to the post.

Defensive backs need to know when to turn and run. We do a drill called "cushion drill" to teach that technique. In the drill, we match a receiver and defender. People want to know when to turn and run. I simply tell the defenders, they need to know the speed of the receiver. If the receiver is 4.5, they have to turn quicker than a receiver who is 4.8. In the cushion drill, the defender starts out with inside leverage on the receiver. As the receiver breaks off the line, the defender backpedals. He weaves to keep the inside leverage if he has to. When the receiver breaks his cushion, he turns and runs. He wants to maintain inside position and on top or ahead of the receiver.

The defender wants his shoulder in the receiver's armpit as they run down the field. He does not want to be behind the receiver. I want him out in front where he can push off his feet and catch the ball.

The next drill is the slant drill (Diagram #7). The slant is the number-one route we want to stop. Teams like to throw this pattern on the goal line. We have to stop it. In this drill, we run two patterns. We run the quick out and the slant. The purpose of the drill is to teach the defensive back where he should be on both patterns. The receiver aligns to the inside two yards off the receiver. If he reads the slant, he jumps the inside shoulder of the receiver and gets inside to take the slant away. We want the defender to rip across the receiver and undercut the pattern.

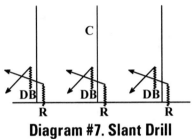

Diagram #7. Slant Drill

The coach stands behind the defensive backs and signals to the receiver which pattern to run. If the receiver plants inside and runs the out, the defender plants and attacks the upfield shoulder. We want to fit over the top of that pattern. The out cut is a hard throw to complete. If the ball is not accurate, it can be six points the other way. The slant pass is an easy pass to complete. That is why we want to undercut the route and make the play. On the out route, we want to be in position to make a play on the poorly thrown ball. We have to honor inside moves and play outside moves. The coaching point is to make sure you work the drill from both sides.

We play cover 2 in our coverage scheme. When we play cover 2, we align our corner on the line in a press alignment. I remember going to a clinic in Chicago and hearing Don Shula speak. He spoke on cover 2. I asked him what he did when the receiver got outside his corner on cover 2. He told me they did not get outside the corner. We play the coverage that way. We do not let any receiver get outside the alignment of the corner. We play hard press and jam them to the inside.

This drill is a jam flood drill (Diagram #8). In the drill, we have two running backs and two receivers. There are two corners aligned on the receivers in an outside press alignment. The coach stands behind the defensive backs and gives directions to the two running backs. The corners jam the receivers and key the running backs. If the back comes to the corner's side, he jams the receiver inside and releases him falling back outside into his flat zone. If no back comes to the corner's side, he stays on the jam and rides the receiver inside. The coach can send a back each way or have no backs in the pattern. He may only send one back. The corners must jam and see the backs.

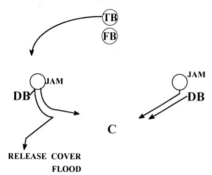

Diagram #8. Jam Flood

The next drill goes with the jam flood drill. We call it "jam sink" (Diagram #9). The defensive back jams the receiver and sinks into his area. The coach has the ball, moves the defender into his area, and throws the ball. The receiver reacts and plays the ball. The jam is a two-step jam and a retreat into the flat zone. To avoid a long throw, we compact the drill. The receivers and the coach are one yard apart with the coach between the receivers and two yards off the line. The defender performs a two-step jam to the inside and sinks into his area. They alternate side and do not go at the same time. It is one side and then the other side.

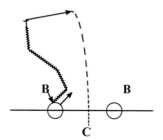

Diagram #9. Jam Sink

We do ball drills all the time. We use a drill called high ball drill. It is a simple drill. You align your defensive backs in a line facing you and have them run toward you. You throw the ball high and make them catch it at the highest point in the arc. We want them to jump and catch the ball at the highest point.

We have a player at our school who is the national high school champion in four hurdle events. He is the national champ in the 60-meter hurdles indoors and the 110-meter hurdles outdoors. He is the 300-meter champ indoors and the 400-meter champ outdoors. He is a defensive back with great speed and cannot catch a cold. He did have a 90-yard interception return this year. He covered the distance so fast it was unbelievable. Even if they do not catch the ball, we want them to go high and try to catch it.

This next drill is a receiver drill (Diagram #10). We align two receivers on the sideline 15 yards apart. The defensive back aligns on the coach in between the two receivers. On the snap, the receivers break downfield on their yard line. The defensive back goes into a backpedal. The coach does not try to fake the defender. He tilts one way or the other and throws the ball. The back breaks on his shoulder movement and goes for the ball. He wants to high-point the ball and returns it downfield.

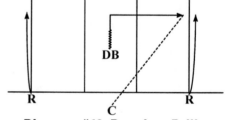

Diagram #10. Receiver Drill

We are trying to teach confidence that the defensive back can cover from hash mark to hash mark. We are also teaching the defender to break on the long arm motion of the quarterback. The quarterback can pump and fake the throw, but when his front hand comes off the ball, we break in that direction. You could do this drill without the receivers in the drill. However, when you put the receivers in the drill, it presents a different look to the defensive back. With the receivers running to the ball, it makes it a more realistic game situation. Some defenders look at the receivers instead of the ball and cannot make the catches. This drill makes the defenders play the ball and disregard the receivers.

The stretch drill is a close-quarters catching drill (Diagram #11). The coach is on the sidelines, and the back is at the bottom of the numbers. The defender backpedals to the top of the numbers. The coach tilts his shoulders, and the defender breaks at a 45-degree angle to the next yard marker. The coach throws a short, five-yard pass, making the defensive back stretch out to get to the ball. It is a simple drill, but it makes the defensive man stretch and concentrate on catching the ball.

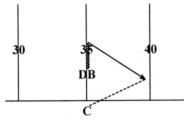

Diagram #11. Stretch Drill

The coach throws the ball to the next five-yard marker. The players want to stretch and see how far outside the five-yard line he can stretch. That can give him confidence that he can cover ground.

The drill we do a lot is the man fade drill (Diagram #12). On the fade drill, we teach them a number of things. He has to cover the fade in man and in zone. To start the drill, we play man coverage with the coach standing on the sideline. Five yards to his left is a defensive back standing on the sidelines. The receiver is outside the defensive back, standing on the sideline. The receiver and defender are facing opposite directions. The receiver is facing downfield and the defender is to his inside in a good stance. On the snap of the ball, the receiver runs a fade pattern. The defensive back opens to the defender with his outside foot. He runs to play the fade, working into the receiver. The coach throws the ball, and the defender plays the fade.

The defensive back turns and runs to the receiver. He is not looking back for the ball. He is trying to catch up to the receiver and makes his play off the receiver. When the receiver looks back and puts his hands up for the ball, the defender uses the

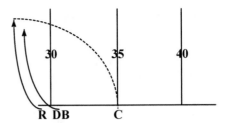

Diagram #12. Man Fade Drill

hand toward the receiver to run it through the outside hand of the receiver. We hope to knock the ball out of the hands. If the ball is underthrown, the receiver cannot get to the ball because he has to come through the body of the defender.

The first mistake the defensive back makes is to look back for the ball. He cannot do that. He has to focus on catching up and playing through the receiver's hands. The defender's body position is played with his back into the receiver, so when he reaches with the inside hand, that is the hand to the receiver side. The receiver can make a one-handed catch with his outside hand but not the inside hand. That is why we go through the outside hand.

On the zone technique, we run the same drill (Diagram #13). The difference is the alignment of the defensive back. He is off the receiver two yards with inside leverage. On the snap, the defender weaves in his backpedal to force the receiver wider and to the sidelines. He zone-turns to the quarterback and stays over the top of the receiver. When the ball is released, he high-points the ball and makes the interception.

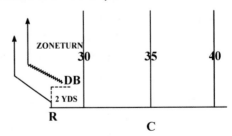

Diagram #13. Zone Fade Drill

During our practice period, we do a number of deep ball drills. What this amounts to be is a pass catching drill for the defensive backs. They start the drill in a backpedal. They backpedal for five to seven yards, depending on which coverage we are assimilating. They use the techniques they use to get into the scheme coverages we play. In this drill, we teach half-coverage techniques. They backpedal, get into their deep coverage drops, and I throw the ball. They make their adjustments to the ball. I do not throw the ball to them. I throw the ball away from them, and they go get it. If I turn them to the post, I may throw the ball behind them and make them speed turn to get to it. As the ball is in the air, the defensive back must assume the ball is for him, and he must go get it.

To play in the defensive secondary you must do other things beside play pass defense. The defensive backs must tackle. We have a number of tackling drills I want to show you.

The defensive back must make tackles in the open field. They do not have to be bone-crushing tackles or perfect form tackles. However, they must be sure tackles. The objective of any tackle is to get the ballcarrier on the ground.

When making a tackle, the defender must have an aiming point that he tries to hit. On an angle tackle, the aiming point is the V of the neck. Most tackles are missed because the tackler does not get close enough to execute the tackle. You have to get as close as possible, then take one more step. The angles in the hips, knees, and ankles are what produce the power. You must see the target and explode through that target.

Another important element of the tackle is the finish. If the back makes good explosion and tries to drag the back down, he may lose the tackle. He has to finish the tackle with his leg drive. The feet must continue to move throughout the tackle. He has to wrap up the ballcarrier and drive him to the ground.

The first drill is a box drill (Diagram #14). I have two tacklers and two ballcarriers. The tacklers and ballcarriers are five yards apart, facing one another. There is five yards between the tacklers and ballcarriers. I stand behind the tacklers and give the ballcarriers a direction. They want to make a 90-degree cut in the direction I point. They take two steps and cut to the outside. The tacklers approach

the ballcarrier. When the ballcarriers cut, the tackler executes an across-the-bow angle tackle. In the tackle, the defender wants to get his head across the body of the ballcarrier and run his feet. We want to make contact, grab, and run the feet to take him back.

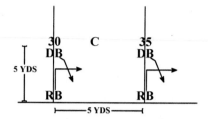
Diagram #14. Box Drill

We do a sideline tackling drill that is similar to the box drill as far as technique is concerned (Diagram #15). The ballcarrier is against the sideline, and the tackler is three yards inside and coming to meet the ballcarrier. The thing we want to do on the sideline tackle is to stay square as long as we can. We do not want to turn and run toward the sideline. If we do that, we give the ballcarrier a cut against the grain. We must approach the ballcarrier, make contact with the backside shoulder, and drive through the ballcarrier. We are almost taking the ballcarrier in a head-on position, working the head across the body.

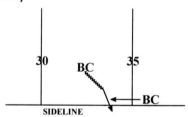
Diagram #15. Sideline Tackle

When you make a sideline tackle, the thing you are trying to prevent is the ball breaking back inside to the middle of the field. We want to keep the ball hemmed into the sideline and make the tackle or drive the ballcarrier over the sidelines.

Gentlemen, I appreciate your time and your attention. I believe in the things we teach, and I believe they are sound. Thank you very much.

Mark Soboleski

THE TRIPLE AND MIDLINE OPTION SCHEMES

McDowell High School, Pennsylvania

I love going to clinics. I just went to a wing-T clinic. When I listen to the coaches talk about the offense, it is all the same. I always try to get one thing that might help me with our program. What I am going to do today is tell you what we do, how we practice it, and how we game plan it. I will give you the base plays that we run. I will give you our twist on the plays and talk about how we incorporate some things in our approach to those plays.

I want to start by giving you some basic philosophy as to why we run this offense. I will tell you what triggered me into this system. I am going to talk about game planning. I want to show you what we do the day of the game. I will talk about how we practice it and pick the personnel we want to fit the offense. One of the biggest things we do as a coaching staff is to sit down and try to find all the pieces and put them in the right spots. In an option system, it is vital to get the right players in the right positions.

I am going to cover the triple option, which is 12 and 13; the midline triple option, which is 10 and 11; the double-option read, which is 10 and 11; and the perimeter option, which is 18 and 19. If I do not run out of time, I may get to the counter option and some of the passing game.

There are a number of reasons we run the offense. This is what we built our system on.

Why

- Equalizer—Can block eight
- Limits the defense—Prep time is short
- Time of possession—Keeps their offense off the field
- Balanced formations—No strength; balances the defense

- Numbers advantage—Blocking angles
- Passing game—Vanilla coverage
- Blitz pick-up—We want them to blitz
- Different brand of football

This offense gives us an opportunity to compete every week. The last two years, we have competed well against high quality opponents. This offense gives us a chance every week. We had some great athletes last year and have some of them coming back next year. We do not block everyone in this offense. We may not block the opponent's best defenders all game long.

This offense limits the defense. To play an option team, you have to stay balanced in your defense. You cannot load up one side. It stops teams from blitzing and makes them play more straight football. That helps us with our game preparation.

We feel in the offense we can score at any moment. For the past two years, we have been explosive. Our players believe in the offense and think we can score.

The offense is a balanced formation. We can go unbalanced in our formation but we do not do that very often. We want to see how the defense will play our offense. Ninety percent of the time, we are in one formation. We may tinker with another formation, but we do not run multiple formations with the offense. We feel staying balanced is an advantage for us and forces the defense to stay balanced.

In this offense, you can gain a numbers advantage in blockers to defenders. We also get great angles in our blocking scheme. The offense forces the defense into vanilla coverages. Most of the time, we only see one coverage from the secondary. We want defenses to blitz. When they blitz you, we feel like they are guessing. They try to run a blitz to make something happen.

This is a different brand of football. For Navy to beat Notre Dame twice in the last four years says something about the system. The advantage we have is the defense does not see the option every week. The defense is not comfortable with the schemes they play against options. Those schemes are not what they are used to playing.

Keys to the Offense

- Philosophy
- Have a package
- Can you fix it?

When you run the offense, those are the things you must consider. I want to show you our base philosophy. I got this from another option coach. I adapted it and reapplied it to the offense we run.

Philosophy

- Run the football.
- When we throw it, we look for the big play.
- We have a system—it is packaged.
- We practice it every week and the players get sound in the scheme.
- Keep it simple.

We have to run the football. It does not matter how many defenders the defense uses, we can run the ball. This year, we averaged 32 yards a completion. When we throw the ball, we look for the big play. When the safeties start to get nosy, that is the best time to throw the ball.

We have a system. I will show you how we package the system. We go into every game with a package for every front we could possibly see. On occasion, we are surprised. After the season, we review the defensive fronts we saw during the season. We record what we did that was successful and what did not work. If we see the front again, we have a reference point about the front.

We practice the offense every week and the players get sound with the scheme. We keep it simple and get as many repetitions as we possibly can. We want the running of our three base plays to be second nature with our players. You get that from multiple repetitions.

Package

- Triple option first
- Every play we do is triple
- Multiple scheme
- Multiple formation
- Play-action

Everything we do starts with the triple option. We install it in April during spring practice. We run it all summer long. We run it repeatedly until we are almost flawless in our execution. We get that done, and then we add the other options. We run multiple schemes of options. We run the counter option, midline option, and perimeter option. We have multiple formations in place, but we do not use them often. The play-action pass is an important part of the triple option. We do not throw it often, but when we do, it is usually for big chunks of yardage.

Can You Fix It?

- Game-time adjustments
- Staff on the same page
- Prepare for possible problems
- Prepare for multiple fronts
- Game day play calling—based on what the defense is playing

I think one of the best things we do is what we call "Can you fix it?". When we start the game, we try to figure out what the defense is doing immediately. We are ready to adjust because we put the time in during the week on possible scenarios they may run. The staff has to be on the same page and talk the same language. We have to recognize the front and communicate it to the players. We have to prepare for multiple fronts. On Monday, we may block a 5-2 defense. If we think there is a possibility the opponent will change defenses, we block the 4-3 on Tuesday. On Wednesday, we block their base defense. On Thursday, we block a junk defense. We throw some kind of unusual alignment or exotic defense. We want the team to think. We do not block the same defense all week.

Overall

- Can score on any play
- Coaches on the same page
- Catalog defenses
- Play-action passes
- Players need to know read and pitchman
- Try not to run a bad play

This offense can score on any play. We sell that to the players in every drill we do. On every play we run, we make the back run all the way to the end zone. It does not matter if we are on the 20 or 40 yard line. They run to the end zone and they do it at full speed.

We want the coaches on the same page. When we talk about defenses, we use the numbering system that has been around for some time with a slight alteration. The techniques played on the guard are 1, 2, and 3 techniques. The techniques played on the tackle are 4, 5, and 6 techniques, and the techniques on the tight end are 7, 8, and 9 techniques. When I talk about a 6 technique, that is the outside shoulder of the offensive tackle. We make sure the players understand the numbering system for defensive techniques. When we align our defense, we use the same numbering system.

We catalog defenses in the off-season. Anything we faced this year that was new, we write it down. We write down the movements and coverages that go with the defense. We played a team last year that stood up the entire defense. Everyone was running around with no real alignment before we snapped the ball. We catalog all the defenses we see.

When you are an option team, you must train your players to recognize the read defender and

pitch defender. There are two reasons for this. If the fullback knows the read key, he has a clue as to whether he takes the ball or the quarterback keeps it. If all the players know the read and pitch defenders, they will not block them.

We try to stay out of the bad play. We run a "check with me" call system. With the "check with me" system, the quarterback changes the play from one side to the other. The call for that is *Xerox*. In camp, we spend a lot of time with our quarterbacks on blitz checks. We match the blitzes with plays. If the quarterback sees a particular blitz, he runs a particular play. We do not want to run a bad play, and we spend the time with the quarterbacks to prevent it.

We stress to our players that they must practice with intensity. Every drill we do is full speed, and we expect our players to go full speed. We want to make practice as intense as possible without a lot of standing around.

Game Planning

- Can be a guessing game
- Look at base defense
- Come up with an option plan
- Defense other possibilities
- Prepare for every defense
- Stay simple
- Use formations to get defenders out of sync
- Use the front that a defense is playing against them

Option football can be a guessing game. Teams will play things that they do not normally play. We have scouted teams that played a 5-2 defense in every game we had seen. When they played us, they came out in a 3-3 stack. We have to switch gears and adjust.

To avoid that situation, we look at the opponent's base defense. When we look at the first film and the base defense is a 4-4 with a cover 3, that is where we start. If I think they may be in something else, we may practice against something we never see. We have to prepare that way because when you are an option team, you never know. Because the defense does not see the option every week, they may make some drastic changes. It becomes a guessing game as to what we will see.

When we decide what they do, we have to come up with an option plan. We make our plan off what we think they will do and how they will defend the quarterback and the pitch. We prepare for everything.

We want to use the fact that we are an option team to take advantage of the techniques of the defenders. We want to take advantage of a defender that is doing something he does not ordinarily do. If the outside linebacker usually attacks but is playing soft because of his responsibility, we want to devise something to take advantage of that.

Game Day

- Identify the front
- Identify the tackle's technique
- Pre-determine game sheet
- Game board
- Identify the option responsibilities
  - ✓ End
  - ✓ Inside linebacker
  - ✓ Outside linebacker
  - ✓ Safeties and corners
- Coaches on the same page
- Eyes tell me what the defense is doing

Game day is hectic for us because we never know what we will see. On our first play, we run 12 dive. We know the front is the normal defense, and we want to see where they go. We want to know if the middle linebacker takes the fullback or comes over the top for the quarterback. We want to know where the safeties and outside linebackers go.

The second thing we look for is the tackle's technique. If it is an odd front, we want to know if he is an inside shade, head-up, or outside shade. If the front is an even front, we want to know where the tackles are playing. Are they shading the nose and a 3 technique? We have to find that out.

We have a pre-determined game sheet for game night. We develop a game plan for any defense we might see. That is what is on the backside of our game board. We have starting plays for all the defenses we have seen or expect to see. We list on the game board all the options, midlines, and passing game. We list our base plays from our base formations.

The second thing we do is find out what the tackle is doing. The most important information I can get from the coaches in the booth are the techniques of the end, linebackers, safeties, and corners. I want to know if the end is squeezing the fullback, coming upfield, playing static, or attacking the quarterback. Is the inside linebacker playing over the top for the quarterback, or is he playing the fullback? Does the outside linebacker have the quarterback or the pitch? They could slow play the outside linebacker and try to play both the quarterback and pitchback.

If the defense brings the safety to the fullback, that changes how we block everything. If they bring the safety to the quarterback, that changes how we will attack them. We have to get that information as soon as possible.

One of the most important things for an option team to do is get the personnel in the right spots. The quarterback has to be a special person. In our offensive line, we put our big players at the guard position. We want big players at the guard so they can get in the way of the Mike linebacker. The offensive tackle has to be more athletic because of the techniques he has to use. We tinker with the offensive line during the season. We constantly change the personnel early in the season until we get what we want.

We have played with different personnel types at the fullback. We look for a bigger body at the fullback because they take a beating during the season. The halfbacks are our wing players. The biggest requirement is that they block. If the halfback cannot block, he cannot play in this system.

Since we are a big school, we are fortunate to get athletes from three middle schools. Each year, we get three freshmen quarterbacks into our program. The middle schools run the three base plays from our offense. They can run anything else they choose, but all of them run the three base plays. The freshmen come into our system knowing those plays. They have some idea about whom and how to read.

When we pick a quarterback, we have to answer some important questions about him. We have to know if he will do the following things.

- Will he get up off the ground after a hit and run the same play again?
- Can he make a play on third down?
- Does he believe in it?

The quarterback has to be unselfish. The ball is in his hands on every play and you must have the right player there. He cannot worry about his stats. He has to put us in the right play and make the reads. He must be an athletic player.

If you plan to run this system, you need to go watch someone practice it. I would suggest you go watch Navy practice. The most critical thing to running this offense is practicing the system and practicing it right. The reason we are successful in this system is the way we practice it.

In the quarterback's individual period, they practice their *steps* repeatedly. You cannot practice footwork too much in this system. We expect him to line himself up with another back in the backfield every play to create a mesh. That takes countless hours of drilling on footwork. If he is too wide, he forces the fullback off his track. If he is too tight, he cannot reach the fullback. He has to be exact every time to make the mesh with the fullback.

The second physical skill he has to master is the *pitch*. We teach the pitch with a thumb-under movement. We snap the thumb under and shoot the ball underneath the hand. We drill the pitch with four types of pitches. We teach *sit and pitch*. In this drill, the quarterbacks sit down and pitch the ball back and forth. They step at the target and pitch the ball. We teach *pitch and protect*. The quarterback pitches the ball and falls away from his forward run.

This is to protect himself from an attacking pitch key.

The *running pitch* is opposite the sit and pitch. We align them on a line and run them down the line. They run at full speed and pitch the ball back and forth to one another. Make sure you have them pitching the ball with both hands and in both directions. The last pitch is *fake and pitch*. We do that two ways. The first way is to dip the inside shoulder as if to turn inside and pitch the ball outside. After he dips, he sits and pitches the ball as he did in the sit drill. The second thing we do is fake the pitch and turn inside. It is the opposite of the dip and pitch.

The next thing we work on is the *read*. In this drill, there is no center or fullback. We work on the quarterback's footwork and whom he reads.

When we go to a group drill, we bring the centers and fullbacks into the drill. If you want to run the option scheme, you must work with the centers or the timing will never work. The timing has to be precise for the play to work. In this drill, we use our alignment strip to make sure the tracks in the mesh are right. You can buy one of them or use an old fire hose. It has the splits of the offensive line marked on the hose. Our offensive line splits are two feet between the linemen.

We start with the midline drill (Diagram #1). We have a center, fullback, and quarterback. The coach aligns as the read key in a 3-technique or 4-technique position. The fullback aligns with his hands at two-and-a-half yards behind the feet of the quarterback. We use three different reads for the quarterback. I will talk about the footwork when I show you the play. The quarterback reads the coach. The first thing is to squeeze on the fullback. The quarterback

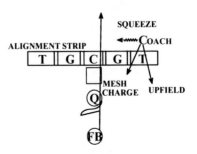

Diagram #1. Midline Drill

pulls the ball. The second read is an up charge by the coach, which is straight up the field. The quarterback gives to the fullback on that play. The third read is the mesh charge. The coach attacks the mesh and the quarterback gives the ball.

If we get the mesh charge, the fullback has to break the tackle of the closing lineman. He gets the ball and has to run hard. The quarterback cannot keep the ball on a mesh charge. The fullback should read the mesh charge and know what is coming. He goes a thousand miles an hour up the middle line and we think we can break that tackle.

The next part of the drill moves the coach to a 5 technique, which is head-up the tackle (Diagram #2). We run the triple option, which is the 12/13 play. The track for the fullback is up the butt of the guard. We use the same three reads when we run the drill. We run this drill repeatedly. You must get the maximum repetitions in these drills to run this type of offense. If you are not committed to running these types of drills, do not run this offense.

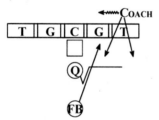

Diagram #2. Triple-Option Read

We bring the halfbacks into the group drill and run a two-ball drill (Diagram #3). In this drill, we run the same drill as before except we add a second ball in the pitch phase of the option. Regardless of the read on the fullback, the quarterback runs the pitch phase of the offense. We have a second quarterback stand outside the first read key. If the read key forces the ball to the fullback, the second

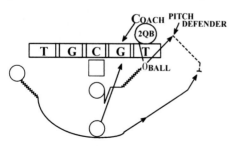

Diagram #3. Two-Ball Drill

quarterback hands a ball to the quarterback. He carries out the drill by running the pitch to the halfback. There is a pitch defender to make the quarterback pitch or keep the ball.

The last drill we do is a repeat of all the drills except we put a secondary and receivers into the drill (Diagram #4). We run the two-ball drill with live blocking on the perimeter. We run this drill from the 20 yard line. The split receiver and halfback block live on the corner and strong safety. They can use their base scheme or switch blocks on them. In the base block, the split end blocks the corner and the halfback arcs on the strong safety. In the switch scheme, the split receiver cracks on the safety and the halfback kicks out the corner. On every play, the fullback, quarterback, or halfback must sprint the 20 yards to score.

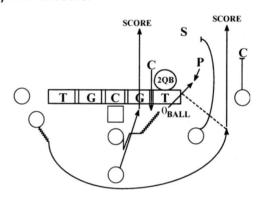

Diagram #4. Perimeter Drill

In those three drills, we want to put pressure on the quarterback. We want to challenge him and make the drills hard. We want to mix the reads and force him to make challenging decisions. I think that is what makes us successful.

When we go to the team drill, we do three different versions of team. We do a team take-off drill. It is a team unity thing. We break the huddle and run an option play. We run two teams in the drill and run six plays a piece.

The next team drill is team option. This is a live drill. We work two groups and everything is live except the quarterback. During this period, we tell the read keys what to do and put a lot of pressure on the quarterback. It is a 15-minute period but sometimes it goes longer because it is a vital period.

The last team period is team plan. This is the last period of the day. We run the game plan during this period. There are about 30 to 35 plays in the drill. After we do this drill, we are done. That is how we practice the scheme. I think we do a good job offensively.

The 12/13 is our base triple option. This is the first play we insert into our offense (Diagram #5). The read key is the first man on or outside the offensive tackle. We pitch off the second man outside the read key. The key to this play is to get vertical push at the point of attack. We want to push first-level defenders into the second level. The halfback goes in motion to get to a path through the heels of the fullback. We want him at full speed when he hits the level of the fullback. Because of the speed differential of players, we coach our players to leave on the cadence that gets them into position—some leave earlier than others.

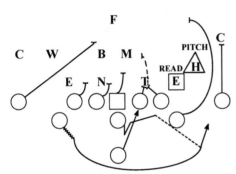

Diagram #5. 12/13 Triple Option

We will always check the triple away from a monster scheme in the secondary. The game adjustment is on a 4-technique tackle. We can block him or not block him. That will be a game-plan or sideline adjustment. If we apply the base rule, we block him.

The quarterback steps at four o'clock to the fullback. We step with the right foot going right. We use a two-step mesh. We step with the right foot and get the left foot on the ground. The left foot does not go straight down the line. It goes back at four o'clock and creates an angle for the fullback to get to his aiming point.

On the first step, the quarterback gets his hands back as far as possible to get into the mesh

with the fullback. We want the mesh as soon as possible. We want the knees bent and the chin locked on the front shoulder. We want both eyes on the read key. That is why we lock the chin on the front shoulder. We do not want them with one eye on the read and one eye on the mesh.

He meshes with the fullback, rides him, and makes his decision. He never goes past his front knee without making a decision—that leads to fumbles. If he needs more time to figure out the read, we allow him to use the hop step before he gets into the mesh. The hop step is with the left foot into the line of scrimmage.

The fullback step is to the crack of the guard. That is his aiming point. He runs full speed through that aiming point. It is a veer course. I do not let them cut in practice until they run 10 yards. In practice, they must run full speed on their angled course. If they dance or cut, I go insane. I want them on that course because there is a reason for it. In game situations and different fronts, that course can change.

In the mesh, the fullback must have a "soft seal." That means he "holds" the ball but he is not holding it. He knows if he gets the ball. The fullback comes over the ball and soft holds it. We tell the quarterback to tap him on the stomach if he gets the ball. It probably never happens, which makes that clinic talk. We tell the fullback, if he feels the pop or the quarterback's back hand come out, to clamp down on the ball.

The playside tackle has to veer block inside or combo with the guard. We refer to our double-team combo blocks as ace, deuce, and trey. The ace is a center/guard combo. The deuce is a guard/tackle combo, and the trey is a tackle/halfback combo. If the tackle has a 3-technique defender inside, he combo blocks with the playside guard up to the frontside linebacker. On this play, if the guard is uncovered, the tackle veer blocks on the linebacker.

We tell the playside tackle to veer block with a 6-technique defender, which is an outside-shoulder defender, on him. If he has a 5-technique defender, he veers until we tell him not to. If that occurs, we may loop the tackle outside for the linebacker. If the tackle has a 4 technique aligned on him, we handle it two ways. We will not block him and treat him as a 5-technique defender or we deuce him and treat him as a 3-technique defender.

The onside guard blocks man-on to inside linebacker. The backside blocks of the play for the center, guard, and tackle are scoop blocks. If we make an *on* call, we block the pitchman with the halfback. If he stands on top of the play, we can block him and pitch off the next threat downfield. That is a call we make, but it is not a rule.

The second base play we run is the midline option. What I am going to show you is the double option (Diagram #6). The read key is the first defender outside the guard. We still want vertical push up the field, and that is why we play our bigger players inside as guards. We check the play away from a 1-technique player. If the defense aligns with two 2-technique players keeping the defense balanced, we run the play. The guard treats a 2-technique defender as a 3 technique.

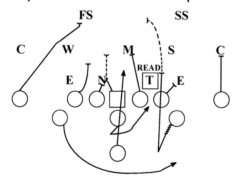

Diagram #6. Midline Double Option

The play is easier to run because there is only one read involved and the mesh is closer to the quarterback. The quarterback steps off the line of scrimmage by pivoting off his opposite foot. He has to clear the path over the center and get the ball as deep as he can to the fullback. He reads the first man over or outside the guard. The mechanics are the same from this point on. He has his chin on his shoulder and eyes on the key. The reads are the same as the triple. He rides the fullback to his front foot. If he pulls the ball, we want him to get vertical almost immediately.

The fullback has to be on the midline and explode upfield. The only time he can deviate from that track is when a nose defender is on the center. We expect him to break all tackles coming from the outside.

The halfback comes in motion and has the playside linebacker as his blocking assignment. If the linebacker disappears, he climbs to the free safety. The playside tackle has a hammer block. That is a turn-out block on the defensive end. We tell him to play basketball defense on the defender. He has to make sure the defender cannot come underneath him. If he tries to come underneath, the tackle shuffles inside and walls him out of the play. If the tackles cannot handle this block, they cannot play.

The playside guard veer blocks to the inside. He looks for the playside linebacker in the gap to the backside linebacker.

The center, against an even front, will use an ace combo to the backside linebacker. We run the play against an odd-front defense. I like the play against that defense. This is good against the 3-3 alignment (Diagram #7). We triple-team the nose with the center and two guards back into next week. We want the nose to disappear. The guards look for the middle linebacker to one side or the other. The fullback drives up the midline and favors the playside. We want him to get skinny and run away from the outside threat.

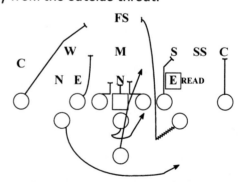

Diagram #7. Midline vs. 3-3

My time is up. Thank you for being here and being so attentive. I am heading for the breakout room if anyone wants to talk more about this offense.

THE 50 DEFENSE: FRONTS AND ZONE BLITZ

Destrehan High School, Louisiana

We are in South Louisiana on the coast, close to New Orleans. I drove six hours due north to get here. It is warm year-round in our area. Sometimes, in December, we are out in shorts. This year, it snowed in south Louisiana two days before the state championships. You never know what you are going to get. You must prepare for everything.

We were a 4-2-5 defensive team when I got to Destrehan. In the 2006 playoff game, our opponent's running back ran for 300 yards. This was my first year as defensive coordinator and they almost fired me because of that. I was coaching the 4-2-5 and did not have all the answers in that defense. We went back to running what we knew best. We went back to the 50 defense to stop the run. Teams were running the football on us. We had good pass coverage and had no trouble stopping the pass. We were having trouble stopping the run.

The major priorities were pursuit angles and running to the ball. We think we do a good job of that and we coach it in every drill. We base the defense on players being able to tackle the ball. To learn to tackle, we start in a form-tackling drill. We teach form tackling like everyone else does.

Form Tackling

- Good fit position
- Bite the bicep
- Grab high cloth
- Roll the hips
- Step on toes

We still do that in our individual periods. We get the form-tackling work for two to three minutes every day.

I want to talk about personnel in the 50 front. Our Sam linebacker has to be an athletic player. He is a strong and physical defensive end. He plays on the tight-end side 90 percent of the time. That depends on what the offensive coordinator on the other side wants to do. We have two defensive ends and we call them Sam and cat. We play the true defensive end at the Sam linebacker position over the tight end.

We call the defensive tackles defensive ends. They do not like the term defensive tackles. Our defensive ends are two-gap players. They are strong and play with good technique. They are responsible for the B gap. In the 50 defense, your nose must command a double-team and he must play two gaps. If your nose guard cannot play two gaps, you will get hurt with the inside run. That is not why we are in this defense.

The cat linebacker has to be the best athlete on the field. In 2007 and 2008, we had two great players, and they both went on to sign scholarships at the next level. Last season, we were 5-6 and one of the reasons was we were not very good at the cat position. We evaluated the players in the spring and we should have stuck with our decision of who to play. We tried to switch players and it backfired on us. We took our lump early in the year. Toward the end of the season, we played better. We did not play great, but we were better than at the beginning of the season.

The Mike linebacker is our true linebacker. He is the fill or plug linebacker. He is slower than the Will linebacker is, and does not have as good of feet. The Will linebacker is the second-best player on our defense. The Will and cat may look alike, but the Will linebacker has to run. We ask the Will linebacker to do many things for us.

I want to talk about technique, but I am going to go through it fast. All even techniques are head-up for us. The nose guard plays a 0 technique, which is head-up the center. We very seldom play a 2 technique in our scheme. We have a G scheme, but we do not use it much. The ends play a 4 technique head-up with the offensive tackles. The Sam and cat play a 6 technique head-up with the tight ends.

All odd numbers are shade techniques. The inside shoulder of the guard is a 1 technique and the outside shoulder is a 3 technique. The outside shoulder of the tackle is a 5 technique. The tight end has three techniques assigned to him. The inside shoulder is a 7 technique and the outside shoulder is a 9 technique. The head-up position on the tight end is a 6 technique.

We letter the gap, moving from the inside to the outside. We letter the center-guard gap as the A gap. The guard-tackle gap is the B gap. The tackle-tight end gap is the C gap and the outside is the D gap. All this does is give you a reference point, so you will know where we play our personnel.

We have the ability to set up different defenses by calling technique numbers. The numbering system ties in with the gap responsibility and the slant package. The *even-numbered* techniques play head-up positions and take inside-gap responsibility. A 4-technique defender is responsible for the B gap. The *odd-numbered* techniques play shades and outside-gap responsibility. A 5-technique defender is responsible for the C gap. We can call the strength to a tight end, number of receivers, to the field, or to the bench. The number called sets the two defensive ends. Sam and cat are always two techniques away for the ends. The noseguard goes to the 5-technique side. The linebackers line up according to the front, usually in a 20 or 30 technique.

If the defensive call is 44, the defensive ends align in a 4 technique to each side. The Sam and cat linebackers align in 6 techniques. They are always two technique numbers away from the defensive end. We generally call our strength to the number of receivers. If we have a trip set right, our call is right.

If we have a 5 in any defensive-front call, the noseguard shades to that side.

The first front is a 44 front (Diagram #1). The defensive ends align in 4 techniques. The Sam and cat align in 6 techniques. The noseguard is in an 0 technique, head-up the center. The Mike and Will linebackers align in 20 techniques head-up the guards at linebacker depth. On rundowns, the free safety moves down into the box. He starts at 12 yards on passing situations and 10 yards in running situations. In running situations, he starts at 10 yards and moves down to six or seven yards in the backside B gap.

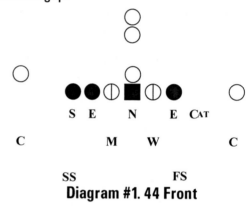

Diagram #1. 44 Front

If I am playing with a younger player at the free-safety position, I take the responsibility to what happens to him. If I roll him down to six yards, and the receiver beats him on a play action pass, that is my fault. You cannot put a player in a pass/run conflict and blame him when he gets beat. An older and more experienced player takes the responsibility for his actions.

In the 45 front, the cat linebacker moves off the line of scrimmage (Diagram #2). There is a split end to his side and he removes himself from the line into a walk-off position on the split end. The defensive end moves out to a 5 technique on the outside shoulder of the offensive tackle. The noseguard shades the center toward the 5 technique. The other defensive end aligns in a 4 technique, and the Sam linebacker aligns in a 6 technique on the tight end or a 6 technique on the ghost of a tight end. That means he has no tight end and aligns as if there were a tight end. He lines up on air.

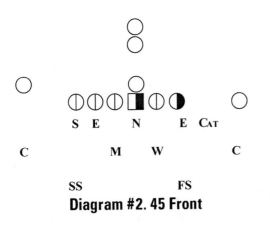

Diagram #2. 45 Front

A 45 ram is a call for the cat linebacker (Diagram #3). On this call, he aligns on the slot or #2 receiver to his side. He leaves the box and aligns with an inside-leverage technique on the slot receiver. Before he leaves, he tells the 5-technique defensive end, "You." That tell the defensive end he has to contain. The cat linebacker aligns on the inside eye of the #2 receiver at five yards deep. The cat wants to jam the #2 receiver as he comes down the field. We play this type of call in a definite passing situation or according to the scouting report.

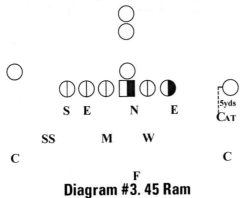

Diagram #3. 45 Ram

We have a 53-G front (Diagram #4). We have many fronts in our package that we work on in the spring and early fall workouts. We have this front in our package, but we have not run it in quite a while. This is a scouting report adjustment. The Sam linebacker aligns in a 9 technique on the tight end. The defensive end to that side gets into a 5 technique alignment on the offensive tackle. The opposite defensive end aligns in a 3 technique. The cat linebacker moves down into a 5 technique on the outside shoulder of the tackle. The G call tells the noseguard to move over into a 2 technique on the guard to the tight-end side.

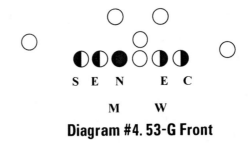

Diagram #4. 53-G Front

The Mike linebacker to the tight-end side aligns in a 30 technique on the outside shoulder of the guard. The Will linebacker is in a 20 techinque head-up the offensive guard.

We play cover 3 behind the fronts I am showing you now. We can play other coverages, which I will show you later.

The next front is a nickel 35. (Diagram #5). In this front, the tight end is to the left side of the defense. We give a left call. That means the left defensive end aligns in the 3 technique or first number of the defensive call. He lines up on the outside shoulder of the guard. The defensive end to the split end side gets the second number, which is five. He aligns in a 5 technique on the tackle. The noseguard always aligns to the 5 technique. He shades the nose to the split-end side.

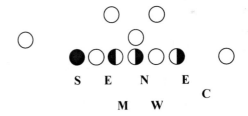

Diagram #5. Nickel 35 Front

The Mike linebacker plays a 20 technique and has responsibility for the A gap. The Will linebacker aligns in a 30 alignment and has the B gap. If the offense comes out in a double set with no tight end, the Sam linebacker aligns in a 5 technique on the offensive tackle.

If we play a dime 55, we have the Sam and cat in jam positions on the #2 receiver to their sides (Diagram #6). In our scheme, the cat linebacker is our drop defender and the Sam is the rush end. That occurs about 90 percent of the time.

If we have a dime call, it is a definite passing situation. The defensive ends move into 5 techniques to both sides. We can play cover 2 behind that scheme. We can blitz or rush three defenders. The Sam linebacker in this adjustment plays like the outside safety on a 3-3 look. We do not often see the formation I have it drawn up against. If there is a tight end, he plays off the line of scrimmage. In the third-and-long situations, we generally see a trip or spread formation.

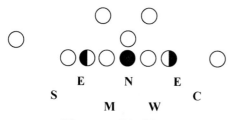

Diagram #6. Dime 55

If we get into a man-coverage situation, we may take the Sam linebacker out and replace him with a defensive back. In normal coverages, he has the curl to flat area. Last year, we did not have the types of players we usually had at those positions. When we went to the nickel and dime situations, we replaced both linebackers with defensive backs. That goes back to putting your players in conflict and asking them to do what they cannot do.

We have a slant package that goes with our fronts. If people are hurting us with the run, we slant the front. In 2007, we won a state championship with our offense. We could score 50 points a game with no trouble. We slanted more because we were not as good on defense. In 2008, we repeated as state champions and won with our defense. We had two good defensive ends. One signed with Alabama and the other one will sign with someone big this year. We score less than 20 points a game and won with turnovers and defensive scores. We did not slant as much with this team. The point I am making is you need to slant more when you do not have as talented players.

We run the 44 slant. We use this against option teams. We align in a 44 front and pinch the defensive ends. They move from a B gap responsibility to an A gap responsibility by pinching inside. When they

pinch, we stay flat and go through the offensive guard's hip. We stay on the line of scrimmage. If the offense blocks down, that is the defensive end's path, because he squeezes on a down block. The noseguard is a two-gap player, and the linebackers play their technique.

If we call 44 all slant, that brings the defensive ends, Sam linebacker, and Cat linebacker on slant stunts (Diagram #7). In south Louisiana, if it is third and three, or fourth and two, we play this stunt. The defensive ends pinch as they did in the slant. The Sam and cat linebackers slant inside, aiming for the hip of the tackle. They are flat and play on the line of scrimmage. The nose tackle is a two-gap player and the Mike and Will linebackers play their technique.

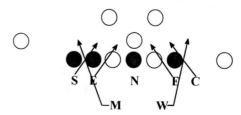

Diagram #7. 44 All Slant

In the secondary, we play cover 3, unless we are inside our red zone. If we are inside our red zone, we play cover 1. If we have a lot of field to work with, we play cover 3 and give up something. I will give up a flat, but I am not going to let the offense go 80 yards playing against man coverage.

This past year, when we aligned correctly, we did not give up the big play. Ninety percent of the big plays we gave up were alignment errors by the defense. When we aligned correctly, we were a good football team. We may check out of the stunt with an empty, but other than that, we are coming. People know our tendencies in this situation and run the ball outside. On the snap of the ball, the Will and Mike linebackers come off the tail of the slanting Sam and cat linebackers. If there is a gap off the Sam linebacker tail, that can hurt you.

We run the 45 slant. The callside defensive end aligns in a 4 technique and the weakside defensive end aligns in a 5 technique. The rules for the 45 slant are the Sam linebacker, 4 technique defensive end, and the nose guard slant to the 5-technique defensive end (Diagram #8). The right defensive end plays a 5 technique and everyone else plays a slant technique. The cat linebacker plays a ghost 9 technique on air. The Mike and Will linebacker play their 30 techniques. The noseguard slants from the A gap responsibility to the weak B gap responsibility.

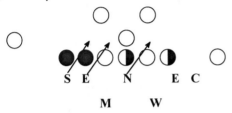

Diagram #8. 45 Slant

If we want to reverse the stunt, we call 54 slant. The strength call is left. The left defensive end moves to the 5 technique and slants outside. The nose slants into the strongside B gap and the 4 technique end slants into the weakside A gap. They all use their slant techniques. The noseguard shades the center strong, aims for the inside hip of the guard, and plays on the line of scrimmage. The Sam, cat, Mike, and Will linebackers play their techniques. The difference in the 45 slant and the 54 slant is the 5 technique slants outside, because he has a tight end outside him. In the 45 slant, the 5 technique plays technique, because there is no threat outside of him. These two stunts are a slant to and away from the strength call. If there is no tight end outside the 5-technique end, he does not slant outside.

If we run a blood stunt, both linebackers blitz their gap. If we run 45 blood, the 4 technique end is left and the 5 technique is right. The nose shades to the 5-technique side. The Mike linebacker blows his strong A gap and the Will linebacker blitzes the weak B gap. Everyone else plays technique football.

If we call a 45 weak blood X, the Will linebacker and the noseguard run an X-stunt to the weak side of the defense (Diagram #9). They reverse their gaps of responsibility. We run this often. It is one of our favorite stunts. The noseguard aligns to the 5 technique and stunts into the B gap. The Will linebacker comes behind him and into the A gap. The

rest of the defense plays their technique. We like this stunt because the Will linebacker is the second-best defender on the team, the nose is a good player, and they can make plays. We put Jimmys and Joes in position to make plays for us instead of X's and O's. We run the stunt with the personnel in mind.

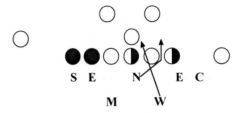

Diagram #9. 45 Weak Blood X

If we want to attack a weak offensive lineman, we run a stunt at him. We are simple when it comes to blitzing a linebacker. If we run the strong blood X, it is the same stunt to the strongside involving the nose and Mike linebacker. The nose slants across the center's face into the strong A gap. The Mike linebacker comes behind the noseguard into the weakside A gap.

The slant stunts are always the same techniques. We slant to the new hip of the adjacent linemen and play on the line of scrimmage. The tags tell us who is involved in the slants. The 45 psycho involves the Sam and cat linebackers (Diagram #10). They run the slant stunt to the inside. They run blitzes for the deepest back in the backfield. A level-one slant is on the line of scrimmage. A level-two slant is as deep as the deepest back. It is a double-crash stunt off the edges. If we call this stunt, we do not check the stunt, unless it is a game-plan check.

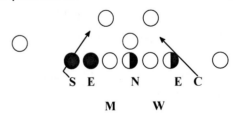

Diagram #10. 45 Psycho

We do not run this stunt often, but when we do, it is effective. We use it in the second half when an offense is hurting us. The Sam linebacker cheats outside to give himself an angle to close off the inside. He aligns head-up and times his movement with the cadence of the quarterback to get outside the alignment. If we call, "psycho-stick," the Sam linebacker comes flat to level one immediately. We run that against option teams to get the Sam linebacker in the quarterback's face immediately.

We run the 45 bam (Diagram #11). This is a strong-safety stunt with the Sam linebacker. The Sam linebacker closes in the C gap and the strong safety blitzes off the edge. Our players love to run this stunt. We play the bam stunt two ways: We give up the flat and play cover 3. That is not as scary for our players. If we want to cover the flat, we call cover 1 and lock up on the receivers. That way, we can cover the fullback to the flat. Normally, when we give up a flat, we give up the flat that requires the longest throw for the quarterback. We play to high school talent with regard to the flat we cover.

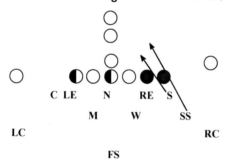

Diagram #11. 45 Bam

When we play an inside veer team, we have to play option technique. If the offensive line tries to split, we adjust our head-up techniques to 4i alignments. If we still had too much area to cover, we moved our defensive end into the gaps and played football. They do not penetrate the gaps. They play on the line of scrimmage and squeeze as if they had a down block. The coaches have to make the adjustments. The adjustments are simple, but we have to make them. You cannot depend on the players to do it. They do what you tell them to do.

On the inside-veer option, the defensive ends have the dive back with help from the inside linebacker. The Mike and Will linebackers play dive, to quarterback, to pitchback in their techniques. The Sam and cat linebackers take the first threat,

which is the quarterback. The strong and weak safeties have the pitchback. The free safety on cover 3 aligns between the hash marks of the field. However, we have adjustments to get him where he needs to go. He reads the uncovered offensive lineman and gets a run/pass read immediately.

We tell him that he has pass responsibility first. That puts him in conflict, but we rely on tendencies, down and distance, and game planning to put him in the best possible position.

If we play the outside veer, the defensive end has to take on the double-team. The Mike linebacker has the quarterback and runs to the pitch. The Sam linebacker takes the first threat to him, which is the dive back. The strong safety takes the pitch.

On our zone blitzes, we are simple. The first zone blitz is 45 storm (Diagram #12). The defensive end to the side of the call slants into the A gap. The Mike linebacker blitzes the B gap behind the end's inside slant. The nose slants into the weakside A gaps. The 5-technique end on the backside has to contain the quarterback. The cat linebacker drops into his coverage. The strong safety runs an edge stunt off the strongside, and the Sam linebacker blitzes off the edge. The strong safety drops into the strong curl to flat zone. The Will linebacker drops into the middle-hook zone and we play cover 3 in the secondary.

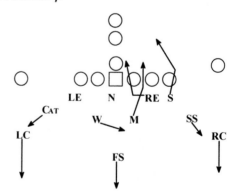

Diagram #12. 45 Storm

When we zone blitz, we give something up most of the time. The Sam linebacker plays run first. However, we will not run this on a running down. We run this in a passing situation.

The 44 cobra is a corner blitz (Diagram #13). We drop the Sam linebacker into the curl/flat zone, as he did on the storm. The defensive end to the weakside slants into the B gap. The Will linebacker blitzes the A gap. The nose and 4-technique end slant into the A and C gaps. The Mike linebacker covers for the Will linebacker in the middle-hook zone. We roll the secondary, with the free safety going to the outside third, and the strong safety going to the middle of the field. We like to bring the corner off the boundary side of the field.

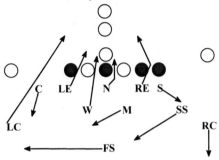

Diagram #13. 44 Cobra

After the storm, we whip out. On storm, the Mike and Sam linebackers are involved. On whip, the Will and cat linebackers are involved. The storm comes from the strongside and the whip comes from the weakside. We run 44 whip (Diagram #14). On the whip, the cat linebacker blitzes off the edge. The weakside defensive end slants into the A gap. The Will linebacker comes behind the slant stunt and blitzes the B gap. The Sam linebacker drops to the curl/flat zone and the Mike linebacker drops to the middle. The free safety inverts into the weakside-flat zone and the strong safety moves into the middle third.

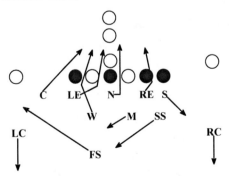

Diagram #14. 44 Whip

The last zone blitz I will show is the 45 freak (Diagram #15). That is the free-safety blitz. We align in a 45 front. The noseguard shades to the 5-technique side and slants across the center's face into the strongside A gap. The 5-technique and 4-technique ends rush through the C gaps and contain the quarterback. The Will linebacker blitzes his B gap. The free safety times his blitz and comes through the weakside A gap. The Sam and cat linebackers drop into the curl/flat zones and the Mike linebacker drops into the middle-hook zone. The corners play the outside thirds and the strong safety drops into the middle third.

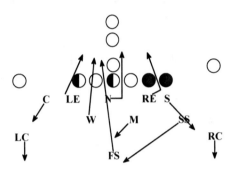

Diagram #15. 45 Freak

We have great talent. We had great athletes this year, but they were not as good as the teams we have had in the past. We have 85 to 90 players involved in our program. We had a down year last year, but we will be better in the years to come. To win back-to-back state championships in 2007 and 2008, and then stumble into a 5-6 season, is not acceptable. We will be back.

I appreciate your time and hope you have a good clinic. Thank you for your attention.

FINDING SUCCESS AT A SMALL SCHOOL

Ubly High School, Michigan

I know everyone here today is from a small school. We all know we have to make a program and system work with the players we get. Our school enrollment is 258 students. We have 140 boys in grades nine through 12. We have won four regional championships. We average 33 points a game and give up 13 points a game. When I got to Ubly in 1996, they had just won a league championship. The next year, we went to the bottom of the barrel. In a school like this, the high are high and the low are low.

I worked for some good coaches who had an impact on me. I used to ask them, "Is football X's and O's, scheme, or brainwashing?" Those coaches had great success, because they got the players to believe in what they were trying to accomplish. It *is* a brainwash. You will see from our scheme that it is not difficult stuff. The Holy Grail is not the 1000 things you do, it is getting the players to believe in the things you do.

Finding Success at a Small School

- 10 commandments of Ubly football
- "Kiss" principle
- Off-season is about getting stronger
- Early season is not a country club
- Season is about getting better
- Simplicity in defense

I am going to talk about the 10 commandments of football. I came up with them about three years ago. I will talk about the KISS principle, which stands for "Keep It Simple Stupid." You have all kinds of players and you have to keep it simple for them. The off-season is about getting stronger. We try to take a 135-pound player and get him to 150-pounds

before the football season starts. You have to get the players out of the halls, but at the small school, there are not many players in those halls. You have to take what you have and make them better.

You have to get players in shape when you are few in numbers. That is physical shape and hitting shape. We may not have the most talented team in our league, but we will hit. We have made the state finals once and the other six times we lost to a state runner-up. We ran into teams that hit and played us tough. You may beat your head against a wall trying to think of what we could have done to win the game. You have to understand that this is what we do. If that is not good enough, then it is what it is.

Ubly Football 10 Commandments

- Out *hit* our opponent.
- Out *block* our opponent.
- Out *tackle* our opponent.
- Be more *disciplined* than our opponent.
- We will be in *better shape* than our opponent.
- We predicate our offensive and defensive systems on *technique.*
- We believe in *ball control.*
- We believe in *demoralizing our opponent.*
- We believe in limiting *turnovers and penalties.*
- We believe in *out working* our opponent.

If you look at this list, there is not much about scheme. I do a lot of reading in the off-season. I read books about old-time coaches. Lou Holtz's book was great. It talked about philosophy, discipline, and finding what works best for every player. I read a book by Joe Paterno. He talked about being able to change everything you do as a coach. However, the one thing you carry with you from a young age to an old age is your philosophy. If your philosophy is to set up the run with the pass, that is what you believe. You may run 15 different schemes, but you will keep that as part of your belief.

I wrote these 10 commandments three years ago when they told me I had to have something to give to the parents that explains our philosophy. This was what I came up with and what we use today. If you want to out hit your opponent, you do tackling drills. The game of football is about out tackling and out blocking your opponent. We went 11-1 this year and the game we lost, we were out blocked and out tackled. We played great defense and shut them down, but we could not do anything against them. If you look at the games you lost, you were out hit in those games.

Our system is simple, which does not allow us to let undisciplined things happen to us. You have to be in better condition than your opponent. We base everything we do on technique. We do not blitz five times a year. We play defense based on technique. The game is about technique, athletic positioning, tackling, and recognition. We do a good job of recognizing what the offense does.

We believe in ball control. There were many years we could only score 20 points a game. When you play good defense, hold the ball for three-fourths of the game, and do not turn it over, you will win. We try to demoralize our opponent. We want to turn the four- to five-yard runs in the first quarter to 10 to 15 yard runs in the second quarter. You have to sell your players on that and it is mental. Is it brainwashing or scheming? I believe 80 percent of it is brainwashing.

We can control the ball because we do not turn it over. We do not get penalties at the wrong time. That is part of our belief. We went to the full T-formation, because we do not turn it over in that set. We do not spend time working on faking until we get to the playoffs and play teams from out of the area. If our players are mentally strong, we will out work our opponent.

We all deal with soft players. That is the way they make them these days. You cannot bitch about it. You have two things you can do. You can find someone who will do it the way you want it done or you can coach what you have and get them to do it.

"The KISS principle states that simplicity should be a key goal in design, and that unnecessary complexity should be avoided." That is the business definition.

Why the "KISS" principle

- We get the parent's best.
- We need special education kids to be successful.
- We need underclassmen to be successful.
- We do not want "paralysis by analysis."
- It has all been done before, so coach what you know and believe in.
- It allows us to focus on the 10 commandments.

We have 22 senior boys in our school but that is the parent's best. We need special education players to be successful. We had a player who gained 1400 yards as a J.V. player. He was a special education student. He was a hard working player. We had to do something to make him a successful player. We took our fullback, moved him to halfback, and played the special education player at fullback. The halfback player was also a special education student. We went to the T-formation to take advantage of what these players could do. You have to coach what you have. You need those kids and you need them to be successful.

Over the years, we have had more success with kids like that than A students. We have more success with players from broken homes than the ones with two parents in the home. The reason is those players are searching for something.

We need underclassmen to be successful. You have to play the best player available in your school. You cannot worry about the senior who does not play in front of a freshman. The best players must play.

We do not want paralysis by analysis. I came up as a wing-T coach and felt like we had to throw the ball to be successful. I studied and watched film, and had the perfect system to install. What happened was paralysis by analysis. I did not realize that I not only had to make it simple for me, I had to make it simple for the players.

Everything in coaching has been done. This is not rocket science. Coaching football is about getting the most out of your players. I have a core belief in football, I know how to teach them, and I believe in them. It took me 12 years to figure it out. I want to do what I know. It allows us to focus on the things that make us successful—the 10 commandments.

The "KISS" Principle in Practice

- Series football out of the "T"
- We base everything we do offensively off the middle trap.
- Rules blocking allows us to get off the ball and utilize technique.
- Common-sense terminology allows us to do many different things without becoming complex.
- Drills and repetition are important.

We have three series we run out of different formations. Our base series is middle trap, cross buck, quarterback sweep, and reverse. We run the 41-42 traps repeatedly in practice until it is second nature for us. When we get to the regular season, we run one or two of those plays a week. The play is motor memory for our players. We start the freshmen teams out running this play and it continues into the sophomore season with the same thing. They will be able to block that play.

Our rules are very simple. We want to protect the inside gap to the hole, kick out, and lead upfield. I will explain that when we get to the spread. We want to use common-sense terminology. That allows us to do many different things without becoming complex. Call your plays what they are. A trap is a trap. I do not say block down on the 3 technique. I tell them to block the down on the man in the gap. Drills and repetition are tremendously important.

I read a book one time and I do not remember the name of the book. However, I do remember what impressed me. They asked the question, "What was the difference between Tom Landry and Vince Lombardi?" These were two outstanding coaches from the 50's, 60's, and 70's. They had completely opposite styles of coaching. Tom Landry was the invocator. He was ahead of his time. The answer to the question was, "Tom Landry could do 1000 things one way. Vince could one thing a 1000 ways." Tom Landry was intelligent and could do many things. We are more like the Vince Lombardi theory. We want to do one thing many ways.

This is our base play (Diagram #1). If the center has a nose guard, he fires off the ball into the nose. If the nose goes backside, the center blocks him that way. If the nose goes frontside, the center and playside guard combo block on the nose with the guard coming off for the backside linebacker. The playside guard, tackle, and end are coming off the ball at a 45-degree angle to the inside. They are wall blockers. We want them to avoid the trap man and get virtually shoulder-to-shoulder to the inside. Anything that crosses their face, they block and destroy it. It does not matter who they block. They cannot allow penetration of the wall by any defender.

Diagram #1. 41-42 Trap

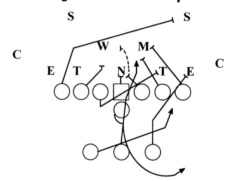

The backside guard pulls and blocks the first man past the center. The backside tackle fill-blocks inside for the pulling guard. The backside end goes downfield for the playside safety. The coaching point for the pulling guard is to take a slight drop-step to get on a 45-degree angle. This protects against a wrong shoulder or sink technique by the defensive lineman.

This is our simple belief. We wall off and kick out. If the defender can blow up one of our blockers, we get beat on that play. If we build the wall, the defenders have to go around it to make the tackle. That is what you look for. Our players do a lot of hunting in the off-season. They understand if you shoot at a rabbit that is running, you do not shoot at the rabbit. You shoot where he is going. They understand that with a defender. You cannot take an angle at the defender. You have to take the angle as to where he goes.

In the backfield, the fullback runs the midline. We want five yards out of this play. The playside halfback blocks the defensive end. The backside halfback comes across the set and fakes an outside run. The quarterback hands the ball to the fullback and comes out the front side to fake the backside halfback. He runs to the playside and fakes the power pass or sweep.

The next play has the same concept. We are blocking down and kicking out. This is the 45-46 play. It looks like the first play. We have three ways we can block this play. The point of attack is the six-hole off-tackle. We have three different ways to block the defensive end. If we call a 46J-block, he uses a J-block and traps the defensive end. If we call 46-end, the playside end blocks the defensive end. If we call 46-regular, the backside guard pulls and kicks out the defensive end.

We want to double-team at the point of attack (Diagram #2). The offensive tackle and tight end double-team the defensive lineman to the playside linebacker. The fullback runs the same path and fakes the trap play. The trapper has to root the defensive end out of the hole. If the halfback kicks out, the backside guard pulls and leads through the hole and blocks the first enemy jersey in the hole. If the guard kicks out, the halfback leads into the hole. If the defensive end slants inside, the end blocks him. The trapper has to be aware of that block. If the playside end blocks the defensive end inside, the trapper goes outside and so does the ball. If the playside end releases the defensive end, the play goes inside.

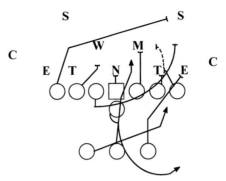

Diagram #2 45-46 Off-Tackle

We ran this play in the state finals. We got to the state finals because we had two great athletes. They are both at Grand Valley State. We will probably never have that chance again. We are like the other small school in the state of Michigan. It was an honor to go, but we did not play well and got our butts kicked. We had a 125-pound halfback executing the J-block on a 310-pound tackle. He could not move him but he got between him and the ballcarrier. When you have those types of blocks, the running back has to tunnel into the hole.

Using these two blocking schemes, I found some other things we could run out of different formations. We are not simply a full-T team. We can do other things from other formations. We put plays in that we could possibly use. We package it into a series. We won a regional game last year running these two plays out of the spread formation.

Out of these two plays, we can run 62 different plays from 14 different formations. If you can master these two plays, you can make the rest of it up as you go along. We have had fun with that.

Conclusion

- We better be able to block the 42 and 46 against everything imaginable.
- We better be able to protect inside to the hole, trap, and protect backside.
- We better get off the ball.
- Everything else we do better not be too complicated.

Use common-sense terminology with all your blocks. Call a block what it is. If it is a trap block, call it a trap block. If it is a fill block, that is what it is. Tag every block. The blocks are drive, angle, and downfield. They are what they say they are. If we ask the backside tackle what his assignment is, he knows. On our plays, the backside tackles will fill-block 50-percent of the time. He fills the inside gap and blocks anyone in there or who comes in there.

We tag everything. If we run a two-man pass pattern, we call hitch-seam. The outside man runs the hitch and the inside man runs the seam. The reason we do that is to take all the guessing out of the game. If you do not have a smart player at one of those positions, this makes it easier for him. If he is on the outside, he runs the pattern called first.

We installed a spread formation. We call it the 400 series (Diagram #3). We had a great quarterback coming and we had to have a passing set. When we went to the spread, everyone got confused. I thought to myself that this does not fit what we do. I changed the set, put a tight end into the formation, and called it spread-400. It is a 2x2 set with tight end to the left side. If we want to flip the set to the opposite side, we call spread-500. If we wanted to run the 42-trap, the blocking was the same as with the full T.

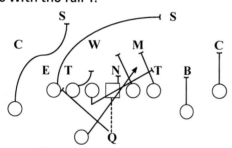

Diagram #3. Spread-442

This fits what we are doing. We have not changed anything for the offensive linemen. They block this play the same way they did from the full T. We can go to trips by moving the wide receiver from the tight-end side to the other side. We call that spread-400-trip. We can flip the back from the left side of the quarterback to the right side by calling, "flip." The quarterback is in the shotgun set.

If we want to run the 45 play from the spread formation, we call Spread 445 (Diagram #4). The blocking is the same. We block down and kick out.

We read the tight end's block to see if we go inside or outside the block. If the play is the J-block, the back in the spread kicks out the defender and the quarterback follows the guard into the hole.

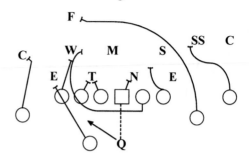

Diagram #4. Spread 445J

We base everything we do off the T. We did not try to learn many different other things. We simplified it, not only for the players, but for the coaching staff as well.

When we call our pass game from the spread formation, we call two routes (Diagram #5). The outside receiver runs the first pattern and the slot runs the second call. If we call slant-wheel, the outside receivers both run slants, and the slot runs the wheel route.

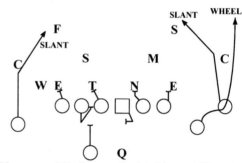

Diagram #5. Spread 400 Slant-Wheel

I have heard this at clinics before. Some things that you learn stick with you. I heard a coach say the reason he ran the full T was that it allows you to get stronger. We do not go to a seven on seven passing camp. We work in the weight room.

Off-Season: Get Stronger

- Every kid can get stronger.
- Make the weight room readily available:
  - ✓ We have two athletic conditioning classes.
  - ✓ The weight room is open every morning and after school.

✓ Workouts vary—in sport athletes and out-of-season athletes.

- Nothing we do in the off-season is mandatory, but it is amazing what *expectation, availability, and visibility* accomplish. All but two of our players in grades 9 to 11 are failing to get their lifts done every week.

- Agilities: We do as many coned agilities, high knee drills, and plyometric boxes as we can during each week. The two most important things in our system, both offensively and defensively are:

  ✓ Exploding hard and low.

  ✓ Changing directions in a position to hit.

- *Maximize* the minimal time you have with kids who are not in the weight class.

We have had zero footballs out this year. It allows us to get stronger. Every player in our program can get stronger. If you are the head coach and the weight room is running, you need to be there. We work four and sometimes five days a week. I am there every day. There is no delegating someone to run the room. If you expect your players to be there, your butt had better be there. When you are there, get involved with them.

How can the players get excited if the head coach is not there? How can the head coach share the team's excitement if he is not there? With the title of head coach, also comes the responsibility to be there.

Our weight room is small. We do our agilities in the hallway. We have no space in our school and it is tiny and old. That cannot be an excuse for not working at the program. If you complain about the facilities and use that as a reason not to run a quality program, you will not win. We just expanded our weight room. It used to be a closet and still is. It has two benches and two squat racks. You make it up as you go along. If you are in a small school, you have to realize that there are things you will have to deal with. That is the way it is and it is not going to get better.

We have to vary our workouts for in-sport athletes and out-of-sport athletes. Nothing we do

in the off-season is mandatory. We have no sign-in sheet at the door. I am there every day and it is amazing how the players show up. It is amazing what the expectation of players, availability of the weight room, and visibility of the coaches can accomplish. If you want the players to sell out, it is up to you to show the same type of effort.

The two most important things we can accomplish in this program are to change directions and hit and to learn how to explode hard and low. We can lift all the weights we want, but if we are not practicing exploding hard and low, we will not do it in the fall.

You have to maximize the time you have with your athletes. At a small school, the athletes play three sports. As the football coach, you want them to play three sports. There is nothing better than having competition. I do not want one of the top athletes on my team only lifting weights for nine months. I want him to compete and get better at competing.

What is the difference between a school with 250 students and a school with 2500 students? You are lucky to have one stud athlete in your school. They have 25 stud athletes in their school. In a small school, the athletes have to play all the sports.

The best way to maximize your time with those athletes is before/after school workouts. These workouts apply to only the players who do not have a weightlifting class. If a player is playing another sport, he comes in during the morning workouts two days a week. He does the weight lifting only. The second day, they do their plyometrics and power cleans. His agility is playing basketball. If players are not in a sport, they come after school three days a week. They do the agility program, weight lifting, and plyometrics.

I cannot emphasize this enough—you need to be there when the players are there. You have to be there to enjoy their success and kick them in the butt when they slack off. The players go harder when the head coach is around than when he is not.

Early Season is Not a Country Club

- Get in shape.
- Get in hitting shape.
- Technique at full speed and we will make everything we do a good habit. The rest of the year, we will tweak what we do.
- Scrimmage-base offense and defense against one another.
  - ✓ Break up the lines—good versus Good.
  - ✓ Tape practice and let the kids know what they are doing, right or wrong.
  - ✓ Point out loaf (lack of effort).

Do not take yourself too seriously. Too many times, we have come off a good year and struggled for the first four or five games the next season. Never assume a player will be better or as good as he was the previous season. Get your team in good physical shape. Teach them proper techniques and then get in hitting shape. The only way you can duplicate game speed is to go live. We are going to be safe, but we are going to hit and scrimmage big time. That is the only way you get better.

Practice should not be a country club. The only time we get dummies out is when we do walk-throughs. We do all our technique work at full speed. You can do techniques at each station for 10 minutes, but they have to do it right. You have to be actively engaged and excited. I get excited. It wears me down, but I get excited. All the coaches need to be actively involved with every drill and every workout.

We have had success in our programs, but the question is, "Will we be able to sustain that success?" You never know. I enjoy the hell out of coaching. I enjoy this time of year. I do not enjoy the practice or game, for that matter. I do enjoy the game when the players are having fun. I enjoy seeing players grow and being a part of that. I enjoy putting a foot in their butt when they need it. People say you cannot do that anymore. If you are visible and put them in a position where it is simple, you can have success. You must have expectations for them and they will play for you.

In closing, I want to say, I have never set a goal for any team. I thought I was the only one who did that. Setting up master goals of going undefeated and winning a state championship is setting yourself up for failure. Our goal is to out hit our opponent. Setting an individual goal of trying to bench 200 pounds is a good goal.

There are too many X-factors to set master team goals. There will be enough people on the periphery to put pressure on your players. That is especially true when your program gets to the point where they expect state championship every year. Your players do not need that extra pressure.

Be careful when you set team goals. If you achieve them, you were supposed to do it. If you do not, you are a failure. However, we all know there are no failures, especially at a small school. Thank you very much.

THE RUGBY PUNT FORMATIONS AND COVERAGE

Whitehall High School, Pennsylvania

It is a pleasure to be here today. I want to thank you for your warm welcome. If you coach special teams, you are a different kind of coach. You have a different mentality than the other coaches on your staff. I listened to Bobby Bowden last night, and he said many great things. I wrote many of them down.

If you are the special teams coach, you have to believe you can win the game on special teams. If you go out and try not to lose the game, you are selling your kids and the program short. It is not about surviving as a team it is about prevailing. My whole philosophy about the special teams is I want to affect the football game with our special teams units.

I want our players to believe that we can make an impact in the football game. To convince your players of that point, you have to talk about the why. You have to teach the why and explain it to your players. You have to teach them *why* special teams are important.

The Importance of Field Position

The kicking game gains importance when you understand scoring percentages. It may sound simple but the numbers do not lie. The more field you make the offense earn, the less likely they are to score points. Special teams impact field position more than any other aspect of the game. The average play on special teams is over 30 yards. The average offensive play is four to five yards. We must make our opponents earn the field and give our offense the best chance to score.

We called our special teams the Special Forces. We started to this when I was at Elon University. Each special team had its own name that related to the Special Forces. I was the special team's

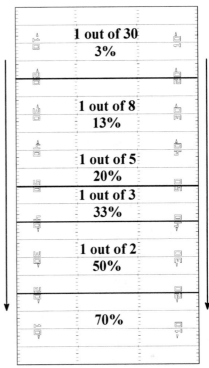

Diagram #1. Impact

coordinator but each position had a phase of the kicking game they were in charge of. That is how we handled the special teams, and we adopted the Marines slogan.

Special Forces—We are looking for a few good men!

- Athletic: Run and hit
- Attention to detail
- Technique: Master of your trade
- Desire: Important to you?
- Reliable: Can we trust you?

It is not about survival. It is about prevailing. If a player does not pay attention to detail, he cannot play on the punt team. We want our players to have good technique and be a master of their trade. I want them to buy into the technique and take ownership of it. Desire has to be important to them. If they do not want to be on special teams, we do not want them on the team. It is your job to convince them that you need them. In the end, if the players do not have desire and it is not important to them, you will not be successful.

The players must be reliable, and you have to trust them. If we put someone on the field, we had better be able to trust them. The coach's job is on the line.

2009 Goals

- Explosive Plays: Kickoff return > 40 PR < 20 turnovers, blocks, fakes +1
- No Penalties: Alignment, See the ball, do not chase.
- Turnovers: Create one; allow none.
- Returners: Field all kicks cleanly
- Punt Pro Pride: Net punting 35 yards
- Punt Rush Swat: Opponent net punting < 30 yards
- Kickoff Cover Delta: Deep inside 25-yard line; sky inside 30-yard line
- Kickoff Return Stampede: Average drive start -31
- PAT/Field Goal: 100 percent inside 27-yard line, 50 percent outside 27-yard line

We use the terms pride, swat, delta, and stampede as the name of those units. We call the punt pro unit pride. The punt team and punt-return team is not about how many yards they average per kick. It is all about net yards. If we punt the ball 50 yards and they return it 20 yards, the net yardage is 30 yards. The net yards are the numbers we look at.

The number of yards the kickoff return gets is not important. The starting position for the offense is the most important item in the kickoff return. Our stampede unit wants to start every drive beyond the 30-yard line. It is not averaging 25 yards on the return. If we can fair catch a short kick at the 35-yard line, that is a win for us.

A 27-yard field goal is one kicked from the 10-yard line. If we get inside the 10-yard line and have to kick a field goal, we should make 100 percent of those kicks. When we get outside the 10-yard line, it becomes a more difficult kick. Kicks from the 15-yard line are 33-yard kicks. If he makes 50 percent of those kicks, he is meeting our goal.

I want to talk about the rugby punt. We use the rugby punt for a number of reasons:

- Coverage
- Center does not block
- Practice time
- Average punter
- Fakes

I got this scheme from Memphis University. The first reason we went to the rugby punt was coverage. In the coverage, you have five gunners. The center does not block. He is one of the gunners. People think the rugby punt is exotic and you have to spend a lot of time practicing it. You do not. In a game situation, you never know what the opponent will do on the punt. The blocking scheme in the rugby punt is very simple. You do not need to look at a ton of different defenses to punt the ball.

You do not have to have a great punter in this scheme. You can rugby punt with an average punter. If you do not have a great punter, you can put your best athlete back there and be in good shape. This year, we did not have a great punter. We put our running back as the punter. A soccer goalie is the place to find one of these kickers.

With the scheme, we can run a number of fakes. We run many fakes and are not afraid to run them. We call our fakes from the line of scrimmage. Many times, we call a fake and we do not like what we see. It is easy to get out of the fake and punt the ball.

We punted 33 times in 2009 from this formation. The punter averaged 38.3 yards per punt. We downed the ball 17 times and had 12 fair catches. The punt-return team returned four punts for 16 yards. We had a net punting average of 37.8, which is good. We also quick punt from the spread formation. If we are near or just inside the 50-yard line, the quarterback can quick kick the ball from the spread set.

In our punt alignment, we have a center and two guards two yards apart at the ball (Diagram #2). The tackles and ends split eight yards from the guards. The center along with the tackles and ends are the five gunners. If you are on the hash mark into the shortside of the field, there is not a lot of room. The eight yards are important because you can identify a creeper slipping back inside to try to block the kick. At five yards from the ball are the right, left, and middle blocking backs. The punter aligns at 14 yards.

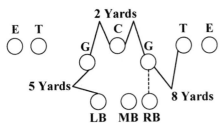

Diagram #2. Rugby Punt Alignment

The center does not block. He snaps the ball and releases to the ball. The right guard was a 6'3", 215-pound tight end. He was very athletic. The left guard was an athletic offensive tackle. The guards do not have to be big players. If you have linebacker, tight end–type bodies, they are the ones you want to play.

The left blocking back was our second-string fullback. The middle blocker has to call the cadences and automatics for the fakes. The players we put in the block like are defensive linemen or tight ends.

Rugby Punt Rules

- Left guard: Backside A gap
- Right guard: #3
- Right back: #1
- Middle back: #2
- Left back: Frontside A gap, back

In a rugby punt formation, you will get a six-man rush most of the time (Diagram #3). The backside A gap belongs to the backside guard. We cheat the guard as far off the ball as we can legally. The guard

kicks inside and protects the gap. The right guard has the third defender from the outside counting inside. If #3 defender is in the A gap, he blocks him. If #3 defender is on his nose, he blocks him. If he is on his outside shoulder, he blocks him. If #3 is in the A gap, that is ideal for us. The right guard down blocks on him and washes him inside. If a defender comes up the middle off the other side, the guard's block catches him in the trash.

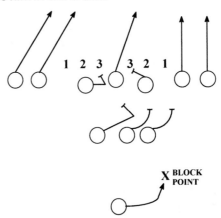

Diagram #3. Rugby Punt Rules

The right blocking back blocks the #1 defender from the outside. The middle blocker blocks the #2 defender on the frontside. The left blocker has the frontside A gap for any penetration. If he has no one in that gap, he blocks back to the backside. The blockers align at five yards and cannot back up. They have to move forward to take on the blocks, not settle backward.

They must stay square on the defenders. The right side blocker is like a pass blocker. He cannot turn his shoulders outside and open the inside. He has to stay square and attack the outside number of the defender. We want the blockers to use all the principles of blocking. They must be physical and have great blocking principles. We want their thumbs up and elbows in as they punch and block the defender. The most important point is to get the face on the outside numbers of the defenders. The three blockers want to block the outside number of the defender on a rush.

The punter catches the ball and false steps. He steps left, right, left, and punts the ball. He wants to keep his shoulders square to the line of scrimmage.

With his shoulder parallel to the line of scrimmage, he presents the ball on his outside hip. He wants the ball to be low at his hip and punt the ball. Sometimes the ball comes out as a line drive and rolls. The roll is what we depend on. Some punter can boom the ball but you do not need a good punter. We want a low drop as opposed to a high drop. Most of the techniques of punting will care over to this style of punting.

The punt block point for the punter is nine yards deep and four yards outside the ball. We do not know the exact point until we select the punter. In practice, have the punter put a towel on the ground at the block point. That tells everyone where the punter will kick the ball. That lets them know what they have to protect.

If the right blocker misses the block, he does not want the defender coming outside. If the defender is inside, we still can punt the ball. The punter should be able to get rid of the ball in 2.3 seconds. On occasion, we call "watch." That means if they do not pressure the punter, he does not punt the ball immediately. He holds the ball and punts it late.

On the punt coverage, the tackles and the center are going to the ball (Diagram #4). They have no contain-responsibility or leverage alignments. The coverage unit when they get close to the return man wants to sink the hips and get themselves under control. They must be square to the return man. The ends sprint down and leverage the ball on their inside shoulders. They are not containing players. As they get under control, they want to keep the inside foot forward as they move to the ball. If the ball tries to break outside, they can open to the outside.

If the defender's shoulders turn to the inside, he cannot pursue to the outside. If the ball breaks outside, his hips of the defenders, lock and he cannot get back outside. The guards cover and aim five yards outside the return man. They are not the contain rusher but aim five yards outside the returner. We have five defenders inside of that five-yard area. The guards are level two coverage

players. They have blocking assignments and will arrive late. The right and left blocker are the contain defenders. The middle blocker is a second level coverage man and keeps the ball in front of him. The punter is the safety.

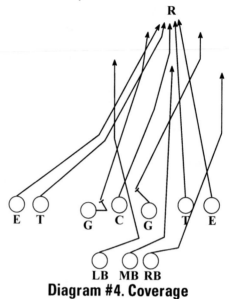
Diagram #4. Coverage

An overload occurs when the defense puts four rushers to the right of the ball (Diagram #5). The left blocker has the responsibility for the #4 defender coming through the A gap. Everyone else blocks their rules.

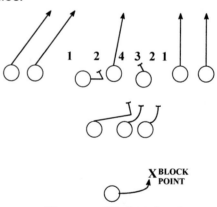
Diagram #5. Overload

If we want to punt the ball to the right, we call "Rambler." The name comes from a youth league program in our community. It means right. If we want to kick to the left, we call "Eagle," which is another youth league team. The "R" in Rambler and the "L" in Eagle means right and left.

We can call a tackle over and move one of the tackles to the other side. We call "tackle over

Rambler" and send them on the field. The signal caller calls out the defensive alignment. He may call 4-2. He looks to the sidelines. I check with the coaches in the box. If the call is right, I give him the thumbs-up signal, and we punt the ball. If the defense overloads to the right and I am not comfortable with the protection, I give an "Eagle" call, and we punt the ball, rolling to the left side. That changes the launch point of the punt to the two-defender side.

If one of the defenders moves in from the outside alignment on your tackle, we call him a creeper (Diagram #6). We count him in the numbering system. He becomes the #1 defender. The right blocker blocks him. The middle blocker takes the #2 defender. The right guard blocks the #3 defender, and the left blocking back blocks the strongside A gap. The left guard blocks the backside A gap, and we punt the ball to the right side.

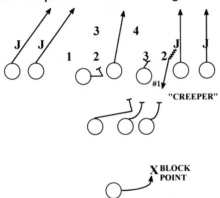

Diagram #6. Creeper Overload

The defender may twist in their charges at the line of scrimmage (Diagram #7). If the #2 and #1 defenders twist in their charges, the right blocking back takes the defender coming to the outside, and the middle blocking back takes the defender coming inside. That is one reason we do not go after the rusher in an aggressive fashion. We want to let any twist or cross charge materialize before we deal with it. They do not back up; they hold their ground and attack the defenders as they threaten their position. That does not mean they are less physical.

If the #4 rusher blows either A gap, the left blocking back picks him up. His rule is strongside A gap to backside.

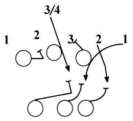

Diagram #7. Twist and 3/4

If we get a four-defender side to the right and we do not like the alignment, we call "Eagle" (Diagram #8). The left guard blocks the #2 defender to his side. We count from the outside. The right guard blocks the frontside A gap. The left blocking back blocks the #1 defender to the left side. The middle blocking back blocks the #3 or #4 defender coming up the middle of the formation. The right blocking back blocks the A gap and back if nothing comes into the A gap.

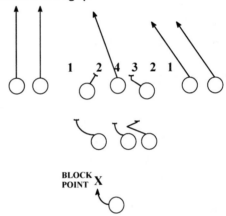

Diagram #8. Left Punt

The punter receives the ball, steps to the left side, and punts the ball. The punter catches the snap, takes the false step, and takes one step before he punts the ball. These techniques for the punter are assuming you have a right-footed punter.

When we use a fake punt, we do it from with a trap play (Diagram #9). The play is not important. You can choose any play you feel comfortable in running. We like the trap play. The diagram is an unbalanced tackle over formation. We do that so we do not have as many defenders to worry about to the trap side. The trips alignment to the right runs off the defenders aligned on them. We snap the ball to the left blocking back. The middle blocking back is the kick-out or trap blocker. He blocks the #1 defender. It should be an easy block because that defender forces the punt. To force the punt, he comes outside and upfield to the punter.

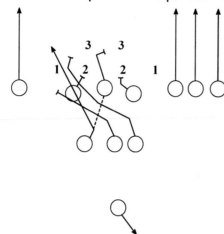

Diagram #9. Trap Fake

The hard block is the right guard sealing the A gap. He cannot allow penetration from the #2 defender in that gap. The frontside guard has a down block on the #2 defender. The center comes up the field and cuts off the backside linebacker. The right blocking back leads into the hole and looks to the inside for the linebacker. The left side gunner releases downfield. The left blocking back receives the ball and gets on the outside hip of the right blocking back. The right blocking is the pulling guard turning up in the hole for the frontside linebacker.

We run a pass fake off the set also (Diagram #10). The tackles are ineligible and must stay in to block. If there is a creeper to frontside, we can use the tackle to block the creeper. The backside tackle can cheat to the inside and may be a factor in the blocking scheme. We do not need him, but he can block. The blocking rules for the pass are the same for the punt except for the center. He is ineligible and cannot release. He takes the place of the left blocking back in the protection. The right guard blocks the playside A gap. The middle and right blocking backs block the #2 and #1 defenders coming from the outside.

The frontside receiver runs a comeback pattern at the distance needed for the first down. The backside receiver runs a crossing pattern, coming across the field at first-down depth. The left blocking back goes through the A gap or takes the best release and runs into the flat area.

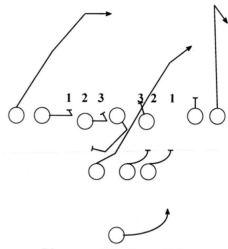

Diagram #10. Pass Fake

Since I have been here, we have had one punt blocked. It happened this year against an undefeated team. We lost the game by a touchdown. Blocked punts will get you beat. The defender came through the backside A gap and blocked the kick. The backside defenders are not blocked, and by operation, they should not be able to get to the punt. When you move the block point, the rusher should not be able to get to the kick.

We made a mistake in protection. The backside blocking back is supposed to block the backside A gap. If there is no one in the gap, he blocks back. The left guard did not move his feet and released his defender in the A gap. The left side blocking back took the defender coming from the outside and let the A-gap defender come free. What should have happened was the left blocking back blocks the most dangerous man. He blocks the A gap and lets the punter get the ball off, avoiding the backside rusher.

If we have trouble in either of the A gaps with speed rushers, we make an adjustment. We allow the center to snap the ball and squeeze the gap and help the guard. We have to do a better job of coaching the guards to get off and move their feet to stay square on the A-gap defender. However, as a game adjustment, we use the center to help the guard.

Another problem that may occur is the alignment of the left guard. If he has a fast rusher to his inside, he feels he has to tighten his split to block the A gap. That shortens the distance from the backside to the block point. That has to be a concern for your punt-coverage team.

If we cannot clearly define the defenders as to their position, the protection team has to communicate. We point to and verbalize the defender we are blocking. The blocking back calls the front and looks to the sidelines. He calls, "3-3 Rambler." If that is the correct call, I give him the signal, and we snap the ball.

We want the center to snap the ball on the right hip or the right half of the punter. If he can snap the ball there, that is where we want the ball. If he snaps the ball to the left hip or outside the framework of the punter, he brings the left side rushers into play. The snap is critical to the operation. The block point coming from the backside is a drastic angle for the rusher to get to the ball. It may look like he is close to blocking the ball, but he is never a threat to do it.

The punter in this protection scheme is not as protected as in other schemes. However, we have never had a roughing-the-punter penalty or had him knocked down. That speaks volumes for the security of the protection. The protection has not been an issue for us.

We want the blocking backs to stay on the same plane and not creep up. When they do strike the rushers, we want their nose on the outside number of the rusher. We can use a man scheme for an overload situation. If the fourth rusher appears in the frontside A gap, we can include him in the count, and the left blocking back takes him man-to-man. If he fakes and does not come, the blocking back checks the backside and covers.

On the schedule this year, we had two schools come after the punt. We know who they are and make sure we are alert to their fronts. This year, we had a third school try to block the punt, and we hurt them. Most of the teams we play do not try to block the punt. They stay back and try to field the ball and stop it from rolling.

The earlier we can run a fake in the punting game, the better it is for us. When we do it, that gives the defense the mind-set that we will fake it. That keeps them from rushing and makes them defend the fake. If we give the punter the "watch" call, he has the option to run the ball out of punt formation.

When you make that call, you must have a smart player doing your punting. We do not worry about down-and-distance but we want good decision-making. I coach him on that situation, but I let him make the decision. When he decides to run the ball, he calls "go" to the protection so they know to stay on their blocks. If he decides to run and sees something he does not like, he can still punt the ball. If he makes the first down, it was a good decision. If he does not make the first down, it was a bad decision.

We like to unbalance with the tackle over. The problems occur when you have to punt the other way. If they overload the callside and make us punt the ball to the other side, we only have one gunner and the center to that side.

The punter may not be a great punter, but when the ball is rolling on the ground, the return team is scared to pick it up. The football does not bounce like a basketball. It takes funny hops. It can bounce into a blocker and make it a live ball. When the ball hits the ground, the coverage team runs away from the ball. That is to our advantage.

Watching the cut-ups of this past season, I was not satisfied with the mechanics of our punt-coverage team. To cover the punt as a gunner, you must have great get-off from the line of scrimmage. To have a great get-off, you have to prefect your stance and fundamentals. We will work on that in the spring and next year.

The beauty of this scheme is you do not have to be good in your protections. You can make mistakes in the protection and not get punts blocked. The good point is we get players down the field in coverage. In our protection scheme, we are not protecting the punter as much as we are protecting the block point. In our punt-coverage team, we gave up one return of 12 yards. The other three punts gained four yards.

I want to talk about the technique of the right guard in the A gap. I covered this briefly. If the right guard has an A-gap rusher, he wants to block him down the line. By being aggressive, he can wash him into another rusher attacking the middle of the protection. It destroys the timing of the rusher. Knocking him off balance means he cannot block the punt.

You should not run the tackle over into the boundary. That puts the defenders too tight to the guards. They can creek off the inside tackle and not show they are coming. We want the creeper to have to change his alignment to get to the punt. If we see him creeping, we count him in our numbering system and pick him up.

One of the reasons we moved our blocking back from four-and-a-half yards to five yards this year was to be able to sort out the twists in the line. The defenders define the stunt by the time they get to the blocking backs. It makes it easier for them to block. Also, by changing the block point from the right to the left side, we can control the rushers. If they do not know which side you will launch the ball from, they are not that aggressive.

When we get inside the 50-yard line and punt the ball, we have to practice sound punt-coverage rules. We want punter calling left, right, short, or middle. That lets the coverage team know where he kicked the ball. The return players will lie to the coverage players and try to fake them away from the ball. If the receiver fair catches the ball, the first coverage player goes past the fair catch and sets up to keep the ball out of the end zone. On the fake, the punter can fake the run to the opposite side or fake the high snap from the center.

We are a no-huddle, spread offensive team. Our tempo is very fast. Any time we get inside the 50-yard line, we could punt out of our doubles formations. We use our three-step pass protection. The first things we do are hard count and try to draw the defense off. If they jump, it gives us a first down or a shorter yardage situation. If they do not jump, the quarterback backs up and punts the ball. The back in the backfield aggressively attacks his blocking assignment. He does not set up and protect. We align the tight end to the right side so there is not a short corner off the edge.

If we have the ball in the middle of the field, we like to go to the trips formation to get the extra player into the coverage. Another thing we do is fake the quick kick. We do everything we normally do except throw four verticals. When teams scout you, they know what you will do. We hustle to the line and use the hard count. When the quarterback drops back, the safeties start to retreat because they think it is a punt. We snap the ball and run four verticals.

For us to be backed up, we must be inside the four-yard line. As long as the punter has 14 yards, we use our regular punt formation. When we get into a danger situation, we are inside the four-yard line. The formation we use is a field-goal formation with two split receivers. We one-step the ball and kick it. We beef up the offensive line a bit to help seal the inside.

The last thing I am going to talk about has to do with the backed-up position. If you have to take a safety, there is a good way to do it. We want to run the clock before we give the safety. We do not want anyone to hit the punter, and he must avoid all contact. He can run with the ball, but he has to be able to step out of the end zone quickly. We tell the offensive line to actually hold their defenders at the line of scrimmage. The worst thing that can happen is you get a half-the-distance penalty if the defense takes the penalty. You used the clock, and you get to do it all over again. They will not take the penalty because they want the ball back.

Thank you very much.

RUNNING THE 3-5-3 DEFENSE: WHY AND HOW

Riverside High School, New York

I want to start with a couple of random thoughts. In one hour, I am going to tell you about the defense in the simplest terms. The most important thing in the 3-5-3 defense is the *noseguard*. The second point is the outside safeties, which we call *spurs*. The third important thing you must have is one good cover *corner*. If you have two corners, you are in good shape. If you do not get anything else from my lecture today, please understand those three things.

I am not trying to sell the 3-5-3 defense, but as soon as I go through the history of our team, it will be an option for you to consider. My defensive run coordinator, Steve Pangallo, introduced this defense to me three years ago. He previously coached at a Buffalo Jesuit high school. They ran the 4-4 defense but were tinkering with the 3-5-3 defense. His head coach at the time did not want to add it as part of their package. They were to play Canisius High School, which was a powerhouse, in the state playoffs. They played them earlier in the season and lost 40-0. They installed the 3-5-3 in one week and took Canisius to overtime before losing.

He came to Riverside High School and brought the defense with him. We went to Georgia Military College to refine what we did. Everything we do comes from GMC. Coaches Bert Williams and Rob Manchester were instrumental in helping us with the defense. At that time, I was a 4-3 team with a cover-2 secondary. Our record over the last three years has been 26-6. Most of the six losses came in the first year when we were installing the defense. Since we have installed the defense, we have been in the state finals two of the three years. In the three years, we have had 17 defensive shutouts. Fourteen of those shutouts are on the record as shutouts. In three of the games, I gave up a safety, a special teams touchdown, and a fumble returned

for a touchdown. So unofficially, the defense gave up no scores. In those three years, we were 7-4, 10-1, and 9-1.

Rationale Behind the 3-5-3

- Personnel.
- You only need a few defensive linemen. You tend to get linebacker/strong safety type of players.
- Speed kills—we want faster players to fit into the linebacker/strong safety type.
- Fewer coverages to learn.
- You remain balanced on both sides of the ball, so if an offense motions to an unbalanced formation, fewer players have to realign.
- You are showing an eight-man front, yet you are still strong against the pass. The emergence of the spread offense causes defenses to remove a linebacker from the box to cover a receiver. This causes a loss of gap integrity.

There are several reasons why we run this defense. The first reason is our players are smart. We have a lot of speed and true student-athletes. The key word in that statement is *athletes*. I was looking for a defense to stop the power running game. We needed something to stop the isolation, counter trey, and other power football plays.

When you play this defense, you need fewer defensive linemen. Riverside is a 2A school but we have a small enrollment. Our enrollment could be Class A football. We get between 60 to 70 players out for our varsity and junior varsity teams. The juniors and seniors are on the varsity, and, after that, I divide the team in half. The sophomores and freshmen make up the JV team. If we have a stud in one of the lower classes, we bring him up to the varsity team.

When we chose the defensive players, we took the fastest 11 athletes and put them on defense. However, I did pick my quarterback first before we did that. Working with a smaller group meant you got more reps in your practices. We are an urban high school and we have a lot of speed. However, you do not need speed to run this defense.

This defense helps you remain balanced on both sides of the ball. If you face teams that motion for a single-receiver side to a double-receiver side, you do not have to worry about adjustments. If the offense uses a trips set, it is no problem to adjust to that set.

We are showing an eight-man front, which helps us in our running game defense. At the same time, we are able to play great pass defense from this defense.

Advantages of Playing the 3-5-3

- Not many coaches know how to block or game plan for 3-5-3.
- It is a very flexible defense. Nickel and dime alignments can be made without disrupting the scheme, and with the right personnel, there is no need for subs.
- The defense is an eight-man front, yet five of the players are speed players (linebackers) and they can defense the pass.
- You can use smaller, faster players.
- Offenses do not know where the pressure is coming from.
- It confuses the offensive line.
- Great adjustment to two-minute offense (personnel does not need to be changed).

Another advantage of playing this defense is that teams do not see the defense very often. That presents a problem for game planning against the defense. In this defense, you can disguise the blitz very well. You can blitz from any number of places in this defense.

It is flexible in the secondary. You can play a nickel or dime in the secondary with no difficulty at all. It presents an eight-man front for the offense.

Our speed players are the linebacker positions. It is a great defense versus a spread team. This is a balanced defense, which lets us get the extra defender on the triple option.

Offensive teams are beginning to concentrate on the two-minute offense. This defense will help you play in those situations. We do not have to worry about substituting personnel in and out of the game. We can play the situations without changing personnel. The calls are easy to communicate. That is important when you play a no-huddle team. The offense may play the no-huddle the whole game or go into it in the two-minute drill. We do not have trouble adjusting because of communication.

Teams that we play have five offensive linemen who must turn around and play defense for them. Most of the times, those players are playing a 3 technique or 1 technique and not one of the defensive ends. You get a lot of punishment playing that way. In this defense, we have one position where we play an offensive lineman and that is the noseguard position.

Disadvantages of Playing the 3-5-3

- Teams lining up and trying to smash your three defensive linemen
- The tight end is not covered
- Sometimes moving out of a cover 3 or man
- Not always giving a multiple look up front

With every defense, there are disadvantages. It is not good against two-tight end power running teams. The tight ends are not covered in this defense. We found this out with the option game. They come inside on the linebacker and get outside on the option. Another problem we had with the tight end was down the middle of the field with the single high safety.

In this defense, you give the same look to the offensive line each time you align. They have to combination block on the middle and outside stacks to block the defense.

Keys to Success

- You have to *believe* in the defense, and then convince your players it is sound. Stats and records help.
- Pressure—the use of many different pressures is the biggest key in this defense.
- Surge—the noseguard is the #1 key. He needs to force a double-team.
- Offensive coaches use valuable time practicing many different blitzes and stunts.

If you decide to run this defense, you have to believe in what you are doing. It gets frustrating sometimes. In the first year we ran the defense, we started out with a 1-3 record. I had to convince myself as the head coach that this was the right defense. If I give you one thing for the day, it is to do your homework and stay with the defense. You have to believe.

This defense is a pressure defense. It puts pressure on the quarterback. If the quarterback is not ready for the one- and three-step reads, he will take a beating. The noseguard has to force teams to double-team him. The first year we played with a short, stocky noseguard that was quick. This year, that player was injured and we played a backup tackle in that position. He was 6'2" and 300 pounds, but he had the same kind of success as the quick player. He took the double-team but also made plays for us.

The center has a problem, particularly if he is a shotgun center. He has to worry about snapping the ball and stepping up for leverage. The 300-pound player is not going to bull rush the center. He is going one side or the other to make the center move his feet and get to a gap. This defense is a place-and-replace defense.

When we pick our personnel to play this defense, we start with the noseguard. He needs to be a wrestler-type player. He plays in a 0 technique on the center (Diagram #1). The defensive ends are agile and fast. They align in a 5i technique on the offensive tackles. That is what people might call a head-up alignment on the offensive tackle. I call

them basketball-type players. In a school like ours, Buffalo has a reputation for good basketball players. They were in the 6'3", 190-pound class. We had some other players that were the 6'0", 205-pound types of athletes. We played with quick players in that position.

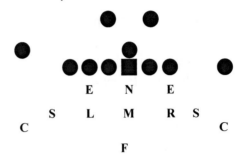

Diagram #1. Base Defense

The Mike linebacker is the prototypical middle linebacker. He stacks behind the noseguard. All he is worried about is stopping the run and has to know how to blitz. He is going somewhere on every play.

The outside safeties or spurs are the best athletes we have on the team and they are the smartest defensive players. They align outside the tight end or uncovered tackle. Their alignment will vary based on situations and the scouting report.

The Lou linebacker plays on the strongside of the defense and the Rob linebacker plays to the weakside. They align in a stack position behind the defensive ends in a 40 technique. The only difference is the Lou is *stronger* and the Rob is *quicker*. These linebackers are the "betweeners" of the Mike linebacker.

The Mike linebacker is going to stop the run. The Lou linebacker has to stop the run, but he also has to get into the coverage. He has to cover the tight end or the #3 receiver coming out of the backfield.

The Rob is the speedster. He is a good player and he's smart. He has to cover the boundary plays in this defense. He is involved with more pass coverage and plays similar to the outside safeties.

The field spur is the best linebacker type. He is like a strong safety. What we did with our spurs was to match them up to the outside linebacker types. If we had a strong linebacker at the outside linebacker position, we wanted a strong pass coverage spur to that side. He could get into the flats and play strong coverage. To the other side, the spur was more of a blitzing linebacker type. He was on the side with the pass coverage outside linebacker.

Our corners are cover-1 defenders. They must be able to play man coverage. The free safety aligns in the middle and calls the defensive adjustment on the coverage. He is the free player in the middle and has to play the alleys to either side of the ball. He is our defensive quarterback.

We align in the base front at the beginning of each play. From the base front, we make our adjustments to what the offense does. We play some of the 4-3 rules from this front. However, you do not want to change the front from a 4-3 to a 3-5 look or go from the 3-5 to a 4-3 look. You will not be successful if you do that. We stay in the 3-5 and adjust the personnel in that scheme. We are not playing a 4-3 although it looks like it. All we are doing is moving the down linemen to different techniques and covering with the safeties or linebackers walking down in the front.

In the solid front, we move the defensive line away from the tight end (Diagram #2). We move the defensive end to the strongside down into a 3 technique on the guard. The noseguard moves to a weakside shade on the center. The designated spur walks to the line of scrimmage and aligns in what we call a 7 technique, which is on the outside shoulder of the tight end. The weakside defensive end aligns in a 5 technique on the outside shoulder of the offensive tackle.

Diagram #2. Solid Front

When the linebackers or spurs come to the line, they align in a two-point stance on the outside shade of the tight end or tackle. They play with the foot to the ball up in their stance. They must be up and ready to shoot the hands from their chest on the tight end.

When you play a defense that plays a 3 technique and a 1 technique, the offense has certain ways to attack that alignment. They want to trap the 3 technique and double-team the 1 technique. That is what we prepare for in this adjustment.

In the under front, we move the front toward the tight end (Diagram #3). The defensive end to the tight end will move to the outside shoulder of the tackle in a 5 technique. The noseguard moves to a strongside shade on the center, and the backside end moves into a 3 technique on the guard. In this front, we walk up the outside linebacker to the line of scrimmage and he plays a 6 technique on the ghost tight end. In this situation, we call the linebacker a *Bat*, which means a backer. You can call these positions anything you like.

Diagram #3. Under Front

We play a tuff front against double tight end teams (Diagram #4). We put the defensive ends in 3 techniques on the outside shoulders of the guards and walk both Lou and Rob linebackers head-up the tight ends. Teams think they can go to the double tight ends and take advantage of the 3-5. If the offense wants to play power football, we adjust our fronts and play.

Diagram #4. Tuff Front

We want to pound the center and slant the defense. This defense is a gap-responsible defense and we cannot two-gap in our scheme.

We can adjust and look like a 4-4 type of defense with a *heads* call. On this adjustment, we bring the linebacker to the tight end side into a 6 technique head-up the tight end. The strong end and noseguard move into 2 techniques head-up the guards. The backside defensive end moves into a 7i technique, which is a wide 5 technique on the offensive tackle. This is a great way to tinker with the offensive linemen with your alignments and it is good in a passing situation. You can run line twists with the 2 techniques and get the linebackers involved with a blitz game.

The eyes adjustment moves the end into a 4 technique on the inside shoulder of the offensive tackles, and the wide adjustment moves them to the outside shoulders of the offensive tackles. The wide is good against the pass because the ends are charging upfield with linebacker help underneath. That allows them to contain or box on the pass.

The next thing I want to cover is the line movement calls. The jacks call is an outside C-gap charge by the defensive ends. If they have a blitz coming to the B gap on their inside, this is the movement they use.

The slant and whip are three-man movement calls by the defensive ends and noseguard. On the slant, they go to the strongside call. If we call whip, they slant away from the strongside.

If we call strong, we get the three-man movement (Diagram #5). The defensive ends perform the jacks movement. They both have an outside C-gap charge. The noseguard slants into the weakside A gap. The Mike linebacker is responsible for the strong A gap on this movement. If we call weak, the noseguard goes to the strongside. The difference between strong and weak is the direction of the noseguard.

Diagram #5. Strong and Weak

The *big stick* is one of our favorite movements (Diagram #6). The defensive end slants from his head-up position on the offensive tackle into the A gap and secures the gap. He cannot take a lateral step. He must attack at an angle that is gaining ground. He is attacking the A gap on any type of block except the down block of the guard. If he gets a down block from the guard, he squeezes off the guard's rear and looks for trap or some other inside block coming to him.

Diagram #6. Big Stick

We ran this from the weakside most of the time. We used it against teams that ran the counter trey or power 0 to the strongside. If they pulled the guard, tackle, or both, the big stick was in the middle of their scheme. If it was a power 0, the defensive end ripped across the tackle's face and chased the guard into the hole. The center has to block the nose, and there is no one left to block back on the slant.

The pinch helps against the power game and on the goal line. The defensive ends slant into the B gaps, and the noseguard slants into the strongside A gap. If we play a dive option team, this is a good movement to use. The defensive ends come down into the B gap and take the dive back. Those are our defensive line movements.

When the noseguard or defensive end is an A-gap or B-gap defender, they are to spill all plays outside. When the defensive end slants inside, he spills everything outside. If the guard pulls away from him, he chases the hip of the guard. He gets in his hip pocket and follows. If there is a double-team block, we want to fight the one-man surface and split the double-team.

On zone plays, we want to get vertical in our gap responsibility and penetrate. If the ball flows away, we want to be active in our cutback gaps. The noseguard wants to beat the center's block. However, if linemen reach him, he plays the backside of the center and the Mike linebacker plays the frontside A gap. On flow away from the defensive end, he gets vertical in the B gap and looks inside for a puller or cutback zone runner.

If the offensive guard drive blocks on the defensive end, he attacks the guard with his hands and eyes. He keeps outside leverage and collapses the gap back to the inside.

The line movement or stunt will determine the gap responsibility of the outside linebackers. If the Rob or Lou has a B-gap responsibility, he keys the guard and reacts off his action. If he has a C-gap responsibility, he reads the tackle.

Linda/Rita B-Gap Responsibility

Flow to:
- Down = Shoot B
- Out = Collapse B
- Pull in = Attack the down
- Pull out = Attack the downhill (call made?)
- High hat = Drop

Flow away:
- Lateral shuffle for cutback or counter

Linda/Rita C-Gap Responsibility

Flow to:
- Down = Shoot C
- Out =Collapse C
- Pull in = Shuffle contain
- Pull out = Attack the down
- High hat = Drop

Flow away:
- Shuffle eyes go to quarterback
- Play quarterback, cutback, counter

When we went to Georgia Military to learn this defense, this is what they taught us. It is what we teach our players. It is simple. The aiming point is the most important thing when you are teaching the slants. It is vital that the athlete works vertical on his second step. That helps him from getting washed inside by a down block. Working vertical helps to get the pads square and puts us in a great football position.

Anytime we go on a 45-degree angle, we always use a big rip move. We never try to swim as a move. Having great pad level is essential and using the big rip will help with those efforts. During practice, I try to use big rips and other hand motions in every drill we do. The goal is to use hand violence on every play. *If they cannot touch you, they cannot stop you!*

When we run the 45-degree vertical, the aiming point is the hip of the adjacent lineman. If the defensive end slants into the B gap, he aims for the offensive guard's hip. He steps with his inside foot at a 45-degree angle, squares his shoulders, and rips with his outside arm through the B gap.

The linebackers in the 3-5 defenses are stacked behind the nose and defensive ends. They align with their heels at five yards from the line of scrimmage. You must teach alignment, reads, blitz techniques, block destruction, tackling, and converge. When we work on tackling, we work on 1-on-1 tackling with an emphasis on open field tackling. We work the six interior defenders together. The spurs and corners work together in numerous drills. The spurs are in the open field more than anyone is. They have to combat the jet sweep all the time. The spurs have to get out in space and make the open field tackle or force the ball back to the inside.

Blitz Calls

Left side:
- Linda = Will (ILB)
- Leopard = LOLB (spur)
- Lion = Both LOLB and Will backer

Right side:
- Rita = Sam (ILB)
- Rhino = ROLB (spur)
- Ram = Both ROLB and Sam Backer

When we call our stunts, we can send the blitz from the left, right, or both sides. We can send two defenders from one side and one from the other. The number of blitzes you can run from this defense is more than anyone would ever want to run. Linda is an outside linebacker blitz from the left side. Leopard is a spur blitz from the left. If we want to send the left spur and outside linebacker, we call Lion.

If we want to blitz the outside linebacker and the Mike linebacker, we call Linda/Mike (Diagram #7). It is a simple blitz. The outside linebacker blows the B gap, and the Mike linebacker blows the A gap. The defensive end to that side knows he runs a jacks movement into the C gap. The noseguard knows the Mike linebacker is going into the A gap to the strongside and he has to slant into the opposite A gap.

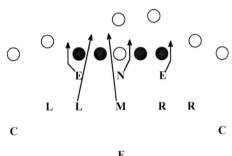

Diagram #7. Linda/Mike

If we want to reverse the stunts of the outside linebacker and the Mike linebacker, we call Linda/Mike X (Diagram #8). The outside linebacker goes first and blitzes the A gap. The Mike linebacker comes off his butt into the B gap. Everyone else in the stunt does the same thing.

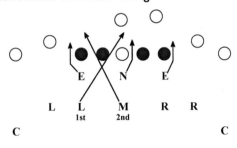

Diagram #8. Linda/Mike X

We can run a three-man game. If we call big stick Linda/Mike, the stunt starts with the defensive end (Diagram #9). On the big stick, the defensive end slants into the A gap. The Mike linebacker blitzes the B gap and the outside linebacker takes the C gap.

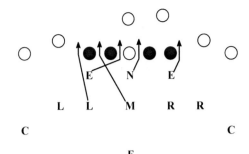

Diagram #9. Big Stick Linda/Mike

If we want to send the spur, we use the term Leopard. On this stunt, I will use a multiple call. The call is Leopard Mike slant (Diagram #10). On this call, the defense runs a slant call to the tight end side. The stunt sends the Mike linebacker into the weakside A gap. The Leopard brings the left spur to the outside off the edge. We could run each component of the stunt by itself or put them all together.

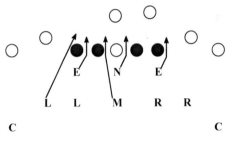

Diagram #10. Leopard Mike Slant

If we want to involve the outside linebacker to that side, we use the term Lion. Lion is a term that sends the outside linebacker and the spur. If we run the big stick Lion, it is the same stunt as I showed you before except the Mike linebacker is not involved (Diagram #11). On the big stick Lion, the outside linebacker blitzes the B gap and the spur comes outside in the C gap. The line movement is the same as before. The defensive end runs the big stick, and the noseguard slants into opposite the A gap.

As you can see, with these three people, the blitz package is as big as you want to teach. If we want to involve the free safety in those blitz schemes, we have the same capabilities. Anytime you want to switch the gaps in a blitz, you simply call X.

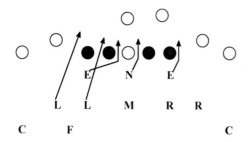

Diagram #11. Big Stick Lion

The alignment of the spurs is 3x3 yards outside the tight end. To the openside of the formation, the spur aligns at 4x4 yards outside the offensive tackle.

Sometimes, we tinker with their alignment and align them at five yards. We have all the linebackers and the spurs aligned at the same depth. If we play a twin set, the spur to the tight end side aligns in a 2x2-yard alignment on the tight end. The spur to the twin side aligns 1x4 yards deep to the inside of the slot receiver in the set.

We teach our corners to deny any inside releases by the wide receivers. We never want to get beat inside. We use the outside hand and foot to attack receivers. The corner accelerates to the receiver the more he widens. We want to put body between the quarterback and receiver. If the receiver's feet chop down, the corner slows and keeps his inside leverage.

If the receiver runs vertical, we want to attack his inside earhole and keep inside leverage. We want to close on the receiver and not let him slip to the inside. We want to knock him off course and use a trail technique. We play the receiver's eyes and hands in our coverage.

We use quarters coverage as part of our secondary scheme as a change-up coverage, but our primary coverage is man. If you have questions, I will be around.

WING-T JET SWEEP AND ROCKET SWEEP SERIES

River Hill High School, Maryland

We have been using the Jet and Rocket series for about 10 years. Fourteen years ago, we put in the wing-T. We expanded to the jet and rocket series and do not run much buck sweep anymore. We have had to add things as we go to keep the defense guessing. We went to some power things and a key breaker that we added to the offense. We try to give the defense different formations and different looks. We are giving he defense some different looks, but we are running many of the same plays.

We have done some different things with the passing game and added some things from the pistol game. The pistol seems to be the hot topic in football. The spin series and some of the single wing plays are starting to come back in today's football. We do some of that from the pistol offense in the four-yard shotgun set.

We started in the wing-T offense, but we have changed our thinking and gone to what we are running now. We changed for a number of reasons.

Why We Changed from the Old Wing-T

- Defenses overloaded to the tight end side.
- Defense reading guards
- Need for an outside play to the split-end side.
- Force teams to defend strong/weak sides.
- Do not need a big team.
- Series-oriented and complementary plays are similar.
- Add more deception to the offense:
  - ✓ Several plays look the same.
  - ✓ Speed motion
  - ✓ A confused player cannot be aggressive.

Teams started to overload to the tight end side and we needed something to run to the split end.

We tried the read sweep, but it was not as effective as the buck sweep to the strong side. The defense was catching up to what we were doing and we needed something to make the defense play a balanced defense. That is when the jet sweep came into play for us. We start fooling around with it in 1999.

When we started running the jet sweep, we ran it to the split end side. We were worried about running it to the tight end side, because it was a wider flank. As we developed the play, it is just as good to run to the tight end side. Because of that, it became a "check with me" play.

Another thing we wanted to do was simplify the blocking rules. When we ran the buck sweep, we had a thick playbook because of all the blocking rules. We wanted to simplify that and make it easier for our players. We have no spring practice. We had to simplify what we did to get more plays into the offense. We did that by simplifying our blocking rules.

With the jet and rocket, the frontside reaches and the backside scoops, so it became very simple. To run these plays, you do not have to have a big team. We are using smaller players at the guards. We are playing more fullback types at the guards, instead of the jumbo offensive linemen. We played this past year with a 165-pound guard. We had a fullback who was the second strongest player on our team but we had no place to play him. We put him at guard and he is fast enough to pull and stay in front of the back.

One of the things that did carry over from the wing-T was the philosophy of having a series. If we put a new play into the offense, I want an inside run, counter, play action pass, and a screen off that play.

I want as many plays that look the same as feasible. They are different plays with the same backfield motion.

We have developed an offense that has more deception. Instead of doing the three-step buck motion, we run the full speed rocket and jet motion. The defense has less time to react to those plays. By using the full-speed motion, we play faster. That helps us get outside on the edge. With all the motion, we confuse the defense. At times, when we snap the ball, we have three players stacked behind the center. When the defense is confused, it takes away from their aggression.

In the modern wing-T, we are in many spread formations. We are a one-back offense. We never have two backs in the backfield. We offset the fullback in this offense. He is behind the quarterback only 30 percent of the time. We offset him behind the tackles, and, at times, we are in the empty set. In the empty set, the fullback will be in the slot. You can do this if you do not run the buck sweep and run jet and rocket.

You have to realize, the jet-sweep play is part of the whole offense. It is not a gadget play. This offense is becoming more popular with Navy and Georgia Tech running this play. Georgia Tech is making a killing with the rocket sweep in their triple-option attack.

The buck sweep was good and lasted for several years before the defense caught up to it. The jet sweep came along, and was a better play. It was faster to the flank, had more plays off of it, and had more deception. The new play is the rocket sweep, and it is the best of them all.

I want to go over the philosophy of the play. We want to get the best athletes on the field. We like this offense because it goes along with our defensive philosophy. We are a 3-5 alignment on defense. We are taking speed over size for the most part (Diagram #1). We try to get our best and fastest athletes on the field. We have taken out the fullback and replaced him with another halfback-type player. That means we play with three tailbacks on the field.

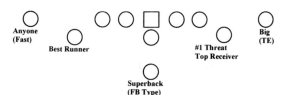

Diagram #1. Best Athletes on the Field

We got rid of the typical tight end. We play with a basketball-type receiver, instead of the tight end. We want the type of player who is taller, more athletic, and better at route running.

We want to be a three-, four-, or five-back offense. If the quarterback can run the ball, we include him in the running attack. The split end changes from year to year. In some years, he is your typical split end. He has good hands and is fast. In other years, he may be the second best running back. This varies with our personnel from year to year.

Last year, our tight end ran the ball for 400 yards and seven touchdowns. By changing formations and moving the tight end around, we were able to give him the ball on some running plays. This type of offense makes it fun and exciting for your players. Almost all the eligible receivers and back can run the ball. It is a team-oriented offense.

Balanced, Ball-Control Offense

• Team-oriented offense
• Five or six ballcarriers on offense
• Series: Same backfield motion for several plays
• Simplified blocking schemes
• Flexible offense:
  ✓ Adjust to fit personnel
  ✓ Feature your best players
  ✓ Take what the defense gives you
• Multiple balanced/unbalanced formations
• Different types of motion; fast motion
• Great misdirection plays and play-action
• Appear complex to the defense

We have the concept of a series. We want four or five plays that look the same. We want an outside play, an inside trap or dive, a counter play, a play-action pass, and maybe a screen. We want all those plays with the same backfield motion. This offense will adjust to your personnel. If you have a great quarterback, you can run the "run and shoot" offense. If you have a stud running back this fits what he can do.

Put Pressure on the Defense

- Difficult to defend and prepare for.
- Make defense defend the entire field.
- Fast motion makes it tough for defense to adjust.
- Create numbers advantage; mismatches.
- Vanilla defense: Easy to read coverage
- How do they react to motion?
  ✓ Widen defensive end, slide linebackers, slant line, roll coverage, and follow motion

It is hard to get a scout team ready to do this offense in one week. We give the defense many different formations. The timing of the offense is so critical, it is hard for a scout team to put that together and simulate it. We do not see as many blitzes and we see some vanilla coverage. The big thing we want to know is how they will handle the motion. Once we figure that out, we are hard to defend.

There are two big keys to the offense. You must use many formations and you must carry out your fakes. We have a drill where we use no ball. We run the play and everyone carries out his fake. The next thing is probably the most important. You have to spend the time with your halfbacks blocking. Too many times, the key blocks are from the halfbacks. We play kids at that position who may not be as fast as other players, but they are better blockers. That is something we work on every day.

The last 10 years, we have tweaked the offense and added plays that have helped us. When we started to use the rocket and jet, our yards and touchdown totals have gone up. The last three years, we have averaged 40 points or more.

In our alignments, we are standard (Diagram #2). We have two-foot splits between the center, guard, and tackle. The tight end splits three feet. Many teams reduce their splits, especially on the goal line. You need to play around with your splits.

You may want to reduce them to six inches in situations. When you run the jet and rocket motion with reduced splits, it puts the back on the perimeter quicker.

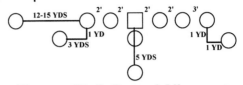

Diagram #2. Splits and Alignment

We want our halfback as close to the line of scrimmage as possible. We want him even with the quarterback when he is under the center. He faces forward in a two-point stance. We want the hand on the thigh pads with the inside foot slightly back. The inside foot is in a heel-to-toe relationship. We do that so we can pivot on the jet motion and drop-step on the rocker motion. We face forward so we can fire out and block downfield. If the halfback is to the tight side, he is one yard outside the tight end and one yard behind him. To the open side, the halfback is one yard deep and three yards outside the offensive tackle.

The coaching point on the alignment of the halfbacks is to get them as close to the line of scrimmage as you can. It will help them with their blocking and a quicker release on their pass routes. We moved the super back (fullback) up to four yards. His heels are four yards from the line of scrimmage.

We adjust the super back position in the backfield (Diagram #3). We offset him to the left and right. We use letters to put him to the right or left. A and B are the letters for left alignments and C and D for right alignments. The A and D alignments are four yards deep behind the tackles. The B and C alignments are four yards deep behind the guards. We do not use those alignments much, but we have plays that go with that alignment.

Diagram #3. Super Back Alignment

We use something new called a "short-wing." The halfback aligns in the B-gap even with the quarterback. We call the short wing "bull." That helps us with our zone plays and we can run the jet with him. That gives the defense a different look. We try to look complicated to the defense, but run the same plays.

Our base formation is red (Diagram #4). The tight end is right with the wing outside of him. We have a split end left and the left halfback is in the slot three yards outside the tackle.

Diagram #4. Red (Right Formation)

We call the mirror set to the opposite side, "blue." Red is right and blue is left. The white formation is a double-slot formation with the tight-end split (Diagram #5). We adjust the formation by reversing the slots and split receivers. We bring the split end and tight end into the slot positions and move the halfbacks out to the split positions.

Diagram #5. White Formation

The silver formation is a double tight end and double wing formation. The opposite of that formation is the empty set. The empty set with the three-receiver side to the right is green (Diagram #6). The opposite set is black. When we go to the empty set, the super back is the outside slot to the three-receiver side.

Diagram #6. Green Empty Set

Those are the base formations, which we can adjust to make them different. If we call red-over, the split end moves from the left side to the right side and we have an unbalanced set. The tight end becomes ineligible, but we have removed the corner

from the backside. If we want to run the rocket sweep to that side, there is one less defender to block. That is a simple adjustment. We add the tag "over" and get a different look. If we want to move the fullback over to that side, we call red-over-D. If we want to run the rocket sweep right, we have many blockers in front of the ball.

Another adjustment we used this year was what we call "nasty." We align in the white formation and bring the split end over. He aligns three yards outside the halfback on the line of scrimmage. He is ineligible, but we have two stand-up players three yards apart who can double crack inside on linebackers. If we move the fullback over into the D alignment, we have a power set to the right with all kinds of blocking angles.

If we align in a blue formation and add bull, we have a left formation with the wingback sitting in the B gap (Diagram #7). We can motion the right halfback and run a zone or isolation play and it is almost like an unbalanced line set. If we incorporate the pistol look with the adjustments, we have the defense guessing and scrambling to align. In the pistol formation, the quarterback is in a three-and-a-half- yard shotgun set with the super back behind him. We can offset the super back by adding an A or D call. This is the single-wing look.

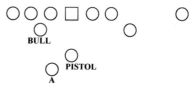

Diagram #7. Blue/Bull Pistol-A

To run this offense, you must have the motion game. The first motion is rocket (Diagram #8). The halfback aims at one foot behind the heels of the super back. That will put him about four and a half yards off the line of scrimmage. We snap the ball when the halfback is behind the fullback. The quarterback uses heel motion to set the back in motion. He rocks the heel, and as soon as he loses sight of the back he says, "Set-go." That puts the halfback behind the super back. It is all timing to snap the ball at the right position. We drill that repeatedly in practice.

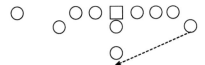

Diagram #8. Rocket Motion

Once the halfback gets behind the fullback, he gets flat to the line of scrimmage. The jet motion goes directly behind the quarterback (Diagram #9). If the play is the jet-sweep, we snap the ball at the outside leg of the onside guard.

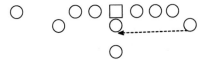

Diagram #9. Jet Motion

If we use the halfback as a lead blocker on an isolation play, we can use jet motion (Diagram #10). The cadence for this play is on two. The quarterback raises the heel and sets the halfback in motion. He calls "set-go" as the halfback reaches the outside leg of the guard. We want the play to look like the jet-sweep. He tries to draw the defense offsides. The back squares to the line of scrimmage at the quarterback and shuffles to the isolation gap. The quarterback calls "set-go" and we snap the ball.

Diagram #10. Lead Blocking Motion

We do not use long motion too much. We use it to get into a pass route or change the formation to a trips set. It is jet motion with the ball snapped as the halfback passes the wing back to that side.

We use a motion called "U-turn" (Diagram #11). This is a combination of both jet and rocket motion. We start the halfback in jet motion, as we did on the lead motion. The quarterback calls the first snap, as he gets to the guard's outside leg. The halfback continues in motion until he reaches the opposite halfback's inside leg. He reverses his motion and goes back in rocket motion from where he came. The quarterback calls the second cadence, as if he were going in normal rocket motion.

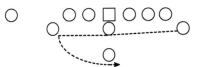

Diagram #11. U-Turn Motion

Before I run out of time, I want to get into the plays we run. The first play is the jet-sweep. We have run this play for nine years and we still run it, because it sets up the play action pass. We also run the cross off this play.

We want to run this play from multiple formations (Diagram #12). The motion is full speed and we snap the ball when the back reaches the B gap. The quarterback reverse pivots at 180 degrees and hands the ball off in the playside A gap. He always *opens to the side of the motion, regardless of the type of motion.* That is an essential point. We only block outside the playside B gap. If you can get three blocks, you will have a good play. The playside tackle reaches the defender aligned on him. The playside guard pulls and looks inside to the outside. He does not always get in front of the back. However, if the back has to cut the ball back, he will get a block.

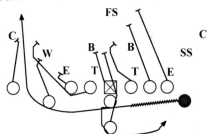

Diagram #12. Jet Sweep/Split End

We were leery about not blocking the B gap defender at first. If the quarterback gets the ball to the running back in the proper spot and the back is running full speed, that defender cannot make the play. The key block is the block of the halfback on the Will linebacker. We want to hook him or push him to the sidelines. The ideal situation is to hook him. We want to get outside. The design of jet sweep is to get outside from the hash numbers to the sidelines. We do not want to cut this play up. On the reach blocks, we have to beat the defender to the spot and seal him inside. The split end stalks the corner and tries to block him inside. The super back runs the trap fake behind the jet back and cuts off the backside. The backside linemen scoop inside. The quarterback gives the ball to the jet back, fakes the super back on the trap, and fakes the waggle pass.

We put the jet-sweep in to have a play to the split-end side, but this is just as good to the tight-end side. We can use the play as a check-with-me, automatic call. The quarterback has to have a flat 180-degree pivot and the exchange is in the playside A gap. If he gives the ball anywhere else, he is slowing the back. He cannot get off the line of scrimmage and force the back deeper.

This is a wider flank play to the tight-end side (Diagram #13). If there is no one covering the playside tackle, we pull both the guard and tackle. The tight end has the reach block on the defender covering him. The halfback has to reach the strong safety or the force defender. The backside scoops. The mechanics for the quarterback and jet back are the same as for the split end. We might want to reduce the splits of the offensive line to the playside. If we set the super back in a D alignment, he leads the play like a pulling guard. If he is behind the quarterback, he runs the trap fake. The quarterback fakes the power pass to the tight-end side after he fakes the super back on the trap.

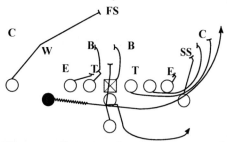

Diagram #13. Jet Sweep/Tight End

We have a number of ways we can block the perimeter. If we block it straight, we block-base on the corner and Will linebacker. If we feel they are rolling a safety, we can change the scheme (Diagram #14). We can crack inside with the split end and bring the halfback outside for the corner. That is a switch scheme. We can crack inside with the halfback and split end, and bring the guard to the perimeter. These types of blocking patterns set up

our play-action passing. The switch scheme sets up the post-wheel pattern.

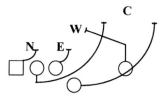

Diagram #14. Switch Blocking

With the offset super backer, we have more options (Diagram #15). The halfback can help the tight end with the defensive end. The corner can crack on the Will linebacker and the super back can lead on the corner.

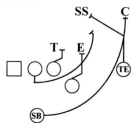

Diagram #15. Super Back Lead

The last one I want to show you is the nasty set with the super back in the D position (Diagram #16). The split end comes over and aligns on the line in a nasty split. We double crack with the split end and tight end and lead on the perimeter with the super back.

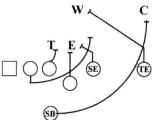

Diagram #16. White Nasty Double Crack

We feel the sweeps and outside game will open up all the inside plays. We have to figure a way to get those things done.

We use the rocket-sweep because it goes great with everything else we run. I think it is a better sweep, because we get wider and deeper. On this play, there are more opportunities for cutback running. All the complimentary plays are the same. This does not require additional teaching with the linemen and minimal teaching with the backs. We can run this play either way. The jet and rocket force defenses to defend sideline to sideline.

On this play, the super back is behind the quarterback and goes away from the action (Diagram #17). The halfback comes in rocket motion. The quarterback fakes the super back on the trap and pitches the ball to the rocket back. It is a dead pitch to start with. We do not want the ball tossed softly. We want some zip on the ball. The back should be over the tight end or the ghost of the tight end when he receives the ball. He is four yards deep at that point. The good thing about this play is we block from the C gap to the outside.

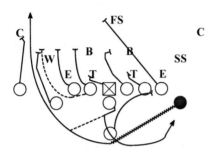

Diagram #17. Rocket Sweep

The tackle does not reach the 5-technique defender. He reaches to the second level defenders. If the 5 technique loops outside and tries to cross the tackle's face, he has to run upfield with him. We receive the ball outside the C gap and we do not want to block back. If we can block the Will linebacker and the corner, we can get 8 to 10 yards on the play. The playside guard is the same as the jet. The backside linemen scoop or reach inside. The halfback and split end have the same assignments as the jet. We can use the change-up blocking on the perimeter.

The main coaching point is with the rocket back. He has to be flat to the line when he passes the super back position. After they catch the ball, they can start to get upfield. We do not want to come downhill until we get the ball. When you practice the play, put a bag down, so they cannot turn up too early.

The rockets and jets are 8- to 10-yard plays. Where you hit the home runs is the inside traps and dives. When we run the inside plays, we have to make some adjustment for different motions. The first play is "dive" (Diagram #18). This is a base-blocked play. We run it with the super back behind the quarterback or in the offset position. When we offset, we run the dive wider and call it "hand-back." The super back aims at the inside foot of the tackle. The quarterback reverse pivots, rides the super back, and carries out his keep fake to the outside. We can run the jet or rocket motion with this play.

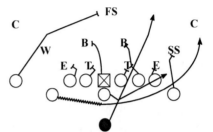

Diagram #18. Dive/Hand-back

The main inside play we run is the trap play (Diagram #19). There are some minor changes based on the motion. This play is the jet-trap. What we want to do is fake the jet in one direction and trap in the same direction. In the diagram, we run jet left and trap left. We have to fake the jet sweep first and hand off to the trap second. When we run this play, we do not want the quarterback to extend the ball. He seats it in his stomach and the jet back makes the fake. The quarterback turns back to the super back and hands him the ball on the trap. After he hands off, he fakes the waggle opposite the jet motion.

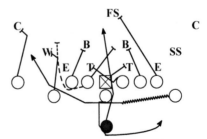

Diagram #19. Jet-Trap

The quarterback always opens to the side in the direction the motion is coming from. On the trap to the right, the super back steps with his right foot and puts it down in front of his left foot. Stepping with the foot to the side of the play, helps align him for a cutback play. If the defense is an odd-front defense, he probably has to cut back to the right. If the front is an even front, he takes the ball up the gut.

If we call rocket motion, we have to give on the trap first and fake to the rocket second. On this fake, the quarterback extends the open hand to the rocket back.

We love misdirection and probably do not run them enough. Ten years ago, this was a trick play. Now we run it five or six times a game. This is a good play to run after a turnover to try to get a big play. We snap the ball earlier to make it easier for the jet back (Diagram #20). This is crisscross right. It is a double exchange and we snap it early to make sure the first exchange is sound. The jet back receives the ball, turns it over in his hand, and hands it to the opposite halfback with an outside exchange. He hands the ball with the hand away from the line of scrimmage. After he hands the ball off, he continues to run and carry out his fake.

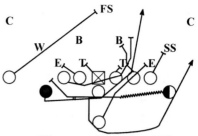

Diagram #20. Jet XX

This is not a reverse. We design the play to go off-tackle. The super back kicks out the end. We pull the backside tackle and he turns up for the frontside linebacker. We base block at the point of attack, using the combinations we need to block the defense. The center and backside guard block back. The tight end blocks the outside linebacker or force player. The thing that makes the kick-out block by the super back is the waggle fake from the quarterback. That gets the defensive end up the field. This is our favorite counter, because it hits quick. The timing and ballhandling are critical, because of the close quarters. We run this play to the tight-end side more than the split side.

Thanks for your attention.

A HOLISTIC APPROACH TO REVIVING A PROGRAM

Durango High School, Colorado

Thank you. For those of you who do not know, Durango High School football does have a proud history of competitive football. Over the past couple of years, though, it has really dropped off. Prior to my coming to Durango High School in 2008, their record was 0-10. The year before that they were 3-7. In a two-year scheduling block, we ended up playing all those teams again. Our turnaround was a lot of fun this year.

One of the challenges we had at Durango was that we had not won a game in nearly two years. Not only my fans, my parents, and my community, but also my players did not really know how to win and did not know what it felt like to win. This year, we went 8-3. We made it to the first round of the 4A playoffs.

The easy explanation as to how we did that was we played good defense. In 2008, they gave up 409 points in a 10-game schedule. In our 11-game schedule this year, we gave up 159 points. That made a big difference. In addition, we held onto the football. In 2008, the turnover margin was probably around -20; this year, we were +9 in turnover margin.

The other thing that we did is we looked at our talent and we knew what we had, so we played the best we could with what we had to work with. We did not have a lot of big guys, but we had guys that could run. We had guys that would work hard. We played ball control. When we could not get first downs, we played field position. Our punter was first-team all-state, primarily because he got a lot of opportunities to punt the ball. He also kicked off and put the ball into the end zone 50 percent of the time.

What I really want to talk to you about is the long-term answer as to how we made our turnaround. I am a big quote guy. I like to give a lot of simple quotes to the kids that they will understand and that will stay with them. Our goal was to win the state championship, and here is a quote I gave to the kids that we talked about a lot.

> *There is a path to the top of even
> the highest mountain.*
> —Afghan Proverb

I did a whole presentation of about 15 minutes on that quote alone. I talked about how important it is to stay on the path and follow your leaders. Things are going to happen if you do not stay on your path. When people get off the path while climbing Mount Everest, bad things can happen—they can die or get lost.

I looked at our program and determined I needed to come up with a holistic approach as to how we were going to turn this thing around. I knew it could not be just one season on the field. It had to be a long-term solution. I wanted to do something that would enable our program to grow and be something we could build on for the long term.

WHAT IS A HOLISTIC APPROACH?

The principles of holistic management involve approaching a challenge by looking at the whole instead of the parts. A lot of us talk about synergy—everybody working together is more important than the individual. It's the same idea.

- The goal of holistic management, in any field, is a long-term comprehensive vision. Again, I don't want to be a one-and-done guy.
- In other words, define the quality of life you want.

- Once a goal is established, success will depend on management, planning, execution and feedback from monitoring. We all do a lot of planning. We plan for practice, we have a game plan, and we manage a lot of details. Not many of us spend time during the season on feedback.
- A series of "testing questions" that look at things like cause and effect, weak links, the source and use of money and energy, sustainability and the effects on society and culture can keep an endeavor on track.
- What is needed is a framework. The particulars of any endeavor are then shaped by the framework. You have to have some type of structure in place in order for this to work.

I am an off-campus guy. I work during the day as a financial analyst. I do a lot of detail work during the day before I come to practice. Also, I have been trained, in my business background, in an area called Six Sigma. It is a very detailed quality-control approach to management. I will not go into all of the particulars because it is very boring and sophisticated. It gives you a different way of thinking and you look at problems in a whole different way when you are trained to break everything down to its smallest part. I think in those terms whenever I have a problem that I need to manage rather than getting overwhelmed by a big problem.

I do realize that, as a coach, I have a lot to learn. I hope you understand that I know I am not the greatest coach in the world. I have coached on different levels—not on the college level—but at the youth and high school levels. I played college football at Northern Arizona University and helped turn around a program. We were able to turn it around and have a very successful four years while I was there.

I have been fortunate to be around some very good coaches and very good programs. One of the guys who I played for—and who has been one of the biggest influences on me—was my quarterbacks coach and the offensive coordinator at NAU, who is now the head coach of the Minnesota Vikings—a man by the name of Brad Childress. We also had a guy by the name of Andy Reid who was the offensive line coach. I was also fortunate enough to be a free agent with the San Francisco 49ers while Mike Holmgren was still there. His GA was Jon Gruden. I learned a lot from all of those guys and many others.

So, how am I as a coach? I would have to say that in this room of coaches, I would be ranked number one in terms of who is the best financial analyst in this room.

My personal belief is that we are coaching for more than wins and losses. We are here to impact young people and we are here to do good things for those young people. In my mind, everything counts. Sometimes you are all those kids have. I really believe that.

Impress upon the mind of every man, from the first to the lowest, the importance of the cause, and what it is they are contending for.
—George Washington

So what are we contending for? Our mission statement is pretty straightforward.

OUR MISSION STATEMENT

To help develop the boys in our program into well-rounded young men who will have a positive impact on their families, our community, and the world, in their chosen field.

It does not say a thing about football there, does it? I believe that if we get down to thinking and doing the right things all the time, we will win some ball games. If we think that it is all about ourselves, we are going to struggle to win football games. If we are working to raise great men, then we are going to win football games.

We are a small community of about 15,000 people. Everybody feels as if they have a piece of the pie. And usually, they have their fingers in the pie all the time. This is how I have broken it down into five constituencies (Diagram #1).

Diagram #1. Constituencies

Community Interaction

- Impacting others
  - ✓ Players speaking at middle schools
  - ✓ Participation in community events
  - ✓ Alumni impacting participation
- Showing appreciation
  - ✓ Acknowledging sponsorship
  - ✓ Website
  - ✓ Players saying *thank you*

The first one is the community. Obviously, we need the community's involvement in a lot of ways. We need contributors. We found people who were willing to donate our equipment. We had to go to a rental company to borrow some generators and some light stands so we could have a training camp.

We worked on a lot of stuff from some of the local restaurants in order to provide food for 40 to 60 kids. A lot of it was saying thank you and sitting down with them and talking with them to let them know what we were trying to do with the program and how we were trying to change it.

Another thing was sponsorships. We are a long way from everybody we play. We have to charter a bus and sometimes we drive halfway to stay in a hotel overnight and drive the rest of the way the following day. We do everything that we can do to try to make it suitable for the kids, but it takes a lot of money. Fortunately, one thing we did not need was a bunch of new coaches.

It was also important that we got to know the media. We are the only high school in town, but they cover a lot of communities. If you have a good relationship with the media, it really helps the kids, and the parents, and the community.

Another great part of our program is we have a lot of community interaction. We do whatever we can to impact others. We have our players go to speak at the middle schools and talk about staying in school and staying off drugs. It really means a lot when it comes from kids and not just from adults. Our kids like to go back to their old school, and it gets them fired up. In addition, the middle school kids feel an attachment to the high school and the football program.

We participate in community events. We have a homecoming parade and every member of the team wears his game jersey while in the parade. We also have a big winter parade and we make sure our kids are visible for that. If there is an event, we make sure that we participate. We go to basketball games, wrestling matches, and anything that the school is involved in as a team.

We keep the alumni involved. We will bring them back to talk to our kids. The alums love to come back to visit. They have been big supporters, and they help contribute to what we are trying to do.

We like to show appreciation and we do that in a couple of ways. We acknowledge all of our sponsors by personally taking them a gift. We make sure they are in our game program. Anything we can do to make sure that we publicize that they are supporting us.

One of the big things we did was create a website. If you don't have a website, you have to get one. Guys, it is so easy to do. We created a website and got our own domain name; go check it out: www.demonfootball.com. It cost us $199 for a year. I think everyone can afford that. My wife is our webmaster. She has never had any experience with running a website before. It has our music on it, we can update pictures, we can put sponsors on it, and we can acknowledge people every week. Again, if you can find someone that has a little time, the website is an easy way to keep people involved, and it is well worth it.

The last thing is having our players say *thank you*. We stress that all the time. If any of our players go out to a sponsor, we make sure our kids express their appreciation for their help. It goes a long way in showing people that all of the things we are preaching about—doing the right thing—they can see in action.

SCHOOL

Goal: To Be Leaders on Campus

- Set the example for all students to follow
- Classroom behavior
- Hallway mentality
- Off-campus behavior
- Football sets the tone for the year
- Get off to a good start

Challenges

- Administrative support
- Overcoming apathy
- Instilling school spirit

Our goal at the school is to be the example on campus. I talk to our kids about this all the time. I tell them they have to be the ones to set the example on campus. This is especially true during the fall when school begins. We want to set the example in terms of classroom behavior. It drives me nuts to have a bunch of kids running around with their hats turned sideways, thinking that they are tough when they are not. After I told them that the first time, the next time we were in a meeting, they all had their hats off. It is just a sign of respect. In addition, it shows the teacher that they have respect for them and their class. We want them to be paying attention in the classroom and not be the guy that is goofing around. We want them there on time and sitting in the front of the classroom.

We talk about how they should act in the hallway. If someone is getting bullied in the hallway, they should go to defend the guy who is getting bullied. It doesn't matter who it is that is bullying him and it does not matter who is being bullied, you have to set the example in the hallway. A lot of times, the bully will not mess with the football players no matter how tough he is.

In a small town, our kids are very visible. So we make sure they know that in the community they have to be on their best behavior. It is also important that we get off to a good start because it sets the tone for the rest of the year. It also keeps the community involved. We won our first two games at home and it was another four weeks before we came back home so it kept our momentum going at home.

One of our challenges was getting the support of the administration. We have a very nice principal, but she is not much of a football fan or much of a sports fan. I think it is important that you know where your administrators stand.

Another area where we had a challenge was our field. Our field was terrible. Two years ago, they decided to sod it and the district decided to save some money and hire someone who did not know what they were doing. Three weeks before our first game, our field was unplayable. I did what every responsible businessman would do—I sent out an email and copied everyone in the world. I told them I was going to forfeit the game unless they fixed the field. I put them on the spot. They did not want to have that on their conscience, so to their credit, they went out and hired someone to get it fixed.

There was not a lot of school spirit before we came in and it was a fractured school. We did some things that really helped that.

Parents

- Gaining "buy-in"
  - ✓ Provide a structured environment
  - ✓ Treat their sons with respect
- Give them an outlet
  - ✓ Parents club
  - ✓ Merchandise
  - ✓ Website

- Setting boundaries
  - ✓ Provide a structured approach to conflict
  - ✓ What you will talk about
  - ✓ What you won't talk about
  - ✓ Treat them with respect
  - ✓ Demand their respect in return

Does everyone have perfect parents for their program? Even though the team was 0-10, the parents had all the answers. I was the third coach in four years that came to the door and told them we were going to turn this thing around. At some point, the parents tended to doubt us a little bit. We had to get some buy-in from the parents. The main thing we talked to them about was that we were going to provide a structured approach for their kids. The coach before did not really have a structured program. They did not know from one day to another what to expect. We treated their kids with respect and told them in the beginning that they would be treated with respect. That did not mean the kids would run the program. We were going to demand a lot. But the team was going to gain a lot in return.

We got our parents involved. Their job, every Thursday and for every away trip, was food. They organized our caravan to our cross-state rival. We want them actively involved in everything that we do off the field, and I stress *off the field*.

For merchandise, we came up with new T-shirts and hats. We gave them away to have an identity as part of the program. We put pictures up on the website of the kids along with statistics and we made mention of their parents.

One of the best things we did was to sit down with each of the parents. We had a horrible type of parent group. It got so bad that they ran the soccer coach off after one year. We have great parents overall, but we had a few squeaky wheels that made it uncomfortable for everyone. We wanted to deal with this right away and to set boundaries that provided a structured approach of how to work out those situations. I went over it with every parent and gave each one a contract they had to sign. This thing was 16 pages long. We talked a lot about everything

that we were going to do in our program. We talked about what they should expect from me and my staff as coaches. It talked about what we expected from their sons as players. In addition, it talked about what we expected from them as parents. That was the most important part of what we did.

We told them we will talk about what things their son could do to get better, and we will talk about it if their son is being abused by a coach or another player. We will talk about health issues that we feel are not being dealt with appropriately. We will not talk about their son's playing time. We will not talk about the performance of an athlete who is not their child. We are not going to talk about schemes and whether we are or are not throwing the ball enough.

We did have some parents that wanted to come and complain at the beginning of the year. All I did was pull out the contract and ask them if that was their signature on it. I said, "Now, let us talk about what your son can do to get better." I let them know that I was willing to stay after practice and help with drills to help them get better. Moreover, we did. We had some players that wanted to get better and they got extra work. We had some that did not want to work to get better.

Coaches

- Building a staff
  - ✓ Hire smarter than you
  - ✓ Define roles
  - ✓ Provide structure
- Growing together
  - ✓ Provide opportunity for feedback
    - ❑ Weekly staff meetings
    - ❑ One-on-ones
- Address issues as they come up
- Make adjustments

In talking about coaches, that was probably the one area I did the worst on. I was dealing with a group of coaches that I was just getting to know as we were coming into the season. That was one of my challenges. In putting together the staff, the most important thing you can do is hire people that are smarter than you are. If you think you have to be the smartest one in the room, then you're already behind the curve. I was fortunate to have a defensive coordinator that had 40 years of experience. It just so happened that he was one of my high school coaches. He also had a home in the Durango area that I stayed at and I told him I was not going to leave until he agreed to be one of my coaches. I was able to give him the entire defense and not have to worry about any of the defensive decisions that needed to be made. That was a huge part of our success this season.

Another important part is to define the roles of each of your coaches. This includes everything from what they do at their positions, what they do in the locker room, and what their responsibilities are for travel. About halfway through the year, I found that I was doing just about everything. Part of it was that I did not take the steps to tell them what they should be doing. I thought some of the coaches would figure it out on their own, but they were waiting for me to tell them.

I want to make sure that we provide structure for the coaches. One of the things that I do is I have a very detailed practice plan. I break it down into five-minute increments. That helps my coaches know how much time they have and what they are supposed to get done in those five-minute increments.

In growing together, I believe you have to provide an opportunity for your coaches to give feedback. We have weekly staff meetings on Saturdays after the kids go. You have to let your coaches speak out. We could have some knock-down, drag-out discussions during those meetings, but at the end of the day, everybody has to come to an agreement. Not that everyone has to agree, but you have to come to an agreement as a whole. I believe as the head coach you have to allow your assistant coaches to give input. Assistant coaches, you have to be willing to speak up. You have to find the appropriate time when it is not in front of players.

It is hard sometimes to make staff adjustments, especially in a small community where everyone

knows each other. But when things are not working, you have to find a different way of going about it. That is one of the things we're going through right now.

PLAYERS

Change the Culture (Off the Field)

- Restore confidence
  - ✓ Team before self
- Do the right thing
  - ✓ "...when nobody's looking." —JC Watts
  - ✓ "Hard work beats talent when talent doesn't work hard." —Tim Notke
  - ✓ Worst to first
- Create a theme
  - ✓ "Rise Up"
- Mental preparation

Change the Culture (On the Field)

- Drill the fundamentals
  - ✓ Technique, technique, technique
- Classroom study
  - ✓ Film study
  - ✓ Game planning
- Execution
  - ✓ Put them in the right place
  - ✓ Let them play
- Be good at the things that take no talent
  - ✓ Know your assignment
  - ✓ Be in great physical condition
  - ✓ Play like your hair is on fire
- Physical preparation
  - ✓ Spring ball
  - ✓ Summer workouts
  - ✓ Daily practice
  - ✓ Provide structure
  - ✓ Demand effort
  - ✓ Demand execution
  - ✓ Don't finish on a bad play

With our players, we had to change the culture. That was a big thing on our part. We had to restore their confidence. We did that by talking *team before self*. We had no individual names on the backs of the jerseys. We took logos off their helmets until they earned them. It is our way of saying it is not about what you look like, it is how you play. Are you going to play as a group or are you going to play as an individual?

In doing the right thing all of the time, my favorite quotes are: "Do the right thing even when nobody else is looking," and "Hard work beats talent when talent doesn't work hard." We had less talent than most of the teams we played. We worked harder and had ourselves prepared to play.

We used "Rise Up" as one of our themes during the year. We used the Tampa Bay Rays as an example. In 11 years as an organization, they never had a winning season. The next year, they went all the way to the World Series. I used this to try to get them to believe that we could go from 0-10 to league champions and play in the state championship game. Every week, our game plan would have *Rise Up* at the top and another statement at the bottom of the page that went with our theme that changed every week.

For our culture off the field, mental preparation was a huge part of it. We spent a lot of time drilling them on technique repeatedly. We spent about 30 minutes every day in classroom study before practice. We spent about an hour to an hour and a half every Saturday to get them to understand how the game works.

We handed out a 12-page game plan every week. I do not think they had ever seen a game plan before. It had scouting reports, tendencies, and pictures of what we were going to do and what the other team had done in the past.

Our motto, as coaches, became "Put them in the right place and let them play." If you don't have a lot of talent, then you better make sure that you know your assignments. We also had to make sure that we were in good physical shape. We played with about 16 guys all year. We had 20 to 30 guys on our roster—about 16 of them played.

Change the Culture (In Their Spirit)

- School spirit
  - ✓ Uniform change
  - ✓ Leadership mentality
  - ✓ Fight song
- Pride
  - ✓ Win with class
  - ✓ Be humble
  - ✓ Lose with dignity
- Success stories
  - ✓ Highest award
  - ✓ Jerry Martinez Community Spirit Award
- 2010 graduates
  - ✓ Kicked out of his home
  - ✓ Now attending class
  - ✓ First in family to graduate

I changed our uniforms when I got to Durango. Our school colors are red and white. The year before, they were wearing black. Black is kind of a tough color, and we were not tough. I went back to our school colors, and that made a big difference in school spirit. We went back to our original school colors and back to our roots and who we really are. I think that went a long way.

We had some good success stories. We gave out our highest award—the Jerry Martinez Community Spirit Award—to a senior who demonstrated great contributions not only to our team, but also within our community. We felt like that was an important way to emphasize what we believe in with our program. We had some other examples of how some of our kids overcame personal adversity to some type of success. We, as coaches, have a responsibility to ensure that happens and it is recognized. Even when a kid doesn't do the things he needs to do to stay on the team, we let him know that we love him and we still care about him and we will try to help him overcome adversity.

THE NO-HUDDLE SHOTGUN OFFENSE: WHY AND HOW

DeWitt High School, Michigan

It is a pleasure to be here today. This is a great clinic. It is the one clinic I have attended over the years. I brought my head freshman coach with me today to assist me with the audio visuals. If anything goes wrong with this lecture, we can blame A.J.

I want to get into our lecture on the no-huddle offense and how we got to where we are today with this offense. In the past 30 years, Dewitt High School has run the following different offenses:
- 1980's and 1990's: Wishbone
- 1999-2001: Flex (military academy option football)
- 2002-2007: Spread shotgun no-huddle
- 2008-Present: Spread shotgun/pistol no-huddle

I took over the program in 1999. We switched from the wishbone to the flex option offense, similar to the offense that the Air Force academy runs. Army and Navy also run the same type of offense today. We ran that offense for the first three years I was at Dewitt. In my first year, we were not any good. The second year, we got a little better, and the third year, we went to the state semi-finals.

You would think we would want to keep the same offense going. We looked at our kids and felt we needed to make some changes in our offense. We agreed we needed to fit our offense to the personnel we had coming back at Dewitt High School. It becomes a philosophy issue. Some coaches say, "This is what we are going to run, regardless of the talent we have each year." Other coaches are willing to change their offense, based on the talent they have each year. We felt we needed to adjust to the personnel we had coming back. So, we switched in 2002 to the shotgun offense. At the time, there were not as many schools running this offense in Michigan. For us, it

was a great move. We were able to go to the state finals that season. Following are the reasons we switched to the no-huddle shotgun offense:
- We did not have much size on the offensive line.
- We had short, but good, throwers at quarterback.
- We had a solid number of receiver- and defensive back-type players.
- We had smart kids.
- We had players willing to make a significant commitment.
- We had parents (for the most part) that understood commitment.
- We knew that hardly anybody else in high school was running it in Michigan.

In the last two years, we have added some of the pistol offense to our scheme of things. We are not running the all-spread offense anymore. We ran a lot of the pistol scheme this year. The reason we did this was because of the personnel we had. I thought we had players that fit the pistol running game. We ran almost 40 percent in the pistol offense this season.

We have been very effective with the shotgun-option attack. We will continue to run this offense, because we think it is a great fit for our kids.

People ask why we went to the Shotgun no-huddle offense. We did have some size this year. Normally, we do not have a lot of big kids. Back in 2002, our offensive line averaged about 200 pounds. That was a big reason we considered going to the no-huddle offense.

I was talking with a college coach a few weeks ago when we were discussing the no-huddle offense. We concluded one major factor in making the decision to run the no-huddle shotgun offense.

If you run this offense, you must have good athletes to be successful. If you are trying to cover up the fact you are not as athletic, it is not a good thing to do. I have seen some good coaches switch to this offense who have not had much success with it. They just did not have the athletes to run this offense. We have been fortunate in that we have had some good athletes and we have been successful running this offense.

We were successful with the offense, because we had some quarterbacks who could throw. If you are going to run the no-huddle shotgun offense, you must be able to throw the football. We felt we had kids who could throw the ball.

We had good receivers in our program. We had a lot of them. We did not have a lot of linemen, but we had a lot of good receivers.

In our school and on the football team, we have been blessed to have had a lot of bright kids. It takes smart players to make all of the checks and reads in this offense. It helps if you have bright kids on your team. I adjust from year to year, depending on what we can and cannot do. This past year, our quarterback was a 3.9 student with a 30 ACT score. However, I have had quarterbacks who were not as talented and did not have the honor grades. They could not do the things that the quarterback we had this year was able to do.

You must have players willing to make a significant commitment. If you are going to run this offense, you must be willing to put a lot of time into it. There is a great deal of time you must be willing to commit to become good in this offense. If your kids are not willing to work, it will be difficult to win. I am not just talking about weight lifting. You have to do speed training and go to individual workouts.

You must also have parents who understand commitment. Even if you feel you have great parents, you still have some who are critics. Our parents are not any different from the ones that you have, but they are supportive. We have a lot of professionals in our community. The work ethic is a big part of the commitment and the parents help in this respect.

When we made the switch to this offense, very few high schools were running it. Now, it is a different story, as most teams are running some form of this offense.

I have listed the advantages of the no-huddle shotgun offense. In addition, I have given comments as to why we went to this system. I am sure these points would apply to other similar offenses, but following are the reasons why we went to the no-huddle game:

- We can control the tempo of the game.
- It is easy for the coach to change the play.
- It is fun for the players and the fans.
- It is easy to recruit players to play in the system.
- It allows teams to score points quickly.
- It gives you more offensive snaps.
- Our opponents' two-way players can be fatigued.
- Defenses must be standardized in the scheme.
- It is hard to simulate in practice.
- Defenses have to spend more time than normal preparing for you.
- It makes it harder to pick up tendencies.
- It causes the opposing defensive coaches to get out of their normal routine.
- The opposing defensive coaches have to decide how to communicate.
- A two-minute offense is built into the offense.
- Defensive personnel changes are difficult (particularly in the red zone).

We are no-huddle, but we can still snap the ball when we want to snap it. We have the ability, tempo-wise, to hurry up or slow down the tempo and control the clock.

When I went to Dewitt High in 1999, they did nothing in the off-season program. They did not have a weight program and they did not do any speed training. They just had good kids and good coaches who got them ready to play each season. To change the culture with what I wanted to do was very difficult. Once we got it rolling, the parents have been great.

We have three coaches who are paid on the varsity level. We have six volunteer assistant coaches. I have nine coaches on our varsity staff. Only one of these staff members is a teacher. All the rest of them are willing to give up a ton of time. They work extremely hard, because it is a year-round job for us. In all of the winning programs that I have studied, the coaches have been willing to put in extra time.

We feel that it is important to have programs within a program that develop team concepts. This is an important aspect of a winning program. We have had great administrative support, and we all know that is important. We feel the off-season strength and conditioning program is vital to a good program.

When we decided to go to this system, we looked at ways to learn about the offense. This is what we did to find out the details about the no-huddle shotgun offense. We went to clinics as much as possible. We read books and articles on the no-huddle. We watched videos of the system. We taped games from TV to study. We talked to other college and high school coaches who were successful running this offense. We spent as much time as possible at several colleges.

We visited and talked with the following coaches and their staffs:
• Northwestern (Randy Walker)
• Grand Valley (Brian Kelly and Jeff Quinn)
• Michigan State University (Dave Baldwin and John L. Smith)
• Central Michigan (Brian Kelly and Jeff Quinn)
• Central Michigan (Butch Jones)
• Cincinnati (Jeff Quinn)
• Florida (Urban Meyer)

First, we had to decide if we wanted to run the option offense. We came up with the following reasons to run the option offense:
• It provided a comfort level for us.
• It forces the defense to play assignment football.
• It is very difficult to prepare for in one week.

• Urban Meyer: Spread & option = trouble for the defense.
• It fits the type of athletes we have.

Next, we had to decide which scheme of the no-huddle option we would run. There were several types of option offense to chose from, including the following:
• Speed option (University of Florida)
• Zone (run based) (West Virginia, University of Michigan)
• Zone (pass based) (Texas Tech, Northwestern, Kansas)
• Military academy option (Navy, Georgia Tech)
• Combo (Oregon)

From our studies and discussions with other schools that ran option football, we felt the ability to communicate what we were going to do on offense was a key factor in all of the different types of option programs.

Communication is the key to a Successful no-huddle offense. We had to develop a system to be able to name and to call these plays:
• Run play
• Pass play
• Pass protection
• Snap count
• Motion
• Shifts
• Audibles
• Formations
• Tempo

For example, we include states, colors, terms, numbers, and right and left directions. We knew we must also have a signal or name for different techniques or schemes. Examples would include perimeter blocking and line calls. You must be able to deceive your opponent with communication. You must have multiple ways to call your base plays. You must have the ability to give fake signals or calls.

We knew we had to develop a strong off-season workout program. This would require a lot of

- H: Two-back set. One-step open then aiming point of frontside guard's outside leg; buzz feet to give QB time. If lined up as slot, must get outside leg of playside guard; 4x2 get shoulders square; once receive the ball, various motions.
- QB: Flat down the line. Pitch key is (gap exchange) C gap player. Not necessarily the DE. Do not attack outside shoulder of DE. If read key squeezes, it becomes speed option.

O-Line Rules

- PS tackle: B gap to backside LB (never pass up run through LB)
- PS guard: A gap
- Center: Block back
- BS guard: pull to frontside LB (continue up if gone)
- BS tackle: gap, seal, hinge block

With gap exchange and shoveling off the C gap defender, if the defensive end squeezes flat down the line of scrimmage with the linebacker exchanging to play the C gap, then the puller can log the defensive end and shovel in from the linebacker. The gap exchange concept also applies for the playside tackle never passing up a linebacker run through (an outside stacked backer blitzing the B gap). We prefer to run to a 1 technique, however, running to a 3 technique has an advantage.

When blocking a 3 technique on the playside, the playside guard and playside tackle double and read through to the backside linebacker. If the backer comes over the top, the guard overtakes and the tackle climbs. If the backside backer comes under for a run through in the B gap, then the guard is off the double-team for the backer.

On double-teaming the 3 technique with the playside guard and playside tackle or a nose with the playside guard and center, if the down defender disappears (stunts away), then climb immediately to the second level. For instance, if the nose stunts into the opposite A gap, then the playside guard climbs immediately to the second level, and the center stays on the block. If the end squeezes, but stays square, we will trap and shovel the ball. If the end wrong arms, then we log block him.

MIDLINE

Offensive Line Rules

- PST: KO EMOL
- PSG: Veer PSLB to MLB
- C: Combination Block C/G (name and call every time) to BSLB
- BSG: Combination block C/G (name and call every time) to BSLB
- BST: Wheel and seal end
- TE: KO EMOL

Change-ups

- G/T Fold: Guard kicks out on EMOL; T is under G to PILB (name and call every time)
- G/T Cross: Tackle veer blocks PILB TO MLB; G KO EMOL

Perimeter Rules

- Both WRS: Crack near safety
- PSHB: Rock/lock motion; lead through B gap to PSLB; if TE, arc to safety
- BSHB: Pitch back; rip/Liz motion and lead through the B gap inside/out
- FB: Run on the midline, slide to the PS hip of C
- QB: Step deep off midline; stab ball deep; ride and decide; keep through the B gap. Give, unless drive key squeezes flat on FB.

I will be around if you have questions. I know everyone wants to go to the tables and win a lot of money. Good luck and thanks for staying around.

NEW!

2010 COACH OF THE YEAR CLINIC NOTES
LECTURES BY PREMIER HIGH SCHOOL COACHES

EDITED BY EARL BROWNING

2010
CLINIC NOTES
Lectures by Premier High School Coaches

Edited by Earl Browning.

$29.95 • 260 pages • 978-1-60679-109-7

Also available:

2005	2006	2007	2008	2009

1-58518-934-0	1-58518-982-0	978-1-58518-074-5	978-1-58518-740-9	978-1-60679-065-6
264 pp. • $24.95	256 pp. • $24.95	268 pp. • $24.95	256 pp. • $24.95	272 pp. • $29.95